ALBAN

This is a volume in the
Arno Press collection

THE AMERICAN
CATHOLIC TRADITION

Advisory Editor
Jay P. Dolan

Editorial Board
Paul Messbarger
Michael Novak

See last pages of this volume
for a complete list of titles.

A L B A N

A Tale of the New World.

[Jedediah Vincent Huntington]

ARNO PRESS
A New York Times Company
New York • 1978

Editorial Supervision: JOSEPH CELLINI

———◆———

Reprint Edition 1978 by Arno Press Inc.

THE AMERICAN CATHOLIC TRADITION
ISBN for complete set: 0-405-10810-9
See last pages of this volume for titles.

Manufactured in the United States of America

———◆———

Library of Congress Cataloging in Publication Data

Huntington, Jedediah Vincent, 1815-1862.
    Alban : a tale of the New World.

    (The American Catholic tradition)
    Reprint of the 1851 ed. published by Putnam, New
York.
    I. Title. II. Series.
PZ3.H923Al 1978 [PS2044.H442]   813'.3   77-11293
ISBN 0-405-10836-2

ALBAN.

A L B A N.

A Tale of the New World.

BY THE AUTHOR OF "LADY ALICE."

" A man of free and active mind will remain tranquil in the peaceful regions of truth, or he will seek it with restlessness and disquietude. If he find only false principles to rest on,—if he feel the ground move under his feet, he will change his position every moment, he will leap from error to error, and precipitate himself from one abyss to another."

BALMES.

" We cannot make this world a paradise, and all its inhabitants saints, as foolish puritans dream."

BROWNSON, *On the Fugitive Slave Law.*

NEW YORK:

GEORGE P. PUTNAM, 155 BROADWAY.

LONDON: COLBURN & CO

M.DCCC.LI.

STEREOTYPED BY
BILLIN & BROTHERS,
10 NORTH WILLIAM-STREET, N. Y.

J. F. TROW, PRINTER, ANN-STREET.

A WORD ABOUT "LADY ALICE."

THE author of the above-mentioned (too?) celebrated book had no reason to complain either of the public for not reading or of the critics for not noticing it, few novels recently published having had a wider circulation, and perhaps none, for a long time having received so much notice from the press. And notwithstanding the extreme severity with which it was assailed, he is not disposed to complain of injustice; the criticism was often one-sided, but it was not, generally speaking, unfair in spirit, or unkind. The author was often edified and oftener amused by it; and, upon the whole, although he would have been glad to have seen some of the positive merits of his literary offspring better appreciated, for otherwise he would have seemed to lack the natural vanity of literary paternity, (and any thing unnatural is monstrous,) yet he could not, except in one instance, have spared any thing that was actually said. He has always meant, however, to take the opportunity, whenever it came, of saying something in regard to the morality of Lady Alice, to the disparagement of which so much has been said; and particularly as he feels a sort of traditional respect for one ancient Quarterly—the "grand-mamma" of American periodicals—in which he was assailed on this score with such unmitigated virulence that it seems as much a duty to make some sort of reply, as it does for one who has been bespattered with mud (I was going to use a stronger word) from any quarter, to brush his clothes before presenting himself again in decent society. Literary people (for scarce any

other will have seen the article) will understand that I allude to
the North American Review.

There is, I think, a limit beyond which the misrepresentation
of a book under review ought not to go in a respectable periodi-
cal. One expects that a hostile critic will take his own point of
view, and sometimes even force a meaning on his author which
was never intended; that he will make sweeping assertions in
regard to the tone, drift, and spirit of a book, quote passages without much regard to their context, and, in short, so distort the
thing that the author would hardly know his own work, and feel,
like Warren Hastings under the unjust castigation of Burke, that
he was the greatest villain in existence. But assertions which
are point-blank falsehoods, without even a shadow of truth to
support them, are a stretch of the reviewer's prerogative, and
when made to support a charge of studied indecency and immorality against a clergyman, as the author was then, convert a
review into a libel. Out of a dozen examples of such "false witness," I select one of the least offensive, uttered (I regret to say)
with the avowed purpose of showing the "thoroughly licentious
character" of Lady Alice. "Promiscuous public bathing of both
sexes," says the reviewer, "is represented as only offensive to a
taste not sufficiently catholic; and 'Clifford, who knew the customs of all countries, and had reasoned on all with the calmness
of philosophy, thought not the worse of the modesty' of the Italian women for their attachment to this custom." Now the promiscuous public bathing of both sexes is a custom of our own
surf-beaten, tide-rolling ocean coast, and our American women,
whether they are attached to it or not, certainly practise it universally, as it is a choice between that and not bathing at all, for
a woman cannot enter the surf with safety alone. At Rockaway,
and I presume at Nahant, one gentleman, or two, is what most
ladies require. But this is not the case on the coast of the Mediterranean; the "sandy floor" of whose scooped and retired hollows "a tideless sea never wets," to quote from Lady Alice.
Here the most decorous separation of the sexes in the use of the

sea-bath exists, is enforced by the police, and is carried out spontaneously by the natural decorum of a southern people, who are "very scrupulous in respecting any spot of the coast that they see to be occupied by ladies, or females of any rank," to quote again. In short, nothing of the sort is said or described or alluded to in Lady Alice, and the peculiarity for which "Clifford thought no worse of the modesty" of the Italian ladies, was simply that they unmade and made the inevitable toilet on these occasions " beneath the open sky." This in fact is what princesses and maidens have done from the heroic times of the Odyssey, and the sacred times of the Bible, on all the shores of this famous sea. But the modern Italian women use bathing dresses, I need scarcely observe, although the only observation to which they are exposed is that of some distant passing boat.

If Lady Alice had not been a girl of spirit, a genius, an heiress, and above all, so *nobly* born, (which has its weight even in America,) she never would have survived all this. But survived it she has, and it is agreed that she is a captivating creature, whether in " the flowing garments of modesty," as the author expresses it, or in the " dreamy elegance" of a "basquined waistcoat and black trowsers of oriental amplitude." From the innocent composure with which she receives a stranger's kiss " on the shore of Vietri," to her conscious blush in the last hour of maidenhood, she shows a courage and frankness, which are not perhaps inconsistent with her piety and chastity, but which render her extremely *piquante*.

And then Louise Schönberg! what an idea to represent her as clandestinely married to Augustus without knowing it— against the laws of England, but in accordance with the laws of God ; breaking off the connection before she knows what its consequences will be, refusing to legitimate it, because its consequences are irreparable, discovering that it binds her for ever just as she is about to commit an unconscious bigamy, escaping from that difficulty by the most improbable, yet probable deception, then telling all this to her maiden friend ; and finally, in that curious and much blamed scene of the gondola, seeking her husband to impart to him the secret of the validity of their union, to confess the folly of which despair has made her guilty, and to implore his pardon and his patience ; ending by marrying him again, before the Church, without his knowing who she is ! These strange, apparently involved, yet really simple plots, in which every step is linked to the one preceding it, amid apparent recklessness of consistency, and the remote cause, the initiative of the mistakes, and the faults, traceable up to a progenitor's sin, are in the ancient rather than in the modern spirit, we confess.

But we really cannot stop to explain or vindicate " Lady Alice." If it deserves explanation or vindication, instead of forgetfulness, reproductive criticism has arrived at such a pitch of excellence in our day, that no doubt justice and more than justice will be done to this singular story. From the dull falsehoods of the North American Review, to the sparkling raillery of the Lorgnette, I leave therefore the critics to themselves, till my day comes, if it ever comes, for appreciation and praise. I cannot blow my own trumpet, nor find " understanding as well as verses." The faults of Lady Alice lie on the surface, like scum on the sea ; it is unnecessary that I should confess them to be faults, or excuse them by showing that there is a pure and deep and cleansing wave beneath. Every body, whose good opinion is worth having, sees, or may see, both.

I may, however, throw out one idea, as not having a merely retrospective bearing. The passion of love may be made interesting, I think, without those conflicts which the moderns love to paint, and which suppose a degrading anarchy in the soul. Nothing has done more to confuse the distinction between virtue and vice than modern English sentimental fiction, particularly that which claims to be moral, if not religious ; and one object which I have had in view in my former, and have pursued in my present work, has been to make the lines sharp and distinct.

New York, *July* 14, 1851.

ALBAN.

BOOK I.

The First Climacteric. The Foundation Laid.

CHAPTER I.

The New England coast is very much indented (as is well known) with fine bays, which the numerous rivers of the Eastern States have united with the sweeping tides of the Atlantic to scoop out in the generally low, but stern and unalluvial shores. These bays are also, for the most part, good harbors—the homes and rendezvous of those adventurous whalemen whose hardy enterprise, three quarters of a century ago, gained the magnificent eulogiums of Burke. Yantic Bay, on the coast of Connecticut, particularly answers to this description. It is the mouth of a beautiful river, which, rising in the above-mentioned State, after a certain course of rapids and waterfalls, unites its waters with those of an equal tributary, and flows navigably for about thirteen miles through rich embosoming hills, when the latter, gaining both elevation and severity of aspect, expand around the bay itself in a wide sweep of woodless and stone-fenced heights, having a white beach, and a long, low, surf-beaten point of bleached stones and shells for their terminus. At the sea end of the point, stands a white light-house : nearly two miles higher up, on the opposite heights, is a still formidable fort ; and near it, (at the present writing,) a colossal monument of some passage in the war of the Revolution, of which that fort was the scene. The bay is also dotted with a few rocky islets. From the absence of wood, and the profusion of stone, the landscape, if bold, is rather severe in aspect, but at the in-flowing of the river, some outjutting points, covered with thick groves, promise a softer inland.

Just out of the shelter of the groves just mentioned, close to the water side, and rising rather picturesquely from it, is situate the ancient town of Yanmouth. The Indian name of the river there emptying, was thus adjusted by the early settlers with an ending of their mother tongue and country, with a felicity rarely to be observed in the geographical nomenclature of the New World. We call Yanmouth an ancient town, but that is as cis-atlantic antiquity goes : it has a date of two centuries. It had not, indeed, quite so much in the year 1815, in which our story opens. At that time several British men-of-war were lying in Yantic Bay, which quite recently they had been engaged in blockading. The men were very often ashore in parties on leave, which broke the quiet of the town, and injured its morals, but, on the other hand, this disadvantage was compensated by the visits of the officers, between whom and the little aristocracy of Yanmouth an agreeable social intercourse had succeeded to hostile relations. There is an aristocracy in every society however limited or inarti-ficial, as there is a top and a bottom to every thing.

It was on a Sunday—and that a memorable Sunday, on which the fate of the world was being elsewhere bloodily decided ; for it was the 18th of June ; and the peculiar calm of a New England " Sabbath" in midsummer, rested on those iron hills, and wide, bright waters, and pervaded the rudely-paved streets of the old-fashioned rural town, half country village, and half seaport. At about ten o'clock, A. M., the silence was broken, but the sentiment of repose rather heightened, by the sound of the church bells answering one another at well-regulated intervals. There were two bells only in Yanmouth then :—that of the old Congregational "Meeting-House" where the mass of the real Yanmouth people, especially the gentry, still served the God of their fathers ; and that of the less pretending edifice, where a small body of Episcopalians maintained what in New England was regarded as a novel and schismatical worship. Both bells were fine toned, though they were different. That which swung in the tall, white Congregational steeple had been captured from the Spaniards by a Yanmouth privateer, a half century before, and was both high and musical. That which answered it with a graver yet mellow accent, from the square bastard-gothic turret of the Episcopals, was the gift of the Society for the Propagation of the Gospel.

Even in advance of the hour for meeting, or church, (as it would be variously termed according to the affinities of the speaker,) three boats had put out from the British frigates, and pulled up the bay to the landing. Two were captain's gigs, out of which got a half-dozen officers, who paired off, and sauntered in the direction of the Episcopal church. The other two contained, besides their crews, about a dozen "young gentlemen," whose course after landing was various. A few, and those the more unfashioned in · face, shape, mien, or dress, followed their seniors ; but a set of neatly-equipped, rather good-looking youngsters, after some delay and mutual consultation, set their coxcombical faces in the direction of the meeting-house. The streets of Yanmouth ran partly parallel with the water side, partly at right angles with, and ascending steeply from, it. They were wide, and lined with large, handsome, old-fashioned, white houses, chiefly of wood. Some were long and low ; some had " piazzas" (*anglicé* verandas) in front. Here and there a high, narrow, red store, with gable to the street, its heavy block and hoisting tackle swinging from under a projecting peak, added to the picturesque variety. Before the principal houses stood old trees—vast and spreading elms, white-armed button-balls, or gigantic weeping-willows. All was now silently stirring, and quietly alive with men and boys in bright blue coats and nankeens, and the gracious wearers of lustrous silk brocade or snowy muslin.

Yanmouth meeting-house stood about half way up one of the rising streets of the town, being built (to use the local phrase) on a "side hill," in a situation, therefore, of great conspicuity. It was built of wood, and painted white, like all New England meeting-houses of the time, and was adorned with the usual double row of green-blinded windows down its sides ; yet being of very ample dimensions, and even grand in proportions, with a bell-tower and spire of gradually lessening galleries, enriched with elaborate balustrades, it stood out against the blue sky a very imposing and almost beautiful object. It had a small church-yard—a green square, two sides of which were occupied by the "meeting-house shed," destined for the shelter of the equipages of such of the congregation as might come from a distance to worship. Hence the other two sides were open to the street, and the trampled turf contained, of course, no graves. The burying-ground is usually quite separate from the church, in a New England village.

The worshippers from the town flocked in, slow but unloitering, exchanging few greetings. The long gray shed also filled up with horses, gigs, and wagons. Their male owners seemed to regard it as a privilege to stand about the doors or under the eaves of the meeting-house so long as the bell continued to toll, but yet without profaning the sanctity of the Sabbath by entering into conversation. At length the bell ceased, and these lingerers also entered ; the noise of their feet mounting the gallery stairs was soon over, (there was no organ, of course, to pour out its volumes of unspiritual sound,) and a profound silence filled the sanctuary. The body of the house was divided into great square pews, so that one half the congregation sat facing the other half. In modern New England churches the seats all look towards the minister, and this seems, at first sight, the most sensible arrangement ; but, in reality, the old one was more in accordance with true New England principles. In the new places of worship there is none of that solemnity which used to be felt from the consciousness of each individual that he was under the grave and unavoidable observation of all his brethren. The downcast looks and formal composure of the females that marked the old congregations have disappeared. Ease has succeeded to awe. But the worst of it is, that the genuine idea of Congregationalism is violated. The centre of action and interest is shifted from the assembly itself to its minister ; and the nature of the action is also changed ; a solemn, if severe, synaxis has degenerated into a lecture ; a church watching over itself has sunk to an audience.

The young officers of Her Majesty's ship of the line Avenger and frigate Tonnerre (captured at Trafalgar) liked the old square pews for the view they afforded of many a lovely New England countenance.   Truly, the summer light, softened by its passage betwixt the numerous green slats of the Venetian blinds, fell on more than one face of exquisite beauty, of a bloom as delicate as Britain could boast, and features of more classic precision than her humid atmosphere permits, at least without a certain hot-house culture.   In many instances this physical beauty was united with that air of saint-like purity and heavenly peace which is often ascribed to nuns, but which is, or was, very common among New England Congregationalists ; proceeding in both cases, doubtless, from the same causes, habitual self-control, and the frequent contemplation of Divine things.

As a general thing it may be doubted whether this spiritual style of female loveliness attracted the regards of our naval friends so much as that which was more mundane.   Their admiring glances were bestowed, however, with great impartiality ; the young Yanmouth ladies were doubtless, in most instances, acquaintance, at the very least ; in some cases, a tenderer, though temporary interest, might be almost acknowledged ; and it seemed that only the successive contemplation of all the fair faces present could satisfy that hunger of the sailor's eye after a long cruise, for the soft peculiarities of feature and expression proper to the other sex.   We have not come to Yanmouth church, however, to observe and describe these profane distractions, which have forced themselves, we must say, unpleasantly, upon our attention. Our own business here is infinitely more serious.

In a large wall pew, which shares with one other in the church the distinction of red cloth lining and brass nails, is a family that claims particular notice. The master sits in his proper place, (that is the corner seat next the side aisle, and commanding the pulpit,) a man rather below the middle height, slight, erect, yet evidently, from his thin silver locks, of venerable years. The head is characteristically New Englandish ; small, rather square than oval ; nose Grecian, with refined nostril, and compressed mouth ; eyes not large, but well set and piercing. The lower part of this face was charged with a florid color which proved that seventy winters had not exhausted a rich and abundant vitality ; but the wide, serene, scarcely-wrinkled brow, was as silvery in tone as faultless in mould. Ideality, causality, benevolence, veneration, conscientiousness, firmness, all well developed ! It is easy to see what character this man will have displayed. He has been the kind father, the admirable citizen, the patriot, finally, the saint.

His *vis-à-vis* offers a striking contrast. It is a man in the prime of life, tall, large framed, but well knit. He is dressed in the fashion of the time and season, a blue coat, with white neckcloth, waiscoat, and trowsers, of an immaculate purity ; his large shirt ruffles are elaborately plaited ;—then the ordinary mark of a gentleman. From this snowy *just-au-corps*, so fresh and clean, emerges a grand, handsome head, oval and brilliant. It would be too vital were it not that the massive, clean, white forehead is prematurely bald ; the activity of the cerebrum has left little more than half of the dark brown locks that once shaded its superb temple.

The interior corners of the pews were occupied by two females, the elder of whom could not have passed thirty. She was short, slight, and pale. She wore what was then *distingué*, a white shawl, of Chinese silk, over her high, lace-ruffed, short-waisted, black silk dress, and a Leghorn bonnet and lace veil, that seemed modish, and even imposing, in Yanmouth meeting-house. Her features were good, but irregular ; the mouth, in particular, was deficient in symmetry, yet was its expression sweet ; one eyebrow was markedly higher than the other, but the eyes were finely cut and of the softest blue ; the nose was a little high, yet beautifully formed. She had the saint-like expression of which we have before spoken. It was, indeed, a very interesting face.

Her companion was like her, but the likeness was a family one ; the mould was the same, but the casting had been more fortunate. In short, the face of the younger lady was as nearly perfect as possible ; but its expression was tinctured with a faint haughtiness, not unusual in features of extreme regularity. Between these fair and gracious personages sat a neatly-attired black girl—black as the ace of spades ;—around her curly head was gracefully wound a bright parti-colored cotton handkerchief. In her arms she sustained a burden of flowing muslin petticoats, and long lace robes, from which emerged the small, fair, slumbering features of an infant—a sleep-bound monthling. These were indications, appreciated, doubtless, by all the congregation, that Mr. and Mrs. Samuel Atherton were intending that morning to "dedicate" their first-born son to God "in the ordinance of baptism."

The aged minister entered the assembly, walked with slow dignity up the middle aisle, and more slowly, yet with greater dignity, ascended the pulpit stairs. He was an old-fashioned parson of the "standing order." His somewhat shrunk legs were invested in black small-clothes and stockings, and he wore great silver shoe-buckles. His hair was long, flowing on his shoulders, and white as snow. After some moments of silent preparation in the deep interior of the wine-glass pulpit, moments during which the congregation became gradually hushed as the grave, this venerable man arose ; all arose with him ; and lifting up his hands, he commenced his prayer.

It is not our intention to report it. It was a good prayer, brief and pointed, in the nature of an introduction to the exercises about to follow. The good pastor had used nearly the same every Sunday morning, for more than half a century that he had exercised the pastoral office over the church in Yanmouth. A hymn was then sung, about dedicating little children, like Samuel, to God. Then the pastor read the passage of the New Testament where the Lord commissions his Apostles to go forth and baptize all nations. Then followed a much longer prayer, very discursive, very theological—like an abstract of the Westminster Confession, united to an exposition of the Book of Revelations. Towards the close of it, however, the speaker narrowed down his theme to the present time, and spoke of the family whose youngest " hope" was to be offered for admission into the visible church. He declared that this unconscious babe, on whom so much of the interest of the present occasion was concentred, was the descendant of a long line of eminently pious and now mostly sainted ancestors, whose graces he prayed that the babe might inherit, as well as their name. He alluded particularly to one living and present, a venerable servant of God, the grandsire, as it seemed, of the babe, now waiting for the call of his Master, ready like Elijah for translation, whose mantle, he asked might fall on this infant descendant. Finally, he expressed great confidence in the real election of the yet unconscious candidate for the baptismal sprinkling, on the ground that a child of so many prayers as had gone before his very birth, and would ever follow him through life, must have been predestinated from all eternity to the enjoyment of the celestial mansions, it being, as he said, the well-known method of the Omniscient and Sovereign Dispenser of all good to stir up his people to ask with fervor those blessings which he had in each instance eternally predetermined to bestow. With the exception, perhaps, of the young English officers, a look of pleased internal acquiescence was visible on all the countenances of the congregation as the prayer concluded.

" The child," said the minister, still erect in the lofty pulpit, " may now be presented by the parents for baptism."

"Who are the godfather and godmother?" whispered a midshipman to a staring Yanmouth youth in the next pew.

"Them are the parents," was the reply, accompanied with an expression of pity ; "we don't have nothing of that kind *you* said."

The ceremony of baptism is not necessarily deprived of its solemnity by the simple manner of performing it customary among the New England people. On the contrary, the mere act of baptism, left entirely to itself, with no benedictions of the water, no promises and renunciations of sponsors, no signing with the cross, not to say, without the numerous rites used in the Catholic church—the salt, the spittle, the insufflations, the exorcisms, the unction, the lighted candle, the white robe—is perhaps even the more impressive. The minister exhorted the parents to bring up their child in the nurture and admonition of the Lord. The nature of the present transaction he described, indeed, as a mere oblation of the child to God ; but he assured them, on the other hand, that God had promised to be a Father to the children of His saints, and that the offspring of believers were the most likely subjects of discriminating grace, a consummation to which their efforts and prayers ought constantly to tend. The father held the babe at the font ; the white-haired old minister dipped the tips of his trembling fingers, sprinkled a few drops of water on the face of the infant, not even waking it from its deep and awful slumber, and said :

"ALBAN, I baptize thee in the name of the Father, and of the Son, and of the Holy Ghost. Amen."

2*

CHAPTER II.

THE British tars sauntered along the quiet streets, rolling on their hips, and squaring their elbows like yard-arms. There were no grog-shops open in Yanmouth on the Sabbath day, and though immoralities of another kind were far from being unknown, there was yet no absolute rendezvous in this comparatively innocent sea-port, where the distraction of equivocal female society could be obtained. The selectmen exercised too strict a vigilance. So, finally, a little knot of the blue-jackets, *ennuyé* with promenading without a purpose, sat down upon the stone door-step of a store, and one of them pulling out of his pocket a pack of dirty cards, they fell to amusing themselves with a game that is a prime favorite with sailors:

Cards are dull without a stake ; so the next thing some of His Majesty's silver pictures were produced, and the shillings and half-crowns changed hands rapidly. Unfortunately the position of the gamesters was commanded from the windows of the meeting-house gallery. They were quiet at first, as they had been strictly enjoined to be, and spoke in under tones, for the hush of the town awed them ; but forgetting themselves by degrees, particularly the lookers-on of the game, they gave way to occasional laughter, with loud talking, to which now and then a ripping oath added its peculiar energy. In the deep pause between the giving out of the last hymn, and the preparatory *fa mi sol* of the volunteer choir, the noise of a laugh came faintly in at the open windows and caught the ear of Deacon Jabez Flint, a zealous upholder of the ancient laws, and one of the selectmen of Yanmouth. To seize his hat—a broad-brim—and staff (it was silver-headed) and go forth to ascertain the cause of these profane sounds, was in fact the duty of Deacon Flint ; and his investigations soon brought to light the enormities that were in the act of commission :—card-playing,

gambling, swearing, and unseemly merriment on the Sabbath in
the open streets of Yanmouth, in meeting-time, with consequent
disturbance of public worship, added to the profanation of the
Lord's day, each in itself a circumstance involving a separate violation of the by-laws of the town, and constituting all together a
complex offence of no ordinary magnitude. What did it matter
that the offenders were foreigners? In the command to sanctify
the Sabbath was there not a special clause including " the stranger
that is within thy gates?" So reasoned Deacon Flint, who had
" set his face as a flint" against such doings ; and he took his
measures accordingly ; the consequence whereof was, to be brief,
that by the time meeting was out, four seamen of His Majesty's
frigate Tonnerre had been arrested by a constabulary force of eight
fanatical Puritans, under the guidance and authority of Deacon
Flint, in his broad-brimmed hat and silver-headed round cane, and
lodged forthwith in the county jail.

From insignificant causes arise, oftentimes, the wars of mighty
nations. The arrest of a few sailors for violating the municipal
laws of a New England town was a matter of no great import
in itself; but construed as an insult to the British flag, under
which those sailors and their officers had landed,—a less thing
might suffice to dissolve the peaceful relations then newly re-established between the two countries. Thus the zeal of Deacon
Flint, approved by some, was deemed injudicious by others. The
British officers were indignant, and some of the juniors proposed
to storm the jail and effect a rescue. This counsel was indeed
promptly rejected by their superiors in the informal consultation
which took place at the moment, as both unwarrantable, and
certain of defeat from the well-known spirit of the people. Some
of the middies said that the commodore would bombard the town
if the prisoners were not instantly surrendered ; but it was an
obvious answer to this prediction, that the British ships themselves
lay directly under the guns of Fort Yantic.

While the people, collected in groups, in spite of Sunday, discussed the affair with the phlegm peculiar to New Englanders,

and the knot of cockpit officers at the boat wharf were holding a somewhat excited, if not angry, colloquy on the subject, the captain of the Tonnerre himself consulted apart with his first lieutenant, in the veranda of an inn that fronted the landing.

"Best to treat it good-naturedly, as an instance of respectable zeal, but ludicrous in our eyes," said the senior officer.

"I call such an instance of zeal, confounded impudence," replied the lieutenant, with deliberate emphasis.

"No doubt, Harvey, no doubt; but the object at present is, to get the matter over amicably, without seeming to pocket an insult. The men must be released though, to-night."

"This Deacon Flint, they say, is as obstinate as a mule;" observed the lieutenant.

"I think I have hit upon a way of managing him," said his superior, looking at the subaltern. The lieutenant in turn regarded his captain with an air of inquiry.

"General Atherton has unbounded influence," pursued the latter. "The people here regard him as little less than a saint."

"Quite so," assented the lieutenant, slightly flushing.

"Deacon Flint would follow his advice implicitly, no doubt, especially in a case like this, which, in fact, is a question of religion," said the captain, gravely. "You know the family, Harvey; you must see the old gentleman. He is a gentleman, every inch of him, and a soldier;—he would enter into my feelings,—into the feelings of a commanding officer."

"General Atherton is very rigid in his ideas about Sunday— the Sabbath, as he would call it," said Harvey, hesitatingly.

"Pooh! pooh!"

"I mean, he might object to one's calling on him to-day, on such an affair;" persisted the junior.

"Nonsense. You will have the goodness to go up to General Atherton's immediately, Mr. Harvey, and make such a representation of the case as will procure his interference to liberate the men at once," said his commander moving off. "I am going to the ship; you won't come aboard without them, of course!"

CHAPTER III.

By this time the bells had begun to ring for afternoon meeting ; for, as many of the congregation always come from far, it is the custom of New England to allow but a brief intermission between morning and afternoon service, seldom exceeding an hour. Lieutenant Harvey did not proceed on his errand till after the evening service therefore, which, for some reason, he attended at church, and though he had often heard the beautiful prayers hastily read before an impending action or gathering storm, when Sunday happened to precede, he had perhaps never more heartily prayed to be " defended from the fear of our enemies," or " from all perils and dangers of this night," than when he was simply going to ask a favor of a particularly quiet New England country-gentleman.

But service was over—it was longer than meeting by at least a quarter of an hour—and the brave lieutenant's way led him into the broad ascending street on which the meeting-house stood. It was lined with great trees and paved with rubble stones, from which the rapid descent of waters in every rain had long since swept away the lighter portions of the soil. Here and there native rock, smooth and flat, appeared above the surface. At the top of this street ran another at right angles, and beyond, the hill extended in an open green terminating in a white court-house, flanked by a stone jail—a square, solid building with grated windows, from one of which the English officer's blood boiled to see the grim faces of his men peering out in durance vile.

This was the end of the town in that direction. Behind the court-house and jail were seen only stone-fenced hills and the sky. But on the right of the court-house green, in the midst of lofty and considerable grounds, stood a large white mansion of brick, having a many-sloped black roof without gables, of which the eaves projecting like a veranda, and supported by massive and square brick columns, formed a huge piazza quite round the house. The white front wall of the grounds flanked the green, and was of brick, stone-coped, and broken by quaint brick pillars, like those of the piazza. There were two gates, a larger one at the lowest point of the hill for carriages, and a smaller one, but more enriched, latticed, and flanked by pillars, above, which served for pedestrians, or even for visitors in carriages, if they did not mind walking a hundred yards, or thereabouts, to the house. Lieutenant Harvey directed his steps to this entrance, and entered by it without using the brass knocker. Within was a small lawn, planted with shrubbery, and a flagged pathway led from the gate to a flight of half-a-dozen stone steps, which brought the officer to the level of a green and shrubberied terrace, with a continuation of the pathway leading to another flight and another terrace, whereon stood the house, the great brick pillars of the piazza having their quaint lofty bases rooted in the turf. Those of the front were wreathed with honeysuckles. Roses bloomed between them, and beneath the open windows. There was a path under the piazza, and on one side was a garden rising in terraces and skirted with fruit-trees ; on the other, the hill descended in a green slope to the carriage-road. and the view was open over the town, to the bay, the wooded mouth of the Yantic, and the gray heights beyond, with their fences of stone and guardian forts.

Lieutenant Harvey raised the bright brass knocker of the double-valved green door. An old negro in a white coat answered the summons. His wrinkled black face evinced great surprise at the visitor.

"What, Massa Harvey! you come to de Cassle a-courtin' on de Sabbat' day! Sir! as sure as my name is Sam'l Ath'ton, the gen'ral no 'prove it."

"I have not come to the 'Castle' to-day a-courting, Sam. I wish to see General Atherton himself on particular business."

"The gen'ral never tend to biz'ness on de Sabbat'," said the negro, letting in the visitor with evident reluctance. "My goodness, Massa Harvey! de Cassle de las' place you ought to come to, to do biz'ness on de Sabbat' day afore sun-down. You lose your crak'ter in dis house entirely."

The vestibule into which Harvey was admitted, was a small, square hall, nearly filled with a broad, well-lighted staircase. The narrow, but very rich foreign carpet with which this was laid, and a hall-lamp of cut glass suspended from the ceiling, gave it an air different from most Yanmouth interiors at that period, although now it would be far from unique. A sword, and an old revolutionary cocked-hat hung on the wall. The negro threw open a door, and ushered the visitor into a spacious drawing-room, —in the vernacular, the parlor.

"Mr. Harvey!" said a soft voice, in an under tone of slight surprise.

There were three ladies in the parlor, two of whom have already been introduced in their pew at the Congregational meeting-house, and it was the younger of these who spoke, and who, at the same time, rose to receive the English officer. The other two remained sitting and silent, but regarded him with a stare of undisguised curiosity.

"I called to see your father, Miss Atherton, on an errand of importance from my commanding officer."

"Your father is in the bedroom, Betsey," said a voice with quickness ; and the young lady addressed left the parlor without further remark.

"The bedroom," in a New England house at that time signified the bedroom of "the heads" of the family. It was generally upon the first or principal floor, and was much used as a more sacred kind of sitting-room, to which all the members of the family proper had access ; but when the best, or drawing-room chamber, was occupied by guests, as happened at this time at General Atherton's, it would also afford a place, on Sundays, or at other times, for devotional retirement ; and such, doubtless, as Lieutenant Harvey immediately understood, was the case at that instant. The reader will also at once comprehend, that the above observation, addressed to Miss Atherton, proceeded from her mother. She was a woman on the shady side of sixty—perhaps nearer three score and ten ; very slight, very straight, sitting erect in her chair by the open east window, without leaning in the least upon the high back for support ; a large book was open in her lap, and she was reading without the aid of glasses. The close cap of the time entirely concealed her gray hair, and surrounded a face that must once have been beautiful. It was still full of vivacity. On the wall directly opposite her hung her own portrait, a few years younger, perhaps, but in the same costume that she actually wore— a dark silk gown and snowy muslin neckerchief, arranged with neat precision. Many other portraits adorned the walls, and we may indeed scrutinize the apartment a little, while we are waiting in solemn silence for General Atherton to appear.

It was a large room, as we have said, and lofty, and the portraits were ranged down one side of it. General Atherton, whom we have already seen at meeting, was there by his lady's side, in the old continental blue and buff, the high, white cravat, and rich frill of '76. The painter had caught well his expression of saintly serenity. There was a head which you would have sworn was his father's, but of harder lineaments ;—the costume plain and citizenish, but otherwise scarcely to be made out ; and another which you might divine to be his mother's,—very soft, and the most youthful in the collection : it must have been taken three quarters of a century before. Probably it was painted by Smybert, who flourished in the then loyal colonies, before the French war. The other portraits were more modern ; one smooth, youthful countenance, almost boyish, surprised you by its association with a parson's gown and bands,—signs of office which the Congregationalist ministers in Boston, and the larger cities of New England still retained. At the lower end of the room, over the very high mantel-piece of dark native stone, hung also nearly a dozen miniatures in oil, exquisitely painted ; evidently all by the same hand. The massive little gilt frames made the wall sparkle ; and they were disposed round a central piece,—a lozenge-shaped coat of arms, worked in gold filagree and blue,—a resplendent object preserved in a glass case. There was very little furniture in the apartment, compared with our modern profusion. An escritoire bookcase of mahogany, polished by constant rubbing into a sort of golden looking-glass, and nearly covered with spotlessly bright and fanciful brass mountings and drawer-handles, stood near the fireplace. A tall, old-fashioned clock, with the moon's ever-varying face moving on its dial, stood in a darkish corner, solemnly ticking in the silence. And there was little else that was ornamental.

The beautiful Miss Atherton returned from her mission, saying, in a low tone, that "Pa" would come in presently, and seating herself by a window, resumed her book. Young Mrs. Atherton had not uttered a word. She sat in a low rocking-chair, meditating apparently, for her air was serious though sweet. Ten minutes elapsed, and General Atherton did not appear.

"Have you been to church to-day, Mr. Harvey, or to meeting ?" suddenly asked old Mrs. Atherton.

"To meeting, madam, in the morning," said the officer.

"Ah ! then you saw my grandson christened," broke in the old lady with animation.

"Saw him baptized, you mean, ma !" said young Mrs. Atherton, faintly, and with a slight winning smile of remonstrance.

"No, child, I mean christened ;—is not that what you call it at home—in *Old* England, Mr. Harvey ?"

"Baptized or christened, madam, is the same, I have always understood," said the lieutenant.

Miss Atherton's lip curled, but she did not look up from her book.

"How did you like the name ?" pursued the old lady, with a courteous but sarcastic air. Harvey said he thought it a very good name, and Miss Atherton's lip curled again.

"It comes from a good source," said the old lady, turning over to the first pages of her book,—"the calendar of the Church

of England Prayer-book—the only prayer-book I ever use.—
Yesterday was St. Alban's day, and I find he was the first
English martyr, so, as I was promised the naming of the boy, I
chose that.   It is better than Hezekiah or Samuel, don't you
think ?"

"Those names are both in the Bible, you know, mamma !"
said the married daughter; "I am sure you really like them."

"I like Hezekiah in your father, Grace."

"And Samuel in my husband, I hope," said the daughter,
with a smile, though somewhat pained.

"He was named after his father, who was President of Congress," said the old lady, "and a signer of the Declaration ;—not
that I think any better of him for that,"—and she glanced out
of the window towards the fort on the distant heights.

"And Samuel in the Bible was one of the judges, and a
prophet of the Lord," said Mrs. Samuel Atherton, with perse-
vering suavity.

"And Alban in the Prayer-book was one of the martyrs, and
a saint of the Lord ;" rejoined her mother.

Truly, it has excited our surprise that this young descendant
of the Puritans, christened in a Congregationalist meeting-house,
should receive the name of a Catholic saint.   But we have not
time to think about it, for at length, the General Hezekiah so
long waited for, comes in from his retirement, and listens with
grave but gracious attention to the British officer's story.

"What you urge is reasonable, Mr. Harvey," said he, at its
conclusion.   " Deacon Flint is a good man, but his zeal in this
instance has carried him further than duty required him to go.
It would have sufficed to reprimand your men, and send them
back to their boat.   I will go with you to his house, and doubt
not to obtain an order for their release."

"It is a work of necessity and mercy," said the younger Mrs.
Atherton.

"I think so, daughter Grace."

CHAPTER IV.

It was almost the longest day of the year, of course, and it seemed that the sun never *would* go down that evening. Gradually, however, the shadow of the hill climbed up the quaint brick pillars of the old Atherton house—the "Cassle," as black Sam called it—and chased the red light up the varied slopes of the black roof, till at last only the gilt points of the forked lightning-rod sparkled in the day-beam. Then Elizabeth Atherton came out among the roses and honeysuckles of the piazza, and sauntered into the garden, lifting her gracious white drapery a little, as she went up the terraced parterres, till her form was seen at their highest point defined against the crimson sky.

It was in the angle of the wall that she stood, where a great rock emerged above the surface; the road ran some twenty feet below on one side; on the other, her father's domain extended, in grass land and locust groves. The land on the farther side of the road was also General Atherton's, except the very topmost slope of the hill, which was fenced off by itself, with a line of trees running along its lower boundary. This separated lot manifested the purpose to which it was devoted, by hundreds of grassy mounds, with numerous white gravestones interspersed. At the date of this present writing, General Atherton, with his wife, and both their daughters—the beautiful Elizabeth herself—repose beneath one of the highest knolls, which is crowned by their tall obelisk tombstones. Be not too sad, reader; for consider that thirty-five years have elapsed; and of those four, one only died in youth. A common fate, late or soon, ingulfs the earthly life of all.

The golden ray (we mean it) at length had ceased to tinge even the highest rampart of Yantic fort; it was positively sundown; and a stir became apparent in Yanmouth. From her lofty post of observation, Betsey Atherton could see many a doorway become enlivened with white dresses and summer trowsers ; now a solitary beau, and then a whole bevy of girls would flutter down or across a street. Laughter was heard in the twilight, and music, and the resounding of gates swung to with a sort of consciousness that the Sabbath was over. Soon a quite numerous party were descried coming up the hill, and crossing the green towards her father's house. They came in at the upper gate talking gayly and loud. Elizabeth saw her father and elder sister go out to meet them on the terrace steps. After a short conversation, two or three girls, and as many youths, broke away from the rest, and came actually running into the garden, the females in advance of their companions. As they flew along the terraces, one gave a faint, hoydenish scream, and another laughed.

"Why *girls!* how you *act!*" said Miss Atherton, reproachfully, in her low, soft voice, slightly drawling the two italicized words.

They were all beautiful creatures, to speak generally, fragile in make, and reaching apparently, in age, from sixteen to twenty. One had a profusion of long, light brown ringlets falling on her shoulders ; another's glossy raven hair was classically twisted ; the third had short crisp French curls all around her forehead and temples. Two of the gentlemen who followed them were English officers, and one of these was our friend Harvey, with whom Miss Atherton shook hands, and said, with a very sweet and gentle, though amused smile :

" I trust you have succeeded in liberating the captives, Lieutenant Harvey ?"

" I wish I could as easily deliver another captive that I know of, Miss Atherton," replied the lieutenant gallantly.

The girls all giggled, and the other gentleman exclaimed, "*All* the captives ! you ought to say, Harvey." And the three girls laughed again, and Miss Atherton said she thought "they were *possessed !*"

We are afraid that if we were to continue our account of the conversation, it would not prove greatly more edifying than the slight specimen we have given. Miss Atherton herself gradually took part in what she at first seemed to consider the undignified conduct of her friends : at least she laughed, though low and musically, as people say, and retorted their silly railleries. By and by it was proposed to promenade up and down the walks ; and the young ladies accepted without scruple the offered arms of the cavaliers. The conversation now became more subdued ; the moon rose upon the rugged but beautiful landscape ; the terraces of turf and stone, and the long, white piazza were partly in shade, and partly in a soft glitter.

" The new world is more charming than the old," said the English officer.

" And you are really serious in your plan of giving up your profession and settling in the West ?"

" Never more serious in my life. Your brother-in-law has promised to sell me a township in the Genesee country, not entirely beyond the reach of civilization either, and for a mere trifle."

" But you first return to England ?"

" We sail on Thursday," said the lieutenant.

" I am very sorry," said Miss Atherton, looking up at him. The English officer was a handsome fellow.

" And I was never so sorry in my life," replied the lieutenant. " To be quite plain—since I am going so soon—and may not have another opportunity, (let us turn up this walk, Miss Atherton,) you are the cause."

The sailor hemmed and cleared his throat. There was nothing sufficiently definite said yet for a lady to answer, but enough for a lady to understand. Miss Atherton looked down of course.

" I ventured to speak to your father this afternoon," pursued the lieutenant, rather vaguely. " He reproved me for mentioning it on Sunday—on the Sabbath I mean—but referred me to you."

" Mentioning what ?" said the young New England lady, with characteristic caution.

" I thought I had explained that, Miss Atherton. What could I mention but my attachment—my respectful, devoted attachment to yourself ?"

The young lady immediately had the air of one very much surprised.   Young ladies are always surprised, and yet somehow they
know very well.   Miss Atherton withdrew her hand softly from
her companion's arm.   She stopped abruptly midway of the walk,
and turning away slightly, looked over the low rough wall towards
the burying-ground, where the gravestones glittered like her own
raiment.   What a question is she deciding !   It is whether she
shall be a wife and mother, and go with a companion whom she
likes, and whom she would easily learn to love with tenderness, to
a clime and soil, an air and mode of life far more favorable to her
delicate, but untainted constitution, than that of the stern New
England coast, and where she would probably have lived as long
as our New England flowers generally do when transplanted to
the alluvial West ; or whether she shall lie soon—a virgin—under
yon moonlit knoll.   She has no conception of this aspect of the
question, yet there seems something deeper than either maiden
coyness in confessing, or womanly reluctance to give pain in
denying, a reciprocation of the feeling with which she has
been addressed.   She does not look at her companion, which is
unfortunate, for he is a manly figure, most particularly good-looking, and now an ardent and sympathetic agitation quickens his
deep respiration, and his fine embrowned features express many
things that females instantly appreciate, and greatly like,—sincerity, warmth of feeling, respectful fear, passionate admiration.
There was clearly a struggle in the maiden's bosom, but it was
brief.

" I am sorry—very sorry—that you feel so, Mr. Harvey,—that
is—I cannot—."   She hesitated.   " You know my principles,
Lieutenant Harvey ; I cannot reconcile it to my conscience to
marry one who is not a Christian."

"Not a Christian, Miss Atherton !   My God ! do you take me
for an infidel ?"

" Oh, no, not an infidel, sir ; but you do not so much as believe
in that change of heart which we think necessary to make a *real*
Christian.   I always resolved," added she, and her delicate pro-

file looked firmness itself,—" I always resolved never to marry any but a Christian."

" But this is a very extraordinary resolution," said the lieutenant, with profound seriousness. " You have three married sisters, Miss Atherton, and not one of their husbands is a Christian, in that sense of the word. Why, there is your own mother, Miss Atherton, who is of my church :—I am as much a Christian as she is, am I not ?"

" That does not alter the right and wrong of the case," said Miss Atherton, mildly.

Others of the party now approached, and the pair resumed their walk, but Miss Atherton did not resume her lover's arm.

" I may venture to think that at least you have no other objection," said the lieutenant. " My family, I believe, is as good as yours, though it may not be so distinguished, Miss Atherton."

" I never thought of comparing them," said the young lady.

" I cannot boast of my million acres of wild land, and my forty ships sailing to the Indies, like your brother-in-law, Mr. Samuel Atherton."

After a few moments' thoughtful silence Betsey Atherton touched quickly with her finger that region of the forehead where phrenologists locate the organ of calculation, and replied, with a mixture of archness and sweet sincerity :—

" My highest aspiration, when I have sometimes thought of wedded life as most desirable for one of my sex, has been to marry a talented minister, settled over some large society, in New York or Boston, like my brother Jonathan, whose income, Lieutenant Harvey, is considerably less than your patrimony would produce, if converted into dollars and put out at the American rate of interest."

CHAPTER V.

THE life of Master Alban Atherton, till he was about eight years old, crept on (the days, upon a child, drop one by one, slowly, like the beads of a novice) between his father's house in the great city and his grandfather's in the rural haven of Yanmouth. At that time, owing to the nearly annual visit of yellow fever, New York was not considered a safe summer residence, and as the commercial difficulties that followed the peace pressed too dangerously on one who had (literally) so much heavy canvas spread as our hero's father, to allow of his remaining long at a distance from his counting-house, and Mrs. Atherton would not permit the long months from May till the frost to separate her from her husband, the boy was naturally sent to his grandfather's. Here his aunt Elizabeth took charge of him ; and it is no slight privilege to know in early childhood the modesty of virginal care. By itself, indeed, it might have proved too cold an influence, under which the young soul would have blanched like flowers exposed only to moonlight ; but at the end of every six months little Alban passed into the warmer arms of his mother, and played his winters through in the glow of his father's hearth. The great parlor at the " Cassle," with its sparse, old-fashioned furniture, and windows shaded but by the honeysuckles and massive pillars of the piazza, was not more different from Mrs. Atherton's winter drawing-room with its crimson damask curtains, its modern sofa covered with sumptuous red velvet, and the sideboard of silver plate and Chinese porcelain which glittered in its deep recess, than was the spirit of the former abode from that of the latter.

Mr. Samuel Atherton was a hearty, genial character, devoted to the world, particularly to the increase of his fortune, fond of good living, hospitable, friendly, generous, confiding, quick in resentments, susceptible of the influence of female beauty. With his intellectual power and his strong passions he might have made a bad man, had he not been endowed with great conscientiousness. His education had been one of great simplicity, and he had always been involved in business. His affection for his wife and son was of the warmest kind. If refinement, gentleness, and a deep sense of religion breathed out upon young Alban from his slight, quiet, blue-eyed mother, the great frame, vital activity, and cordial laugh of his father inspired qualities, as well physical as moral, of a far different order.

There was a difference of system as well as of persons and things between New York and Yanmouth. At both our young hero learned the rudiments of religion from the Westminster Catechism, but at his grandfather's, twice a day, the household were assembled round what is called in New England, metaphorically, the family altar : while at his father's, a grace before meat, of extreme brevity, constituted the visible domestic worship. Mr. Samuel Atherton was not a "professor," and in fact, rather went beyond the New England notion of consistency, in one as yet unacquainted with the power of vital godliness, even by saying grace at his own table. The Sabbath was observed in both houses with equal strictness, but (it was a less point, yet by no means an unimportant one) at Yanmouth, Saturday evening was "kept;" in New York, Sunday evening was reckoned "holy time." So, at a very early age, the boy learned that at Yanmouth the church of the family was Congregationalist, but in New York, Presbyterian ; and that these churches differed not in "doctrine," as he was told, but "*only*" in church government." The longing for unity, which is one of the strongest instincts of the human mind, compelled his young soul to puzzle itself over this mysterious diversity, and unable, as children always are, to think that two ways to heaven can be right, he inwardly, even at that early age, exercised his power of choice, and finding the mere claim of authority doubtless a proof of its validity, he accepted Presbytery, and placed Congregationalism, as such, under his childish anathema.

At Yanmouth, too, a mystery of another sort became an element of young Alban's imagination. It is that geographical mystery which children and peasants,—all ignorant minds,—feel as so attractive, yet so awful. What lay beyond the circle of hills that bounded on the north the view from his grandfather's terraces? Alban, at seven years, had journeyed by water, but never by land. And then there was the Yantic, that came flowing out of those hills, with rich woods overhanging its eddying stream—what sort of region lay about its sources?—who dwelt around its fountains?

"What do they call the place where the river falls, aunty?" he asked.

"It is called Yantic Falls, my dear."

"That is not the same Yantic Falls where uncle and aunt Hezekiah live, and cousin Rachel, is it aunty?"

"The very same, Alban."

"Oh, is it the same?" said the child. Then, after some minutes' meditation, "And grandpa lived there too, a great—great while ago, did he not, aunt Betsey?"

"Yes, yes, my dear child, he did. All the Athertons lived first at Yantic Falls. Your great-uncles—your grandfather's brothers—live there now; and a great many other Athertons, who are your relations, more or less near."

"Is Yantic Falls so large as Yanmouth?"

"Yes, Alby, it is larger."

"It is not so pretty, is it, aunty?"

"Yes, my dear, it is a much more beautiful place—the most beautiful I ever saw in my life."

"And do my great-uncles all live in houses just like grandpa's?"

"No, my dear:—they, with others of your kindred, live in the old Atherton homesteads, where our ancestors have lived, ever since the family came here, that is, almost for two hundred years."

"What are ancestors?" asked the child.

"Our grandparents, and our great-grandparents, and our great-great-grandparents, and our great-great-great-grandparents, and so on, as far back as you like to go, up to Noah or to Adam," said his aunt, soberly laughing.

"And homesteads—what are they?"

"A homestead is the house where our ancestors lived, one after another, and which belonged to them, with all the land round it. But you have asked questions enough for the present. Some day I will take you to Yantic Falls, and then you shall see the old homestead,—our own, I mean—the old homestead of all."

"But I cannot see our ancestors, aunty, for they are dead."

"No, Alby, but you shall see their graves."

It was a great event when little Alban was taken by his aunt one Saturday afternoon to Yantic Falls. One of Elizabeth Atherton's married sisters was "settled" in Yanmouth, and it was young Mansfield—a nearly full-grown nephew, and Alban's cousin, who drove them in General Atherton's chaise. The chaise, alias gig, and the pleasure-wagon, were nearly the only carriages then known in Connecticut. It was about a century, in fact, since the great-grandfather of General Atherton had set up at Yantic Falls the first chaise ever seen in the colony, and the family had never since used any grander vehicle. The distance from Yanmouth to the Falls, was only a dozen miles or thereabouts; the road was hilly, indeed, but in fair order, and wound its way through a half-wild, and highly picturesque country, that showed, however, at every step, more of fertility and of culture. The little Alban evinced a quick eye for scenery. Every gray rock overhanging the road, every copse, with its sweet spring gurgling over living green by the road-side, every glimpse of the winding river, with its shadowy islets, elicited expressions of delight which made Tom Mansfield laugh, and charmed the quiet heart of Betsey Atherton. But it was when, about half-way to the Falls from Yanmouth, they suddenly came upon an Indian village in an ancient clearing, belted with the oldest woods of the region, that Master Alban's transports could scarcely be restrained. Here was indeed a new world which no one could have suspected to exist within so short a distance from Yanmouth. Not but that the Indians frequently came down to the port, with fruit and fish, or moccasins, and baskets of birch-bark, braided with porcupine quills; and sometimes a blanketed squaw, with blue trowsers under her single short petticoat of the same color, and a man's hat on her head, her patient papoose bound to a straight board between her shoulders, would stray into the kitchen of the " Cassle," and sit in silence, (till black Hagar as silently brought cold meat, or perhaps some cast-off finery of her mistress,) scorning to beg, and departing with a stately "good morning" by way of thanks.

Alban was familiar with this; but an Indian town! the huts, the yellow gourds, the half-naked little boys; it was quite like one of grandma's stories. He almost wished that he had been an Indian. Betsey Atherton's beautiful face also lighted up with intense feeling of some sort, as they passed out of the old Mohegan village.

" When you are a man, Alban, if you are a true Christian, as I hope you will be," she said, " you can be a missionary, and teach the Indians to love Christ."

The " Falls" answered very well to Elizabeth Atherton's description. Alban was silent and attentive, as the strong bay horse drew the chaise up the hill that led from the " Landing," or business part of the town, to the " Plain." Under the hill-side covered with junipers, across the wide greens shaded with elms, they trotted along with the stealthiness peculiar to gigs. All the houses were of wood, double and two storied, and painted white or yellow. They stood in green shrubberied court-yards, with white railings, and noble trees in front; gardens in the rear. They stopped at one which seemed older than the rest, for it was more deeply embowered. Before Thomas Mansfield could help his aunt and Alban out of the chaise, the yellow front-door was opened, and a young lady came out exclaiming, " Why, Bessie, how do you do ?" and ran to meet them at the gate.

" How do you do, Rachel ?"

The ladies kissed each other with great seeming affection, and Rachel kissed Alban two or three times, but the great Thomas Mansfield once. The passing by of one or two persons, who gave the arrival a look of curiosity, did not seem to embarrass at all these cordial welcomes. Rachel led them into the house, and at the door met them a middle-aged motherly matron, who kissed all the new-comers.

" You come in good time, sister," she said to Miss Atherton. " Dinner will be ready in half an hour, but if little Alban is hungry, as he must be after his ride, he shall have a piece of gingerbread immediately. Do, Rachel, get Alban a piece of that gingerbread hot from the oven."

In fact, the house was fragrant with the recent " bake." It was Saturday, you know.

4

CHAPTER VI.

"I LIKE exceedingly the plan of taking Alby to see all the Athertons, and the old Atherton homesteads," said Rachel Atherton to Betsey. "It is a very wholesome thought that we belong to a race rooted in the land for many generations—a race which God has multiplied and blessed."

"I thought that it would teach the child what is meant by the God of his fathers," said Betsey Atherton, with her sweetest smile.

"To whom I trust that he will be faithful as his fathers have ever been, in spite of his being named after a Catholic saint," said Rachel's father.

This conversation occurred at dinner.

Deacon Hezekiah Atherton was Elizabeth's oldest brother, the sterner image of their father, yet of a singular and almost enchanting suavity in his occasional manner. Rachel was but a few years her aunt's junior, and their intimacy was sisterly. She was in her maiden prime then,—scarcely turned of twenty ; tall, a dark, bright face ; fine eyes, sparkling teeth, a smile of irresistible sympathy. Rachel Atherton was what is called an intellectual girl. She had imagination, enthusiasm, and great moral energy. She was by no means so beautiful as her aunt ; her figure though passable, wanted the charming undulations of Betsey Atherton, whose every line was harmony, and her every motion grace ; yet Rachel had already twenty admirers to Elizabeth's one.

"You don't find our table so elegantly furnished as yours at the ' Castle,' sister Betsey," said Deacon Atherton.

"I am afraid Bessie finds more serious fault," said Rachel, glancing at the slice of fresh bread, by the side of her aunt-friend's plate, of which the crust only had been touched. "My bread is sour to-day."

"Rachel has so many books to read, and so many enterprises of charity on hand, that her housekeeping suffers;" said her father.

"The bread is raised a trifle too much," said Elizabeth, candidly, "but I get along very well. Pa is so particular, that *I* am obliged to be as particular myself at the Castle, as you say."

"And you have no pictures to paint," said her brother, glancing at the numerous water-color copies of celebrated pictures which decorated the dining-room.

"No ; I do not possess Rachel's enviable talent in that respect," rejoined Betsey, with an admiring glance at a finely-colored "Deposition," after Rubens.

Indeed, it was not only the sour bread that betrayed to Bessie's experience some neglect of the fine details of New England housekeeping ; but she knew her friend's infirmity. Cutting an over-sweetened tart, (which Master Alby—little epicure—left on his plate,) Rachel informed her friend that after dinner she would accompany her in a general visitation of the Atherton families, and would take the opportunity to unfold to her a scheme of which she was full, and which Bessie, she was sure, would approve. The chaise was brought to the door ; the two girls took their places, with Tom Mansfield sitting between them on the edge of the two cushions just where they met ; Master Alban had a stool placed at his aunt's feet. It was a load, but the bay horse was strong. Away they go, under the lofty elms that line the road. On one side of the broad green are the white houses amid their gardens ; on the other rises the steep hill, covered with juniper and pine. They are to call on at least a dozen families, all owning the name of Atherton, all more or less nearly related to little Alby, either on the father's or mother's side, all in a circuit of some four miles square,—a beautiful *rus-in-urbe*, so mingling farm and town, fair streets, wild hills, thick groves, romantic waterfalls, lonely meeting-houses, and factory villages. The burying-ground of Indian sachems lay in a wood near one of the finest mansions, and many a strange tradition was told by Rachel of Indian battles and sanguinary acts of vengeance, of which she pointed out to Alby the precise localities. Then the manners of the people, which Alby was too young to appreciate :—the blended urbanity and rusticity of his kinsmen,—people who had never known a superior, and acknowledged none but their Maker, dwelling in the old homesteads which had never (so they boasted) passed out of the name ; or swarming in new hives, destined, as they hoped, to a similar permanence. Everywhere Alby was made much of : all said that he must be very happy to live with his grandfather, and that they hoped he would one day be as good a man. It being Saturday afternoon, all invited him to stay to tea, and promised him a dish of local celebrity, which on the eve of the Sabbath smoked on every decent supper-table in Yantic :—baked beans and pork. Alby wanted to accept the first invitation, but finding that he was sure of the regale anywhere, he declined the subsequent invitations with the best grace. Upon the whole, it may be doubted whether any scion of English aristocracy was ever more impressed by a visit to the stately manorial residence of his race than was our Alban by his, to the rural city founded by his Puritan and republican ancestors, who, indeed, had been the founders, not of that single community only, but of vast commonwealths.

It was not till they had finished the round of calls, and had turned their faces homeward, the day-star being already sunk beneath the wooded hills, that Rachel opened to Betsey Atherton the scheme with which her mind was now profoundly exercised. It was two-fold. First, she wanted to establish in the family a weekly " concert of prayer," for the " conversion" of all its members :—this met Bessie's warmest approval. Secondly, she wanted Bessie to unite with her in a project for converting the Indian village between Yanmouth and the " Falls" to real Christianity, and for giving them the regular institutions of the gospel.

" It is most desirable," said Bessie ; " but how are *we* to accomplish so good an object ?"

"We are to go and live among them," replied Rachel; "teach the women and children,—hold regular prayer meetings with the former."

"But how is my father's housekeeping and yours to go on meanwhile, my dear Rachel? Our mothers depend on us, you know."

"Why," said Rachel, "Ma is as zealous as I am in the matter; she has agreed to take weeks with me; you must do the same with grandmamma; and then *we* can reside alternately a week at a time at Mohegan Town."

"What, alone!" exclaimed Bessie, in alarm. "Oh no: I could not. Besides, *my* mother, you know, is too far advanced in years, for the fatigues and care of housekeeping. Really, it does not seem to be my duty to throw them upon her every alternate week, in order that I may go teach the Indians."

"What is to become of the Indians, then, in the next world, Betsey?" asked Rachel Atherton.

"Very true," said Betsey, much perplexed. "But to take weeks with me would soon kill mamma."

This checked the ardent missionary for a moment, but she soon returned to the charge. "Why cannot the house go on for a week at a time without *your* superintendence? Some things might not be quite so well done as you would do them, but with servants so well trained as yours, it could not amount to much, and grandpa is so good a man, I am sure that he would cheerfully submit to it for the sake of saving souls."

Bessie laughed outright.

"You know nothing about the care of superintending a house full of black servants, dear Rachel. Your Esther will get along well enough in your absence; she is a sharp New England girl; but to think of Hagar and Sam being left to 'rule the roast;'— 'de Cassle' would be topsy-turvy in half a week! What do you think, Alby; could you do without aunty a week at the Castle?"

"I wish you could go and save the Indians, aunty," said the

child, who felt the contagion of his cousin Rachel's enthusiasm, more than the justice of his aunt Betsey's reasoning.

" *My* opinion is," said Tom Mansfield, who had been giving the bay horse a good many cuts with his whip, while the discussion proceeded, "that the weeks aunt Betsey went to Mohegan they would have to eat sour bread at the Castle."

CHAPTER VII.

RACHEL ATHERTON was not a girl to be defeated by any thing short of impossibilities in a scheme that had once thoroughly engaged her enthusiasm. After failing in every other argument, she had one sure card in the peculiar family pride of the Athertons —a pride which attached itself far more to the high religious character of their ancestors than to their worldly position. It was a source of unacknowledged, but more real, self-complaisance to Elizabeth Atherton herself, as we may have seen reason to suspect, that her race was distinguished by an incontaminate piety and saintly devotion, than that it appertained to the gentry of the land. That the first Atherton in the colony had enjoyed among his fellow-settlers the exclusive title of *Mister*, that they had given a President to Congress, Governors to States, Judges to the Supreme Bench, Generals to the army of the Revolution, and, brightest distinction of all, a " Signer" to the Declaration, was nothing in comparison to the number of devout and learned ministers they had produced, and to the fact, often mentioned in their annals, that the blood of an early apostle to the Indians flowed in their veins. In addition to these glories in its spiritual escutcheon, the family was always conspicuous for the piety of many of its female members : more than one volume of " Memoirs," illustrating the remarkable Christian graces of some daughter of their house, gone to the grave in her virgin bloom, perhaps in a holy childhood, or of some lovely matron—the scion of another tree transplanted into the Atherton inclosure—who, if she had not drawn her blood from them, had infused into them of her own, enriched the hagiography of New England. But as yet the name had produced no female missionaries, and the missionary character was separated from every other to a New England apprehension, as if its possessors were almost of a different species. The popular idea of these laborers of either sex, especially when their self-devotion had been consecrated by a premature death, approximated to that of the saints among Catholics.

Rachel made a visit at the Castle, and staid a week. She talked of her missionary project the whole time, and appealed successfully to the feelings which we have described, the more successfully, because unconsciously, as one who was profoundly influenced by them herself, without being aware of it. Old Mrs. Atherton, indeed, was entirely deaf to all that her granddaughter could urge, but her opposition was almost passive, or at least, confined itself to sallies of witty ridicule, while over her grandfather, who was fond of her, Rachel gained a complete victory. He was very assailable by the idea that he might be suffering considerations of his own temporal comfort to stand in the way of the eternal welfare of his benighted fellow-creatures. Mrs. Atherton's old-fashioned high churchmanship, associated, as it was, with a scarcely concealed Toryism in politics, rendered her influence in the family, on a religious question, *nihil*. Rachel quite plainly intimated that grandma's indifference was akin to that of Gallio. Even Betsey feared it was a proof that her mother had not experienced a vital change of heart. It was out of the question, however, she said, for *her* to take part in the new enterprise, as long as Alby remained under her care. It would be betraying a trust to quit him in order to teach Indians. But she promised that in the autumn, when he returned to his parents for the six months, she would allow Jane Mansfield to take her place on the alternate weeks at the Castle, and become Rachel's co-laborer at Mohegan.

Jane Mansfield was the hoyden of sixteen introduced to the reader on the Sunday evening described in the third chapter of this book. She was the granddaughter of General Atherton, of course, and their almost daily visitor, but to consent to her being substituted for his daughter was no doubt a great sacrifice to the claims of Christian charity. A more serious one was in store for General Atherton. It often happens that when good men make a formal resignation of any possession to God, scarce expecting, perhaps, to be called upon to make it actual, he takes them at their word.

The autumn came, September blowing eastern gales, and October breathing southern airs. The parents of our little hero came on to Yanmouth with their younger children, to spend a fortnight and keep Thanksgiving. There was a round of dinners and teas in the ancient town, and the mutual hospitalities extended even to Yantic Falls. " Woe worth the day" to the turkeys, as the first Thursday in November approached. General Atherton entertained at dinner at least twenty of his relatives, chiefly his children and grown-up grandchildren, besides as many more juveniles. The principal table was spread in the great parlor ; the children feasted in the smaller ordinary dining-room. The Rt. Rev. Dr Richard Gray, Mrs. Atherton's brother, an " Episcopal bishop," (as the Yanmouth people pleonastically termed him,) said grace before, and the Rev. David Atherton Devotion, the new pastor of the Yanmouth Congregational church, made a long prayer, by way of grace, after dinner ; almost as long as that with which he had opened the morning service. Some of the guests, females of course, who had never seen a bishop before, except at confirmation, wondered that Dr. Gray did not wear his robes on this occasion. Dr. Gray and Mr. Devotion were extremely cordial, though the bishop thought the minister unordained, and the minister returned the compliment by thinking the prelate unconverted. Both did justice to their host's Thanksgiving cheer, and (especially the bishop) to his fine old wines. With what consummate grace old Mrs. Atherton presided ! how well, apropos to some obsolete plate, she told (for the hundredth time at least) the story of her entertaining the Duc de Lauzun, the Marquis de Lafayette, and half a dozen more French officers of rank, at a dinner, " not nearly so good as this, you must know," at Yantic Falls, in the Revolutionary war ! With what an air of unaffected pity for the present generation, she declared that the Duc was "truly" a gentleman, and with what a gracious mixture of sadness and sense of the historical dignity of the event she alluded to his subsequent fate. "You know," she said, (every body knew it,) "he was guillotined in that terrible French Revolution."

They observed early hours in those days. Dinner, even on Thanksgiving day, was served at two o'clock, P. M., and at half-past six, "the drawing-room" (opened only on such occasions) was already lighted up for the evening party that followed. This apartment, so famous in Yanmouth, was adorned with a cream-colored carpet of roses, in a single piece, and high-backed chairs, gorgeously worked on yellow satin, by the hands of patient female Athertons. But it could not suffice that evening for the company which overflowed into all the apartments of the floor ; even the sacred recesses of "the bedroom," converted into a depository for gentlemen's hats and overcoats, admitted parties of both sexes, seeking rest after dancing. For they still danced in New England, even in pious families, although the line was already beginning to be more strictly drawn. But the voluptuous dances of Germany and Russia had not yet obtained a footing in the new world. Cotillions and country dances sufficiently interested the youth and the youthful beauty at General Atherton's ; besides that, two ladies of the old school, in matronly brocades, performed a minuet.

The week after these festivities Betsey Atherton commenced her missionary labors. On one Saturday evening Rachel came to Mohegan-town from the Falls ; on the next, her aunt arrived from Yanmouth to take her place ; and thus through the winter they alternated, regardless of weather, of the discomforts of their temporary abode, of the solitude of their work. Frequently, they both went and returned from their mission on foot. Coarse was their diet ; hard their couch ; comfortless their crowded school-room ; tedious their task of instruction, with pupils who had the primary habits of attention to acquire, as well as the simplest elements of knowledge. They were cheered by each other's presence even only for an hour or two on the Saturday,— hours which they sanctified by devoting them to united prayer for the objects of the mission. They then held a female prayer-meeting for the squaws, of about a half-hour's duration, begun and closed with a hymn sung by their own sweet voices only; then fervently embraced, and parted for another week.

The solicitudes of Rachel Atherton were not limited to procuring for the neglected people she had undertaken to Christianize, merely such religious and temporal instruction as two young ladies could bestow; she would not be satisfied with any thing short of seeing the Mohegans converted into a community of Congregationalists, with a church and settled pastor of their own, a permanent school, and all the elements of New England civilization. To realize these objects, she resolved to apply at once to the government of the United States. She boldly wrote in her own name to the Secretary of War, to whose bureau all Indian affairs belong, to advocate the claims of her *protégées*. A nephew of General Atherton, and of course the cousin of Rachel and Elizabeth, had a seat in the Federal Senate. She obtained his support without difficulty; and a petition which the secretary might have found reasons for evading if it had been urged in any other way, became irresistible when it was advanced in the name of two young ladies, who had first devoted themselves with so much self-denial to the cause which they advocated. A sum was granted from the Indian appropriation to build a meeting-house and parsonage, and support a minister among the remnant of the Mohegans. In the spring with the rains that softened the frozen soil of the Yantic valley, a shower (as Rachel and Betsey believed) of divine grace descended to soften the colder hearts of the half-savage inhabitants of the Indian village. Several adults of both sexes gave, in the language of the country and the time, " no equivocal tokens of being the subjects of a gracious work," and when thorough examination by the church at the Falls had sufficiently proved this, as was thought, they were baptized.

Such a work as this could not be carried on in secret. The enterprise of the Misses Atherton became a topic of conversation in all the religious circles of New England; its success was prayed for in monthly concerts ; sympathizers in remote towns sent contributions of money, books, and clothing, in aid of the interesting and successful mission. The youth and personal loveliness of the missionaries could not but transpire. Unmarried ministers felt their interest peculiarly excited ; and some of these were in a position to allow of their manifesting it.

The Rev. President Hopewell was a distinguished preacher and divine, whose reputation at the age of thirty had placed him at the head of a rising New England college. He was in search of a wife, and he came to Yantic Falls to apply for the hand of Rachel Atherton, although he had never seen her. He was handsome, intellectual, self-confident, a man much coveted ; he made his advances with graceful skill. But Rachel was far above being thus diverted from her work. She thanked him with enchanting expressions of sympathy, and recommended him to try a friend of hers who had leisure to be married and who was far more fitted than herself to adorn the station he offered. Before taking this advice the President went down to Yanmouth to see Elizabeth. Betsey Atherton was withheld by no such lofty notions as those which influenced her friend in the rejection of every kind of matrimonial project ; but Betsey Atherton had, what even Rachel had not—a purely virgin soul, to which not this or that wedlock, but marriage itself, was a thing to recoil from. It was not that she lacked the tender instincts of her sex, as we have seen in the case of Lieutenant Harvey. She was proud, not cold ; delicate in her thoughts, and therefore exacting in her ideal. She would have been perfect, if in the way she had been brought up she could have apprehended the living object which alone can absorb the heart without defiling it,—of which she could have said, *Quem cùm amavero, casta sum ; cùm tetigero, munda sum; cùm accipero, virgo sum.*

Betsey Atherton was one of those, who, as the proverb is, are "not long for this world." She caught cold in her visits to Mohegan-town. The school-room was crannysome, and full of draughts. In the spring she had a cough—fatal sign on the

New England coast. Our young Alban was with his aunt again in the summer, at her urgent wish, though she was already marked visibly for the grave. She had one of those beautiful, rapid declines of which we mostly read in books. After the first shock of learning her danger, she neither hoped to recover, as most do, nor feared to die. Her frame of mind was even sweeter as her disease advanced, and her death was triumphant. Its effect upon our Alban's story is what we have here to note. For General Atherton did not long survive his daughter's loss; the Mansfields moved into the Castle, now become old Mrs. Atherton's house; and it ceased to be one of our hero's homes. We must follow him to another.

5

BOOK II.

School; or, the Basement.   The Hero Assimilates.

––––––––––––•––––––––––––

CHAPTER I.

IT came about the time of the great September gale, and was
very like one in its effects. As sometimes it is one of the
mightiest trees that is uprooted by a hurricane, so often it is a
colossal fortune that is prostrated by a crisis.   Ever since the
unexpected peace had toppled down half the commercial houses
in the United States, Samuel Atherton had been gallantly fighting for his credit.   Knowing himself to be solvent, it was hard
to strike under a sudden broadside from an unexpected enemy.
The treason of a confidential agent, whom he had just made his
partner, and who absconded after using his name to a fearful
extent to cover his own private losses at the gaming-table, was
the immediate cause of Mr. Atherton's stopping payment.   We
may as well say at once that he ultimately paid every thing, but
for the time all was lost.   He saved nothing for himself.   Even
his wife's fortune, just paid by her father's executors, was
swept into the vortex.   Plate, library, pictures, carriage, of course,
went under the hammer, and from the fine mansion in State-
street, hitherto so hospitable in the worst of times, the family
were forced to remove into a small house in the jail liberties, to
avoid at least a prison ; and from that safe point Mr. Atherton
began as a poor man to reconstruct his fortunes.

The aspect of New York at that time was very different from that which the city exhibits at present. The neighborhood of the Battery (then a safe and delightful play-ground for children) was the aristocratic quarter of the town, occupied by large and well-built mansions, and distinguished by its air of seclusion. In Whitehall, where now a dozen omnibuses at once are thundering at every instant down to the South Ferry, over a pavement shattered and gullied by their incessant wheels, the grass then grew in the middle of the street. Wall, William, Beaver, Broad, and the contiguous streets, were full of little old Dutch houses, with high gables, rising in narrow steps to their apex. There were no palaces then on the yet unknown Fifth Avenue, rivalling those of the merchant aristocracies of Italy ; Mr. Upjohn had not thickly sprinkled the city (the half of which did not exist) with those churches of brown stone, so beautiful in detail, of which the material will always excuse the architectural defects. Mr. Atherton, then, attended public worship in Wall-street, in the First Presbyterian church, which the rising generation will know nothing of, though it has not ceased to exist, having been transported like Aladdin's palace, as it were, without displacing a stone, into New Jersey. On Christmas, which Presbyterians then did not observe, the children were taken by their nursery-maid to old Trinity, to see "the greens," enjoy the mysterious music of the organ, (equally unknown as yet to Puritan assemblies,) and wonder at the under-ground murmur of the responses, at the minister's "white gown," and the strange and almost awful change to black which preceded the sermon. In those days the reality of Santa Claus was unsuspected, and Alban with his brothers suspended their stockings over the chimney-piece on Christmas eve, earnestly begging that a candle might be left burning, whereby the good-natured visitant, the lover of children, when he descended the chimney with his reindeer-sledge, might not fail to peruse the certificates of good conduct carefully pinned to the carved wooden mantels.

Poetical elements mingled in the existence of the young Knick-

erbockers in those days of which our vulgar modern New Yorkers
know nothing. What a glorious region for Alban and his set
was the district of rocky heights and wild ponds within a boy's
afternoon walk of the City Hall! What kite-flying in spring on
the former! what rare skating in winter on the latter! How
the clear ice-tracts embraced the snowy islets, and formed endless
labyrinths among the thick, leafless marsh bushes, where it
was a pleasure to be lost! What a place for fun and fear was the
City Hall itself, with its long vaulted corridors, its mysterious lob-
bies, dark basement cells, its marble staircases, echoing dome, its
gallery and terrace. Every Saturday afternoon they played in it,
ignorant as it was of the blackguards and loafers who now loiter
about the Park, and fearing only lest "Old Hays" should seize
them for climbing too adventurously along the perilous basement
ledge under the windows of the public offices, or for trampling
down the grass of the Park, by "double base," or "every man to
his own den."

"The army," said Uncle Toby, "swore terribly in Flanders."
School-boys swore terribly in New York in the days of which we
speak, and they did not limit themselves to swearing. A language
even worse than profane was but too frequently on their lips.
The ears of our Alban, at this period of his life, became familiar
with a phraseology to which at Yarmouth he had certainly never
been accustomed. At first it shocked, then it amused him; by
and by he took a certain pleasure in hearing and repeating it;
(we are sorry to record these infirmities, but historic truth obliges
us ;) and although a sense of delicacy in part, and in part an honest
fear of being wicked, withheld him from both profanity and coarseness *de proprio motu*, yet we fear that he was often ashamed of
his own timidity. There was one peculiarity of his position at this
time which deserves to be noticed. Alban had no sisters, and
from the retirement in which his parents lived he could not boast
so much as the acquaintance of any young persons of his own age,
but of an opposite sex. His school intimates were boys either sis-
terless like himself, or whose sisters had grown up, or at whose

homes he was not allowed to visit. He had the sweet recollection of his aunt, and he knew the reserved tenderness of his mother; but apart from these influences, it was a hard, a boisterous, and a far from refined society in which he lived. Yet all agreed that Alb Atherton, though foremost in sports, for innocence of manners and sweetness of temper was the girl of the school. And he was the notorious favorite of the masters. There was nothing that he could not learn, and he got on so rapidly that he read the Enëid through for pleasure while his class were working at the first book. The mathematical teacher was forced to give him recitations apart, he devoured Euclid with such impatience.

Indeed, our young hero displayed an insatiable appetite for every species of knowledge. On the heights where he flew his kite, the strata of which the fatal process of grading for new-invading streets had already laid bare, he mineralized in his small way, and his spare cash (not much to boast of) went to augment his specimens or to enrich a tiny collection of shells and coins. The huge volumes of the British Encyclopedia were for ever littering his mother's sitting-room, while Alban, as far as he could without assistance, patiently mastered its elaborate treatises, which he could not know were, in the march of science, already obsolete. At this time the Waverley novels were issuing from the press, and his father got them from the libraries as they appeared; but the perusal of Waverley, when he was about nine years old, so excited the boy's imagination, that Mr. Atherton would not even allow his son to hear another of the series. But there was an old copy of the Arabian Nights, saved with the Encyclopedia from the sale; and one birthday, his father gave him a large Pictorial Pilgrim's Progress :—at twelve, Alban knew these and Shakspeare almost by heart.

" This boy has no moderation in any thing," said his father; " he tires himself to pieces with playing in the streets, and then he buries himself in a corner with a book till he is almost blind."

" I wish Alban would not play in the street at all," said his mother, " or at least that he would keep in sight of the house

Grey-street is quiet, (for it is not a thoroughfare,) and it is almost as clean as our own yard. I should think it would be a great deal better for any plays than Hudson or Greenwich, or that odious Park."

"You can't keep such a boy in bounds, in a city like New York."

"That is what I am afraid of," replied his mother, "that he cannot be kept in bounds. I don't like all his associates. And he is getting into bad habits already—" ("Bad habits!" ejaculated Mr. Atherton)—"why only last night he and Bob Simmons were out till nine o'clock, double knocking at all the doors, and ringing all the bells for a dozen squares."

"What, Alban!" exclaimed Mr. Atherton, with a hearty laugh.

"Certainly; they call it playing the Old Harry! Bob wanted to break a pane of glass in every house, but Alb would not consent. Robert Simmons is a *very* bad boy," said Mrs. Atherton emphatically. Mr. Atherton laughed again.

"The Simmonses are our next-door neighbors, you know, my dear, so that Alban would not avoid Bob, even if he never stirred out of Grey-street. Mr. Simmons is alderman of the ward, and a member of the church; and he is rich. You can't forbid our son associating with his. Boys must take their chance."

"I believe that a city is a bad place for the education of boys," replied Mrs. Atherton. "See the young Mortons. If Alban should turn out dissipated like one of them, it would break my heart."

"Would you be willing to send him away to school?" asked her husband.

"If poor Elizabeth had lived, he might have fitted for college at Yanmouth," was Mrs. Atherton's indirect reply. "As it is, I don't know where I could be willing to send him, unless to your Sister Fanny's, at Babylon."

Our hero was destined to owe a great deal to maiden aunts. The virgin sister of his mother had watched over his childhood;

the virgin sister of his father was to preside over his incipient manhood ; for it is somewhere, we think, from twelve to sixteen, that young Americans begin to be men.   Aunt Fanny lived in her own house at Babylon, which was a small country village in the green heart of the State of New York.   She had brought up already one generation of young Athertons, motherless cousins of Alban, and was now trying her hand on another—her great nephews and nieces—with whom, in point of age, our hero might be classed.   Aunt Fanny had a very poor opinion of Mrs. Samuel Atherton's domestic management, and had been anxious for a long time to extend to the latter's children the benefits of her own experience.   To send Alban thither, to finish his preparation for college, was therefore an eligible plan, and to execute as easy as talking.

Babylon, an ancient colonial fort of great fame in the early Indian wars, had been effectively settled soon after the Revolution by the paternal uncles of our hero, who had migrated thither from Yantic with their flocks and herds, or, in plain English, with the proceeds of their patrimony converted into continental currency.   The rich farms of the vast township belonged chiefly to them, and from one of them, in solemn but characteristic jest, it had received its ridiculous name.   The village boasted a select school of high provincial repute, founded under their patronage and chiefly sustained by their liberality.

CHAPTER II.

" HE is a —— fool," said young Alban.

The blank was filled up at the time by a profane expletive, with which we would not willingly sully our pages.

The first oath ! It was the first, and Alban had not uttered it in a rage, but with cool premeditation. He did it to seem manly. It was for the same reason that he had tried to smoke cigars, unsuccessfully, for his cerebral temperament was absolutely intolerant of the narcotic. " He is a —— fool." The expression was neither scholarly, nor gentlemanlike, nor Christian, nor even intelligible, and Alban thought of it a good deal that night in bed, before falling asleep.

The day following Alban swore again, not faintly as at first, but *ore rotundo*, and that two or three times. He is getting on. But it was that evening that he learned from his father that he was going to Babylon to school.

" I have begun to swear just at the wrong time," said Alban to himself. " That last —— to-day really came out without thinking ; what if I should get into a habit of it before I go to Babylon. They are all so very religious at Babylon. There has been a great revival, and I don't know how many have joined the church. My cousin Henry is a convert, and George St. Clair —the only fellows there that I do care about. George has written me a long letter about religion, and saving my soul. What will they think of my swearing ? I must certainly break myself of it at once. Certainly the habit of swearing is a dreadful thing. Every body says so. People have been struck dead for swearing. What would Aunt Betsey say to my using such expressions ! Perhaps she saw and heard me at that moment. God saw me at any rate, and heard me too. I believe I have been very wicked, and very silly. Oh, our Father in heaven !" he concluded with himself, "help me not to swear any more, and give me a new heart, so that I may not wish to swear."

Alban prayed to this effect very earnestly. The prime and moving reason doubtless was the fear of disgracing himself in the sanctified public opinion of young Babylon, which, after the great revival, must be so very different from that of young New York. But this primary influence of human origin awakened also the slumbering conscience, smiting it internally with the rod of the sudden perception of the Divine Presence. Under this impression he wrote a very pious letter in reply to George St. Clair's, a letter which filled Babylon—young and old—with rejoicing, and which caused Alban, when about a month after he arrived there, to be greeted universally as a "young convert." Wicked boy! little hypocrite! not for resolving, although from motives partly human, to avoid profane language; not for resolving to be as good as possible in future; in both which he was of course right :—but for allowing himself to pass as one mysteriously sanctified, in a society where the notion of such a supernatural change was current.

The greatest difficulty in going to Babylon was the physical one of the journey; not a serious one by any means, but neither so short nor so easy as at present. Our little hero embarked at New York on a steamboat, at nine o'clock one fine May morning, under the protection of a Babylonish uncle. It was thought to have been a good passage when they disembarked at Albany at three P. M. of the day following. The next day conveyed them by stage up the wild Mohawk valley. It was only on reaching the central table-land of the State, that a canal-boat offered to Alban the delight of a yet untried mode of travel. It was at noon of the fourth day that they arrived at Babylon.

Alban forthwith received a class of very little boys in the Babylon Sunday-school; he was invited to attend the "young converts' prayer-meeting," composed of about a dozen boys of from twelve to sixteen years, all "hopefully pious," and all (but himself) already "church members;" and Mr. Jeremiah Cant-

well, a candidate for the ministry, and beneficiary of the Ladies'
Benevolent Sewing Society, which had called him from the occupation of a journeyman hatter to pursue his studies at Babylon
school, and who presided at the aforesaid young converts' prayer-
meeting, called upon Alban the very first night to "lead in
prayer."

Tremendous moment! our hero would have given worlds to
decline ; but before he could utter a syllable the whole meeting
was on its knees, each young convert with his face buried in his
hands, and his elbows supported on his chair. There was a
moment's dead silence, and Alban, desperate, plunged *in medias
res*. His quick perception took in at once the situation with all its
proprieties, and if from the utter want of experience his prayer
was somewhat unique in Babylon, it was not on that account less
refreshing. He warmed as he got on. He had in fact opened a
new vein. Recollections of his maternal grandfather's daily
fervent appeals to Heaven shot like lightning through his mind—
a torrent of devotional eloquence flowed forth.

"What a prayer you made, Alban!" said his cousin Henry,
as they walked home arm in arm. "We had no idea of your
having such a gift."

Aunt Fanny's cottage was an irregular, rambling structure,
the several members of which had been erected at different
times, as convenience or necessity required. It was of wood,
and painted white, of course, and stood on the skirts of the
village, in the centre of an ample garden, orchard, and green
shrubbery tastefully laid out. The moon shone bright on the
gravelled walks as the young cousins flung behind them the
swinging gate ; and before they reached the open front door,
a little girl in a white frock came out upon the steps to meet
them.

"Have you had a good meeting?" she asked.

"Very interesting," said Henry Atherton.

The child took the answerer a little apart from Alban, and
whispered in his ear. Henry replied in the same tone.

"No secrets," said Alban, rather awkwardly, for he suspected the subject of the conference.

"Oh, it is no secret," said the young girl, putting her hand in his. "Come, let us all sit down on the sill. There! you, Henry, on this side, and Alban on the other, me between you. There is just room for us three."

They did so. She was a pretty little creature, nearly of Alban's age; with large blue eyes, the most dazzling skin, and long flaxen ringlets, flowing nearly to her waist. She put one of her white bare arms round Henry Atherton's neck, but she only looked affectionately from time to time at Alban as he sat very, very close to her side on the door-sill.

Thus we may leave them; Alban being, as it were, in a new world.

CHAPTER III.

ALL the young converts at Babylon kept journals. Henry Ather-
ton did ; Jane did ; and so Alban did. Here is a leaf from
Alban's. It will give us a notion of him at that period of life.
Some of it is spicy.

"Aug. 15." (There is no Anno Domini, but he is thirteen
and a half years old.) "I have been now three months at B.
When I first arrived, I remember being puzzled by St. Clair's
asking me in Sunday-school, whether I had yet experienced any
decline in my religion. I suppose I understand now what he
meant. My heart is very cold, and I certainly no longer feel the
same pleasure in prayer that I used. By George's asking the
question, it is a regular thing, I take it.

"Sept. 15. Aunt Fanny entertained me to-day with an explanation of the Book of Revelations, which she understands, as
she does the whole Bible, in a sense quite peculiar to herself.
She thinks the seven Churches of Asia, denote the seven Christian denominations of the present day, viz. : the Catholic, the
Episcopalian, the Presbyterian, the Methodist, the Baptist, the
Congregationalist, and the Quakers. She pretends to fix each
Church. Thus the Laodiceans are the Episcopal Church, because
it is ' neither cold nor hot ;' the Quakers are the ' Church of Philadelphia,' of course ; the Presbyterian, (on which she is very
severe,) is the ' Church at Sardis,' for it has the name of being
alive, and is dead, yet has a few names which have not defiled
their garments. The Methodists are the ' Church of Thyatira,'
because its works are mentioned twice, showing that they believe
in perfection. The Roman Catholics long puzzled her, for
the description of each of the Churches seemed to suit them
exactly, one not more than another ; but at last she concluded
they must be the ' Church at Pergamos,' because ' it dwells where

Satan's seat is.' It seems to me there is a good deal of fancy in this, but I love to hear her talk. There is a new servant—'help,' I mean—come to-day, a tall, handsome girl, with black eyes : I must find out if she is a Christian.

"Nov. 5. I am afraid that Jane is going back as well as I. I have long kept up, under the sense of my own declension, because I thought *she* would not fall away. A girl—that is, like my cousin Jane—seems so pure a being. I can't imagine her having one of the thoughts that daily come into my mind. Then she never hears the language that I do. To be sure, I don't associate much with boys of my own age. I wonder if girls ever use bad language when they are by themselves.

"Nov. 10. Jane is always in the house with Polly and Maggie. They are very good servants, but not fit companions for a young lady. It can't be well helped in Maggie's case, for they are of the same age. Indeed, till Polly came, we all amused ourselves together, and very innocently. Now the girls keep by themselves, and I cannot help suspecting mischief. If so, Polly, with her black eyes and pouting red lips, is at the bottom of it. She is eighteen years old, four years older than any of us, and she ought to know better.

"Dec. 10. Just a month since I wrote last. It was the very next day that Jane first hinted to me privately that Polly amused them when they were alone by telling them ludicrous stories. I had a great mind to tell Aunt Fanny at once, but finally concluded to tax Polly herself. In her defence, she told me one of the stories, at which I could not help laughing. From that it has gone on, till we have come to listen and repeat,— all of us. Even Jane will repeat the 'funniest things,' as Polly calls them, before my face, without a blush. We spend thus almost every one of the long evenings in that great kitchen, with its bright floor and roaring fire of logs. It is a curious thing that that little German, Madeleine, whom aunt employs for charity, and who cannot speak pure English, will not hear a word bordering on indelicacy. At the first hint, she sticks her

6

fingers in her ears, and runs off. She puts us all to shame, I must say, for she has scarcely clothes to her back, can neither read nor write, and prays to the Virgin Mary, I believe, every night and morning. With all our superior light,—for even Maggie reads her Bible daily,—we are not so good as this ignorant and superstitious child.

"Dec. 20. I have been trying to convert the little Madeleine. I wanted her to let me read the ten commandments to her out of our Bible, that she might see the wickedness of worshipping images, but she would not listen, any more than to Polly's equivocal stories. She said she had learned the ten commandments in her catechism, and that was enough for her.

"'But, Madeleine,' said I, 'your priests leave out one of the commandments. I only want to read you that one, to show you what a sin you commit in worshipping the cross and the Virgin Mary.'

"'I guess there is one of the commandments left out by your priest, Mr. Alban,' replied the little sauce-box, 'or else you don't tell him of your carryings on with Polly and Miss Jane, when you go to confession.'

"'We never go to confession, Madeleine,' said I, rather red, I guess, for I was cut, and speaking sharply too,—'that is one of your popish corruptions.'

"'Ah, Mr. Alban,' she said, 'I thought you didn't go to confession, or you would know some things to be sins, which now, perhaps, you think are not.'

"'And why do you pray to the Virgin, Madeleine, instead of to God?' She was cleaning her knives, and could not get away, or I believe she would have run. After a while, as I persisted in questioning her, she answered, very pertinently, I must admit, 'I *do* pray to God.'

"'Why then do you pray to the Virgin too? Do you think that God cannot hear you? or that the Virgin is more willing to answer your prayers than He?'

"She looked puzzled, and only after some time answered, in the words of the catechism, doubtless,—

"'The Holy Virgin and Saints, hear us *in* God, and God's charity makes them *willing* to pray for us!' With what a touching foreign accent the poor girl said this. It is no answer, of course, yet I did not know exactly how to meet it.

"Dec. 25. Christmas, and no dinner! My father always has a Christmas dinner. I went to the Episcopal church last evening, for the first time in Babylon, although it is directly opposite aunt Fanny's. It is merely a long room, and a very low ceiling; but dressed with the greens, and lighted up, it looked really beautiful. The pulpit had a canopy, like a crown, of evergreen mixed with white artificial roses. The roses formed the name IMMANUEL. The pulpit, too, and the desk under it, (I like having a prayer-desk,) were a mass of dark foliage; and the communion table, which is not bigger than aunt's workstand, being covered with white, and having all the silver vessels on it, was a kind of sparkling centre right in front of the desk. The rails were hung with heavy festoons of spruce boughs, and white drapery to match. I must say I liked it, and more particularly that reading the psalms alternately by the minister and the people. Old King Nebuchadnezzar, as the boys call him—the church-warden, uncle says he is—gave me a prayer-book, and found me the places. I dare say he was pleased to see one of the Atherton boys come to his church. I was almost ashamed to join in the reading at first, but by degrees I grew accustomed to hear my voice, and, ' responded' as they call it, with the best of them.

"Dec. 27. Sunday. I have been to the Episcopal church again to-day, with B——, who is allowed to go because his family are Episcopalians. Aunt don't like it, I see, but she says nothing, except that the Episcopal Church is lukewarm, like that of Laodicea. The Episcopal service takes hold of me wonderfully. It is so pleasant to have something to do in church besides stand up and sit down. But I am afraid there are few spiritual Christians among them. I call to mind grandpa, and aunt Betsey, and cousin Rachel, and all the shining Christians I have ever known. None of them were Episcopalians. Our cousins, the Greys, in New York, are of this Church, but they do not seem so pious and saint-like as my mother, who is a Presbyterian. And I perceive that it is since I have declined in religion that I feel myself so drawn that way. When I have been carrying on, as Madeleine says, with Polly and Miss Jane by the kitchen fire, or stealing a kiss from the latter on the stairs, as she is creeping up to bed on Saturday night, all dewy with the recent ablutions, (sweet child that she is !) though I know—at least I believe—there would be nothing wrong in the last, if we had not been *talking* so, why, the next morning, somehow, I feel as if I wanted to go to the *Episcopal* church. The Presbyterian Church is for saints, but the Episcopal is for sinners.

"Dec. 31. It is the New Year to-morrow, and I mean to turn over a new leaf. I am nearly fourteen years old, and a companion for young men grown. G——, R——, W——, and K——, are all past twenty, yet our standing in the school is the same ; we are fitting for the same class in college ; we associate on equal terms. I beat them all in composition, and yield to none of them in debate. F—— is a full-grown man, yet I believe I have more influence over him than any body in the world. Why, then, for very shame, do I not control myself, and refrain from doing what I know I shall repent of when it is done ? It must be that I am not a real Christian : I have never been truly converted. If there is a revival here this winter, I shall give up my hope, as Jane tells me she has already given up hers, and try for another. Polly, who is a Methodist, says she has no doubt I ' had religion,' but I have ' fallen from grace.' Her advice is to enjoy myself now, not to lose time, but to attend the next camp-meeting, and go into the 'anxious circle ;'—perhaps I shall get religion again !'"

Here occurs a long hiatus in the diary, which we must supply. The revival which Alban looked for to set him right came that very winter. First, the Methodists held a camp-meeting in the wild woods near Babylon. The Presbyterian-Congregationalists, (for they had a compromise of the two systems at Babylon,) despised this movement as fanatical. Alban visited the camp with one of his mature school-friends, and they both agreed to call it a kind of spiritual orgie. But the ground-swell of the commotion soon communicated itself to the haughty Presbyterians. It was ascertained that there was a seriousness. Prayer-meetings were held every morning before light, for the awakening of the Church. A renowned revivalist was sent for, and his coming was the signal for deep excitement. Anxious meetings were held, to elicit and concentrate the interest of the unconverted. The primary symptom of a great work was, that nearly a hundred professing Christians in this large church gave up their hopes, which, besides its other effects, removed the scandal hitherto occasioned by their inconsistent lives ; for it now appeared they were not real Christians at all. Alban and his cousin Jane, though not church members, were in the number of those who thus renounced their claim to the possession of a new heart. Both were said to be under the deepest conviction, but it was very brief, for they were among the earliest of the new conversions, and both found peace on the same day,—a bright Sabbath of February, the sun glittering on fields of stainless snow, and on trees hanging with icicles. Alban was converted in the morning, and Jane in the evening.

The cousins threw themselves into each other's arms in transport, when they first met, after Jane's happy change was announced. Certainly they were both happy, for they believed themselves emancipated from the corruption of human nature. Alban, particularly, to whom it was entirely new, although hitherto remarkable for his cool propriety, was thrown quite off his balance, and for nearly a week acted like a fool. It was only expected, however ; young converts are always somewhat extravagant, and are wisely allowed a spiritual honeymoon.

As the work progressed, the operations of business were suspended, from the intensity of the excitement. The school was closed, and the school-house, slightly darkened at midday, was occupied, early in the morning, at noon, and in the evening, by meetings of the scholars for prayer, with reference to the revival. The girls were on one side, as in school hours, and the boys or young men (for nearly half the scholars of both sexes were grown-up young men or women)—the young men on the other. They led in prayer alternately. Jane's sweet voice learned to raise itself, tremulous with excitement, so as to be heard by the whole breathless and kneeling school. Different individuals, sometimes at their own request, were prayed for by name. The preaching was chiefly on Sunday, when there were three sermons ; but the interest was prevented from flagging during the week, by an impassioned discourse in the evening, on two of the intermediate days. The zeal of Alban directed itself to the conversion of Polly, from the first moment of his own, and after a fierce, prolonged struggle, it was accomplished. Hers was one of the very brightest and most evident transformations that were effected in the revival. But though " brought in" under Presbyterian influence, Polly joined the Methodists.

CHAPTER IV.

It is the school-house ;—a pretty, white Grecian building, standing in a yard among young acacias. It is the school-house
in the long summer vacation. Alban is its sole occupant. It
consists of a single room, lighted on the four sides. There are two
long ranges of clean white desks, and two short ones. There is a
middle space, with a stove, a table for some older students,
and a high desk for the master in one corner. In the opposite
corner is the small vestibule. The windows look out on cottage
villas; on some dark, unpainted houses, standing in vegetable
gardens, embowered in hops, beans, and alders ; and on the green
school-house yard. This last is divided into two portions by a high
board fence, one portion for the boys, one for the girls. But Alban
is now sole lord of the whole. He can take one of the girls'
desks, if he likes ; he can lie on the shady grass, on the sacred,
tabooed, screened-off girls side of the play-ground, or he can walk to
and fro the whole length of the school-room in revery, such as fifteen is prone to, and Alban above all youths of his age. Alban is
luxurious in his free range. His Æschylus, lexicon, and Greek
grammar are on one desk ; a trigonometry lies on the much-
whittled table, under the blackboard chalked with diagrams ; and
his writing materials are disposed in a third quarter. The school-
house is the private property of one of Alban's uncles, by whom
the master is also in a good degree supported. Alban has finished
his day's work, and writes. Let us look over his shoulder. 'Tis
his journal. We shall not confine ourselves to this day's record.

"Aug. 5. In two months I am to enter college. I have been
at Babylon more than two years, enjoying singular privileges.
How have I spent them ? I fear I have not improved them as I
ought—not even the last eighteen months, since I obtained, as I
hope, the great gift. The waste of precious time which I cannot

recall, now gives me the liveliest sorrow.   The brief, monotonous
entries in my journal show how I lived :—in the spring, fishing ;
in the summer, riding, bathing, and playing ball with the unconverted ; in the autumn, out shooting, (a daily record almost ;) in
the winter, skating, snowballing, and sleighing.   I considered that
these things were necessary for my health, but my motive, I fear,
was amusement.   Last winter I read hard, to be sure, but I fear
it was more from ambition than a sense of duty.   This summer I
appear to have lounged away.   Relying on being already two
years in advance of the class I am to enter, I have neglected my
studies to pass the hours in light reading or unceasing revery.

" It is since Jane left us in the spring for Mrs. W.'s great school,
that I have been so dreamy.   I am irresistibly impelled to be ever
constructing in imagination my own future destiny linked, as I
hope, with hers.   I fancy the four years of my college life, the
three years of professional study, which I hope to reduce to two.
Yes, at twenty-two I may very well, with my quickness, be admitted to the bar.   Jane will then be turned of twenty.

" Sept. 1.   I have worked pretty well during August ; dreamed a trifle too much.   This month is the last.   I will try to keep
clear of revery altogether.   Instead of imagining the future, I will
endeavor in the hour of revery to recall the past.

" I have had a thousand imaginary love-scenes with Jane, but
notwithstanding all our cousinly familiarity, and living so long under the same roof, I never had the courage to hint such a thing to
her ; once I wrote her an absurd letter, (it was a year ago,) but I
had the sense to burn it.   It makes me blush at this moment to
remember it.

" 2. I have appropriated the desk which used to be Jane's,
and which was next to mine.   They were two privileged fellows
who had desks next the girls' row, with but this narrow passage
between.   How often when she was writing her exercise where
my journal now lies before me, I have watched her long, fair
ringlets, glossier than silk, now drooping over the paper, and now
falling back on her neck.   And the hussy was so careful never to

look round towards the boys' school, any more than if it did not exist. I cannot remember catching her eye in school-time more than once or twice, all the time that we sat daily next each other, though sometimes her frock would brush my desk as she passed.

"Sept. 18. It appears that my father can afford to send me to college. This is an immense relief to my mind. I had feared that some one of my uncles was to do it. I think I would have rather learned a trade or gone behind a counter. Well, Henry and I are to pack next week for New Haven. I pretend to be a candidate for eternal happiness, yet I am conscious that the coming ten years reach to the farthest boundary of my wishes and hopes. The first seven I mentally devote to preparation and anticipation; the following three to a quick bloom of success—and to the perfect bliss of being married to Jane. Beyond stretches a misty region which I have no wish to penetrate so much as in thought."

The hour when Alban should quit Babylon for college was indeed at hand. His cousin Henry, and George St. Clair, a scion of the house on the female side, the cousin of both, were to enter the same University at the same time, so that a general family sympathy was excited, which extended itself through the community, about to lose for a time the very flower of its youth. Alban went the rounds of the principal families of the village and of its vicinity. to take leave. All hoped that he would spend as many as possible of his vacations at Babylon. Those who knew about him expressed the hope that he would be the valedictorian of his class. The old schoolmaster even ventured to predict this, not only to Alban, but to others.

"I have fitted a great many young men for college," he said to his favorite pupil, "among whom were several of your family. Most of them have done me credit. Some have graduated with honors. But I have never had a valedictorian among my scholars. I count upon you, Alban, to procure this great gratification for an old man's pride."

Alban promised that he would try. It was his own secret

ambition. He had also to bid farewell to about twenty female cousins, ranging from seventeen to thirty, and distributed among four or five households. Some of them were plain and shy, some were graceful and chatty, some beautiful as the morning. Alban kissed them all. It was the custom of the country between so near relations. In their calico morning-dresses, without any ornament but their neat, beautiful hair, and their white hands, they came out into the wide halls of their fathers' houses to meet him, and accompanied him to the trellised front-doors to bid him renewed farewells. They all sent their love to his father and mother. They begged him not to injure his health by study. Rose St. Clair was the youngest of all Alban's Babylonian cousins, and she did not live strictly at Babylon, but at St. Clairsborough, a beautiful village about ten miles distant. She was the youngest of his own generation, for Jane was one degree farther removed. Rose was seventeen, and by universal acclaim the beauty of the county. The boy had gallantly kissed all his other cousins, but with Rose he hung back coyly, though he had just saluted her sisters. She laughed and blushed, and holding his hand, offered her red, beautifully pouting lips.

"When I see you again, cousin Rose," said Alban, "you will be married, I dare say."

"Why, you see, cousin Alban," she replied, "I can't wait for *you*. By the time you were old enough, I should be an old maid."

Aunt Fanny's parting advice had reference chiefly to the religious views which her nephew had adopted while under her roof.

"You may hear revivals, and particularly Mr. Finney's system, unfavorably spoken of, where you are going, Alban," she said; "but you have had an opportunity of forming an opinion on these subjects for yourself. In regard to the Episcopal Church, to which I thought you at one time inclined, I am very glad that you did not unite yourself to it. For although I believe there are real Christians among Episcopalians, as well as in other denominations, yet I think the number is comparatively small; and, generally speaking it is not uncharitable to say, that their church system tends to make people satisfied with the mere forms, without the life of piety. Episcopalians also, very commonly, if not universally, disapprove of revivals, which I must consider a very bad sign. As I have mentioned to you, their Church, in my opinion, is pointed out in the Revelations by that of Laodicea, which was lukewarm, neither cold nor hot, and which Christ therefore threatened to spue out of his mouth. That signifies that unless they embrace the system of revivals, and the other benevolent operations of the day, they will be cast off as a Church. I am very *sure* that this is the true meaning," said aunt Fanny, looking over her spectacles with great earnestness.

"I have not an idea at present of joining the Episcopal Church, aunt," replied Alban.

"I hope you will always continue as zealous, Alban, in all the benevolent operations of the day, as you now are," continued aunt Fanny. "I will say it to you now, that though so young, you have done a great deal here, especially for the Tract cause. I consider that the miracle of the loaves and fishes, Alban, is significant of the multiplication of knowledge through the efforts of the Bible and Tract Societies. I believe you are President of the Juvenile Foreign and Domestic Missionary Society, and Corresponding Secretary of the Babylon Auxiliary of the American Sunday-School Union. You must not lose your interest in these things at college, Alban, as so many do."

"Oh, I am sure I shan't, aunt Fanny."

"Much alarm is felt by ministers and others," continued his aunt, "at the great increase of Catholics in our country, in consequence of immigration. If the ministers understood the Scriptures in their spiritual sense, I think they would feel less alarm. It is very clear to my mind that the Apostle Peter represents spiritually the Roman Catholic Church. As Peter denied his Master, so the Church of Rome has become apostate ; and as Peter dissembled at Antioch towards the Gentile converts, so has the Church of Rome taken away the word of God from the common people; and Paul withstanding him to his face, signifies the Protestant Church opposing the errors of popery. But Peter afterwards repented, and then the Lord gave him the charge of the flock, and commanded him to strengthen his brethren; which shows that the Catholic Church is to be reformed, after which it will strengthen other Churches, and feed the whole world.   We have not yet a Catholic church at Babylon, but the number of Germans of that religion increases here so much from immigration, that I should'nt be surprised if they had one in a year or two, which will distress our people, but will give me a great deal of pleasure.   We shall then," concluded Aunt Fanny, with a look of peculiar satisfaction, " have all the seven churches in the Revelations in this town."

" Were you ever in a Roman Catholic church, aunt Fanny ?" asked Alban.

" I never saw the outside of one, that I remember," said his aunt, smoothing her gray hair thoughtfully under her prim, snowy cap.

" It appears to me, aunt," said Alban, abruptly and energetically, " that the Presbyterian Church neglects too much the moral education of young people, both before and after they are converted."

Aunt Fanny looked at her nephew in great surprise.

" Yes, their moral education, aunt.   We need minute superintendence over what we say, and what we think.   They cram us with the Bible till we are surfeited with knowledge.   I tell you what, my dear aunt, I would be willing at this moment not to know A. from B., to have a right clear conscience."

Aunt Fanny stared.

The servants, or rather the *help*, felt most keenly the departure of Alban and his cousins for college.   It was true that in the Atherton households these domestic appurtenances had always been obliged, by the irresistible, because quiet, haughtiness of the family, to forego the privilege which in that region was then generally accorded to native American servants, of associating with their employers both at the table and in the drawing-room ; but this did not prevent the children, as we have seen, from making the ample and cheerful kitchen their play-room, and the young " ladies" engaged in its respectable occupations, their play-mates and confidants. Even to Alban, accustomed from infancy to the privileged familiarity of black house-servants, this seemed quite as much a matter of course as to his Babylon cousins. But Polly and Maggie were well aware that when Mr. Alban and Mr. Henry came back from college, young gentlemen grown, the case would be entirely altered. They resigned themselves to the loss of their friends ; still it was painful. Even the plain and resolute little Madeleine, with her blue petticoat, and the yellow figured handkerchief crossed over her modest breast, cried as the carriage rolled away from the gate.

7

BOOK III.

College: the First Story. The Architectural Plan appears.

————— ◆ —————

CHAPTER I.

THE city of New Haven is, or was, (for it is many years since we saw it,) most characteristically a New England capital, and not unworthy to be the site of New England's most Puritan, and most New Englandish University. For the information of our Old English readers, we may observe that it is situate on Long Island Sound, (an arm of the sea, which washes the southern boundary of Connecticut,) on a bay where the great ranges of the White and Green Mountains terminate, a few miles apart, in two bold and beautiful bluffs rising like the crests of breaking waves above a vast green plain. These are called East and West Rock. New Haven lies between them, some two miles from the beach.

According to its original plan, New Haven is a square, laid out in squares, the central one forming an immense green. The houses stand chiefly in gardens ; the streets are lined with noble elms, forming a series of arbors, ever crossing. On the upper half of the declivitous green are grouped three graceful churches, and a state-house copied from the Temple of Theseus ; and this collection of public buildings is overlooked on the north by the long line of brick colleges embowered among trees.

Altogether, if it cannot compare ever so distantly with that wondrous relic of the middle ages on the banks of the Isis, the

locality of Yale is stately and academic.   In early October,—the
streets all waving overhead and rustling under foot, with bright
colored leaves,—its aspect was almost poetic.   Alban and Henry
were soon installed in pleasant rooms in an old college.   The
professor who had examined them, observed, with a smile, in designating their apartment, "That college was built by your
grandfather, young gentlemen, and has since served as a model."
Alban was pleased to find the names of several Athertons cut on
the window-seats.   The University (which the boys went over)
bore several other marks of connection with his race, and already
blended in his fancy with those images of a patriotic and pious
ancestry, by which from infancy he had been surrounded.   He
observed with pride the name of his maternal grandfather among
the donors of a fine full-length of Washington, adorning the
Philosophical Chamber.

   " I passed the first eight years of my life in his house at Yanmouth," he said, exultingly, to Henry ; " I assure you it is a
famous place, there is nothing like it at Babylon."

   The young Athertons themselves were regarded with great
interest by both the faculty and the undergraduates.   It was but
two years before that one of the family had taken his degree with
the reputation, always coveted in an American college, of the " best
writer" in his class.   Alban's own tutor had been this Atherton's
generous rival, and the Senior class still cherished the tradition of
the brilliant themes, and the eloquence in debate which had fascinated them as Freshmen.   Was either of these innocent-looking
boys,whose simplicity now provoked the smiles of wise Sophomores
and dignified Juniors, going to prove as "talented" as their cousin ?
There were not wanting those who already affirmed with positive
certainty, that the "little" one would even be valedictorian.
Meanwhile, Alban and Henry were visited in their new rooms by
the Sophs, and unmercifully quizzed.   Their being " members of
the Church" was a fact that soon transpired, and became the occasion of infinite mirth.   One Soph pretended to ask a history of their
experience ; another gravely introduced the poor boys as " pious

young men" to some tall, gaunt, nasal beneficiary of the Education Society. Alban was privately advised by one to keep the fact of his being a " professor" a strict secret, as it would subject him to cruel persecutions. This information was confirmed by others. Smoking-out, ducking, window-smashing, and riding on a rail were the least of the inflictions with which (by their account) the hapless church-member was sure to be visited.

"Let them try it, by George," said Alban, with more of the impulses of the old man than of Christian submission in his youthful breast. "They won't try it twice, I guess."

A more serious disadvantage of his religious position soon threatened our hero. Some fellows, who hated religion in the abstract, and believed that all who professed it were either ninnies or hypocrites, said that Alb Atherton would be a *blueskin*. Some other fellows of his own division, jealous of his recitations, took it up, and declared that Alb Atherton *was* a blueskin. It needs very little to blacken an unknown character in the eyes of the multitude. A few determined slanderers are quite sufficient. With the exception of the charity-students, and of a few self-supporting scholars of humble origin, but resolute industry, such as are always to be found in a New England college, Alban's class were shortly persuaded that he was by nature, if not yet by actual transgression, one of that much-hated fraternity, blueskins, trucklers to authority, spies on their fellows. Alban soon perceived the light in which he was regarded. Some young Southerners with whom he had begun to contract an intimacy, suddenly avoided him. A couple of Yanmouth boys who had at first proudly claimed his notice, cut him. The fellows who sat next him in division did not speak to him. One day, as he entered the division-room, there was a half hiss. Henry Atherton partly shared his cousin's unpopularity, and although stolidly indifferent as respected himself, he felt indignantly for Alban, whom he ardently admired and tenderly loved.

Some lads droop under such an influence, which it is vain to think of resisting. We have known a young man of the most amiable character actually die from the depression and misery thus occasioned. Alban Atherton shrunk into himself, walked haughtily past his classmates, chased ball by himself on the green. He would not even suffer the affectionate Henry to keep him company. Fellows who would not speak to him, would speak to Henry.

One day, as he was approaching his college at noon after a solitary promenade, half a dozen Sophs approached him from his own entry, two of them bearing a long, rough rail. Alban stepped aside upon the grass to let them pass.

"Now, have him," cried they all in a breath.

Two of them seized him by the collar and waist; a couple more caught his legs, and the others placed the rail under him in a trice. In the States there can be no more ignominious punishment inflicted on the object of popular odium. At the South it has often been the fate of the itinerant abolitionist or fraudulent pedlar. It is painful too, and even dangerous. Elevated to the height of the bearers' shoulders, the unfortunate victim is held down to the rail on either side by his feet, and compelled to hold on with both hands, to save himself from torture.

Alban had never fought a regular battle in his life. For the last three years, having been a professed Christian, he had not, perhaps, doubled his fist. But he was agile of limb, supple as India-rubber, and now ireful as a savage. Little did he regard the agony of bending himself back till he could reach the face of his hindmost bearer. In the twinkling of an eye, before one could see how it was done, the rail was flung on the grass, and Alban rolled over with the Soph's cheek between his teeth. He fought "like mad," with very little science, but terrible execution. He broke the nose of one assailant, doubled up another by a furious *coup de pied*, knocked another flat with a huge stone on the temple. The fellow whom he had bitten—a tall creole from Arkansas—now approached him with a drawn knife, calling out with frightful curses, that he would kill him, and a minute more would undoubtedly have ended this history, but at that instant a cheer, or rather a yell, broke from a throng of some thirty or forty Fresh, who had

rushed from various quarters to look on ; and with the yell they
threw themselves forward as one man to the rescue of their young
classmate.

" Fresh !   Fresh !   Fresh !"—

" Soph ! Soph ! Soph ! Yale ! Yale !" were the fierce resounding cries.   It was the most public hour of the day, and the most
public place in college, and in a few minutes, a couple of hundred
fiery youths were arrayed against each other.   On the one side,
the creole, with drawn knife, still swore he would kill the cow-
ardly blueskin, and was hardly restrained by those around him
from rushing alone into the thickening phalanx of Freshmen, who
were now headed by their bully.   On the other hand, Alban
stood in the midst of his new friends, with arms folded, slightly
panting ; his curly head bleeding disregarded, his turn-down collar and shirt-bosom torn, and covered with blood that was not
wholly his own.   Forgetting entirely their prejudices, the class
were in transports of rage at these marks of violence ; a fight was
imminent ; the bully's singular authority alone restrained them.
Alban approached this functionary, who was exerting himself to
keep his class on the defensive.

" I don't want a fight about me, Mr. Hayne.   Let me go to
my room, while you keep the rest here.   I am not afraid of Laurier's killing me."

Several loudly opposed this proposition, but the bully said ;
" You may try it, Atherton.   We shall be in time to save you, if
necessary."

Alban walked quietly off toward his college ; the creole, Laurier darted instantly after him, but was again caught by his own
friends.   Alban turned at the noise.   There was a general shout
from the Fresh, bidding him cut for his room.   But after a moment's hesitation, our young hero walked up to the party from
whom his enemy was still violently struggling to free himself.

" Laurier," said he, in French, " what a big fool you are !
If you did not struggle, they would let you go of their own
accord."

"You be off, and be ——— to you," said Laurier's friends, who did not understand a word ; but Laurier himself became quiet.

"Let us shake hands for the present," continued Alban, in the same language as before, "and afterwards we can settle it like gentlemen."

Laurier replied with a curse of unutterable coarseness, but added to the others, turning away as he said it, "Let him go ; I will find a time for him."

And now the scene was very characteristic of a college commotion. The Freshman class was the most numerous, and, physically, by far the most formidable in the University, having an unusually large proportion of full-grown men. The attack on Atherton was unanimously voted to be an affront to the whole class. It made no difference, it was fiercely said, whether he was a blueskin or not, the Sophs had no right to interfere. But the public feeling towards him was entirely altered in a moment by the spirit he had displayed. His *successful* resistance of the infamous insult offered to them all in his person, elicited a triumphant sympathy, and the severity of the injuries he had inflicted on the enemy inspired a ferocious delight, that exalted him positively into a champion. A meeting of the class was called in the Rhetorical Chamber after dinner, to consider what was due to their own honor. Atherton was greeted on his entrance with enthusiastic cheers. He was called out for a speech, and he had too much native tact not to speak at once to the point of the "slanderous imputation" which had been cast upon him, "of being a blueskin." Amid the laughter of the class he drew a sarcastic portrait of the blueskin character, but affirmed that even the blueskin was more estimable than the slanderer ; for the former, he said, might possibly be acting "under a kind of a sneaking sense of duty"—this expression called forth uproarious applause, and Alban repeated it with emphasis, amid renewal of laughter and cheers—but the slanderer of a classmate, in his opinion, must be actuated by unmixed, diabolical malignity. This speech, aided by a black patch on the temple, at once made

Alb Atherton the most popular man in college. They declared
" he was a talented fellow," and "real spunky," and that " he
had pitched it into the Sophs, first-rate."

With tolerable reason to be satisfied, even as matters stood,
the Freshmen did not propose any measure of serious hostility
against their foes. Something, however, must be done to express
the resolution of the class to hold its own. They and their rivals
sat in chapel in the same aisle, but made their exit at its opposite doors. It had been a common piece of insolence for
Sophomore classes, to make a rush on the Freshmen after prayers,
and push them out. An ineffectual attempt of that kind had
once been made by the present Sophs. But after prayers on the
day signalized by our hero's affray, occurred a thing without precedent, the Fresh making a successful rush on the Sophs. Young
Alban was placed, against his will, nearly in the van between
two of the most athletic of his classmates, and the whole body
pressing on with irresistible force, he was borne triumphantly out
of chapel by the Sophomore door.

CHAPTER II.

ALBAN had thus an exciting *début* at Old Yale, but after that, his college life flowed on in collegiate tranquillity. It is true that there were some violent academical storms in his time,—one fierce riot between the students and the townspeople, in consequence of which some of Alban's class were expelled, and afterwards taken back ; one fierce rebellion, ending in the expulsion of half a class ; one mighty revival, gathering half the college into the " College Church :" and our hero's light sails bent and fluttered, his slender mast creaked, his graceful bark danced like those of others in the gale, but it was only sympathy. He took all the first prizes in his division ; he was universally admitted to be sure of an " oration" when his class graduated ; and men said that Atherton *might* be valedictorian if he wished. He did not wish it. He had started for it at first, but his ambition soon took another turn. He acquired, almost without effort, a more fascinating and very peculiar reputation. If he rose to speak in a debating society, every body listened ; if he had an address to deliver at a college anniversary, the chapel was thronged ; his themes were the topic of conversation, his name was the brag of the college society of which he was a member. There is no political or literary eminence of after life so gratifying. With this academical success a personal trait developed itself in Alban Atherton which one would not have foreseen. He became shy. He had no social brilliancy. Other men of his standing addicted themselves very much to the society of New Haven, which then boasted some celebrated belles ; but even when Alban had got into his junior year, and had consequently passed his nineteenth birthday, he seemed only to have grown more diffident. If he saw ladies fluttering down the elm-shaded street towards him he would turn immediately into another.

Neither did he form any permanent college intimacy, although he had always many devoted personal admirers. The nearest approach to confidential friendship which he enjoyed was with some of the hard-handed, coarse-grained, but often true-hearted, earnest students, known as "charities." As a professor of religion he knew them all, and with one or two was on terms of very familiar intercourse. They loved the highly-nurtured, gifted, and pious youth, who sympathized with their indigence and religious zeal. To them Alban appeared a "rich student," for he knew no embarrassments about his bills, boarded in the upper commons, dressed like a gentleman, and with Henry and St. Clair, indulged freely in the expensive pleasures of riding, driving, and boating.

Among the fellows of his own proper standing in the intracollegiate world, Alban had not a permanent intimate. He cronied for a time, when a Freshman, and even up to the third term of his Sophomore year, with several fellows in succession, but hardly one of these friendships lasted more than a term. He continued to treat one or two of the individuals as familiar acquaintance after the violent intimacy had ceased ; but others he dropped entirely. No one knew exactly why, unless perhaps in some cases the parties themselves. Henry and he were chums, and the affection of the two cousins was constant.

Our hero's vacations were variously spent : the spring and winter mostly with his parents in New York, the long autumnal one in travelling with them, or at least with his mother. In the May vacation of his junior year he visited Yarmouth and Yantic Falls, where his piety, his college-prizes, his modesty, his purity, and the great warmth of his affection for his kindred, caused him to be received with unparalleled cordiality by his relations, old and young. His uncle Hezekiah alone shook his head, for he found that Alban had become infected with the heretical theology of New Haven.

" That is not the faith of your fathers," he said, with a sternly beautiful smile ; " abandon it, Alban, at once, if you wish to be the hope of your family."

"Nay," said the enthusiastic Rachel, beautiful as ever and more than ever sought, though vainly, "there must be something in the New Haven theology which fascinates cousin Alban by its partial truth. I rather like what you say, cousin Alban, about conversion being a rational act. It corresponds with my own experience."

Alban did not feel that shyness with a cousin some twelve years his senior, which made him shun young ladies more nearly of his own age, not related to him. He had several topics in common with Rachel Atherton, and their mutual love for the memory of their aunt Elizabeth was a strong bond of sympathy. Rachel made him take her out to drive in the ancestral chaise, which had now come into her father's possession. She wept as she spoke of Betsey Atherton. She smiled—her father's beautiful smile softened by her womanhood—when she told him that this visit would make her think of him more than she had done for years. She promised to pray for him more particularly than for others of her young male cousins; she engaged him to unite in the "concert of prayer" for the unconverted members of their family. Alban left Yantic with a more intense feeling than ever of proud love for the old Puritan line from which he was doubly descended.

CHAPTER III.

IT was about six months after this visit to Yantic, (the date is not unimportant,) and our hero had arrived at the first or fall term of his senior year. The city of elms was leafless, but the Indian summer still permitted rides to East Rock. Alban had just returned from one on a Saturday afternoon, and was crossing the green from the livery-stable to the colleges. He overtook a classmate. It was an undersized fellow of delicate features, but with a wasted look about the eyes and an uncertainty in his gait that betrayed premature excess. He had formerly been one of Atherton's inseparables, and they were still on good terms although the intimacy had ceased.

" You walk a little stiff, Atherton.   Been riding ?"

Alban assented.

" You are out every Saturday.   You don't visit at all.   I wonder you don't get a gig or buggy instead of a horse, and ask out some young lady.   It would cost you no more."

" It would not be half so good exercise, Shepherd."

" Well, I never saw a fellow like you.   Every other man in the class that is a man, (except the charities and future theologs,) is either dissipated or in love with some New Haven girl.   You are neither.   By George, I sometimes think that you are a girl yourself."

" I am a professor of religion, which amounts to the same thing."

" That's true.   Nothing but religion can keep a man out of it, and religion does not always.   There's not a man in the senior class, in fact, except you and Henry, and the *charities,* that does not dissipate.   See all those fellows in our division that joined the Church last spring during the revival.   This winter two-thirds of them have been disciplined ; and the other third ought to be.

There is little Edwards, and Bob Winthrop, they are worse than ever."

"I have pretty much lost my confidence in religion," said Alban, as if impulsively. "I ought not to say so though."

"Lost your confidence in religion!" said his companion. "So have I. All the intellectual fellows in the Senior class are infidels. But really, Al, I did not expect to hear it from you. Why, do you know what they say of you? That you are the only sincere professor in college, except some of the charities. You are the only man in the class that is pious and popular too."

"I am not so pious as you think," replied Alban.

"Oh yes, you act on principle. Come, I know it, if no one else does."

"You know, Shepherd, that I acted as principle would have dictated in a particular instance, but after all, my motive may have been pride. I am as proud as Lucifer. If I had weaknesses like Edwards and Winthrop, I should be very careful to keep them to myself."

"No, you would not," returned Shepherd, acutely. "Some fellows might ; but *you* would lose that kind of pride. It is odd that you have doubts about religion."

"I have none about morality, Shepherd. It is the New Haven theology that has subverted my faith, not a wish to live like you fellows."

"Professor —— preaches it every Sunday morning in the chapel, but I can't say that I know the difference between the New Haven theology and any other. What is it? I am curious, if it has made *you* skeptical." Alban bit his lip.

"The New Haven theology," he replied, after a moment's thought, "is, that we are not sinners till we actually sin."

"Why do we sin at all then?" demanded Shepherd, waking up.

"Because the will always follows the strongest motive," replied Alban. "Consequently, as soon as the will begins to act, the motives to sin in this fallen world being stronger and more evident than those for obedience, we sin."

8

"Why, that's what our fellows say. The motives to vice being so much stronger than those to virtue, we cannot help falling into it. I have heard Bob Winthrop say so fifty times."

"He is a good theologian. But he forgets the other part of the theory, which is, that God can heap the virtue scale with motives till it weighs down that of vice ; that is to say, He can, by His Spirit, so present to the eye of our reason the supreme advantages of goodness, that we *must* choose it :—which produces the phenomenon of conversion."

"A very clear explanation," said Shepherd. "For my part, the Spirit has never presented to me the advantages of virtue in that irresistible light. On the contrary, vice appears to me so sweet, that, as Winthrop says, I couldn't give it up if I were sure of going to hell in consequence."

"To me vice is repulsive," said Alban.

"The theory seems to suit you exactly, then. How has it shaken your confidence in religion ? That is what I don't understand."

"For one thing, it is contrary to the Bible. And for another, Shepherd, it is possible to be very far from inwardly just and pure, without being plunged into the mire where you and your set wallow like unclean animals :—forgive me."

"Oh, I'll bear any thing from you, Alb."

"How it is possible," pursued Alban, "for a man who has sisters, or fair cousins, so to contaminate his eyes, hands, and lips, and make himself unfit for the presence of modesty, not to say the pure kiss of consanguinity, passes my comprehension."

"Well, I wish I was as good as you, Alb. I wouldn't trouble my head much about theology."

The young men parted at North College to seek their respective entries. Alban paused at the door of his, and gave a look at the chapel porch. The bell for evening prayers was just beginning to ring.

"Certainly," said he, running up stairs two or three steps at a time,—"certainly I will go to the Episcopal church to-morrow morning ; come what will of it."

CHAPTER IV.

It was usual, in reference to the monitor's reports, to call off the delinquents after lecture, and hear their excuses. Monday morning the Professor performed this duty as usual. A. Atherton should have been the first called out, but the Professor began at B. Alban thought he was passed over. At the close, however, the Professor observed—" I wish to speak to A. Atherton." Alban waited. The Professor merely said—" Come to my room after tea. I want to see you."

The Professor was a young man who had been tutor of Alban's division till the class completed its junior year, and had then been elevated to his present position. He was already noted as an able man, and has since attained celebrity. Alban was his favorite. In fact, as tutor, Mr. B. had indulged him too much, so that men said, Atherton might do what he liked, no notice would be taken of it.

The Professor shook hands with his young friend and pushed him a chair by the blazing Franklin.

" You are looking very well this term, Atherton ; better, I think, than any other man in the class."

" Horseback exercise agrees with me much better than the gymnasium, sir."

" The gymnasium is not a bad thing either. I remember when I was a Senior and could practise there, my muscles were like bundles of ropes. I felt like knocking down every man I met, and jumping over every fence I passed."

Professor B. laughed with a quiet, intense enjoyment peculiar to him.

" Your other habits agree with you too, eh ?" he continued. " I like to see such clear eyes as yours in a Senior. It is a good sign."

Alban had been rather ugly for a couple of years, but he was now got to be a very handsome fellow again. His features were well-cut, spirited, and of a poetical cast. His blue eye, open, and as the Professor said, very clear. The brow was fit to enchant Spurzheim, and the masses of chestnut-hair carelessly thrown off from it, slightly tended to a glossy curl. The keen eye of the Professor scanned this fine countenance of downy nineteen by the shaded light of his study lamp.

"You were absent from chapel yesterday morning, Atherton. I did not want to call you up before all those dissipated and irreligious classmates of yours ; not that I doubted you had a good excuse, but because it was better," said the Professor, slightly laughing again, "that *they* should not know you needed one."

"I went to the Episcopal church yesterday morning," said Alban, quietly.

"Umph ! You had forgotten, I suppose, that it was Sacrament Sunday."

"Does that make any difference, sir," said Alban, with a demure, but penetrating glance at the professor.

"Why—why—the violation of the college rule in being absent from chapel without permission, of course is the same."

"I thought so," observed Alban. "I have been often absent before, but never was questioned about it, although, I suppose, the monitor did not fail to report me."

"Yes, but you were never absent on a Sacrament Sunday before."

"No, sir ; but you have just said (pardon me) that that does not make the breach of college rules any worse."

The Professor was a little embarrassed, and perhaps somewhat displeased. There was a profound silence of some minutes.

"You have many privileges, Atherton, which are accorded to you because it is known you will not abuse them. You have been tacitly allowed to attend church in town without asking permission on every particular occasion ; I wish you to continue to do so ; but perhaps you have not considered that your absence

on a Sacrament Sunday may have a bad effect. Your influence
is very great, Atherton."

"I staid away purposely, sir. I have felt a great reluctance
for some time to come to communion."

"You surprise me. But why?"

Atherton did not reply. The professor waited for him a
while, and continued :

"It is hardly possible that you can be affected with those
morbid doubts of your conversion to which some are subject.
Your mind is too healthy."

"Oh, I adopt the New Haven system, sir, so far as that. I
think conversion is an act of the will. If I thought I had never
yet submitted to God, I would submit now. My mind was made
up long ago that if there really were such a thing as being a
Christian I would be one."

"So I supposed," said the Professor, cheerfully. "We have
talked these things over before, Alban, and always seemed to
agree."

"My doubts," said Alban, clearing his voice a little, but
speaking huskily after all,—" my doubts—respect the truth of the
Christian religion itself."

"You have been reading Gibbon, perhaps?" said the Professor,
in a low tone.

"Oh, it is not any books that have made me skeptical," said
Alban, speaking more freely. "It is my becoming a Taylorite,
sir, that has led to it. Ever since Dr. Taylor's sermons in the
revival last winter, I have been working the system out by
myself."

"You are a very young man, Atherton. Nineteen last summer, I think! Last winter, is it? You are very clever, I know,
but this is a disease of your age, not a legitimate conclusion of
your intellect. You will outgrow it. I have gone through the
same thing, myself."

"But I cannot go to the communion while I feel these
doubts," said Alban, with a look of distress.

8*

"Have you mentioned the matter to any one else?" inquired the Professor.

"Yesterday I let something fall to Shepherd, unguardedly. My mind is so full of it. It requires considerable self-command to keep it in."

"I hope you will keep it strictly to yourself. It would injure you, Atherton, very much, to have it known that you feel such doubts, which, I repeat, you will outgrow; and it would injure the cause of religion in College still more. As for coming to the Sacrament," added the Professor, "it will be two months, you know, before there will be another occasion. By that time, I trust, your doubts will be removed, but if not, stay away. You shall not be troubled. Take time, and do not commit yourself."

The unburdening of his mind, and the Professor's kind (though certainly also politic) treatment, softened Alban. He shed tears.

"And pray, what logical sequence have you discovered," asked his friend, by way of diverting his attention, "between New Englandism, as B—— calls it, and a skeptical conclusion? Give us your syllogism."

Alban was at first unwilling to bring forward his difficulties; but when the Professor remarked that Christianity ought not to be made to stand or fall with the doctrine of any school, he was drawn out.

"I have always believed Christianity," he said, "because I had been taught it from a child. And I believed it just as I was taught it: the hardest doctrines as well as the simplest. The Trinity, election, particular redemption, and the eternal damnation of non-elect infants, were, or would have been, just as easy for me to believe as the inspiration of the Bible or the sanctity of the Sabbath. I put no difference between doctrine and doctrine. I believed them altogether."

"I dare say. That could not last, of course," said the Professor.

"That's just it, sir. Dr. Taylor and President Edwards overthrew my faith in Regeneration. Dr. Taylor uses the *word* Regeneration, but he denies and disproves the *thing*.   The revival last winter was conducted on the principle of the young men needing to be converted, not to be regenerated.   We all, following the Dr.'s lead, urged the unconverted to make an act of submission to God.   We set before them the motives.   That is the line I took with F—— and C——."

" I remember your zeal."

" But, sir, when I had succeeded in *converting* them, I found I had lost my faith.   I had before supposed myself to have undergone a mysterious change in the substance of my soul, when I experienced religion.   I had now learned to understand it as a change in my will under the influence of motives.   I could not hold this theory as I used to hold the other.   I have been forced consequently, to enter into an examination of every other point of my religion.   Now, I do not feel sure of any thing."

" I must suggest to the President to begin the lectures on the evidences," said the Professor.   " You have never studied the evidences, Atherton."

" I am looking forward to that to restore my *faith* again," said Alban.

CHAPTER V.

ALBAN was President of the Brothers in Unity. This is the most ancient of three literary societies which exist in the bosom of Yale. The Presidents, who are chosen every term, and are not re-eligible, must be always of the Senior class. The most honorable presidency is that of the first or autumnal term, which is, indeed, the most brilliant of intra-collegiate distinctions. A profound secrecy, however, is observed in regard to all that passes within the Societies, by their respective members. The names of the Presidents and other officers, the subjects of debate, the decisions, the writers and performers at their exhibitions, and the time of the latter coming off, are spoken of only *sub rosa*. They are all facts which transpire, at least in process of time, but even then are not openly admitted by members of the Society. This mystery wonderfully heightens the interest inspired by these venerable institutions. No member of the Faculty can ever be present at a debate ; but the exhibitions, one in each term, being principally dramatic entertainments, are usually graced by the presence, not only of the Professors, but, at a second performance, held specially in their favor, of the ladies of New Haven. The Societies all possess fine libraries and beautiful rooms.

Alban left his room in North College, as usual, one Wednesday evening, after tea in Commons, to attend the regular weekly meeting of his Society. He was soon joined by classmates sallying forth with the same purpose. The night was cold, the stars shining keenly through the leafless trees, as they went down Chapel-street. The Brothers' room was in the town, at a considerable distance from the colleges.

" How clear it is," said Alban.

" Yes, I wish it would snow," replied his companion. " I

want to have a sleigh-ride with a whole lot of young ladies. You used to go last winter, Atherton?"

"Never."

"Oh, you are not a ladies' man. It is capital fun. We dash over to East Haven in no time; run by moonlight, or the Aurora, some dozen miles in about an hour, and then get a supper of oysters and mulled wine, which makes the dear creatures as lively as possible coming back. You are all snug and warm together under fifty buffalo robes, you know."

"And you sit by the young lady you are in love with, I suppose, Winthrop?"

"Provided she is pretty, I don't much care who it is."

"No? I should fancy that would make all the difference in the world," said Alban.

"There are so many of us what is called in love with the same girl, that some of us must be disappointed," rejoined a companion at Alban's other arm.

"I have heard that Miss Ellsworth is very much admired," said Alban.

"The new belle—Miss De Groot of New York—cuts her out en-tirely," said Winthrop "Half the Senior class are desperately in love with Miss De Groot. Perhaps you know her, Alb, as you are from New York."

"Not I," said Alban, half contemptuously.

"Don't say any thing to Atherton about Miss De Groot, I beg," said his other companion.

"You must go to the fair next week," persisted Winthrop. "It is for the new church, you know. Miss De Groot and Miss Ellsworth will both have tables, and you can inspect and compare them at your leisure."

"No, don't you go, Atherton; they will only take all your spare cash for mere nonsense."

"I certainly can't afford to go to fairs where beautiful young ladies take tables," said Alban, innocently laughing as they mounted the stairs of the Society's rooms.

"St. Clair, they say, is smitten in the worst way with Miss De Groot," said Winthrop.

"What, George! Well, perhaps, I *will* go in that case—to take care of my cousin's pocket."

The room of the Brothers' Society was a long and lofty chamber with a coved ceiling. About the middle of the room, opposite the doors of entrance, was the raised tribune for the President's chair, rich with cushions, curtains, and canopy of crimson damask. Below and in front of it was a long table. The settees for the members were ranged in rows on either side, leaving the carpeted space in front of the tribune free. The apartment was well lighted by gilt lamp-chandeliers, the windows at the extremities hung with crimson, the walls adorned with handsomely framed engravings. Perhaps fifty young men were already assembled when Alban and his companions entered. They talked freely, but not loud, till some one moved that the President take the chair.

There was considerable miscellaneous business, during the transaction of which the room gradually filled. The first literary order of the evening was then announced to be a criticism by Mr. E. O. Dwight, of the Senior class. A tall, awkward, black-haired youth, with a very sardonic expression and an open shirt-collar, advanced to the green table in front of the President's desk, seated himself at it, took out a manuscript tied with pink ribbons, and announced that his subject was "Don Juan, a Poem by Lord Byron."

Very great attention was paid to the reading of this criticism. The critic made an able analysis of the poem, extolled the flexibility of the style, the wondrous facility of versification, the force of the descriptions, the rapid movement and natural conduct of the story, its irresistible humor, its pathos, the beauty of the ideas it suggested. Above all, he became enthusiastic in giving a vivid prose transcript of the character and story of Haidée,—the impersonation of love under its double aspect of ardor and disinterestedness. Removing entirely from our thoughts, he said, all pro-

fane associations and every base desire, it was so that in idea
every one must wish to love and be loved. Then he passed to
the consideration of the imputed immorality of the poem ; he
admitted that it contained some freedoms, but he maintained that
it was the freedom of vitality ; that the story, as it stood, was but
a transcript, fresh and original, yet of a more than mirror-like
fidelity, from life itself. He compared the reviewers who thus
declaimed at the morality of this exquisite and unrivalled poem
to those coarse critics of art, who, standing before the Venus of the
Tribune, forgot all the matchless charm of those outlines which
the divine Artist Himself had primarily evoked out of all beautiful possibilities into actual existence, to gloat over and point at
the circumstance of the statue's nudity. The critic was often
interrupted, especially at the last, by lively marks of approbation,
and closed amid general applause.

This choice of subject, its treatment, and the reception it met
with, were highly indicative, no doubt, of the prevalent sentiment
in the most orthodox of New England Colleges ; yet it would be
wrong to suppose that all the audience shared in the sentiments
of the majority. A good many grave, and for the most part,
rustic-looking, yet not unscholarly young men, some of them pale
and spectacled, looked or whispered disapprobation. The features
of the young President were illumined with a smile, half of sympathy and half of dissent. He bent down and said something in
the ear of the secretary, while the renewed plaudits of the Society
accompanied the critic to his place, and then announced with
calmness the business of the evening—the " Catholic debate."

" The question before the Society for debate this evening, is
the following : ' Does the probable increase of the Roman Catholic religion in the United States, by conversion and immigration,
threaten the liberties of America ?' The secretaries will read
the names of the gentlemen appointed to debate."

There were eight names, two from each class, of whom four
had been appointed to sustain the affirmative, and four the negative of the question. They were called up in order, beginning

with the two Freshmen, neither of whom, though present, answered to their names. It was not expected of these new members to flesh their maiden swords so soon. Both the Sophs appeared, and argued with their usual self-sufficiency. The negator of the proposition took the line of denying that such an increase of Popery *was* probable, and consequently that it could endanger American liberty. The Society listened with evident languor.

The Juniors followed. The affirmative here was a debater of rare powers. It was a sallow man of about eight and twenty, with a slender body and a massive head already inclining to baldness. This young man's eye was black and piercing, his voice deep and sonorous. He drew a fearful picture of Popery as the ally of European despotism, and then proceeded with masterly array of causal analysis to show that this feature of Romanism sprang from the essential principles of the Catholic Church in regard to faith and opinion. It was necessary, he observed, to seize the radical difference between Protestantism and Catholicism, in order to comprehend the difference of their results. Protestant faith was the result of rational examination ; Catholic faith was the submission of reason itself to infallible authority. There was no doctrine of religion so sacred but the consistent Protestant dared to subject it to the test of rational inquiry ; there was no dogma of the Church so absurd in the eye of reason or so contradictory to experience, but the consistent Catholic must receive it with unquestioning submission. It was from the diametrical opposition of the interior states thus produced—the mental independence of the one, and the subjection of the moral and rational powers themselves in the other, to an external law—that their opposite political spirit necessarily derived. The Protestant would submit to no law which did not virtually emanate from his own free choice : the Catholic, on the contrary, would be as ready to submit to God *governing* him by another's will, as to God teaching him by another's intelligence. " Our institutions," concluded the speaker, " are but the political blossoms of our religion ;

when we cease to be Protestants we shall cease to be internally republicans ; and no institution can long survive after the spirit which it represented has passed away."

The other Junior rose impetuously on the opposite side of the President's chair, without waiting to be called. His appearance presented a contrast to his opponent in every respect. He was of Herculean frame, with a sanguine complexion, light blue eyes, and auburn hair. His features were handsome but peculiar, and, in that company, unique. The moment that he said " Mr. President," with great distinctness, you perceived that his Celtic physiognomy did not belie him.

" Mr. President," he said, " I myself have the honor to be a Catholic, and I feel therefore the greater pleasure in refuting entirely the observations of the gentleman who has preceded me, whose premises, sir, are all correct, but they prove the very reverse of his conclusion." Here there was a general laugh, in which the Irishman good-naturedly joined.

This imported American was, in short, at the same time a Catholic (the only one in the society) and an ardent republican. There was not a great deal of argument in what he said, but a great deal of fervent assertion, which, with many, had all the effect. If he did not prove his view, he at least illustrated it with infinite humor and eloquence, and sat down amid lively applause. These were the interesting speakers of the night, for the two Seniors were heavy. Each of the regular debaters was allowed a reply, which did not occupy much time, and then the question was thrown open to the Society. Half a dozen spoke on it. Two or three of the speeches were highly interesting. The points made on the affirmative side were, the restriction of mental liberty by the Catholic Church—the anti-democratic constitution of the Hierarchy—the claim of dominion over the conscience —the known opposition of the Church to the diffusion of knowledge—the actual ignorance and superstition of the mass of Catholics—and the general tendency of the human mind to a blind faith and passive obedience, of which the Church would not fail to take advantage, and which would prevent her policy from being essentially modified in the new world. On the negative, it was contended that Catholicism had more to fear from the general Protestantism of the American people than they from it—that it could not stand before our universal intelligence and education— that the children of Catholic emigrants did not grow up in the ignorance of their fathers—that, in fine, vast numbers of the emigrants themselves were already hot republicans, and that even in Europe the downfall of Popery and monarchy both was surely at hand. Except on the part of our Irish friend, of whom it was almost assumed that he could not really believe his ostensible religion, there was not an intimation—not a suspicion was ever so distantly expressed by the speakers on either side—that the religion whose political tendency they were discussing could be otherwise than false. That point was taken for granted by all.

The Society now became hushed and still, to hear the President's decision. Alban had occasionally made a note during the debate, and he began by summing up the arguments on both sides with great fairness and precision. Each debater felt that more justice was done him than he had done himself. Without any thing original in this part of the decision, it was at the same time so flowing in utterance and so accurate in style as to enchain the attention. You might hear a pin drop.

But next was to come the President's own view, and it was thought that Atherton's were sometimes almost inspired. The question before them, he said, looking round on the Society, involved two problems, each of which had exhausted the resources of genius in its attempted solution, and which transcended all others in interest, viz.: the true origin of religion and the true origin of government. It was necessary, he thought, to ascend higher than had been done in the debate, and ask whence political liberty was derived;—was it an acquired or a natural right? Were we entitled to our inestimable franchises, as men, or had we inherited them as glorious and distinguishing privileges from our special ancestors, as the fruit and the reward of their virtue, over

and above other nations and other men ?   Had the Negro or the
Hindoo, strictly speaking, the same right to freedom as ourselves ?
For his part, he was not willing to concede that freedom, political
or personal, was a natural right of the human being since the
Fall, and it appeared to him that the theories which claimed it,
were over-boastful, infidel, and practically ignored the corrupt
and forfeit state of human nature.   (Here there were murmurs of
dissent, mixed with applause.)   " As an American freeman," said
the young President, firmly, " I do not stand on the natural rights
of man—I disdain such a source of my franchises—but on the
hereditary privileges of the race from which I have the honor
and happiness to be descended.   We Englishmen of the New
World are not freedmen, but free born !—*generosi*, not *libertini !*
The question before us this evening, gentlemen, is, whether the
increase of the Roman Catholic religion in America threatens the
subversion of those hereditary privileges of ours,—of what I may
call that *ancient* freedom, which is the haughty heir-loom of the
great Anglo-Saxon race."   Lively and general applause followed
this adroit popular turn.

Alban then proceeded to treat as trivial and evasive the
ground assumed by the negative of the question, that Romanism,
namely, was not likely to spread in America.   The probability of
this increase of Popery was taken for granted, at least as an hypothesis, by the terms of the question, and the effects of such an
increase on our liberties were the only fair domain of the debate.
He might add that it was the only interesting one for them to
discuss, and he marvelled that only one individual had been found
to defend the paradox, that the Roman Catholic religion was the
natural ally of the people against power, and the bulwark of
civil and religious liberty.   He thought that more might have
been said in defence of this position.   It was sustained by some
striking facts in the History of Europe, and it was in accordance
with that theory of political freedom which he had vindicated as
the most sound.   A society which rested on prescription was the
natural advocate of all acquired privileges, but it would by instinct,

defend chiefly the rights which belonged to the bulk of its members, and in the Roman Catholic Church that was the people. Thus it was that the Church had exerted itself with such irresistible force to abolish servitude. As for liberty of religious opinion, he thought it might be justly contended on the side of the Roman Catholics, that no one could ever acquire the right to believe a false doctrine, or disbelieve a revealed truth, consequently it never could be a violation of any right to punish the obstinate advocates of religious error.

"In truth, gentlemen," continued Alban, "it has struck me painfully to hear it said this evening, that the Roman Catholic religion alone demands of its votary a submission of the reason to the authority of faith. What, then, shall we say of the doctrine of the Trinity, or of that of the Incarnation? We believe them because we think we find them in the Bible, and we believe the Bible to be the Word of God. What difference in point of principle is there between this and believing what the Church teaches, because we believe the Church to be the living Prophet of God? I may doubt the infallibility of the Church, and may doubt the inspiration of the Scriptures, but to accept *either*, or *both*, involves precisely the same submission of reason to faith; and if that submission be incompatible with our spiritual freedom, then all revelation is a miserable imposture." Here the applause was warm but partial.

"I conclude, therefore, gentlemen," said Alban, "as I began, that this question is not capable of being solved, without running it up higher, and discussing the truth of the Roman Catholic religion itself. A *false* claim to teach in God's name, must, if it succeed, produce all the pernicious results which have ever attended religious imposture. The first result will be a false faith; the next will be a great depravity of manners; the next will be a loss of all those institutions from which the life will then have departed, of those privileges won by virtue, which vice will have rendered hateful. It is thus, gentlemen, that kingdoms as well as republics have ever fallen; and it needs no argument to prove, that if the Roman Catholic religion be false, which, however, it would be very unbecoming in me, in this place, to assume, its triumph in America would render our liberties nominal, even though our government should still be administered, like Rome under the Cæsars, with all the empty forms of popular sovereignty."

The moment the decision was finished, men began to go out, and during the brief business that followed, such as choosing new questions, appointing debaters, &c., the room thinned so rapidly, that at the moment of adjournment scarcely a score of members remained. It was after eleven o'clock, and the town was still, the shops closed ; the empty streets echoed only to the regular tread, and occasional voices of the young men returning to the colleges.

"Atherton gave a splendid decision to-night," said one.

"Splendid ! but rather anti-republican, eh ?"

"Rather anti-protestant, I thought."

"Baker, and the other religious fellows, looked a little blank at some parts of it, I noticed."

"Yes, I saw Baker staring at Atherton through his spectacles, with his great mouth wide open."

"Ha ! ha ! Well, suppose we go to E's, and open *our* mouths for some champagne and oysters."

OMNES. "Agreed."

9*

CHAPTER VI.

WHEN money is wanted to pay off the debt of a church, or for any other object of piety or benevolence, the unfailing resource, at least if it has not been already tried too often, is a Fair. The New Haven ladies had had several fairs, but then they could very well have one at least once in four years, as they would be sure at any rate of its being a novelty to all the under graduates, upon whose patronage they naturally a good deal rely. The one now in contemplation was for the benefit of a new Episcopal church ; but those were days of liberality, when the high claim of exclusive spiritual jurisdiction had not excited the alarm and indignation of Congregationalist New England ; and the Congregationalist ladies of New Haven worked as hard as those connected with *the* Church, to produce articles for the approaching sale.

The important day at length arrived. The ball-room of the Tontine was the place, and very tastefully was it arranged. A party of students, pressed into the service by irresistible solicitations, had hung the walls with green festoons. The private conservatories contributed fresh flowers ; and the tables groaned under piles of pincushions, pen-wipers, pocket-books, purses, and guard-chains. There was a post-office where letters could be received on inquiry, charged with a postage of half-a-dollar apiece ; and a fortune-teller, who required you to cross your hand at least with a dollar bill. In the evening, the sale-room was brilliantly lighted up, and at that hour—the crowd being greatest—the tables were tended by some two dozen of the prettiest girls in New Haven, " of all denominations." These saucy tradeswomen, who were in pairs to keep each other in countenance, made it a rule never to give change. A perpetual stream was flowing up and down the Tontine staircase, and at the door the squeeze was so great that it was almost a fighting matter to get in or out.

Alban went with George St. Clair; but when they had reached the top of the stairs they were speedily separated. St. Clair pushed on, mercilessly crushing some ladies who were trying to get in, or, to speak more accurately, crushing the foundation muslin of their enormous sleeves, (then the tasteless rage,) while Alban held back, and, indeed, twice ceded his own chance of entrance in favor of a gentle struggler, more anxious about her silken wings than her slender person. But at last he was rewarded by being borne softly on in the very midst of a whole party.

Our hero went so little into society that he knew none of the damsels behind the tables, and he moved round the room without venturing to stop, because he felt an awkwardness in buying any thing of a young lady to whom he had never been introduced. At length, however, he was addressed by one who was already surrounded by customers.

" What, Mr. Atherton, are you going to pass my stall without buying even a guard-chain ?"

" Certainly not," said Alban, coloring, but making an effort to appear at ease, " unless your price is too extravagant."

" They are of all prices to suit customers," said the young lady. " This is five dollars, and this," holding up one exactly similar, " is only one. Take your choice."

" I take the cheapest," said Alban, paying for it.

" Oh, but surely you will buy something else of me, Mr. Atherton. See, here is the prettiest watch-pocket ; 'tis but two dollars, and worked by me—no, by Miss De Groot. She will add your initials and send it you without any additional charge. Of course you will take it."

" Why, of what use is it ?" asked Alban. " I carry my watch in my waistcoat. Certainly I can't need a guard-chain and a watch-pocket too."

The young lady laughed.

" You affect ignorance, Mr. Atherton, to make me explain.   I am sure you know what a watch-pocket is for as well as I do."

" Not I, upon my honor, unless it be to carry a watch," said Alban, with a puzzled air.

" Really, I must tell Miss De Groot.   Mary," turning to her partner, " here is Mr. Atherton (Miss De Groot, Mr. Atherton) pretends not to know the use of a watch-pocket."

Several of the gentlemen who were talking to and making purchases of Miss De Groot were preparing to explain ; but that young lady, who had bowed slightly to Alban as her friend introduced him, was before them, and said, taking it in her hand, without looking at him—

" It is to hang your watch in at night, sir, instead of putting it under your pillow, which is a very dangerous practice.   If you hang it against the wall, you know, the ticking disturbs you. In this nicely-wadded pocket it makes no noise though ever so close at hand."

" After so clear a statement of its advantages, I must buy the watch-pocket," said Alban, laying down a half-eagle.

" We never give change, you know, sir," said the young lady, with a quick glance at him instantly withdrawn, and dropping the gold into the money-drawer, " but you may take any thing else here that you like for it."

" The choice is easily made," said Alban, trying to catch her eye and bow.

" What is it ?" replied Miss De Groot, looking at the myriad articles on the table, but not at Alban.

" No matter," quoth Alban, biting his lips.   " I wish you much success."

" Thank you, sir," said she, curtseying, but never raising her eyes.   She took up a purse to offer a fresh customer, and Alban moved on.

The next stall was the fortune-teller's, personated by a most enchanting damsel, full of mirth, and attired as a gipsy, and there was a crowd round it.   Alban stopped as if he wanted to see, but really to look back stealthily at Miss De Groot. Having heard that she was a belle, he was surprised at her appearance.

He had expected a young lady of some nineteen or twenty, but Miss De Groot could not be more than sixteen. She was fragile and undeveloped. Alban thought he could easily have spanned her waist just where the blue cincture confined her loose white muslin dress. Her rose-tipped arms and neck of lilies were bare and slight in mould. It was the face, then, which caused her to be so much admired, and lovely it was beyond dispute—faultless in every feature, and of a resplendent beauty of color. Its glance was quick and shy, but the mouth, a trifle haughty in repose from its exquisite perfection, became sweet as an opening rose-bud the moment she smiled or spoke. Its charm was then beyond all beauty. The eyes, of whose glances she was so chary, were large and dark-gray, set beneath brown-pencilled eyebrows, a shade lighter than her beautiful, abundant, very dark hair, which she wore brushed off her temples in a loose waving mass, half hiding her ears, and twisted behind with a careless native grace. George St. Clair came up while Alban was gazing at her, and laid a hand on his shoulder, saying,

"Did you ever see so beautiful a girl in your life?"

"I think Jane is quite as beautiful," replied Alban, with some confusion.

"Jane!" cried George. "Oh, no, you don't think so. It is impossible. I dare say Jane will turn out a finer character. Our Babylon cousins, Alban, have an infinite deal of dignity and purity, and all that. Between ourselves, Miss Mary De Groot is a bit of a coquette."

"They all seem coquettes to me. I am not at ease with any of them as I used to be with Jane," said Alban, with simplicity.

"Let me introduce you to Miss Ellsworth," said George, patronizingly. "She will put you at your ease at once. I want you to get over this confounded diffidence, Alban. In a fellow with your advantages it is too absurd."

"Very well; introduce me to Miss Ellsworth. Is not her name Mary also?"

"Her name is Mary also," said St. Clair.

St. Clair led Alban through the throng to the other end of the long saloon, where stood a table of refreshments. Miss Ellsworth was serving it. She, too, was young, but not quite so youthful as Miss De Groot. Her form was developed, her attire rich and showy. Low-cut dresses were then the fashion, and Miss Ellsworth's shoulders were so well formed, her neck so full and snowy, that she probably could not resist the temptation to comply with the mode. She seemed gratified by Alban's being introduced to her, and helped him immediately to a cup of coffee.

"Do you take cream and sugar, Mr. Atherton? Please help yourself. A superb tea-set you think? It is mamma's. She lent it for the fair, on condition that I would preside at the coffee-table and take care of it. By the by, mamma says that you are a relation of ours, Mr. Atherton. Grandmamma's maiden name was Atherton, and mamma says that she was first cousin to your grandfather. Yes; that makes us third cousins. Not very near, true; but blood is not water, after all. The Ellsworths are very clannish, and so are the Athertons, I believe. The fair is going off capitally, as you say. I think we shall make a great deal of money. You pay what you please for refreshments."

Alban had got on so famously with Miss Ellsworth that he was in a mood to be generous. He took another gold piece out of his purse. It was only a quarter-eagle, however Miss Ellsworth received it in the palm of the whitest and prettiest hand imaginable. He was about to retire after that, but she contrived to detain him. She said that he had overpaid extravagantly his cup of coffee and bit of sponge cake; he must at least eat an ice. He preferred some more coffee, for Miss Ellsworth poured, sugared, and creamed it with so much grace. With this second cup our hero gained additional confidence. He rallied some of his classmates who came up for ices and lemonade, in a very sparkling manner. He positively jested with Miss Ellsworth, he laughed, genuinely laughed, at a remark of hers. In fine, he staid at her table three-quarters of an hour, went away and came back again, and at length offered his services to see Miss Ellsworth home, which she accepted on the score of their relationship. So when the sale was closed, that is to say, punctually at eleven o'clock, P. M., Alban helped Miss Ellsworth get her things in the ladies' cloak-room ; she took his arm in a very confiding manner, and joining themselves to a party composed of similar pairs, they took their way to her father's house. It had been snowing at last, and the path was covered to the depth of two or three inches. So the girls went along laughing, and talking, and holding up their dresses. Miss De Groot and a cavalier were just in advance of Miss Ellsworth and Alban, but the former young lady refused to take her beau's arm on the plea that she must hold up her dress. She did it very decidedly, and made a rather singular figure, for she had a white opera-mantle (a capuchin) thrown over her head and shoulders, a thing seldom seen in those days, and below it were visible only a white dimity petticoat, somewhat short and scant, and the extremities of her muslin pantalets. But Alban thought that Miss De Groot stepped very gracefully through the light snow, and when they arrived at Miss Ellsworth's gate, she turned and said " Good night, Mary," in a frank, innocent voice that won his sympathy.

Our hero accompanied Miss Ellsworth through the shrubberied court-yard to the very door. It was a large house, the white front enriched with a good deal of old-fashioned carving about the windows and pediment, as you could see by the setting half-moon and the reflection of the snow. Miss Ellsworth herself threw open the door, which was neither bolted nor locked.

" Won't you walk in, Mr. Atherton ?"

" Not to-night, I thank you, Miss Ellsworth. But I shall soon give myself the pleasure of calling."

" We shall be very happy to see you, Mr. Atherton. Good night, since you won't come in."

The young lady enters a quiet house, for the servants are gone to bed. She locks and bolts the door after her. The hall stove diffuses a genial warmth, but she stamps her snowy feet on the mat, opens a door, and enters a sitting-room where a wood fire is blazing on the iron hearth of a Franklin. The apartment has no other light, but rays issue from an inner door that stands ajar.

"Mary," cries a voice, "is that you?"

"Yes, mother."

"Have you locked the front-door?"

"I have, mother."

"Oh, very well! Who came home with you?" in a lower tone.

"Mr. Atherton, mamma."

"Oh, very well! Now *do* go to bed immediately, for it is almost midnight." And the bedroom door was shut.

Miss Ellsworth took off her "things," i. e., a large cloak, thick hood, and moccasins. Then standing in the firelight she looked at herself in the mantel glass. It was a serious inspection; she twirled her brown ringlets over her fingers, and then let them fall upon the shoulders that beamed so clear and well defined in the dark mirror. She was satisfied that so far as that fair, well-formed bust was concerned, her young rival could not vie with her. But what of the face? That light coming from below was so trying! Still it could not spoil her regular mouth, fluted nostril, and black, sibylline eye. Young Mr. Alban Atherton had certainly been very much pleased with her, yet she remembered that his admiring and somewhat untutored glance had fallen oftener on her shoulders than her face. She would like to form his taste and manners. The last were good essentially, save a college gaucherie, arising from his having kept away from ladies' society since he had been at New Haven. He was worth forming, for all agreed that he was the most "talented" man in his class. He was very young to be sure—not more than twenty, Miss Ellsworth guessed—but then to an experienced young lady of twenty-one he was all the safer for that.

An old clock in a corner struck twelve, and Miss Ellsworth, roused from her revery, considered that she had better retire. But

as there was no fire in her bedroom she deemed it prudent to say
her prayers in the parlor.   So she knelt down speedily at a large
rocking-chair, in one corner of which she buried her ringleted face
for some fifteen minutes, during which period she once fell asleep,
then sprang up again, unfastened her dress, put her hair in
papers with drowsy rapidity, lit a candle, and, gathering up her
things, stole up stairs, where she was soon, we presume, dreaming
of handsome, intellectual, shy students, and of dreadful rivals in
white capuchins, short skirts, and pretty muslin trowsers.

10

CHAPTER VII.

THE snow on the night of the fair proved the first of a storm, which, in a few days, cleared up cold, with splendid sleighing. Fortunately, too, it had come with the moon. No foreigner can imagine the brilliancy of an American winter-night with a round moon riding in the zenith, and a surface of crusty snow, two feet deep, spreading all round to the horizon.

St. Clair, Winthrop, Hayne, and Alban Atherton had invited Miss Ellsworth, Miss De Groot, and two other young ladies, to take a sleigh-ride. The last young lady called for was Miss De Groot, and it was about half-past seven when they dashed away from the door of the mansion where she was a guest. Three ladies sat on the back seat, three gentlemen on the front; a gentleman and lady, who were Hayne and a sister of Winthrop's, occupied the driver's seat, and the driver was on his legs. There was a driver—for it is infinitely too cold an amusement to drive one's self with the thermometer nearly at zero. The ladies were enveloped in furs and covered with buffalo robes, and the whole bottom of the sleigh, by St. Clair's care, had been laid with hot bricks wrapped in flannel. There never was so comfortable a party, all agreed. The countless bells on the collars and girths jingled merrily; the horses dashed forward in excitement, and were scarcely to be restrained from a gallop; the houses flew by; in an instant they were out in the open country, and soon flying along the base of East Rock, the cliffs and woods of which loomed up grandly in the effulgent night.

Very sweetly the three fair faces on the back seat peeped out of their close winter bonnets. Miss De Groot, as the youngest and slenderest, was in the middle. She seemed to enter into the excitement of sleighing more than any one. She exclaimed with astonishment at the wonderful brightness of the moon, counted the few visible stars with the most eager interest, never failed to express a new delight whenever they passed a fine hemlock or spreading pine, with its evergreen boughs laden with glittering snow. Alban's notion was that this girlish pleasure was affected, as a means of fascination. At all events it was wonderfully successful in attaining that end. St. Clair, full of courtesy to his *vis-à-vis*, Miss Ellsworth, could not keep his eyes from wandering to her youthful neighbor, with the air of one perfectly enamored ; and Winthrop, whose style was more off-hand seemingly, but really more guarded, while he cultivated most assiduously the good graces of his opposite neighbor—a very handsome girl, whose surname was Tracy—gave from time to time a glance at Miss De Groot, which Alban wondered how the latter could bear. Our hero was so new that things struck him crudely which people used to society hardly notice. It was difficult, though, for either of Miss De Groot's admirers to catch her eye ; and her raptures about the moonlight she addressed chiefly to her newest acquaintance, which was Alban himself.

"See, Mr. Alban,"—so she called him all the evening— "another great snow-tree is coming ;"—or at a glimpse of the far-off Sound, with moon-tipped waves flashing against a white, ice-bound coast,—"Is not that very, very beautiful, Mr. Alban ?"

Miss Ellsworth also took every opportunity of addressing our hero, not in her friend's open, undisguised way, but in a tone of confidential intelligence that won Alban more.

"We count on you, Mr. Atherton, to help us dress our church." —They were talking of the variety of evergreens with which East and West Rock abounded.

"On what day of the month does Christmas fall this year ?" asked Winthrop, who was a pure Congregationalist.

"On the twenty-fifth of December, I believe," replied Miss Ellsworth, looking at Alban.

"What an ignoramus you are, Winthrop !" cried St. Clair. "Do you imagine that Christmas is a movable feast ?"

"Mr. St. Clair is better instructed," said Miss Ellsworth. "He has been studying the Prayer-book so diligently of late."

"I *admire* the Episcopal Liturgy," said Miss Tracy. "Don't *you*, Mr. Winthrop?"

"If there was nothing but the Liturgy," responded Winthrop; "but the other parts make the service too long, in my opinion."

"Winthrop means the Litany," again interposed the accurate St. Clair. "The whole service is the Liturgy, my dear fellow."

Miss De Groot, who was listening for the first time to the conversation of the rest, smiled, Alban thought contemptuously.

"Miss De Groot does not agree with you there, George," he observed, with more than usual promptitude. "I suspect that she and Miss Ellsworth think you as ignorant as Winthrop."

"Oh, *I* know nothing about it," said Miss De Groot, hastily. "I am not an Episcopalian."

"Mary is hardly a Christian," remarked Miss Ellsworth, with a smile and sad shake of the head.

Miss De Groot's dark eye flashed angrily, and she turned her beautiful face to her neighbor's with warm indignation.

"I believe in Christ as truly as yourself, I suppose, if that is being a Christian, although I cannot believe contradictions about Him, and don't believe that mere outward forms are necessary to salvation."

"Some outward forms are commanded by Christ Himself, you know, Mary," replied Miss Ellsworth, with an irritating calmness, "and you *must* believe what seems a contradiction to your short-sighted reason, if it is revealed in God's word."

"Then why do not you believe in Transubstantiation?" retorted Miss De Groot, hardly suffering Miss Ellsworth to finish. Some quicker blood than Saxon evidently stirred in her veins.

"Because it is not taught in the Bible, Mary."

"Just as much taught in the Bible as the divinity of Christ," rejoined Miss De Groot. "I appeal to Mr. Alban, if it is not."

"If you take the Bible literally, Miss Mary, you may certainly say so."

"And if you don't take it literally, Mr. Alban, you may as well explain away one passage as another."

For the first time she looked him in the face steadily and brightly. Her irritation was gone, and she seemed to have forgotten it. She repeated her words earnestly.

"We must explain one passage by another, and by the general tenor of the Bible, Mr. Alban,—must not we? The Apostles never speak of worshipping Christ; never pray to Him after His ascension, but only to God. He Himself says, 'My Father is greater than I.' 'I go to my God and yours.' What can be plainer than that?"

"Extremely well put," said Winthrop, who had not a spark of religion, and liked any thing that hit hard at orthodoxy. St. Clair looked horrified at Miss De Groot's talking Unitarianism. Alban alone, who had been in the background all the evening as respected vivacity and small talk, answered in a gentle but slightly patronizing manner,

"If the Bible be an inspired book, Miss Mary, we must not treat it in that way."

"You speak as if you doubted its inspiration, Mr. Alban."

"No, that is not what Mr. Atherton means, Mary."

"Every sect understands the Bible in its own way, and you never can make them all understand it alike," said Winthrop.

After this theological burst, the party were whirled on in comparative silence; but Hayne and Miss Winthrop, on the driver's seat, inattentive to what was going on inside, conversed inexhaustibly, and with so marvellously slender a store of topics, that Alban could never admire their facility enough. At last the horses drew up in great style under the piazza of a country tavern. All got out, and the mulled wine was ordered. St. Clair made the inn people take out all the bricks to heat over, whereat they grumbled. The ladies threw off their hoods and outside wrappings, and appeared in becoming demi-toilettes; such pretty worked collars on their necks! such tasteful kerchiefs round their throats! such well-chosen silk and challis dresses! Let Yankee girls alone for not missing their points on such occasions. Only the young New York beauty with the old Dutch name, was somewhat plain in her garb. When Miss De Groot had removed her furs, (the envy of her companions—she said her papa brought them home from Russia,) and the pelisse which she wore under them, nothing had she to show but a little black silk frock (with a touch of the pantalets) and her own graceful shoulders, which gleamed as if they had been carved out of elephant's tooth and gold, in contrast with that dark, scant vesture. So they all sat round the blazing Franklin, with their tumblers of mulled wine, quizzing the rosy maiden who served it, and laughing at every thing "countrified" which their sharp eyes detected in the appurtenances of the inn, or the manners of its inmates. There is probably not another country in the world where four young ladies of the same social rank would be intrusted thus to the protection of as many young gentlemen. The only pledge given to propriety was, that two of the party were brother and sister ; for these were not " any sort" of girls, but belonged (always excepting the young New Yorker) to distinguished branches of the *gentes majores* of Connecticut.

Winthrop was the first to observe that Miss De Groot was not so taken up with the flowing cheer and mirth within, but that she had a longing eye for the freezing splendors without. The inn-parlor looked out upon a small, half-frozen lake, with woody shores rising into snowy hills. Miss De Groot went to the window with her foamy tumbler, and Mr. Winthrop followed her. Miss Tracy, who was a funny girl, began to tell a story, (she was famous for that,) and all eyes and ears were soon given to her.

Of a sudden there was the sound of a smart blow—it could be nothing else ; Miss Tracy stopped with a little shriek, and every body turned round with a start. Miss De Groot was coming hastily back to the fire, spilling her mulled wine on the carpet ; the fire was not half so red as she. Winthrop followed her with one hand laid to his cheek.

"Upon my word, Miss De Groot," he said, amid the exclamations of the rest, "you understand the use of your hands."

The young lady made no reply to him, but looking excessively
angry, said in an audible whisper, as she seated herself between
Miss Ellsworth and Alban, "I hope it will teach him the use of
his."

"Why, what have you done to Miss De Groot, Winthrop?"
cried the gentlemen, St. Clair turning white and red.

"Nothing, on my honor," said Winthrop, affecting to laugh,
"but what I have done fifty times before to other young ladies,
without incurring a similar punishment."

"Why, what *did* he do?" inquired the ladies in whispers, of
the offended fair.

"He put his arm round my waist," replied the latter, very
straightforwardly, but with a suppressed sob. "I asked him once
to remove it;" with a little resentful shake of the head, peculiar
to young girls,—"I did not ask twice."

"Winthrop," said Alban, "you must beg Miss De Groot's
pardon on your knees."

"I declare I am very willing," cried Winthrop.

The other ladies expressed much indignation at him, particularly at his saying that he had done the same thing before, fifty
times, without its being resented. "Never to me," said Miss Ellsworth, scornfully. "Nor to me," said Miss Tracy, coloring. "I
presume you mean to me, Bob," said his sister, with a half laugh.

Winthrop went down on his knees to Miss De Groot with a
very good grace, and Hayne, a gigantic Southron, interceded for his
friend in the most polished tone of chivalric deference. St. Clair,
an uncut diamond, half waggishly and half sincerely observed that
for his part, if he had been guilty of the offence, which Heaven forbid, he should have considered the punishment a reward. He
never before knew the case in which he should have been disposed literally to obey the precept, when one cheek was smitten to
turn the other also. He quite envied Winthrop the honor of having
his ears boxed by Miss De Groot.

"I view it quite in that light," said Winthrop, "though I can assure any one who likes to try, that Miss De Groot hits hard."

Miss De Groot did not show herself implacable, but she kept close to Miss Ellsworth's side the rest of the time that they staid at the inn. It had been proposed to sit differently in returning. Hayne would not come inside, but Miss Ellsworth and Miss Winthrop changed places, and Winthrop himself wished to exchange with one of the ladies; whereupon Miss De Groot insisted that it should be with herself, of course that she might not be obliged to sit next him; and because she would not be opposite to him either, she quietly took the outside place, to the disappointment of St. Clair, who found his cousin Alban between him and the object of his adoration. Miss De Groot seemed to have lost all enjoyment of the beautiful night; Miss Tracy and Miss Winthrop rallied her on continuing to be so disconcerted by a trifle, and Alban caught sight of a tear on her averted face. He desired to soothe her, and (his skepticism did not alter what had become a moral habit with him) to do her good.

"Did I understand you, Miss Mary," trying to divert her attention and confer a benefit at the same time, "to avow yourself that very unpopular character here—a Unitarian?"

"My father is a Unitarian, sir, and I have been brought up to think as he does."

"We all believe at first as our parents believe," said Alban.

"In Boston the first families and the most cultivated people are Unitarians," said Miss De Groot.

"But you, by your name, are pure New York."

"Papa was educated at Harvard."

"Ah, one naturally takes up the system that prevails in one's university," said Alban. "Is your mother not living, may I venture to ask?"

"Mamma died when I was little more than two years old," turning a little towards him and looking him in the face less shyly than usual. "I remember her though perfectly. I wear her hair and miniature together in a locket."

"Do you !" said Alban. "Have you no brothers or sisters ?"

"I had a little brother who died just before mamma. He was only a few days old, you know, Mr. Alban. I have his hair too, in the same locket with mamma's, and it is as dark almost as mine."

"And was your mother a Unitarian ?"

"No," said Miss De Groot, "she was a Roman Catholic ; and that is what I will be if ever I change my religion, which I don't think I ever shall, Mr. Alban."

"Oh, really !" said Alban, rather shocked, for it was hard to tell which faith he regarded with the greater horror. A Papist was a more unpopular character than a Socinian, and here was this young Miss De Groot avowing that she was resolved always to be either one or the other. Alban began to consider to what sect, for her own sake (for his feeling was purely disinterested) he would like to convert her. He could not make up his mind exactly, though he thought of the Episcopal Church, and he pursued, "You will think *me* a true Yankee, but I must really ask you one more question. Was your mother a native American, Miss De Groot ?"

"Oh, ask as many questions as you please. There is no impertinence in your curiosity, Mr. Alban, No, my mother was Irish. I am very proud of my Irish blood. You have seen that I have something of its quickness."

"After all," thought Alban, "there is a good deal in you, and I don't believe that you are such a coquette as they would make out."

But Miss Tracy said, laughing, "What a decided flirtation between Mr. Atherton and Mary De Groot ! Mr. Atherton did not give into it at first, but ' beauty in distress' has proved too strong for him."

For some reason or other the young lady's native temper did not rise at this imputation. She only replied, so mildly that Alban wondered at her again,

"Since you all say that I am a flirt, there must be some foun-

dation for the charge, but I hope that Mr. Atherton will not believe
it merely on your authority."

"Oh, he has better evidence, I think, Mary," said Miss Ellsworth, turning round from the driver's seat ; for she was so near
her friend that their backs almost touched.

"You, too, Mary Ellsworth! Now that is really unkind !"
said Miss De Groot, smiling in the moonlight, but speaking with a
tremulous voice, as if she were hurt. "I must not ask you, Mr.
Alban, if you think I have flirted with you this evening, but I do
assure you that nothing was further from my thoughts. I have
spoken to you more than to the other gentlemen, because I have
an aversion to Mr. Winthrop," (that gentleman bowed,) "and
Mr. St. Clair, I am afraid,—has an aversion to me," she added,
laughing. "Haven't you, Mr. St. Clair ?"

"The greatest !" said St. Clair, with a comic contortion.

"And Mr. Hayne is outside," continued Miss De Groot.

"I was your only resource," said Alban. "It is quite clear.
I feel extremely flattered."

"So do all the gentlemen, no doubt," observed Miss Tracy.

"Myself especially," said Winthrop. "For next to a lady's
preference, give me her aversion."

"Let us part friends," exclaimed St. Clair, in a mock heroic
tone, "for we are approaching rapidly to the end of our journey.
For my part, I forgive all the injuries I have received."

"I bear no malice," said Winthrop.

"Nor I," said Miss De Groot, with a smile of fascination,
principally bestowed, however, on St. Clair and Alban.

The sentiment of a vanishing pleasure subdued our party to
silence as the horses renewing their homeward pace, approached
New Haven. As Miss De Groot had been called for last, so she
was set down first, the mansion where she was a guest being out
of the town. They had to drive in at a gate and ascend a gradual
carriage sweep to get to it. Her friends discussed her character
when they had lost her presence. Miss Winthrop and Miss Tracy
were pretty severe. "Bob was saucy," said his sister, "but it

was a *very* unlady-like thing for her to slap him, in my opinion."
"My belief is that it was all done for effect," said Miss Tracy.
"Just to seem extremely dainty."—"How hard they are on their
own sex!" said St. Clair. "It seems to me that nature gave you
your hands, ladies, as well as your nails and teeth, to defend yourselves from impertinence, if the occasion require, as well as for
other purposes."—"The occasion did not require such a use of her
hands on the part of Miss De Groot," rejoined Miss Tracy. St.
Clair and Hayne maintained the contrary, although with many
expressions of deference for the sentiment of the ladies.—"How
you all talk!" said Miss Ellsworth. "Mary De Groot used her
hand to punish Mr. Winthrop's rudeness just from instinct, without stopping to think about the pros and cons."—"Exactly," cried
St. Clair; "it is just as a cat scratches, or a cow hooks at you
with her horns. I told you so."—"I think that Miss De Groot
afterwards regretted having boxed Winthrop's ears," observed
Alban.—"It was only one ear that she boxed," said Winthrop,
"and quite enough, I assure you. I was bending down to whisper
a compliment, you know, about her eyes being brighter than the
moon, or some such nonsense; and I did'nt put my arm round her
waist, as she said I did, but just touched her with my open hand,
as one does in taking out a lady to waltz, or in passing her into a
carriage,—nothing more, on my honor,—and she said as quick as
a flash, 'Please take your hand off my waist, sir,' with so much
haughtiness that, by George, I wouldn't at first, and then she
drew back and struck me as if she would have knocked me down.
I declare I had no idea that a girl of her slender build could strike
so hard."

Winthrop had evidently received a deep impression. The rest
of the party laughed at his story, in various tones, while the sleigh
cut along an arcade of leafless elms. One by one the other ladies
were deposited at their homes, and in a trice after that, the young
men got out together at North College gate. It was a reasonable
hour;—not quite midnight.

CHAPTER VIII.

The approach of Christmas excited far less interest in New Haven than that of the Brothers' Society exhibition which was to take place soon after the festival. The work of rehearsals was going on secretly but zealously at the Society's room, and many were the rumors afloat respecting the interest of the new tragedy by ———, (the name could not transpire,) the murderous fun of the farce by ———, and the splendid additions which the committee on the exhibition had made to the Society's theatrical wardrobe. The members of the other societies were intriguing furiously for tickets, and all the young ladies who had not yet been privately invited, were in a fever of nervous excitement lest they should be left out.

Whether Alban had worked so hard at his tragedy, (for *we* are not bound to keep the secret of the Brothers' Society,) or at the Evidences, for he confounded the Divinity Professor by bringing every day some fresh and subtle objection to be solved, or whether the image of Mary Ellsworth, or that of Mary De Groot, (since the sleigh-ride,) visited him in dreams and rendered his sleep less refreshing to his body than agreeable to his imagination, or whether the fare in Commons, as he averred, was really execrable that term, it is certain that about the first of December he had suddenly become aware of having lost his appetite, digestion, color, and elasticity. He called on his physician, wisely thinking that it was the business of a professor of the healing art to save him from all care concerning his clay tenement when it got out of order. To employ another's ministry in our ailments, whether of body or soul, enables us to avoid dwelling unhealthily upon them ourselves.

The doctor felt the pulse, looked at the tongue, thumped the chest, peered into the eyes, inquired into the functions.

"Circulation irregular—mucous membrane slightly disordered. You have not been dissipating in any way? You smile. Well, I think not, with that clear, bluish-white *conjunctiva* and girlish blush. Then you have been working that fine brain of yours too hard. What have you been doing?"

"Writing a tragedy, doctor."

"Enough. All accounted for—the pain in side included. Excites the passions as much as dissipation, and draws more fearfully on the nervous energies. You must give it up."

"I have got through my work now, doctor, and am really recruiting; I make a call in town every morning."

"That's well."

"The main difficulty, sir, is the stomach or the liver. I have an idea that I need some blue pill."

"Blue nonsense! You want some old sherry, a change of occupation and a change of diet. Go board at Mrs. Hart's. I will write you a certificate this minute."

Alban lost no time in availing himself of the doctor's certificate. The President, on its being presented, gave him leave at once to board in town; he gave notice to the Steward that very morning, and at one o'clock punctually he was entering Mrs. Hart's dining-room.

The single large table neatly spread with linen damask, was as wonderful to him as if he had never seen the like in his life. The mere glow of the decanters warmed his stomach. The very location of the salt-cellars between crossed silver spoons was appetizing. The knives and forks regularly laid, the tumblers and wine-glasses, the bright plated castors, the napkins in rings of silver or ivory, refreshed his vision, accustomed to the nakedness and disorder of the Commons' tables. How cosy, too, appeared the old-fashioned japanned plate-warmer by the fire! What a savory odor from the not distant kitchen saluted his olfactories!

"I declare," thought he, "I did not realize in what a piggish way we live in Commons."

For three years, saving the vacations, our hero had lived in such a piggish way, a good deal distressed by it in his early days of Freshman simplicity, but accustoming himself to it by degrees, till he was himself grown considerably careless, a fact which his dear "particular" mother puzzled him by lamenting. The manners as well as the arrangements of Commons were very unrefined in those days ; the rude haste, the unseemly neglect of forms, made the tables even of the higher college classes most unlike the old Catholic refectories, which, plain as they were, were schools of decorum as well as of simplicity. Still, it had been better for Alban than luxury, or the fastidious ostentation of the moderns.

Presently came in Mrs. Hart—a tidy dame of forty—whose looks commended her own cheer. The boarders dropped in quietly, and Mrs. Hart introduced Alban to some of them. The first of these was a fresh-looking, well-conditioned, closely shaven young man of some six or seven and twenty, carefully dressed in a black suit and white cravat, whom our hero at once recognized as the assistant minister of the Episcopal church. The other male boarders were Southern students,—fellows of whom Alban's principal notion was, that they were planters' sons, and boarded "in town." There were also several ladies,—one a stately Southern matron who had a son in the Freshman class, and had come on to be near him ; the rest were single, of whom the prettiest and youngest was a niece of Mrs. Hart's, a young lady of extremely affable manners, and very nicely dressed. Indeed, Alban, who had come to dine quite as a matter of business, and in his wonted recitation gear, observed that his fellow-boarders and companions of both sexes were all clothed literally in purple and fine linen. Most of the fellows in the Senior class dressed a good deal, but our hero had never given in to it. His shirts were still fashioned in the simple domestic form which had reigned in Babylon in his boyhood ; his neck was encircled by a plain black silk handkerchief, tied in a careless bow ; a blue frock-coat, threadbare at the elbows and whitish in the seams, had seemed to him good enough even for a morning call on Miss Ellsworth. Now he perceived his mistake. He resolved that he would have a black suit and a large flowered blue cravat, and, to say the least, a set of new collars.

But soup was served, and the Rev. Arthur Soapstone said grace in a brief, rotund style, which said as plain as manner could, "This act derives its efficacy from my legitimate ordination;" which our hero, however, being used to the "personal piety" manner, did not quite comprehend. His reawakened appetite did not allow of his dwelling much on the subject, and very soon the appearance of a magnificent roast turkey, accompanied by a truly American profusion of nicely cooked vegetables, and counterpoised by a superb Virginia ham, dappled with pepper and adorned with sprigs of curled parsley, completed the temporary victory of gastronomy over all other sciences in our young friend's estimation. It was not till the third course (Massachusetts partridges, &c.) came on, to tempt too far his yet delicate palate, that Alban began to open the ears of his understanding to the conversation.

In spite of his white-seamed blue coat and primitive shirt-collar, not only the pretty Miss Hart, but stately Mrs. Randolph Lee, was very gracious to our hero, the fact being, that his plain and worn, but scrupulously neat garb harmonized exactly with the idea which (unknown to him) all had formed beforehand of the "talented" Atherton. Mr. Soapstone remarked to Alban that he had heard of him before, through some young ladies of "the parish." Miss Ellsworth, Alban presumed with a blush. She was one. Mr. Soapstone inquired if he were not a member of the " College Church," as he believed it was called. Alban assented, adding,

"I thought you had been a Yale man, Mr. Soapstone."

"Certainly, sir," said Mr. Soapstone. "I belonged to the Class of '26. I remember I had a classmate of your name. Mr. Hez-e-ki-ah Atherton, I think."

"There was no 'College Church,' I suppose, in those days," said Alban, in perfect good faith.

"Oh, there was what they *called* the 'College Church,' the same as now," replied Mr. Soapstone.

Alban was puzzled. He was not yet aware that the Congregationalist Churches (so called) in New England were not real churches, but only conventicles. However, we are all ignorant till we are taught. We hope our High Church readers will not give up Alban yet on the ground of this pitiable lack of ecclesiastical information on his part; he may live to be as great a stickler for Apostolical succession as they can desire. He may learn to call the " New England Churches," as they were termed by his ancestors, " synagogues of Satan," and to talk of schism and heresy as confidently as the best of them. Alban, however, perceived that some insulting sense lay couched in Mr. Soapstone's emphasis, so he tarried not in replying.

" You mean to imply that it is improper to speak of a ' College Church ?' "

" I mean," said Mr. Soapstone, " that a mere association of persons who are mutually satisfied of each other's personal piety, and who agree in their religious opinions, cannot constitute a Church."

" No," said Alban, " of course they must also unite in Christian ordinances."

" That will not make them a Church," replied the clergyman, with a bow of triumph, " unless they have power to *administer* the ordinances."

" Do I understand you, sir," said Alban, " to assert that the College Church has not the power to administer the ordinances ?"

" I do assert it without hesitation. Allow me to take a glass of wine with you, Mr. Atherton. I hope we shall some day have an opportunity of discussing the grounds of my assertion, which, I perceive, surprises you."

" It seems to me ridiculous," said Alban, very good-naturedly, filling his glass at the same time. " I dare say you can prove it, though, as convincingly as Professor F—— does the inspiration of the Scriptures; which I could believe more easily for their own glorious sake, than I can upon his arguments."

In fact, Alban, when he found there was an Episcopal clergy-man at his new boarding-house, had immediately thought of the opportunity it might afford him to obtain a new solution of his doubts, and a better one perhaps, than all the elaborate historical deductions of his Divinity teachers could supply. After dinner, he drew Mr. Soapstone again to the topic, in which all the Southern-ers, although perfectly irreligious young men, joined with great interest. But Mr. Soapstone seemed unable to enter into the question of the Christian religion itself. He was too much occu-pied with that of the right to administer its Sacraments. At first, indeed, he took a ground which seemed novel, by saying that he believed the Scriptures to be inspired, on the testimony of the an-cient Church ; but when pressed to say how he knew that the ancient Church had not been deceived in that respect, he was unable to answer.

"The canon of Scripture," said Alban, "was fixed, you say, by the Church, in the fourth or fifth century. If we take it then at her hands, because she could not err, why we ought to take in the same way every thing else that the Church teaches, and then we shall be Roman Catholics at once."

"That's a fact !" cried the Southerners.

"If she _could_ err," continued Alban, as Mr. Soapstone was silent, "then we must not accept her decision blindly. We must examine the question for ourselves. And so we get back to the historical argument again, which, to me, is wholly uncon-vincing ; and it perfectly revolts me," said he, warmly, "to be told that my salvation depends on my being convinced by it."

"You are an infidel, then," said the clergyman, waving his hand, as if such a being were unworthy of an argument.

"No," said Alban, seriously. "I am not an infidel, but a Christian sadly perplexed. I do not know how much I ought to believe. I do not know why I ought to believe it."

"Submit to the Catholic Church, Mr. Atherton, and she will tell you what to believe," said Mr. Soapstone, rising, and speaking with animation ; "I mean to that pure branch of it which is established in the United States." So saying, Mr. Soapstone retired to his room.

"The man is crazy," observed one of the Southerners.

"On that subject I should think that he was," said Alban.

The young men, who at first had regarded our hero suspiciously, not overlooking the white-seamed coat like the ladies, seemed now to have imbibed a quite new idea of him. They were not of his class, and being Calliopeans, of course they knew nothing of him as a Society man. They had only understood that he was a religious fellow and a Northerner. They now broke out into warm expressions of their distaste for religion in any shape, except as a necessary part of virtue in girls of good family.

"My God!" exclaimed one of them, with the rude energy of his class and country, "would I have my sister an infidel? I reckon not. I should like to see the man that would *presume* to talk infidel to a sister of mine. I would shoot him as I would a dog."

Alban was so taken by surprise that he could not help laughing at the oddity of their expressions, but he was shocked at their sentiments. It seemed to him that both sexes had the same interest in truth, and the same obligation to purity. This they hooted at, not, however, in an unkindly way. Indeed, though they could not make out Alban, they took a great fancy to him. They had never seen a Northern man they liked so much. Alban's strong propensity to do good made him reason with them on their bad principles, and while they maintained that love was only lust, and that virtue in young men was a physical impossibility, they unconsciously envied him as he vindicated the purity of female affection, and warmly protested that he would rather die than violate the laws of chastity. Atherton would always try to cut blocks with a razor.

It was nearly four o'clock when he left Mrs. Hart's, and these lower class men had to go to recitation. There was no Senior lecture, and he was strongly moved to call on some of his new female friends. Mrs. Hart's boarding-house was on that side of the town where (but just out of it) Miss De Groot's friends lived. He had never yet called upon her. It was a duty neglected. He found that it would be just a pleasant walk up the leafless avenue half choked with snow. The mansion stood on an eminence with lawns around, an extensive wood and hill in the rear. It was of gray stucco, with an Ionic portico, from which the view was fine, especially by that evening light. Alban was admitted immediately, and ushered without much form into a sitting-room that looked towards the west, where he found Miss De Groot and another lady, sitting by a window that came down to the floor; the former was reading aloud and the latter was at work. Miss De Groot put down the book and rose to greet him. When she had introduced him to her hostess, and resumed her seat in the window, her lovely face was flushed, and her eyes were bent upon the carpet, with that shy look which he had observed at their first meeting. It was not one of the houses where young students felt themselves at liberty to call without ceremony, and Miss De Groot's shy manner made Alban feel some doubt as to his position, particularly as she had never, like Miss Ellsworth, invited him to call upon her. There was nothing said either, that tended to relieve this awkwardness. Miss Everett—the hostess of his young acquaintance—a maiden lady of a certain age, sat very quietly on her ottoman, working at an embroidery frame by the fine western light, with her richly flounced black silk dress spreading around her in great state, her gold watch-chain, gold keys, gold pencil, dangling at her waist, and seemed to think that she was not called upon to say any thing to the student who had called to see Miss De Groot. Alban was obliged to open the conversation by remarking upon the beauty of the winter weather, the continuance of the sleighing, &c., hoping that Miss De Groot did not take cold after their sleigh-ride.

"A slight one," replied Miss De Groot, raising her eyes from the carpet, "but I got quite over it a fortnight ago."

"Is it so long since our sleigh-ride?" said Alban with embarrassment.

"How long is it since I took that sleigh-ride with Mary Ellsworth and the girls, cousin Harriet ? Oh, it must be more than a fortnight since."

"'Twas a fortnight last Tuesday," said Miss Everett.

"I have been so busy preparing for the Exhibition," said Alban, "that time has slipped away insensibly."

"Mary Ellsworth told me as a secret that you were writing, or, as I understood her, had written, a tragedy. I believe you are very well acquainted with Miss Ellsworth, Mr. Atherton ?"

"My acquaintance with her dates from the fair at which I had also the pleasure of seeing Miss De Groot for the first time," said Alban.

"But that's a month ago," said Miss De Groot, "and you have seen her almost every day since, have you not ? No ! Well, I hardly ever see Mary that she doesn't speak of your calling the day before."

"Have you been invited yet to our Exhibition, Miss De Groot ? If not, I shall be very happy to send tickets for Miss Everett and yourself."

"Thank you, Mr. Atherton, three or four gentlemen have already made us the same kind offer."

"But you have declined it from them all, Mary," observed Miss Everett. "Don't you mean to go to the Exhibition ?"

"I can not only send you tickets but reserve you places," said Alban, "although, from my duties on the night of the Exhibition, I can not personally wait upon you, ladies, to the Society's room."

"That would suit us exactly," said Miss De Groot, addressing her hostess. "We really do not need a beau on the occasion, so I think that I will accept your offer, Mr. Alban, if Miss Everett is willing."

"Of course I shall go on your account, dear," said Miss Everett. "I really want you to see one of the Exhibitions. We are very much obliged to *you*, Mr. Atherton, I am sure."

Alban did not feel particularly flattered at the manner in which

his offer had been accepted.   Was Miss De Groot vexed that he
had deferred so long calling upon her ?

   " I should have taken the liberty of coming to see you much
sooner, Miss Mary," he said, resolved to try this tack, " if I had not
been afraid of Miss Everett."

   " Miss De Groot's friends are all very welcome here, I assure
you, sir," replied that lady, slightly smiling at this sally of the
young student.

   Miss De Groot blushed, and said, " I should have been very
happy to see you if you had called, Mr. Alban."

   " How have you enjoyed your residence at New Haven ?"
asked Miss Everett, wishing to be civil to him since he had
promised them tickets.

   " I never liked any other place half so well."

   " You are like Mary.   But she has only seen it in winter, I tell
her.   She can form no idea of what it is in summer."

   " It would have the same charm for me at all seasons," said
Miss De Groot, looking out of the window towards West Rock.
" Do you know, Mr. Alban," turning to him, " that I do so wish
I were a young man, so that I could be a student.   Every time
that I see one in my walks, entering one of those old colleges, I
quite envy him."

   " I think I have seen you at the chemical lecture," said Alban,
wondering if after all Miss De Groot were not a flirt.

   " She is crazy to attend them," said Miss Everett, " but she
complains that the students look at her too much when we come
away."

   " Oh, that is not fair !" exclaimed Miss De Groot, crimsoning
to the temples.   " Really, cousin Harriet !   But I hope Mr. Alban
will not repeat such a thing."

   " Certainly not," said Alban, " although I think it is very
rude in our fellows.   For my part, I have always kept back,
although I had the honor of knowing Miss De Groot, fearing
that it would be an annoyance to her to be saluted by so many
young men."

" Papa has told me, and so has Mr. Everett, of Italian ladies of birth and beauty," said Miss De Groot, addressing Alban with animation, " who went regularly through the University, attending the lectures in scholars' gowns, and taking all the degrees, yes, and lecturing afterwards, themselves, to learned audiences. That (except the last) is what I should like."

" College would be an enchanting place with such classmates," said Alban.

" Ah, Mr. Alban, you put down my enthusiasm with a compliment. I see I must be resigned to being a pretty girl and knowing nothing. If **it had** but pleased Heaven to make me plain, it would have suited me better, I assure you. It is so humiliating to be made a toy of, when one is thirsting for knowledge."

The young face glowed with indignation and pride, and the fine—excessively fine—eyes were raised to Alban's with a degree of spirit and courage which he had never observed in them before. Indeed, they shot fire. Miss Everett glanced from her to Alban, with an expressive shrug.

" You ought not to repine, Miss De Groot, at the part assigned to your sex by the will of God—ought you ?" said Alban.

" It's *not* the will of God, Mr. Alban, that we should be regarded in the light I complain of. It is *your* will, and our weakness." She was still angrily flushed, so that Alban thought involuntarily of that cherub " severe in youthful beauty." " What right," she exclaimed, "have you thus to confine us to frivolous pursuits—to persecute us with thoughts that destroy our self-respect ! On every side it meets us, and for my part I should be glad to go into a convent or anywhere, to be environed no longer by this degrading admiration."

" My dear !" said Miss Everett, reprovingly, for Alban was completely silenced, " you are ungrateful to talk in that manner. How many girls would be glad to have half the beauty that procures you so much notice. Most, indeed, complain of nothing but neglect."

Miss De Groot sprang up hastily from her seat, book in hand, ran to the pier-glass, (there was one that came down to the floor,) and surveyed herself in it. She was attired in the same plain, somewhat scant black silk which she had worn at the sleigh-ride, and, as then, it was wholly unrelieved by any of the light ornaments or trimmings with which females take so much pleasure in setting off their charms. Such was then the mode for school-girls, but young ladies brought out like Miss De Groot, seldom adopted it unless in the retired hours of the morning. But her exquisite loveliness defied the sombre and in itself ungraceful garb. She looked at herself steadily a few moments, while Alban wondered. Not the slightest shade of self-complacency was discernible on the soft, girlish countenance which he saw reflected in the mirror, but her sparkling resentment gradually subsided into melancholy sweetness—a sort of self-pity, and her eyes sank modestly as she resumed her seat. She addressed Alban as if she had forgotten the singular excitement under which she had uttered things so remarkable for a girl of her age, and, as Alban thought, scarcely feminine in sentiment.

"Do you understand German, Mr. Alban? I was reading a German romance to Miss Everett when you came in. It is called *Ondine*, and is very, very beautiful."

There was something very pretty in her way of saying this. At Alban's request she gave him an outline of the story, which interested him.

"The manner in which it is told is every thing," she said.

Alban had frequently glanced round the apartment with an observant eye during this conversation. It had an aspect of urban luxury, not usual in New Haven. A sea-coal fire blazed within the mantel-piece of black marble; there were silken draperies, rosewood furniture. On one side of the high, polished mahogany door, stood a piano open. He ventured to ask Miss De Groot for some music. He had heard of her singing and playing as something quite superior.

"It is," said Miss Everett. " Do, Mary, play something for

Mr. Atherton, to show him that you are not quite such a little savage as he suspects."

" No, not to-day," said Miss De Groot, in an absolute way. " The next time he comes to see us I will play for him as much as he likes."

The college and the town clock struck five, and the chapel-bell began to ring for prayers cheerily. Our hero rose to go.

" Ah, that is for chapel, is it, Mr. Alban ?"

" I am sorry you are not obliged to be in your place among the Freshmen," he replied smiling.

" So am I," she answered, rather gravely, although her lips smiled. Her dark eyes looked up to him more sad than merry for a half minute, and then were withdrawn according to her wont. " I would wear a thick green veil to the chemical lecture," she added, " if I were not afraid somebody would divine my motive. Please, Mr. Atherton, keep my little eccentricities to yourself."

" How much character she has !" he thought, as he hurried down the avenue. " Rather more than I like, but I don't think she can be a flirt : time will show."

CHAPTER IX.

CONVERSATIONS with Mr. Soapstone occurred daily, and more than once a day. Breakfast, dinner, or tea seldom passed without Mr. Soapstone finding some occasion to insinuate or proclaim his views of the Church, and Alban made so many hypothetical admissions that the clergyman was the more irritated, and yet urged on, by his obstinate skepticism. On one point the High Churchman speedily obtained a victory. He convinced Alban that Baptismal Regeneration was the doctrine of the New Testament ; but this, in the latter's peculiar state of mind, only set him to weighing how far the Apostles and Evangelists themselves were worthy of credence, in matters, as he said, of opinion. Meanwhile Christmas week arrived, and one evening after tea the Episcopal minister broke off his customary argument to visit the chapel which was his special charge. He invited Alban to accompany him, and our young friend, who liked to hear Mr. Soapstone talk, readily consented.

" The chapel is gothic, you observe, Mr. Atherton," said the clergyman as they approached it. " Mark the picturesqueness of its hooded towers against the night sky ! How superior to those poor Grecian fronts with wooden spires erected by the schismatics on the green ! It was the Catholic Church that perfected the glorious pointed architecture."

" Of which the Protestant Episcopal Church in the United States is the modern representative," observed Alban.

" Say rather the purest modern Branch," said Mr. Soapstone.

" That is what I meant to say," returned our hero. " The other branches are rotten, and he who hangs by them will be apt to catch a fall. *If one could only be sure that this one was sound.* However !"

They entered the chapel by an obscure vestibule choked with

greens. The interior presented a white-walled oblong, with a plaster ceiling. A gallery, painted in imitation of oak, and carved in a running ogive pattern, ran round three sides, and was already hung with heavy festoons ef evergreen, intermingled with the huge letters of an inscription. The aisles (an incorrect term, as Mr. Soapstone observed) were littered with boughs of pine, spruce, and cedar, and a large party of young gentlemen and ladies were dispersed through the church, tying wreaths, dressing columns, or planning where to place inscriptions. There was a good deal of talking, and occasionally a laugh.

The principal operators were collected in the chancel. A couple of young ladies were in the pulpit. They were covering the purple-velvet book-cushion with white, which was to be trimmed with evergreen. Below them, a young gentleman mounted on the reading desk, was affixing a sacred symbol in laurel to the front of the pulpit, an operation which other young ladies were anxiously watching from below. On one side, a long slender ladder rested against the wall ; and in front of the desk, between the communion table and the rail, some six or seven young people of both sexes were consulting about the mode of putting up the chief inscription by which the chancel was to be adorned. Some sat on the rails ; one young lady was half sitting on the holy table itself, which had on it besides, some evergreen twigs, a pair of scissors, and a ball of twine. A lamp or two along the gallery, and tallow candles on the desk, illumined this scene.

" Hats on !" was the first low exclamation of the minister. He walked hastily up the middle aisle. " Do you know." said he, addressing a young man, " that this is a consecrated building ?"

In a few minutes, by dint of like reproofs, and of the signs which the guilty individuals made to others, all the hats were removed. Mr. Soapstone approached the chancel.

" What, young ladies ! sitting on the communion rail ! sitting on the altar ! Miss Reynolds !"

."I declare I didn't know that it *was* an altar, Mr. Soapstone!" said the young lady, starting up with a blush.

"Where is Miss Ellsworth? Pray, Miss Ellsworth, let those articles be removed from the altar. This is really a—desecration of which I should not have expected Church people to be guilty."

Miss Ellsworth was conversing with Mr. St. Clair on the culture of the sentiment of veneration by the usages of the Episcopal Church, and she colored violently at this address.

"We must have *some* place to lay things," she said, rather shortly, "and I suppose, Mr. Soapstone, there is no peculiar holiness in the table itself."

"We *always* laid the things we used in dressing the church on the communion table, and Mr. —— (naming Mr. Soapstone's predecessor) never reproved us for it," cried Miss Reynolds.

"Are we to put the ball of twine in our pockets?" demanded a black-eyed gipsy, "and set the young gentlemen hunting for it till they find it? That will be the best way, I think, Kate," flinging back her curls.

"Now this shows the importance of the appropriate arrangement of chancels," observed Mr. Soapstone to Alban. "If the altar here were a foot higher, a young lady *could* not sit on it; and if it were set against the eastern wall, as it should be, and raised a few steps above the chancel floor, no one would think of laying things upon it. I hope to see it done yet, and the pulpit and desk turned out altogether. The chancel, Mr. Atherton, should be appropriated to the altar alone."

Miss Ellsworth dissented from these principles. She thought the pulpit would be very inconveniently placed for hearing and seeing, anywhere but exactly where it stood. Mr. Soapstone and she argued the matter at some length. He pronounced the existing arrangement of the chancel *Genevan*, and said that it savored of "anti-sacramental heresy." She was afraid that her pastor's ideas about the altar savored of anti-protestant superstition. Nor was she, it may be imagined, disposed to be complying when Mr. Soapstone suggested that a pair of plated candlesticks should be put upon the altar when it was dressed. Miss Ellsworth thought that candles on the altar were a symbol of Popery. She was sure it would give offence ; she would not have any thing to do with dressing the church if it were persisted in ; she had been decidedly opposed to a cross among the decorations ; candles were worse. Mr. Soapstone was obliged to yield the point for the present. The only voice raised to sustain him was Miss De Groot's. She had first suggested the cross, and she approved of the lights. Both, she thought, had a beautiful significance. But as Miss De Groot was a Unitarian, her support rather injured Mr. Soapstone's cause.

The Christmas dressing meanwhile proceeded. The inscription was got up, and was beautiful :—EMMANUEL, in letters formed of wild laurel, on a ground of white artificial roses. The chancel was gradually converted into a bower of evergreens mixed with flowers.

" There is one other point," observed Mr. Soapstone to Alban, " that I should like to press, but I abstain on account of Miss Ellsworth's irritation. The young gentlemen have taken off their hats, which is well ; but the young ladies, on the other hand, should put on their bonnets. All those ringleted and braided heads in the very sanctuary are extremely out of place."

" Miss De Groot keeps on her hood."

" She has a fine sense of propriety. She would become a consistent church-woman with a little instruction. I think she has already a tendency. I must lend her some books. Let us go and speak to her."

Miss De Groot had retreated with the Miss Reynolds who had sat on the altar, to a distant pew where they were working together on a wreath. Some young gentlemen who approached them had already been sent away with short answers. Alban followed his reverend friend slowly, as doubting whether the young ladies did not prefer to be left alone. Miss Ellsworth also detained him by asking his advice. He came up to the retired party in time to hear Mr. Soapstone say, " Were you baptized in the Unitarian denomination, Miss De Groot ?"

" I was never baptized at all, sir."

" Never baptized, Mary !" cried Miss Reynolds.

" Never baptized, Miss Mary !" exclaimed Alban.

" Papa does not believe in infant baptism."

Mr. Soapstone seemed less shocked than our hero expected.

" If you become a church-woman, Miss De Groot," he said, " you will have no schismatical baptism to give you scruples."

" But this makes Miss De Groot absolutely a heathen, does it not ?" asked Alban.

" She is not worse off than half my flock," replied the Episcopal minister, coolly, " who were originally Congregationalists, and have never received a valid baptism."

" Like me," said Miss Reynolds.

" Mr. Soapstone puts us in the same category, Mr. Alban," said Mary De Groot, looking up with a smile, " so you need not look down on me so pityingly."

Alban was silent, pondering the mystery of his own inconsistency, how, while he was questioning the truth of Christianity itself, he should be so much shocked at another's wanting its initiatory Sacrament.

" There," said Miss De Groot at last, holding up the result of her industry, " whether I am a Christian or not, I have made you a cross of native holly, Mr. Soapstone."

Mr. Soapstone was delighted. Alban, even after all he had seen of him, was a good deal surprised at the undignified eagerness with which he caught at the prospect of setting up a cross of evergreens over his altar, although well aware that it would give great offence to at least half his parishioners. He seemed to think that if the material symbol could once be set there, it was a great point gained in the progress, as he expressed it, of Catholicism in the Church.

The cross, nevertheless, was finally placed *over* the communion-table, and then, as Mr. Soapstone could not bear to leave his work unfinished, the candles were set *upon* it. This procedure caused many heart-burnings in the parish, although the Protestant mind was then far less sensitive than Puseyism has since made it. Miss Ellsworth, who "had set her face against the cross," as Mary De Groot said, was highly displeased. Alban was curious to know from what motives the latter young lady had acted. They seemed to be mixed;—a little malice towards Miss Ellsworth, some wilfulness about having her own way, the love of what was in itself beautiful and perfect, and, at the bottom of all, a lurking, hardly conscious devotion to the Cross as the symbol of redemption. As they were all leaving the church, she turned back, and unobserved, except by Alban, who was furtively watching her, slightly bent her knee towards the simple altar.

"In what light *do* you regard Christ?" asked Alban, as he walked by her side. "Do you regard Him as in any sense your Saviour?"

"Why, Mr. Atherton, what a question! Of course, I do. Does not the Bible say that the Lord Jesus Christ is our Saviour? Do you really suppose that Unitarians are heathens?"

"But does not God say in the Bible, '*Beside me there is no Saviour?*' If Christ is our Saviour, it appears to me that He must be our God."

"It is a sweet idea," said Mary De Groot, "that Christ is our God; I could adore Him with all my heart if I were not afraid of committing idolatry."

"The real idolatry, it seems to me, would be in ascribing salvation to a creature."

Miss De Groot half apologized to Alban for accepting his escort home, although she had taken his proffered arm as a matter of course.

"I have been here almost all the afternoon," she said. "I had no idea of being kept so late."

"To see you home is an envied privilege, Miss Mary—if you will overlook the compliment."

"Oh! I overlook a great many every day," she replied.

Our hero's theological notions were now so completely topsy-turvy that he refrained from speaking of Miss De Groot's unbaptized condition, although he kept thinking of it. She herself, after replying absently to several observations of his on light topics, alluded again to this.

"Is it worse to be unbaptized than to be a Unitarian?" she asked.

"According to Mr. Soapstone it makes you a child of wrath, Miss Mary."

"Oh! do you believe in original sin, then?"

"It was the doctrine of the Apostles."

"Then, for example, I am a totally depraved creature. That must be false," she exclaimed, indignantly. "I know I have faults. You may call them sins, if you please. But I have some virtues too. I always endeavor to act justly by others. I am conscientious about myself—far more so, Mr. Alban," she added proudly, "than these young ladies who say that I am no Christian. I would sooner die than utter a falsehood, or admit an impure thought." She spoke in a sweet, sweet voice, but with vehemence.

"You never told a lie?"

"Never deliberately, since I was a very little girl, Mr. Alban. And I have told the truth a thousand times when I was sure to be punished or ridiculed for it."

"From pride, perhaps," said Alban, "which is the sin of sins."

"Because I wish and mean to be a good girl,—if that is pride."

"The true motive would be the love of God, who forbids and hates lying," said Alban.

"Do you always act from that motive, Mr. Alban?" she demanded, after a pause, and half sobbing like a child reproved.

"Indeed I fear not," said Alban, soothingly.

"Papa taught me when I was little that it was noble to tell the truth, and that a liar was despicable," said Miss De Groot, recovering herself. "But I *try* to act from the better motive you spoke of just now, Mr. Alban, for I had a friend who taught me to. *She* used to say that truth and purity were no virtues if they proceeded from any other ; but that vexed me to hear. '

" Do you then expect to merit heaven by your good life, Miss Mary ?" said Alban, as a last resource.

" No, Mr. Alban, I expect that from God's infinite goodness. He gave me my being and a thousand good gifts for which I daily thank Him, without any merit of mine. He will give me, I trust, a blissful immortality in the same way. In that sense, as papa says, I allow that salvation is of grace."

" There is more truth in your way of thinking than many of my friends would allow," replied Alban. " But where does Christ come in, on your system ? How is He your *Saviour* ?"

" Mr. Alban, I will be candid. I am not contented with my own thoughts about Christ, nor with my father's explanation how He saves us. I say my prayers in His name, but what that means, is dark to me."

At the foot of the avenue they met Mr. Everett, Miss De Groot's bachelor host, coming for her. Alban, therefore, reluctantly resigned his charge, who, on her part, however, bade him good night with no outward sign of regret. As he watched them from a distance going up the snowy avenue he heard them laughing gayly.

Mary De Groot was giving her new companion a droll account of the scenes at church. When they reached home, she had to tell it all again to Miss Everett, and again there was much pleasantry at the expense of the Episcopalians. Perhaps it was rather unsympathizing and contemptuous in its tone. A glass of cold water and a dry biscuit were brought in for Miss De Groot, who had not supped, and then, without prayers, but with very affectionate good-nights, the brother and sister and their youthful guest departed to their several chambers.

Mary De Groot did not linger in the sitting-room to put up her hair, say her prayers, or unhook her dress ;—perhaps, because there was a hickory fire and Miss Everett's maid waiting for her in her own room. Her simple night-toilet was soon dispatched, she was left alone, and, kneeling down at the side of the French bed which graced the Everetts' elegant guest-chamber, blessed herself, as a Catholic would express it, *i. e.*, made the sign of the cross from the forehead to the breast, and folding her hands, said " Our Father" slowly in a low voice. Then she blessed herself again, as her Catholic mother doubtless had taught her in infancy, and so with this simple devotion laid herself to rest.

Fair child of the first Adam ! but not unconscious haply of the faint impulsions of prevenient grace, and saved *yet* by the sign on thy forehead from the adversary *qui tanquam leo rugiens circuit, quærens quem devoret,*—may pitying angels guard thy virgin repose.

CHAPTER X.

THE chapel which our young friends had assisted to adorn was excessively crowded at the service on Christmas Eve. The chancel was much admired, particularly the effect of the numerous lights of the pulpit, desk, and communion table, glittering among the fresh evergreens. The centre, however, of this illumination, was Mr. Soapstone himself, first in the desk in his surplice, and then in the pulpit in his gown. Mr. Soapstone, though a resolute Laudian, (for the name of Puseyite was not yet familiarly known,) stuck to the gown. He looked well in it, and particularly well that evening. The white "choker," as O'Connor profanely called Mr. Soapstone's cravat, and the cambric bands were beautifully relieved by the black cassock, and the ample silken sleeves of the gown gave scholastic dignity to the preacher's graceful gestures.

The sermon was capital. Mr. Soapstone had talents of no ordinary kind, and on this occasion, knowing that there would be a great gathering of "Dissenters," he laid himself out. His subject was the Divine Institution of the Festival System, and the point he made was, that in instituting the Festivals of the Old Law, the Divine Prudence had instituted the *system*, and sanctioned the principle, which the Church had carried out in new Feasts, the Memorials of new Mercies. Substituting, perhaps, cause for effect, he was inclined to connect the preservation of orthodoxy with the use of Festivals, and concluded by charging upon the Puritan rejection of the Festival system, the rise of that baleful heresy of Unitarianism, which so much infected the Congregationalist Churches of New England. Some of our student friends warmly discussed the sermon as they moved on with the outpouring crowd.

"Abominable to abuse us in that way," said Winthrop, "after

we had helped to dress the church for him. I'll be hanged if ever I do it again."

" As if there had never been any Socinians in the Episcopal Church," exclaimed a charity student. " Why, the fact is just the reverse."

" Yes, but it arose undoubtedly from neglecting to dress their churches properly with Christmas greens," observed St. Clair.

" It wants something deeper than this mechanism to keep alive faith," said Alban.

" You are right there, Mr. Atherton. It wants grace, sir," cried O'Connor. " Carroll and I are going to sing carols to-night. As your sentiments are satisfactory, will you join us ?"

Here our friends had to cross a street, and were stopped in a heap by a sleigh with ladies in it, from the church door, dashing by in the dark with loud jingling bells. A lady waved her hand.

" It is the Everetts and Miss De Groot," said Winthrop. " I wonder how *they* liked the slap about the Unitarian heresy."

The Everetts and Miss De Groot were much displeased. Miss Everett wondered (as if she had never wondered before) at the illiberality of the orthodox. She thought that after Mary had helped to dress the church, and had made the very cross for Mr. Soapstone's " altar," when none of his own flock would do it, it was downright insulting. Miss De Groot was not so warm as was her wont when any thing occurred to rouse her high spirit, although she could not suppress (perhaps she did not try) a slight bitterness in commending Mr. Soapstone for his candor and consistency. If he really believed our Saviour to be God, he must treat them as heretics. She went on to confess that the service was so beautiful, the lessons, the collects, the chanting and all, were so impressive, so devotional, (Mary was seldom so wordy,) that several times before the sermon began she had wished herself an Episcopalian. But hearing such uncharitable opinions expressed had completely repelled her. Mr. Everett observed with emphasis that it was language which would be appropriate in the mouth of a Catholic ! He could find nothing to say more cutting !

"I wonder," said Mary De Groot, "why we do not adopt some of the Episcopal forms. What right have they to monopolize every thing beautiful?"

"At the Stone church in Boston they *do* use a liturgy," remarked Miss Everett, "and they dress the church for Christmas, which is rather against Mr. Soapstone's theory."

"They are much attached to it," said her brother. "I wonder, as Mary says, that it has never spread."

"*Is* it true, as Mr. Soapstone mentioned, that there is a Unitarian New Testament with the story of our Saviour's birth put between brackets—?"

"As of doubtful authenticity. Well, I have seen such a book, Mary, but it is a calumny to say that it is in use. It was first edited by an English archbishop, too, I have heard, and Coleridge, who is a great Church-of-England man, and a stanch Trinitarian, rejects the account of the miraculous birth of Jesus with contempt."

"But that is shocking," said Mary. "One might as well give up the whole Bible at once."

"One can't well enlarge upon it to you, Miss Mary, but it is a hard doctrine to believe."

"Fie, James," said Miss Everett. "How can you?"

The sleigh jingled on amid a silence of the party in it, and dashed into the avenue to Mr. Everett's house. But as it began to ascend the heavy carriage sweep, Miss De Groot suddenly burst forth in her warmest manner, as if giving way to a feeling which she had pent up from girlish delicacy.

"I as firmly believe," she said, in a voice that trembled with passion, "that the mother of our Saviour was always a spotless virgin, as that I am at this moment, and I declare it makes my heart swell with indignation that any Christian should dare to question it."

She would hardly take Mr. Everett's hand when he offered to help her out of the sleigh, she was so angry. Perhaps to make his peace, Mr. Everett went to his library, and presently returning with a thin quarto, bound in red morocco, handed it to his quick-tempered young guest with a penitent smile.

"That is the 'Chapel Liturgy,' as they call it, Mary."

Mary took it eagerly, and began turning it over.

"Why, it is a kind of abridgment of the Episcopal Prayer-book."

"The addresses to the Trinity, and all prayers to Christ or to the Holy Ghost, are left out or altered, you will find."

"Ah," said Mary, "I have heard papa say, that the Prayer-book is the Mass protestantized, and I suppose that the 'Chapel Liturgy' is the Prayer-book socinianized." She smiled, looking at Mr. Everett, as if they had always been the best of friends, and she had not been so angry with him the moment before as to resolve never to speak to him again except with mere civility. "Thank you, Mr. James. I must take it to my own room, if you please, and look it over."

13

CHAPTER XI.

THE white dimity curtains of bed and window in the youug guest's room had a cold but virginal air, like the white Marseilles quilt, in spite of the thick blankets it covered. She herself looked the same in her clean (Thursday) night-gear, the dark hair low and smooth on her pure brow, and holding out one of her rosy feet to the fire, working its little toes, like an infant's, in the warmth. The toes were pretty enough to have rings on them, or bells, like the aged heroine's in the nursery rhyme,

"With rings on her fingers and bells on her toes,"

but Mary De Groot had none even on the former, i. e., no rings. Her virgin hands were absolved from all ornament save their own beauty, not only when undressed, as now, but at all times.

After playing thus awhile as a child might, without aim, and so serenely that she might seem either an angel or quite soulless, she suddenly turned round from the fire to her chair, assumed her little maidenly wrapper, thrust the fairy feet into their dear little slippers, and seated herself at a little table or stand, whereon were placed her candle and the " Chapel Liturgy." Having read the preface intently, bending down upon it in a very school-girl fashion, like as if she had been conning a lesson, she looked up and said aloud,

" My Unitarian friends excuse the alterations that they have made in adapting the Episcopal Prayer-book to their own use, on the same ground which the Episcopalians allege to justify the changes in their own service, from the old English Book of Common Prayer ; and both cite the latter itself."—Looks at the book and reads—" '*Every particular Church has a right to ordain, change, and abolish ceremonies or rites of the Church, ordained only by man's authority, so that all be done to edifying.*'—

What more reasonable! I declare, I should like to see what changes the American Episcopalians have made from the English Prayer-book. That should be very instructive to a little girl like me."

To think and do were the same thing with Miss Mary De Groot. She rose quickly, drew the silken cords of her wrapper tighter round her waist, tripped with her candle to the chamber-door, and peeped out into the corridor. Mr. Everett's boots lay outside his door.—"After all, he is only an old bachelor!" said the girl of sixteen, and fluttered down stairs. She is in the library with her candle.

"Now, how in the name of goodness am I to find it? Who knows if Mr. Everett has got one? Ah, here is the theology—sermons—Channing, Clarke, Newcome, Tillotson,—ah, here it is! But my! it is a thick quarto—big enough for a church! Oh, here is another that is smaller—never been used, I guess. Oh, Mr. James, you are not very devout! And the American Prayer-book close by it, not near so well bound. I must have them both, Mr. James."

She returned exultingly with her prizes. The beautifully bound "Common Prayer," when unclasped, lay open of itself on the broad quarto page of the Chapel Liturgy; the rigid American Prayer-book she held in one hand. She must spring up again to fetch from a drawer a well-worn volume of the pocket-size—the Manual of devotions which had belonged to her Catholic mother. It was in French, and contained among other things the ordinary of the Mass, with a translation in parallel columns. So the young girl began to collate and compare with a grave and singular patience, having the old Roman Mass—the venerable Liturgy of St. Peter, and much of the daily Office, at one extreme, and the Socinian Chapel Liturgy at the other, as the final result of Protestant improvements. In a very short time, perplexed by having so much before her at once, she devoted herself to those changes made by the American Episcopalians, in regard to which her curiosity had been primarily excited.

" What singular alterations are these !" she exclaimed aloud, in her way. " What could have possessed the people to make them ! How vulgar, how unpoetical,—really—how impure they are !—" She put both her little hands before her blushing face, as if her delicacy had been shocked.—" Oh, if I were an Episcopalian and knew that these things had been changed so, I should feel so ashamed !"

As she got on she grew more excited and perplexed. Here was the creed of St. Athanasius, which the Church of England ordered to be read on all the great Feasts, cast out of the American Prayer-book altogether.—" Is it because it takes away all hope of salvation from us poor Unitarians ? How kind in the American Episcopal Church to decline pronouncing so severe a sentence ! Oh, Mr. Soapstone ! you ought not to be so hard upon us since your Church will not say that we shall be condemned. Really how precise this Creed is on that point !—' *He that will be saved, must thus think of the Trinity.*'—' *Which faith except every one do keep whole and undefiled, without doubt he shall perish everlastingly.*' Well, I like that," said Mary, characteristically. " We know what we have to expect. If, after such a warning we persist in being heretics, we shall have nobody to blame but ourselves when we are sent to a bad place."

Mary De Groot actually cried over these plain and stern denunciations of the Church Catholic. They were tears of pride, but mingled with humility. She did not like to venture her salvation on the chance of Unitarianism being true ; for if it were false, it was clear that she, Mary De Groot, dying a Unitarian, would be *damned*—dreadful word—more dreadful thought ! Was it for that awful end that she had been brought into existence ?

The omission of the Athanasian creed by the American Episcopal Church enabled even so inexperienced a mind as Mary De Groot's to see in its true light the next thing that naturally met her as she pursued her comparison through the morning and evening prayer, and that was the rejection of the Evangelical Hymns.

She would not have expressed her perception in those words, but she saw well enough that it indicated the ritual degeneracy which as certainly follows the loss of faith as bodily decay follows enfeebled vitality. The Church's joy in her Divine Saviour—her mystical but real joy, ever fresh and new—was lost when the Song of Zachary was cut down into a Jewish psalm by leaving out its personal peculiarities, when the Hymn of the Blessed Virgin exulting over the Incarnation, was cast aside as fools throw away a precious gem, and aged Simeon's canticle, uttered with the Holy Ghost in his heart and the Lord in his arms, was dropped out of Even Song as inappropriate for the modern Christian's *Nunc dimittis.*

The intelligent and, in her way, highly cultured, though prejudiced, young girl had begun her investigation with the notion that ritual was unconnected with doctrine in any vital way. She had fancied that whatever was beautiful in the Episcopal worship might be easily accommodated to the wants of her own Church. A faint æsthetic idea had floated through her mind, of a Unitarian chapel in New York, either for the Chapel Liturgy, or something yet nearer to the Episcopalian rite which had so interested her that evening. Now a new light altogether had broken upon her. She saw that the old worship of the Church, from which by mutilation and corruption these Episcopal forms had been derived, was built upon the *faith* that Christ was GOD.

" If that faith be true, what an insult to Him is this Chapel Liturgy," she thought.

But what was the " true Church" doing at the moment when this insult was offered ?—and in the same land ?—Casting out the Athanasian creed, mutilating *Benedictus*, throwing away *Magnificat*, ignorant why *she* ought to rejoice nightly at the " Light to lighten the Gentiles, and the glory of thy people Israel," thinking it bootless for *her* to sing any more " For mine eyes have *seen* thy salvation."

Thus Mary thought, without framing her thought any more into words. Her head was confused and her heart perturbed.

13*

Although it was already midnight, she was about to take up her Catholic mother's manual of devotion, when a strain of sweet, animated, soul-cheering music suddenly broke the silence of the hour. She remembered that it was Christmas, and, putting out her light, went to the window, opened the shutters, and looked out upon the snowy lawn where the carollers stood.

There was a violin with manly voices.   She opened the window a little, and to her ear came words which sung of the Babe of Bethlehem as the Mighty God.   It had been the faith of ages that Heaven and Earth were espoused on this sacred night,—that God had appeared at this time in the nature of man to be the Saviour of men.   Mary made haste and knelt with her face to the starry sky where angels carolled eighteen centuries before.

"O GOD," she exclaimed, "of the substance of Thy Father, begotten before the worlds!   MAN, of the substance of thy Mother, born in the world!   I believe in Thee—I adore Thee.   Teach me Thy will.   Lead me in Thy way."

CHAPTER XII.

CHRISTMAS Day came, and the weather had changed again. Snow fell in great soft flakes, thick and fast, piling the streets with huge drifts. There was good cheer within, not so general as on the national festival of Thanksgiving, but still to be found in houses where no other notice was taken of the commemoration of the Saviour's birth. Some families, indeed, took a pride in not deviating a hair's breadth from their every-day life, but, on the whole, the time was gone by when the Puritans (although that was not in *New* England) appointed the Nativity of the Lord a public fast. The shops, however, were not generally closed, nor were any places of worship open for divine service, except the beautiful Episcopal churches and one small chapel in the poorest part of the town, plain as a Methodist meeting-house, and which might have been mistaken for one but for a wooden cross that crowned its gable.

Mary De Groot was puzzled what to do that day. She longed to repair to church to honor her new-found Saviour, new-born that day in the Church's affectionate forgetfulness of time, and new found by herself, a prize of her heart, a treasure of her faith, secret but dear, as to Her who first knew that wonder of wonders. Should not she repair to Bethlehem and worship at the manger? But whither?—*Vere tu es Deus absconditus, Deus Salvator*—words found, with a translation, annexed to the act of Faith in her mother's manual—was a sentence that ever trembled on her lips.

If she had been in Boston (inconsistent as it may appear) she would have gone to King's chapel to worship her "hidden God," even in the forms of the "Chapel Liturgy;" or if there had been a Congregationalist meeting-house in New Haven open that day for worship, she would have attended it; or in New York, she would have hastened, not unjoyfully, to the old South Dutch church, where

the old De Groot pew was still retained, though seldom visited by
the family ; but she was in New Haven, and her friends took it
quietly for granted that she would not wish to attend either of the
Episcopal churches after the evening's experience.   This taking-
for-granted was a mighty obstacle in the young girl's path, harder
to overcome than the snow which blocked up the avenue.   She
could not propose walking, and on what pretence ask for the
sleigh ?

" They will think I want to see or be seen by some of the students who will be there.   Mary Ellsworth, I know, will say so if
I come out in all this storm, not being an Episcopalian.   I have
no right to go anywhere.   And I won't expose myself to such an
imputation from those girls."

Tap, tap, tap, went the little fingers on the frosty pane of the
breakfast-room window.   The garden paths, the paths of the leafless wood beyond, were choked with snow.   The frozen linen on
the clothes-lines swung stiffly in the wind.   Mr. Everett came to
the window, shrugged his shoulders hopelessly at the dreary scene,
remarked that it was going to prove a stormy Christmas, and that
he was glad they were not going to dine out.   Then he looked
down at his slippers, worked by Mary and purchased by him at the
fair at an extravagant price, and said he should adjourn to the
library, where perhaps his guest would by and by make him a visit
in search of an old novel for this gloomy day.   So he took himself
off.   Calm, cold, handsome, heavy man of five and forty was Mr.
Everett.

Miss Everett sat on the edge of a chair with one foot on the
grate-fender, and one hand protecting her knee from the fire.   She
was glad, too, that they were not going out, and she meant to spend
the morning in answering letters.   She looked up at her blooming
guest who had glided to her side, and wondered for the five hundredth time that Mary never put her hair in papers, it would look
so beautifully, curled in her neck, and she liked to see it in girls of
her age.   The " Middle church" clock began to strike nine.   The
College clock told the solar time, and then, instead of the vocifer-

ous College bell for study hours, commenced a deep, deliberate, church-going peal from the gothic tower of Trinity—the first Episcopal bell. The young girl's heart began to beat, and she was trying to frame a petition that she might be sent to church after all, since it *was* Christmas, when sleigh-bells jingled suddenly in the background, and, glancing out of the window, she saw David and the horses dashing off with a wood-sled, and she knew that he had been sent to draw a load of pine. She suppressed her petition, and departed with an excuse to her own room.

CHAPTER XIII.

" MERRY Christmas, Bridget."

" Thank you kindly, miss, and many more of the same to your-self," said the housemaid, who was finishing Miss De Groot's room.

" Have you seen my presents, Bridget ? Well, you must come into the drawing-room by and by, and I will show them to you,—the most beautiful English holiday books from papa, a set of corals complete from mamma, a gold pencil from Mr. Everett, and from Miss Everett an elegant copy of a book that I admire very much. Besides it all, papa has sent me a beautiful Paris box of bonbons, that is, sugar-plums, with a picture of the Holy Family on the lid, which I know you will admire very much. They are all arranged on a table to show Mr. Everett's company at dinner to-day ; but you must go in and see them, Bridget."

" *That* I will, miss ; but you can't be more plased with your fine presents, miss, than I and Sally Ann was with the beautiful collars you *give* us. I haven't thanked you for it before, Miss Mary, and sure I'm very much obliged to you for thinking of *me* at all."

" You don't go to church to-day, I suppose, Bridget ?"

" Indeed I've been to five-o'clock mass, miss."

" Do you mean to say that you had church at five o'clock this morning ?"

" Surely, miss. The *first* mass—that's the midnight mass in Ireland—was at five o'clock. In this country I've niver known a mass properly at midnight."

" And when is the second mass ?" inquired the young lady with interest.

" The second mass was directly after the first, miss."

" They are both over then !" with disappointment.

" There's the third mass at half-past ten, miss."

"You have mass again at half-past ten, Bridget?" said Miss De Groot, with animation.

"With music, miss, and Father Smith will *praach*. Being the only Catholic in the house, none of the servants wants to go to church to-day but myself. And Father Smith doesn't come very often, miss. It is a month, come Sunday, since we had a mass before."

"Is that why you have three masses to-day, Bridget?"

"Oh, no, bless you, miss. 'Tis on account of Christmas. Every priest says three masses on Christmas Day, because Christ was first begotten of His Father from all eternity, and secondly born of the Blessed Virgin to-day, and thirdly every day in the hearts of believers." Bridget said this in such a tone as made it easy to see she was repeating something often heard. There was a little innocent pride, too, in understanding her religion, which made the young lady smile.

"I want to go to this third mass with you, Bridget," said Miss De Groot, "but you must not say any thing to any body of my intention. I know that the walking is very bad, but I shan't mind that in going to *your* church."

In her sober walking apparel of dark-green merino and tartan shawl, and with her hood drawn close over her face, she may pass for a young servant girl. By Bridget's advice she has drawn on a pair of coarse woollen socks over her boots, for in the drifts the snow is knee-deep. Here she toils till her breast is filled with sharp pain at every rough breath she draws. Even in the streets of New Haven, the deep-lying snow is not shovelled off the sidewalks, and they go, although more easily, yet with fatigue, in the middle of the street. By and by they strike into a well-tramped path. People are following it in single file. On the steps of the plain church with a cross upon its gable, the females shake the snow from their garments, and stamp it from their feet.

The interior of the chapel (it scarcely merited to be called a church) was rude. Instead of pews were rows of benches with backs. The men were on one side and the women on the other, and both sexes spread their handkerchiefs on the floor (at least many did) to save their clothes in kneeling. The altar was of plain unpainted deal, and yet it was rather solemn from its elevation and furniture. The chalice was upon it, under a veil of white silk very richly embroidered in gold and colors. There were no lights except a taper that burned in a common glass tumbler.

Mary De Groot has knelt down by Bridget, has crossed herself in imitation of the latter, and because, in fact, she is used to do so in her private prayers, and has opened her *Journée du Chrétien* to find a fitting devotion. In her life before she has never offered one like that which first meets her eye, being the first morning act in the manual. The young convert from Unitarianism uses it with a beating heart.

"Most holy and most august Trinity, one only God in Three persons, I believe that Thou art here present. I adore Thee with feelings of profound humility, and render Thee, with my whole heart, the homage due to Thy sovereign majesty."

The doctrine of the Trinity was one that she had not yet thought of. To her it had always seemed to be a doctrine of three Gods. But she remembered that stern Athanasian creed—"*He that will be saved must thus think of the Trinity.*"

"I submit," she cried, internally, and bending herself adored the Triune God.

The act seemed to liberate her soul, and give it a freedom before unknown. With a generous courage, offspring of divine faith, she followed the rest of the prayers in her book, at once with her heart and her lips.

"My God, I most humbly thank Thee for all the favors Thou hast bestowed upon me hitherto. It is owing to Thy goodness that I see this day; I will therefore employ it in serving Thee. I consecrate to Thee its thoughts, words, actions, and sufferings. Bless them, Lord, that there may not be one which is not animated by Thy love, or tends not to Thy glory.

"Adorable Jesus! divine model of the perfection to which we should aspire, I will apply myself as much as I can to make myself like Thee: meek, humble, chaste, zealous, patient, charitable, and resigned like Thee.

I will use every effort not to fall to-day into the faults I so often commit, but which I sincerely desire to correct.

"My God, Thou knowest my weakness. I can do nothing without Thy grace. Refuse it me not. Give me strength to shun every ill Thou forbiddest, to do all the good Thou requirest, and to suffer patiently whatever afflictions it shall please Thee to send me."

"If an angel," thought Mary, "had descended to teach me prayers for this morning, what else could he have said?"

These prayers were in French, but next came some in Latin, and not knowing where to find the translation, she skipped until she came to the Litany of Jesus, where the two languages ran side by side. She had just finished reciting it with a great deal of fervor, for it was just what she wanted, and the *Agnus Dei*, which so many say coldly, moved *her* to tears, for the first time supplicating Christ as the Lamb of God, when the great candles were lit.

"Do the Catholics have little clergymen?" thought Mary, with an innocent smile, but pleased, when six young boys in cassocks and white cottas entered with the priest.

The lace of the latter's albe, and the embroidery of his vestment also caught her female eye, and made her throw a glance around the church. She had been so absorbed that she had not observed it filling. Every part of the floor was occupied by men or women, all kneeling, all of the humblest class of society. Their demeanor was the most devout she had ever witnessed. And now the music attracted her attention. She could not help looking back at the organ gallery, and saw that it was full of foreign music-teachers of both sexes, connected with the schools of New Haven. As she did not understand what was going on at the altar, her eye sufficed to attend to it, and her whole mental attention was absorbed by that wonderful *Kyrie*. She perceived that the words were the same with which the litany she had just said, began, *Kyrie eleison, Christe eleison, Kyrie eleison!* without end. At length it was done; the congregation rose; the chasubled priest sung something in a singular tone; the choir recom-

14

menced, and in a minute all sat down as if to hear it through.
Bridget saw that Miss Mary was bewildered, and showed her that
it was the *Gloria in excelsis.*

"Oh, yes," she thought, "that is the song of the angels at the
Saviour's birth. That is what I came here to sing, at least in my
heart. They are singing it in the mass."

Turning over the index of her little prayer-book, Mary had
found the *Messe de Noël ;* and when the priest intoned the collect,
epistle, and gospel, she was able to follow, while her familiarity
with the Scriptures enabled her to understand it all very fairly,
although the words were in a dead language. But in the gospel
certain words were printed in Italics, *Et Verbum caro factum est,*
and when the priest, solemnly chanting, arrived at that point, he
and the surpliced boys and the entire congregation bent the knee ;
in a moment after, he took off his vestment, turned round to the
people, still standing, and having received another book from one
of his youthful assistants, said,

"The gospel which has just been sung at mass is taken from
the first chapter of the gospel of St. John."

He read it in English, down to the words *And the Word was
made Flesh,* &c., and added, as he returned the book to the minister, "You know, my brethren, that it was at these words we all
knelt just now when they were sung at mass."

"Ah !" thought Mary, "they believe in the Incarnation in
this Church !"

CHAPTER XIV.

MARY was charmed and grateful when Father Smith took these words for the text of the discourse which he now delivered from the steps of the altar. It was the very theme which she desired to hear more fully treated—the dogma in which she newly believed—the Incarnation of the Eternal Word. Father Smith's manner was fervent; he gesticulated a good deal; his accent was foreign ; but his thoughts were fresh, and his method singularly perspicuous. The congregation hung upon his lips.

"In these words," said the popish priest,—"THE WORD WAS MADE FLESH,—is contained the Root and principle of all that the Catholic Church believes and teaches; and yet this Root itself springs from a deeper ground, if I may say so, and is planted in the doctrine of the Divine Nature."

This exordium interested Mary deeply, and still more so when by throwing the idea into several shapes successively, the preacher rendered it distinctly intelligible not only to her, but, as she felt, to his entire audience. God, he explained to them, was one, and no unity was so simple or so perfect as His. The Divine Substance was one simple undivided, indivisible essence, one simple indivisible Spirit, Which yet existed in Three Persons really distinct, without ceasing to be the Same in each ; a truth which we could not know except by particular revelation, but which when revealed contradicted neither consciousness nor experience, for both these were silent before it. The text declared that One of these Divine Persons became Flesh. The means by which this sublime union of Godhead and Manhood was accomplished was a creative act of the Three Divine Persons, whereby the Word and Son of God, according to the Will of His Father, and with the co-operation of the Holy Ghost, assumed into Himself the whole and perfect human nature, and became the Son of Man ; so that Jesus

Christ, the First-born of creation, the Anointed in respect to the Holy Ghost Who dwelt in Him, was in Himself the Everlasting Son of the Eternal Father, His Wisdom and His Word, by Whom He created all things, and Whose every earthly word and action was a Fiat of Almighty God.

From this statement of the pure revealed doctrine of the Godhead and Incarnation, the preacher proceeded to unfold its doctrinal and practical consequences. A divine fact like that, he observed, could not stand alone in a barren solitude ; it was fruitful as the Divine nature itself. Neither could it be believed alone in its naked simplicity ; it was but the seed of a joyful and abounding faith. Because the Word was made *Flesh*, we saw a visible Church, we heard an audible teaching, confessed a human priesthood, sacraments with a sensible form and matter, saints working sensible miracles, vocal prayers, bodily penances. It was necessary to salvation not only that the heart be purified by faith, but that the body be washed with water. The Word made Flesh had ordained these things and filled them with virtue ; and the Church knew their value, because, believing Him to be God, she understood all His words in their divinest, mightiest, most enduring sense. The Church never attached a common, weak, human meaning to any saying or any action of the Word made Flesh. When Incarnate Wisdom bade her "*teach all nations*," she knew that she became His organ and therefore infallible ; when the Mediator between God and Man declared " *Whose sins you shall forgive they are forgiven*," she knew that Penance became a Sacrament ; when the Creator pronounced "*This is My Body*," that Transubstantiation became a truth ; when the Pontiff after the order of Melchisedech, added, "*This is My Blood which shall be shed for the remission of sins*," that the Mass was to be a sacrifice. For the whole doctrine of the Church had distilled from the lips of Christ, as her whole life was breathed into Her by His grace.

While Father Smith was saying this, Mary De Groot was entirely convinced that these high dogmas of the Catholic Church did indeed flow necessarily from the Incarnation of God; but the objection recurred to her mind that that Church which so faithfully accepted the consequences of the Incarnation, did also make it null by setting up creature mediators, like the Virgin, and enthroning them in the place of the Saviour. Father Smith suddenly approached this theme in winding up his discourse.

"In nothing, my dear brethren," he said, "is the faith of the Incarnation more manifest than in what the Church believes concerning the exaltation of the Saints. Christ declares that they shall reign with Him, that they shall sit with Him on His throne. So the Church understands that He is not injured by their glory —His own gift, nor disparaged by the intercessory mediation, which is but their promised participation of His. For He is their God and Lord, and cannot be excluded from any thing that they do. She knows, therefore, that He is *in* His Saints, is glorified in them, is invoked, intercedes, obtains graces, works wonders, and in a word, *reigns* in them; so that while they really share His mediatorial throne, He, notwithstanding, wholly fills it, God and Man, the Saint of saints, and Crown of them all."

This was very startling to our young friend, but she saw its truth. Yet what followed was by no means unnecessary for the complete satisfaction of her mind.

"Above all," concluded the father, in a softer voice, "it is on the doctrine of the Incarnation that depends our love and veneration for that Blessed One whose womb bore the Eternal, whose paps this day gave Him suck. MARY is our mother because she is the Mother of our God. On the throne of the universe, He is constrained by the truth of His humanity to confess Himself her Son. And as it was through her individual faith, as the Scripture testifies, that we received the Person of the Word into the bosom of our nature, so it is in her exaltation that our nature gains the highest glory which the Word made Flesh diffuses in His members without losing in Himself. How vainly do men admit a truth under one form of expression while they betray their unbelief by denying it in another? When the Eternal was found

14*

as an infant of days, do they still wonder that a woman is acknowledged as the Mother of God ? If the Son of Mary were
an exalted creature, our love for her might do Him an injury,
but since He is the Creator of Mary, the Author of her merits,
and their Infinite reward, all our homage to her but magnifies
Him the more. The Catholic Church knows very well that
Mary is a simple creature, and that she has nothing which she
has not received. She is but the ark of the covenant, the gate of
heaven, the golden mansion of our God and King. As such we
revere her, but her Son is our God and King himself, and Him
we adore.

" See then, my brethren, how simple in its principle is that
holy faith, every article of which is guaranteed to you by the
Divine veracity. Adhere to it with unshaken confidence, because
God has revealed it. Believe on the Word made Flesh under
every one of these lowly manifestations in which it has pleased
Him to hide His majesty, that you may become the sons of God,
according to the promise that has been read to you in the gospel :
—a blessing which I wish you all, In the name of the Father,
✠ and of the Son, and of the Holy Ghost."

The priest turned to the altar, threw the rolled up back of
the chasuble over his head, replaced the maniple on his left arm,
and the people rose.

" Credo in unum Deum."

CHAPTER XV.

"It is my new faith," said the young girl, "which I came here to confess. The priest has said it at the altar; they are singing it in the choir. I follow it in my heart. When the priest came to the words which confess the Incarnation, he and all the people with him knelt. Shall we do so again, I wonder, when the choir arrive at that part? See, it comes, and the music pauses. Yes, the priest rises with the white-and-scarlet-vested boys; they go to the front of the altar and kneel, and we kneel also. Et Incarnatus est. This is awful. Et Homo factus est. We rise again. Wonderful Church! Which believes the mystery and so comprehends all truth. Did not I read in the Protestant Episcopal Prayer-book that the Nicene creed need *never* be said by them but at the option of the minister? Counterfeit Church, I know you by this hesitation! Wolf in sheep's clothing and false prophet! well may the anathema expire on your trembling lips."

Mary found no difficulty now in following in a general way the course of the glorious sacrifice. It would merely have distracted her could she have traced more minutely an action at once so full and so rapid, in which every word has a value, every gesture a sense, whose boundless scope takes in three worlds, and darts from Abel's offering to that of the present moment. She knew that there was an oblation, for she saw the lifted chalice. She saw the priest purify his hands, and prayed instinctively that her soul might be purified by grace, and her body washed with pure water, that she might be worthy to adore so awful a mystery. *Sursum corda* "lifted her heart" to the Lord, and the sweet tones of the Preface of the Nativity:—but lo! *He comes in the name of the Lord, God and Lord like Him by Whom He is sent!* She saw the lights and incense, (offering of humble zeal to grace this much-loved day,) and she hasted to bow her head, while the choir was hushed, and the bell alone broke the deep stillness by its quick and awful warning.

The last thing at mass is, that after the benediction the priest reads a second gospel;—as a general rule, the beginning of the gospel of St. John, in the reading of which, as has been already noted, all kneel at the concluding sentence (*And the Word was made Flesh*) in honor of the Incarnation.   But as the reader will already have observed, this gospel is the proper gospel for the third mass on Christmas Day, and so another is read at the end, taken from St. Matthew, and containing the visit of the Magi to the infant Redeemer.   One of the females near our young convert, perceiving that she was a stranger to the worship, offered her here an English missal, with the place found, and pointed her to this gospel.   Though exhausted and languid after so many emotions, Mary gratefully read it, understanding of course that it was the same which the priest was reading at the altar.

" Faithful Church !" she again cried to herself, as she perceived whither this second gospel tended, " she never loses sight of Him whom her soul loveth !   Her last glance is the same as her first.   She was about to depart, but she turns to Him yet again, her Divine Spouse !"

For at the words "*and falling down they adored Him*," all again genuflected, and Mary saw that it was so enjoined in the book.

CHAPTER XVI.

FATHER Smith had been up all night hearing confessions: the little church having been crowded with penitents from six in the evening till the early mass. He had sung mass twice, and said one low mass between, giving communion to nearly four hundred. In the interval, he had administered Extreme Unction and the Viaticum to a dying woman, (Death waits not for festivals,) and although it was past midday, except in purifying the Chalice in the last mass, he had of course not broken his fast since midnight, by so much as a drop of cold water. His human nature had a right to be exhausted. But he has yet to make his thanksgiving for that Bread which whoso eats shall live for ever. He kneels in his long black soutane at a desk in one corner of the sacristy, with his face hidden in his hands. His close-cut hair is thickly sown with premature gray, and a bare spot at the crown is not the tonsure, which in the mission is not worn, but the commencement of baldness. Two of his young assistants are noiselessly engaged in putting away the sacred vestments. There is a knock at the door which communicates with the church. One of the boys opens it. A young lady—a young girl, one would say—is there. She desires to speak to Father Smith. The boy motions her to come in, and points her to a chair. She takes it, and gazes around timidly. The priest kneels on in his corner. In the other is a low screen, with a sort of grating in it, a kneeling-board in front, and a chair behind. There is perfect silence. Her heart sinks within her. She looks up for help. Her eye falls on a large crucifix fixed to the opposite wall, over a table. "He died for me," she thinks, "died on a cross! Nothing shall prevent me from confessing His name!"

At last, Father Smith rose. He saw the young girl, and approached her with a look of inquiry. Mary rose, but she was voiceless. She could not utter a word ; she knew not even what she wanted to say, and so she just looked down. The father glanced at her dark, plain hood and blanket-shawl, and the knit socks drawn over her shoes.

"You want to go to confession ? Very well :"—pointing to the confessional. The boys left the vestry, and Father Smith was going to put on his stole.

"No, sir, I do not want to confess," said Mary, in a choking voice, and trembling from head to foot.

"What then *do* you want, my dear child !" rejoined the priest, with some surprise, and some quickness. "My time is precious, but if I can be of any assistance to you, speak. If you have any thing on your mind, you had better go to confession at once."

"I wish to be baptized, sir," said Mary.

"Ah !" The priest observed her more narrowly. She had broken the ice, and now looked up courageously. "You are a Protestant ?" asked he, gently.

"Not now," said Mary.

"Sit down. How long is it since you came to this resolution ?"

"This morning, sir."

"Ah, at mass, I suppose. God is very good. But your friends—they know nothing about it. Are your parents living ?"

"My father is living. My mother was a Catholic, sir."

"God is *very* good !" said the father, with an upward glance. "But have you never been baptized at all ?"

"Never."

"Is your father in humble circumstances ? Has he any religious belief ? Do you live in New Haven ?"

"We live in New York, sir. My father is a Unitarian. He is not poor," said Mary.

"I think that you must be careful not to act precipitately. You must consult your father, and you will yourself need to be instructed, probably, in our holy faith. If God has really touched your heart with His grace, a short trial will only make your faith more firm and pure. What Catholic books have you read?"

Mary handed him the little "Journée du Chrétien." He glanced at it. "Is this all?" he asked, with a smile. "Well, it is enough. God's grace can employ the feeblest instruments. But you will certainly need instruction. And I don't know who will instruct you. Where are you staying? At Mr. Everett's. Oh, I understand. Is there a Catholic servant in the family? Ask her to lend you her catechism. You need no better prayer-book than this for the present. It will be a month before I shall be here again, for I have other stations to serve."

"A month, Father Smith! Oh, I cannot wait a month."

"Oh, yes, you can. It will soon pass. If your faith continue firm, and your desire of baptism is sincere, your soul will be in no danger from the delay. You must write to your father; and, meanwhile I would say as little as possible to others. Do not commit yourself. It is not necessary. Pray a great deal, and particularly make the act of faith every night and morning with fervor and attention. Now go, my dear child. God has been very merciful to you. You can never love Him enough in return."

Mary De Groot dropped on one knee. Father Smith blessed her, and bid her be of good cheer. She went out joyfully; Bridget had waited and wondered in the church.

The good people of New Haven, and the student community of Yale College, passed their Christmas morning in a very different way. The Episcopal churches had been crowded on the eve, but the morning congregations, partly on account of the weather, were thin. The students lamented that the holiday was thrown away on a storm. Smoking, card-playing with locked doors, and kindred amusements, filled up the time of many. Reading novels, lounging in each others' rooms, and all sorts of corrupt conversation, occupied others. The ambitious "studied," as the American phrase is, i. e., read hard. The Professors and Tutors had a day for their private use, unbroken by lecture or recitation. The

Professor of Chemistry shut himself up in his laboratory; the Professor of Natural Philosophy pursued his experiments on the construction of stoves; the Rev. President corrected his last mathematical text-book, and the Divinity Professor recreated himself with a novel. Among the five hundred and more members of the University, there were probably not above five and twenty who went to church on Christmas morning, in the year 1834.

Among the five and twenty was our friend Alban. He had indeed two invitations, one from Mr. Soapstone, to hear his sermon; one from Miss Ellsworth, to sit in her father's pew; and the latter he accepted. It was in Trinity. There was something exceedingly comfortable and old-country-like in the whole thing, that pleased Alban, and reminded him of Washington Irving's beautiful descriptions of English Christmas. There was no new-fangled "Catholicism" in the arrangements at Trinity, no Puseyite innovation, as people would now say : no candles, no crosses, no shams of any sort. It was an old-fashioned church, dressed for the cheerful festival in an old-fashioned way. A young deacon read the prayers in a very graceful manner, and the excellent rector preached an old-fashioned sermon, in which he clearly proved to his hearers from the Scriptures, the Divinity of Him whom he called the great Founder of their religion. His text was the same as Father Smith's, which was not a surprising coincidence, since the same gospel was read in the Communion. The English reformers in arranging their new service, took for Christmas Day the old gospel for the third mass *in Nativitate Domini.* In the well-cushioned pew of the Ellsworths, with Mary Ellsworth's shot-silk dress rustling by his side, occasionally, her delicate, gloved hand pointing out the place, our hero was very well off. There was literally nothing to disturb his enjoyment. There were no low people near at all events, to pollute the air with their breath, and with the peculiar odor that emanates from the unchanged garments of the poor. The sweet breath of Mary Ellsworth, with a fine fragrance of cologne from her clothes, was all that mingled with the fresh smell of the spruce, cedar, and balsamic pine that drooped in deep festoons along the gallery. The Brussels carpet under his feet harbored none of the small but active gentry from whose persecutions poor Mary De Groot suffered all day.

Alban was engaged to dine with the Ellsworths, and when service was over accepted a seat in their sleigh. It was still by the beautiful daughter's side. They were going directly to dinner, for the communion had made it late, as Mr. Ellsworth remarked.

" How fatiguing it must be for the clergy to have so large a communion," observed Mrs. Ellsworth with matronly consideration.

" Particularly if they were fasting, as Mr. Soapstone says they ought to be," said Alban, smiling.

" Mr. Soapstone is a—most preposterous young man," said Mr. Ellsworth.

" Did Mr. Soapstone fast this morning?" asked Mary Ellsworth, answering Alban's smile.

" Why not exactly. But he explained to me at breakfast, that in the present anomalous position of the Church the rule could not be strictly followed ; and he really did not think he could get through the whole service alone on an empty stomach."

" I wonder he should think of it," said kind Mrs. Ellsworth, while her husband laughed bitterly and Miss Ellsworth gayly. The sleigh swept round a corner, dashing between two girls who were crossing the street, and in a moment the bells ceased jingling at Mr. Ellsworth's gate.

The rector and the deacon were among the Ellsworths' Christmas guests. Wine flowed ; the Church was lauded ; the denominations received many mortal thrusts. Even the poor Papists did not wholly escape. The cross and candles at Mr. Soapstone's chapel were canvassed and condemned. After dinner, round the dining room fire, the gentlemen filled up an hour and a half or so, with smoking, politics, and anecdotes of rather dubious edification. Tea and coffee and the ladies succeeded, and the evening of games and music, dancing, laughter, and mulled wine. Alban was Mary Ellsworth's partner in the games and in the cotillion, and his hand trembled when it touched hers in bidding her good-night.

The Everetts' dinner company was naturally of a different cast, Professor S——, P——, the poet, several ladies of a somewhat literary and scientific turn, and a young Marylander of the Senior class, who was a connection. The beautiful maid of sixteen was silent at dinner as a rose in a vase; but in the evening she sang like a Virginia nightingale in an aviary. Young Carroll got beside her after some manœuvring, and she blushed as she asked him if there was not a cathedral in Baltimore.

"Of course, Miss Mary, since it is the see of an archbishop. You should visit Baltimore, Miss De Groot. You would form a very different idea of Catholics from what you get in the North. The best families in Maryland are Catholics."

"Are they really? The faith is the same as that of the Catholics here, is it not?"

"Certainly—oh, certainly, the faith is the same. But we fancy that we are a little more refined than the low Irish you see here."

"Of course you did not go to mass this morning among all the low Irish?" said Mary.

"Oh, indeed, you are very severe, Miss De Groot. Of course I went to mass—at five o'clock. Some of us sung Christmas carols under your windows at midnight, and we staid up for mass, I assure you;—at least O'Connor and I did."

"But at half-past ten?" persisted Miss De Groot.

"Why to tell the truth, at half-past ten I went to the Episcopal churches, first to one and then to the other, in the hope of seeing you, Miss Mary; not for the service, I assure you. But I suppose you found the weather too unpleasant to go out."

"A pretty way of spending your Christmas morning, Mr. Carroll! Is that your Maryland refinement? Would your Catholic friends in Baltimore approve of your turning your back on High Mass at the cathedral, and ranging from one Protestant church to another in quest of an heretical young lady?" She glowed all over, brow, cheek, and neck. " I don't take it as a compliment that I was the person you sought, if indeed I was. I was at the third mass, Mr. Carroll, and I can tell you that I think Protestants excusable in the vile things they say, because they are ignorant, and know no better, but not a Catholic who knows what the mass is and neglects it."

Young Carroll, who was really a good fellow and a thorough gentleman, had great difficulty in making his peace. He insisted strongly on his having satisfied the precept of the Church by hearing one mass, that he was not obliged to hear another, and that he went to the Protestant service (he urged that) purely to see her. He had not taken, nor would he take on any account the least part in their worship, so much as in thought. Nay, to feel the slightest devotion in a Protestant church would be a moral impossibility for him. Mary was silent while he related the history of several attempts to convert him since he had been at New Haven. It was very amusing, for out of pure contempt, the easy Marylander had let himself be argued with, and plied with books to almost any extent, just giving encouragement enough to draw on the zealous proselyters who desired to save him from the scarlet lady.

" But I knew," said the young planter, with gentle animation, " that if I had been blown into ten thousand atoms, the faith would have been found entire in every separate fragment."

" That's the best thing you have said yet, Mr. Carroll," said Mary.

Professor S——, with the instinct that shrewd Protestants have in regard to the danger of conversing with Catholics about their religion, yet influenced by that uneasiness which leads them always to attack it, interposed and asked Carroll some questions in a calm tone of superiority.

" What is the reason, Mr. Carroll, since the Pope possesses the whole treasure of indulgences, that he does not apply it at once to let all the souls out of purgatory ? Why does he demand to be paid for each one separately ?"

"Because he possesses no such power," replied Carroll, with the greatest good humor.

"What, the Pope cannot let as many souls out of purgatory as he pleases?"

"Decidedly not, or it would be very cruel in him not to do it. You don't seem to know, Professor, what the doctrine of the Church is on the subject of indulgences."

"Pray enlighten my Protestant ignorance, Mr. Carroll."

"An indulgence as applied to the souls in purgatory, sir, is only an application of the merits of Christ and the saints in their behalf in the way of a prayer to God. The Church has no jurisdiction over the dead, sir, and the Pope can no more release a soul out of purgatory by any direct act of authority than you or I can."

"That I believe," said the Professor, sarcastically. "You only think, then, that the Pope can pray people out of purgatory, not that he can open the door with his big keys?"

"Certainly," said Carroll, "we believe that there is a purgatory, and that the prayers of the living are useful to those who are detained there: both very consoling truths to poor sinners like me, though not to saints like you, Professor, who will of course go straight to heaven when you shake off this mortal coil."

Mary De Groot laughed, and whispered to Carroll that she was glad he had the courage to defend his religion so manfully.

"I cannot want that," replied the young Marylander, coloring and smiling, "while I am true to the grace of confirmation. I am sorry to say that I don't practise my religion so well as I might, but I should have courage to die for it, if necessary."

After the mulled wine had been duly honored, Miss De Groot returned young Carroll's good-night with abrupt cordiality. She drew back coyly indeed from the hand which he extended with Southern frankness, and made him a deep curtsey instead of taking it, but she gave him one look in saying *bon soir*, that was winged with girlish admiration, due partly to his great personal advantages, partly to his manliness and spirit.

"We must not have Charles Carroll here too often, Mary, or he will convert you to Popery," said Miss Everett, laughing, when the guests were gone.

"Not he," replied the young girl with a blush at her own evasion. But bold as she was, she dared not confess herself a convert to the Church of Rome.

15*

CHAPTER XVII.

In addition to the profound religious questions which now interested him, and the novel excitement of mature female society, our hero was at this time almost overwhelmed with the perplexity and trials of authorship. He had imagined that to write his tragedy was all he had to do ; he was not prepared for the far more difficult business of getting it up. Distributing the parts, inciting the industry and correcting the dull misapprehensions of some actors, repressing the vivacity and self-will of others, superintending the rehearsal, all were new, and tiresome enough. He became heartily sick of his own work, and anticipated nothing less than a total failure on the night of performance. He never thought of the time as drawing inevitably near without a sickness at heart. The only hope he had, was, that his new female friends would be prevented from attending the Exhibition to witness his exposure. The last rehearsal, in the presence of a chosen few, somewhat encouraged him. His friends, indeed, pointed out to him several faults in his play—an excess of plot, over-refinement in the sentiments, and occasionally too great plainness of language—an unsophisticated, unveiled expression of love, which they thought required to be softened so as not to offend the delicacy of the fair audience before whom the Exhibition was to be repeated. Alban said it was too late to correct these faults, but he had no doubt that his critics were entirely in the right. He confessed that he was very inexperienced, and he wished a thousand times that he had had his fingers cut off before he attempted to write that unlucky tragedy. He proposed that the Exhibition should not be repeated, and was but slightly consoled when his principal confidant assured him that in a first effort much would be forgiven.

At length the night of the Exhibition arrived. Alban presided in his chair of state ; the Society's room had been converted into a simple but convenient theatre. Every sitting or standing was occupied. The crowd was suffocating. The tragedy was highly successful, and Alban observed, to his surprise, that the points which had been so severely criticised by his friends in private, were precisely those which elicited from the full theatre its liveliest applause. It was voted a brilliant thing, and wonderfully more spirited, more racy, than could have been expected from so serious a fellow as Atherton. His own friends said that the surprise occasioned by this contrast between the author's well-known character and the impassioned dialogue of his work, was the secret of the success which it obtained before the student assemblage. There was some truth in the remark, for nothing else was so much talked of as this novel feature in a performance of Atherton's. The *experimentum crucis* remained, however, yet to be made, in the presence of nearly two hundred young ladies.

It was a brilliant *coup d'œil*, the theatre on the second night, at the rising of the curtain :—row rising on row of lovely faces on a background mostly of white muslin, mingled occasionally with richer fabrics, but all festive, while a framework of dark manly costume, varied with white waistcoats, inclosed the whole on the sides and rear. The President's seat of dignity commanded a view of both the stage and the audience. In front of his chair three seats were reserved in the middle of a settee for Miss Ellsworth, Miss Everett, and Miss De Groot. The first arrived early, looking very beautiful in her low cut dress and finely-drooping shoulders. Miss Everett and her youthful guest came just as the curtain rose. For various reasons they were sure to attract attention, which their being late increased. Miss De Groot's color rose as she made her way with some difficulty to the place reserved for her. She got seated at last, and looked towards the stage, while Miss Ellsworth, whispering " How late you are !" glanced at the dress of the rival belle. An oration and a poem were to be delivered before the commencement of the dramatic performances, and the orator was already in the full tide of declamation.

The title of the tragedy on the printed bill of the exercises, was "The Fall of the Inca;" an American subject, but admitting the richest European costume of a romantic age. The heroine was the Princess of Peru. As the female parts were necessarily performed by young men, this idea presented great means of effect. The Princess was enacted by a Louisianian, a handsome, dark boy of sixteen, and a Calliopean. His sex was a positive advantage, by warranting that strictness of savage costume which otherwise would not have been allowable. Young Badeau, of mixed French and Indian ancestry, wore in front his own straight black hair, femininely parted, and rendered with infinite spirit the wild passion of the Inca's daughter. The part of Pizarro was played by a young man of dissipated tendencies, but great histrionic talent, who subsequently went on the stage. The lover of the piece was also a capital actor, now an eminent evangelical clergyman in the Episcopal Church. The play, therefore, was well cast. But we must not forget the Inca himself. A pious classmate of Alban's, whom no one would have suspected of such a talent, and at whose name most smiled when it was announced, a candidate for the Congregational ministry, in fact, and a man past thirty, personated the Indian Sovereign—the Child of the Sun—with admirable success. Alban's heart went beating triple time during the whole representation. The last two acts were of thrilling interest; the incidents exciting. They passed rapidly amid breathless attention, and received, at the close of the scenes, the meed of soft plaudits, not unmingled with sighs and blushes. The death of the Inca was wonderfully well managed, and when the Princess swooned on the body of her lover, one of the young ladies, who had never seen a play before, fainted, and had to be carried out. This real incident added to the eclat, and the curtain fell amid enthusiastic applause. Black waiters now brought in ice-cream and other refreshments for the ladies, and the President, quitting his chair of state, tremblingly approached his fair friends. They welcomed him with all their hands.

It does not boot to relate all the flattering things they said. Miss Everett, however, fought shy of a topic on which Miss Ellsworth rallied him, namely, the impassioned love-scenes. Whence had he drawn his knowledge of ladies' hearts and ladies' ways? His Indian princess was a true woman, and Miss Ellsworth appealed to Miss De Groot. Mary had risen for a change of position and was regarding Alban as if in a revery. She started at Miss Ellsworth's question, made her repeat it, and answered with a blush,

"I thought the princess a little too forward,—but then I never saw a play before."

"That was meant to be a part of her character as a princess accustomed to boundless submission and indulgence," observed Alban.

"Oh, it seemed to me all very real, so much so that it made me quite—" she hesitated.—"Christian delicacy does not grow wild in a woman's heart, of course, Mr. Alban. I think that you have painted what we are by nature very truly."

Her face glowed, and it was impossible not to be struck with its cherubinical intelligence brought out by the novel excitement. Mary Ellsworth abruptly drew attention to her friend's dress.

"You have departed from your ordinary simplicity in honor of the occasion, Mary. Mr. Alban ought to appreciate the compliment. I wonder you have never worn that lovely pink satin before. You should make her always dress as becomingly, Miss Everett."

Miss De Groot was in fact arrayed with an unusual care. Her hair was relieved by a slender gold band, over which its dark thick waves seeme struggling to rise. She laughed girlishly at her dress being noticed, and said something awkwardly about having out-grown all her dresses since she came to New Haven, and then the beautiful eyelids drooped.

"What a child she is after all," thought the President of the Brothers' Society, and turned to Miss Ellsworth.

The comedy produced much merriment. The principal character was a raw New England farmer. The wit was not very refined, but the truthfulness of the representation in respect to accent and dialect, and the reckless fun of the preposterous incidents

rendered it irresistible. Every body laughed. Mary De Groot
laughed till she cried, and Miss Everett nearly ruptured a blood-
vessel in the vain attempt to preserve her dignity. Mary De
Groot's uncontrollable convulsion sunk her again in the grave
estimate of Mr. Alban, while Miss Ellsworth proportionably rose
in virtue of the expressions of disgust wherewith she avenged herself for an occasional surprise.

The performance was not concluded till nearly two o'clock.

Miss Everett and Mary waited for the crush to be over,
and Alban, as their inviter, kept near them.

"Are you going home for the vacation, Mr. Alban?"

He had thought to spend it at New Haven. The Sound was
not pleasant at this season; there was sometimes danger from the
accumulation of ice; and it was his last winter vacation.

"But I should think it would do you good to get away from
New Haven for a fortnight."

Here Miss Ellsworth elbowed her way out of the cloak-room
and approached, all muffled, to take leave of the President.

"We shall expect to see you every day in the vacation, Mr.
Atherton."

Alban thanked her, shook hands, and bade her good-night
with a gratified and admiring air. Following with his eye her
receding figure, and watching her gracefully take up her dress to
descend the carpetless stairs, he forgot Miss De Groot, until the
latter appeared in her snowy capuchin, and with the pink satin
carefully gathered up.

"And I must say 'good-by,' I suppose, Mr. Alban."

"How so?"

"I am going home on Monday—to New York."

Accompanying them down the stair, he learned that this was
settled, Miss De Groot having only waited for the Exhibition.
She had written to her father that very day to meet her at the
wharf on Monday evening.

"The idea of her going home alone on that frightful Sound,"
said Miss Everett.

"I wish you were going down for the vacation, Mr. Alban," said Miss De Groot. "Why can't you change your mind, and be my escort?" she added, in a sportive girlish manner.

"With the greatest pleasure," answered Alban, gallantly.

"Will you, really? Oh! you are only in jest, Mr. Alban. New Haven has too many attractions for you to leave it."

"It loses one of its greatest in losing Miss De Groot, who does not think me capable, I hope, of accepting such an invitation in jest. After all, my mother would be disappointed not to see me this vacation."

"Ah, Mr. Alban, if you have a mother who expects you, I shall do a good turn by persuading you to spend your vacation in New York. You can get permission to go on Monday, I suppose?"

"The vacation does not begin till Wednesday, but there will be no difficulty about that," said Alban, half feeling that he might get off on this score, if he chose, and he thought of spending the evenings at Miss Ellsworth's, around a table for games, with all the too agreeable incidents sure to follow; nor did he not remember the morning *tête-à-têtes* which he might hope so much more frequently to enjoy. But Miss Everett took up his offer, and observed, that if Mr. Atherton were really going down for the vacation, it would be quite a relief to her mind. Atherton promised to call at the Grove on the morrow and complete the arrangement; Miss De Groot thereupon expressed her satisfaction without any disguise, and the sleigh glided away with its jingle and slide.

"These rich and proud people seem really to make use of one," thought Alban. "It is rather selfish in Miss Mary to make me quit New Haven to wait upon her on the steamboat. Still, she is a young lady, whom, for what I have seen of her, I sincerely respect."

CHAPTER XVIII.

THE day after an exhibition, men sleep over and get marked
by the monitors ; but Atherton, having a favor to ask, was in
his place at the head of the Seniors, (being A. A.,) just as the
chapel-bell ceased tolling, and Henry Atherton, who was Senior
monitor, and never failed to note his cousin and room-mate's ab-
sences with rigid impartiality, smiled gravely as he rose and took
out his chapel book. Our hero was at the President's lecture and
got the permission he required, the good Doctor observing that
Atherton had been hard worked this term ; but indeed Alban
was never refused any thing. It was the only thing which injured his general popularity, that he was such a favorite with the
"dons." He made his arrangements then in the afternoon, and
in the evening called at the Grove agreeably to his promise.

The small, lofty drawing-room, looked cheerfully manorial
with its high mahogany doors, crimson satin window curtains
drawn, blazing grate, pictured walls, and open piano. Alban
had seen so little of Miss De Groot that he did notice she had
grown since he first saw her at the fair.

She declined an invitation to attend the College Chapel the
next day, but offered to take a walk with Mr. Alban in the afternoon, if he would call at the Grove. She strove, it was evident,
to make herself agreeable to him. She went to the piano and
played. Mary was one of those gifted individuals who play by
ear and catch a piece the first time they hear it. Doubtless her
refined musical organization was connected with that quickness
of temper which we have noticed. Her voice was neither con-
tralto nor soprano ; but soft in the lower register, bird-like in the
higher. As she sung, her well-formed chest played freely in its
easy vesture. It was curious, though, how quietly she sat on the
music-stool—like a child. Miss De Groot paid so much respect

to the vicinity of the Sabbath as to play only sacred music. She performed admirably the *Kyrie* which she had heard at mass.

Alban's ear was pleased, but he was so uncultivated that he knew not whether what he had heard was very good or not; so he was silent.

Mary began some grave and solemn unisons—a sublime Dorian chant. She added words as before. It was the Preface of the Nativity.

"What kind of music is that?" asked Alban, with emotion, when the strain abruptly closed.

"You feel that, do you? It is the intonation of a part of the mass," said Mary, in a low voice. "And this is more of it." She toned off the *Pater noster*, with one hand, singing the words.

"Mary spends her Sunday mornings singing mass," observed Miss Everett.

"Not exactly," said Miss De Groot, bending over the piano.

"You must take care how your father hears you amusing yourself in that way," continued Miss Everett.

"Trust me for that," replied the young girl quickly, and turning merely her head towards the speaker.

"Ever since Mr. Carroll dined here on Christmas Day, Miss De Groot has done nothing but read Catholic prayer-books, and sing Catholic hymns," said Mr. Everett, with a smile and shrug.

"I won't play another note after that," cried the young lady, springing from the piano with her wonted crimson flush when touched. And dropping upon a low seat by the centre-table, and resuming some light work, she added with a spirited toss of the beautiful head, "I assure *you*, Mr. Alban, that Mr. Carroll has nothing to do with my Catholic reading or music,—at least—" she added,—"nothing in the way of personal influence."

"If you were not so strict about truth, I should say that was a fib," thought Alban; but he merely observed that Carroll was a favorite with the ladies, whereat Miss De Groot colored still more, and he inferred that whether conscious of it or not, she was no exception; but that opinion he was wise enough to keep to

16

himself. After all it did not interest him greatly, and soon after he took leave, reminding her that he should call the next day after evening chapel.

The Sunday afternoon walk was pleasant. While the path lay through the wood, as it did at first, they were obliged to go in Indian file ; but as soon as they gained the open road, they walked abreast in the double furrow worn by the sleighs, with a little mound of snow running between. They walked fast. Mary brushed the snow with her short dark green merino. Sometimes they had to turn out for a sleigh, and the people, as they flew by, gave them looks of curiosity. The sun cast a red, setting light on the woods, precipitous cliffs, and snowy back slopes of East Rock. Nearly three miles out they approached a picturesque half-frozen mill-stream.

" Beautiful New Haven !" exclaimed Mary De Groot.

" And yet you run away from it," said Alban; " very unnecessarily, as I gather from Miss Everett."

" Are you sorry to feel yourself under a chivalrous obligation of being my escort ?"

" Nay," said Alban, " I must return in a fortnight, you know, and then I shall not find you here."

" But you will find Mary Ellsworth. You have not been such a daily visitor at the Grove as to miss me much."

" I have been somewhat neglectful of you, Miss Mary, I confess, but you know how busy I have been with my tragedy."

" Oh ! I don't complain. A little school-girl like me (for I have had masters every day, you know) has no pretensions to receive visitors like Miss Ellsworth. It would have interfered with my lessons too much. That is one reason why I had to excuse myself from seeing Mr. St. Clair so often as he called. I do not like a great many gentlemen friends like Miss Ellsworth. But apart from your tragedy, Mr. Alban, it is evident that if you call almost every evening or morning on one young lady, you cannot see much of any other, unless you give up your whole time to visiting. How often in a week were you at the Ellsworths ?"

"Seldom more than twice, really," said Alban, blushing a little under this frank catechising.

"Ah! twice too often," exclaimed Miss De Groot, with quickness.

"Well, why so, Miss Mary?" said Alban, reddening still more.

"Why, Mr. Alban, distinguished as you are in your class, you can't be seriously 'paying attention,' as the girls say, to a young lady like Miss Ellsworth, a couple of years older than yourself. And you can't have the vanity to suppose that courted as she is, she is going to think seriously of *you*, much as she may like you and admire your talents. I am a mere chit; I have no experience in such matters; but an instinct warns me that you are betraying your own dignity."

Our hero looked sheepish.

"Mary *tells*, and laughs at, the compliments and soft things you say to her," pursued Miss De Groot, with girlish malice. "I myself believe that if the truth was known, she gives you in private plenty of encouragement. Now that is treating you shamefully. *I* would never do so. If it were me you admired, I should keep it to myself, and if I showed the least sign of particular regard for you *then*, it would—mean a great deal, Mr. Alban."

"Many thanks for your honest revelations, Miss De Groot."

"I hope I have not offended you."

"Not the least."

"And now I must tell you what brought me to New Haven, and what takes me away," continued Miss De Groot, diverting his attention to another subject. "You must know, Mr. Alban, that I have a stepmother. She is not unkind to me, but you are aware that my temper is infirm. Mamma used to try it. She is a bigoted adherent of the religious views in which you have been educated, and she used to reflect very severely (no doubt she thought it her duty) on papa's sentiments, in which, as you know, I have been brought up, while (I really could not bear that) she called my own mother an idolater. Mamma and I quarrelled, in short, and papa took my part. Then I begged to be sent to school or any where, and papa, finding it was necessary, consented to my passing the winter with the Everetts, who are distant relatives. Now for why I am going back. It is partly because I have learned lately from a good source that it is best not to shun such trials, but to learn humility and patience by taking them as they come, even if one has the mortification of often displaying one's weakness. So I am going home to be a better girl if I can, and to bear the disgrace of being a bad one, if I can't."

Our hero was gratified to be the depositary of such a confidence; at the same time that there was a force of will, and an independent clearness of thought in this young girl, which prevented him from feeling any thing like sentiment in her regard.

" May I ask a question, Miss Mary?"

"Fifty. I shall use my discretion about answering, Mr. Alban."

" Your music last night suggests it. Is your mind turning to your mother's faith?"

" It is the only true religion," said Mary.

" Really! have you got so far already!"

" I am indebted to you, Mr. Alban, for the first word, as far as I know, that prepared me to believe in the Divinity of my Saviour; and that, I believe, includes every thing."

" It may be that you are right there," observed Alban, regarding her with interest and surprise. " A Church founded by an incarnate God ought to be infallible, particularly as He promised it perpetual inspiration, a fact of which I am surprised that Protestants take no notice. If Christ was divine, His Church ought to be the pillar and ground of Truth."

" What a little way you are from the truth, Mr. Alban! I am *sure* you will come to it," said she, earnestly.

" Well, I shall not be guilty of assailing a young lady's religious convictions, if I say *now*," replied Alban, " that my difficulty about Christianity for some time past has been, that if it be true, Popery follows. No intermediate ground is strong enough to bear the weight of a God-man."

" That's it, Mr. Alban!"

They mounted the stile which marked the boundary of Mr. Everett's domain. Again they passed in Indian file along the woodland snow-path, the young maiden leading the way. When they came in sight of the house a covered stage-sleigh was driving out of the avenue.

"An arrival!" exclaimed Miss De Groot, with a tell-tale blush.

Alban went in with her of course. A portmanteau stood in the hall.

"Papa!" she exclaimed. "I thought so,"

CHAPTER XIX.

ALBAN had a vague idea that the father of Miss De Groot was the representative of a race of manorial proprietors on the North River; that he was also the owner of an old farm residence on New York Island, on the ponds of whose domain he had skated as a boy. He remembered at that period a large house at the lower end of Greenwich-street which bore such a name on the door-plate; and far, far back among his dimmest recollections of the time when his father lived in State-street, and he went to a woman's school, appeared the image of a little girl with dark ringlets, and a passionate temper, for whom, on rainy days, a carriage was sent, or, when it snowed, a buffalo-robed sleigh, to convey her the distance of two or three squares which intervened between the aforesaid mansion and Madam ———'s. These reminiscences assumed really for the first time a definite conscious existence in his mind when his eye rested on the figure of Mr. De Groot in the Everetts' drawing-room. It was a form, face, and even a garb, familiar to the young New Yorker in days gone by.

Mary's father was a man above the middle height, having a spare but well-knit frame, slightly stooping, and a classic head. His dark brown hair, cut short and curling massively, his splendid brown eyes, and largely moulded, but regular features, combined to form a commanding, and, at the same time, attractive physiognomy. He was dressed in an obsolete fashion: a blue, gilt-buttoned coat and buff waistcoat, a frilled shirt and white cravat. Between him and his daughter existed, besides some other variations, the ineffable difference of sex and youth.

Their meeting was tender without being very demonstrative. Mary introduced Alban with a slight embarrassment and yet with perfect openness.

" Mr. Alban Atherton of the Senior class, papa. Mr. Atherton had kindly offered to take charge of me, sir, on the boat to-morrow. And so you came in an extra from New York to take care of your little girl yourself."

"Not so little," said her father. "You have grown, Mary. Mr. Atherton is very kind, though, as you say, and I am much obliged to him."

Alban was about to withdraw, but the Everetts politely urged him to stay for tea; Mary warmly, although with a rising color, seconded the invitation, and her father, at whom he involuntarily glanced, said, bending his rich brows, and speaking in a rich voice, "Stay, Mr. Atherton."

They sat round the table for the Sunday tea, and there was a beef-steak for Mr. De Groot, who had arrived hungry. He partook of it sparingly, but drank many cups of weak black tea, conversing the while in a very agreeable way with his hosts. At length he turned to our hero, and asked him a quiet question touching the new religious theories which had been promulgated at New Haven.

"The point of the new school," said Alban, in an explanatory way, which he judged level to the apprehension of a Dutch Unitarian, "is to get rid of the mysteriousness which has hitherto attached to the doctrine of original sin, and the new birth, and the influence of the Spirit in regeneration, and make it all plain to our understandings."

"And how is that done, may I ask?" said Mr. De Groot, gravely, while his daughter slightly reddened.

"Oh, in the neatest manner," replied the student. "Original sin is explained thus. The will being as the strongest motive, unhappily the motives which are first presented to the youthful stranger arrived in this world are such as to compel him to choose what the law of God forbids. The New Birth is the turning of the will from these forbidden objects to the service of God; and the agency by which the will is thus turned about, is the presentation of the motives to obedience in so strong a light by the Spirit, that holiness is necessarily the resulting choice."

"The thought of New England," said Mr. De Groot, when Alban had finished, "may be compared to mountain rills, some of which leap boldly over the precipitous face of high cliffs; others follow gentle and sinuous declivities, but all unite in the common valley. The theory you so well state differs but verbally from that of Dr. Channing, which is, that man is a being who requires *moral culture.* The pure and earnest thinker will yet arise to teach all the different schools their inward identity. The old Church"—glancing at his daughter—"had a true meaning when she asserted the Divinity of Christ; and, indeed, the more purely we contemplate God in Christ, forgetting the mere man by whom Eternal Wisdom sought to instruct and elevate our race, the nearer shall we be to the soul—not of course to the mere dogmatic body—of the ancient Faith."

This style of speculation was new to our hero, and altogether he was somewhat taken by surprise. He was silent from modesty and admiration, but Mary De Groot replied to her father with feminine promptitude.

"How can I be near your soul, papa, by true sympathy, and your body not be precious to me too? Suppose I were to love in you the father abstractedly, but regard Mr. Eugene De Groot as a common acquaintance."

The Everetts laughed. They did not relish Mr. De Groot's pantheistic refinements. They hated the orthodox doctrine soul and body both. Mr. Everett said he never could believe Unitarianism and Trinitarianism to be at bottom the same doctrine.

"I do not say they are the same in form," responded Mr. De Groot, "but they exemplify the same spiritual impulse, that of finding God to be all, and all to be God," and he looked at Alban.

"Then God is sin and error, papa. He is falsehood and hate. How dreadful!" exclaimed Mary, growing warm.

"Sin and error, falsehood and hate," answered her father, with a calm smile, and in a rich triumphant intonation, "are but the discords which are resolved into the harmony of God."

"Let God be true and every man a liar!" quoted Mary, shaking her cherubic head. "Ah, my dear father!"

"Mary's feeling is right," returned her father, a little coldly. "A right feeling is the strength of Trinitarianism. I own that those love most warmly who do not so clearly distinguish. The hottest rays of the spectrum do not coincide with the most luminous."

"But the undivided ray of the sun both lights and warms," answered Mary, with surprising quickness.

"Let us change the theme," said Mr. De Groot.

He did not change it much. Reverting to original sin, he ridiculed the idea of hereditary guilt in the creatures of the All-good. Then he dilated with eloquence on the sole necessity of an interior change in ourselves from the first selfishness of ignorance to the disinterested love of God and Man, in order to make us at one with the Just and True. Christ first had triumphed over selfishness and sensuality, and sacrificed all to that disinterested love; and therefore was He said to have redeemed mankind: for in Him man was reconciled to God, *i. e.*, had attained a divine disinterestedness, for it was man only who was reconciled to God in Christ, not God—the ever-benign—who was reconciled to man. His voice became full of vibration and sweet cadences as he proceeded.

"Paul was inspired, but what is inspiration? In its highest expression you must look for a human element. Read your Bible on your bended knee, but read it not servilely. The great teacher of the Gentiles well explained the Mosaic records as symbolizing a spiritual system. The time has come to explain Paul, as he explained Moses. Inspiration is not, never can be, withdrawn from our race, no more than God Himself. But the inspired, who ever feel a sacred confidence in their own thoughts, are few. Time also must seal their prophecy; time unfold it. The prophets are always men of a remote age, and their writings are ancient. A Bible will take a millennium to compose; another to be accepted."

15

"You think, papa," said Mary De Groot, between laughing and crying, "that a thousand years hence you will pass for a prophet."

Mr. and Miss Everett were overawed by the melodious eloquence of their guest. Mr. De Groot was, in fact, one of those splendid Unitarians whom their own circle nearly deified, and whose daring transcendentalism, although not accepted as sound by the body at large, composed for the most part of hard, literal thinkers, and controlled by a most New England materiality of conception, was nevertheless listened to by them all with something of that reverence which the Orientals pay to the utterances of the insane.

The Everetts were very urgent with Mr. De Groot to induce him to stay a few days at New Haven. His arrival had necessarily superseded the attendance of our hero upon his daughter; but he inquired with courtesy if Mr. Atherton meant at all events to go down to New York on the morrow. Alban recalled his conversation with Miss De Groot respecting Mary Ellsworth, and promptly replied in the affirmative.

"We shall go too," said Mr. De Groot, quietly. "The boat starts at six, I believe. You are all ready for the journey, Mary? And of course I am."

CHAPTER XX.

On Monday morning, while Alban was dressing by candle-light, Mr. Everett's sleigh-barouche stopped at North College gate. Then he remembered that the arrangements made on Saturday had not been revoked. Mr. Everett's servant came for his trunk. Alban was sensible of an extreme awkwardness in taking the vacant seat in the sleigh. It was too dark to discern the faces of his companions, and he fancied that their salutations were frigid.

The engine of the Fanny was in full play when they reached the wharf, snorting like a racer, and churning the water behind the boat into a furious foam. Her cables creaked, and the foot-plank swayed to and fro with every stroke of the paddles. Mary attempting, like a giddy girl, to go on board alone, was nearly thrown off—would have been, but for Alban's timely aid. It was so dark that no one saw it but themselves. Without withdrawing his arm from the waist it had clasped to save her, he guided her through the crowd of boat-hands and porters to the door of the ladies' cabin. Mr. De Groot came on board with a grim aspect, wrapped in Russian furs.

Mr. Everett followed with a courteous but formal air, to take leave of his lovely guest. The girl of sixteen, coyly bending under the swinging lamp of the ladies' cabin, gave him the tips of her fingers and the sweetest smile. The bachelor of forty-five thawed before it. "All aboard that's going!" thundered the captain of the Fanny from the wheel-house." Mr. Everett ran off like a man of five and twenty.

The cables were slipped; the Fanny moved past the wood-piled wharf. Soon they were in the icy bay; then in the tossing Sound. By daybreak nothing could be seen above the horizon, even in the north, but a white land-streak, the snowy coast of Connecticut.

The Fanny felt the winter rocking of the Sound. Mr. De
Groot's dyspeptic stomach did not bear it too well. He was glad
to leave his daughter and Alban at the steamboat breakfast-
table. Even they broke their fast daintily, and were glad to get
on deck again, where Atherton arranged a sheltered seat for Miss
De Groot, while her father, with his furs almost hiding his face,
lay near them on a bale of merchandise. The familiarizing influence of travelling in company is proverbial, particularly under
circumstances of bodily discomfort. The young people sat very
near to each other by tacit mutual consent. Mary De Groot's
cloak of sables became a matter of contention between them.
She, being very warmly clad, insisted on Alban, who was the reverse, throwing it over his lap. They compromised by sharing it.

" Why, you have only that wretched, scanty, faded camlet, with
such a queer velvet collar standing above your ears. I don't mean
to laugh at your student garb, Mr. Alban."

" I thought my camlet was rather a fine thing when I got it—
two years ago, 'tis true."

" I can fancy it being fine for you two years ago. But now it
is short, and has lost its color. You must get a real Spanish full
circle of fine blue broadcloth, and a pelisse trimmed with furs."

" I can't afford such things," replied the young man. " And
if I could, my father would think me stark mad to wear them."

" Would he really ? Now papa thinks nothing good enough
for me. But I hate being dressed up like a doll. It is my pride,
I suppose. Now that I am going home I shall take up with
wearing my fine clothes—as an act of humility." She laughed.
" But, Mr. Alban, are you really skeptical ?"

" It would be an affront to confess it to a young lady—unless
to one like you, who, I fear, have too much faith."

" I should take it as an affront, in general."

" For the just reason that such an avowal by a young man is
usually equivalent to a profession that he rejects the restraints of
morality," replied Alban. " But that is not my case. What has
destroyed my confidence in Christianity is precisely that it does not

keep its promise of making me good and pure. I am as anxious as ever to be both."

Miss De Groot rose and went to her father to inquire how he did.

"No better," was the laconic reply of the sick philosopher, without opening his eyes.

When the young lady returned, she insisted on her student-friend's taking the sable cloak to himself, declaring that it really oppressed her. Alban was warmer, but not so happy, as when the rich heavy garment lay over Mary De Groot's knee as well as his own. The maiden probably minded the looks of the thing more than the reality, as there was always a little cabin-stool partly interposed between them, on the rounds of which she rested her feet. The acquaintance ripened hour by hour. One might suppose that the youth rapidly fell in love. But mystery is almost essential to excite the imagination at that age. Mary's absence of disguise and clearness of apprehension on every topic, left no recess of her mind or heart into which the pure light of Heaven did not seem to shine. Moreover, a sense of honor led Alban to refrain from every word or act which might be construed as taking advantage of a half-grown girl's inexperienced fancy. And a little, it must be confessed, her apparent preference elated his vanity, and this is the feeling most opposite to love, in which a natural humility and self-distrust ever mingle.

The shores of the narrowing Sound began to attract their attention. They passed slowly through fields of ice. Sometimes the scene was quite Arctic. Coming upon a long white building with wings, lying under the shelter of a bold promontory, a bell slowly tolling like a chapel bell saluted their ears

"Look, Mr. Alban, what a site for a convent!"

17

CHAPTER XXI.

" WOULD you like to be a nun ?"

"Not I."

" They say that nunneries are bad places."

" I have heard Protestant girls say so, but I knew a girl who had been educated in a convent, and she was the best girl I *ever* knew. My own mother passed all her life in a convent till she was married, and I have always heard papa say that though bigoted, she was the most innocent creature that could possibly be.

" But, like other young ladies, you wish and expect to be married one of these days ?"

" Girls have a horror of dying old maids, you know," blushing and laughing. " So have I ; it is reasonable, Mr. Alban ; for old maids are neglected and pitied by every body. But I would not mind—I'm not sure I don't prefer—dying a young maid."

" A sweet idea," said Alban, " but shocking. You mustn't mention it."

" I had a friend—the dearest school-friend I ever had—who died so—in her virgin bloom. She was just turned of twenty, and five years older than I, although we had been room-mates for two years. The most conscientious girl I ever knew ! You have heard me speak of her before. I owe her every thing. She was to me a friend, a mother, and a sister, all in one."

These school-friendships are generally so exaggerated, especially when death has dissolved them, that Alban gave more credit to Mary's fancy than to the real excellence of her school-mate for the warmth of this eulogy, although its sincerity was attested by tears. He observed that it must have been an inestimable advantage at Miss De Groot's age to have had such a friend at school.

" You may well say that, Mr. Alban. I feel it more than ever now, knowing the source of Alexandrine's angelic virtues."

"She was a Catholic?"

"She was. But she never tried to convert me. She had promised when I was placed with her that she would not. We were two and two in a room throughout the establishment, each having a separate cot. There was nothing peculiar about her, you know, except that she said her prayers kneeling before a crucifix instead of in bed, as most of the girls used, and that at night she recited the Rosary. I wonder it did not make a greater impression upon me then; but I was so prejudiced against worshipping Christ, that I always regarded her as an idolater, although I used to stand up for her when her religion was attacked by the orthodox girls."

Mr. De Groot's stomach had become tranquillized in the smoother waters of East River. He got up, approached the young people, and announced his intention of going on the promenade deck. The wind had shifted to the south, and the temperature had become comparatively mild as they approached New York. Mary instantly offered to accompany her father to the hurricane deck, to which he assented, but requested Atherton to give her his arm. So Mr. De Groot walked rapidly up and down on one side by himself, while his daughter and Alban, equally glad of the opportunity of stretching their legs, promenaded arm in arm, on the other.

"Your idea of dying unmarried comes back to me," said Alban, perhaps unfairly probing her thoughts. "Have you no day-dreams, then, Miss Mary, of pure, romantic love, in which every thing is noble and perfect, your lover a hero, yourself adored by him, and so forth?"

"Alexandrine used to say that castle-building was a vice, and yet I do build castles in the air sometimes, Mr. Alban. And you are very penetrating to know that there is a great temptation to have a hero, and I own that in spite of Alexandrine's warnings I have not always had the virtue to resist it. But, since you are so curious, my romance is always a tragedy : the heroine dies."

"It was Alexandrine's death that put such ideas into your head."

" O dear, no ! I have had them these three years—but let us talk of something else."

By a little teasing he got her to pursue the subject. She was shy of it, yet willing to be persuaded.

" To tell you the truth, it was a singular dream I had three years ago, which first suggested to me the idea that I should die —not exactly unmarried—but I can't well explain it to you, Mr. Alban."

" You know I have always tried to do you good," said Alban, in an insinuating tone.

" You have, Mr. Alban. I feel it, I assure you. Well, I will tell you my story. But let us stand out of the wind : it flutters my clothes so that I can't hear myself talk. The thing occurred when I had been a few months at school. Papa and my present mother were in Europe, you know ; so that I was like an orphan, and it was the first time in my life that I had even been away from home. There were more than a hundred girls in the school, and among so many, some of course would be bad. But I must say, Mr. Alban, that our public opinion was against badness, and those who were openly wicked, or were known to be secretly so, were kept at a distance by the others. We had a great deal of pride, and there was no end of foolish talking about fashions, and society, and beaux, and so on, but I never knew in *my* circle of intimates the slightest approach to impropriety in word or conduct that was not frowned down at once. But those who were bad and had the tact to conceal it, were dangerous friends, as you may suppose. My first room-mate was of this description. Papa and mamma had chosen her for me, because our families were acquainted, and because her manners were so lady-like. She was about two years my senior. There is no telling you in how many ways that girl was unprincipled. I shudder to think what a risk I ran during the three or four months that I was her room-mate. Indeed, I did not quite escape. Is it not strange, Mr. Alban, that evil companions always do us harm, although without our own consent they can do us none ?"

" It is very true."

" Henrietta was idle, vain, mendacious—does not that say all ?
A liar is already every thing bad. She was mean, a petty thief—
she stole confectionary and fruit from the girls, and even once, a
trinket, which I discovered and returned to the owner—and—she
was not modest. She was always on her guard in the school, for
she loved popularity—no one louder than she to condemn any thing
amiss in others—but before a little girl like me, her room-mate,
who knew necessarily most of her faults, she betrayed even this.
You must remember that I was only a few months past thirteen.
I was afraid to tell of her. I could not bear to be a tell-tale, of
all things ; and insensibly I began to be less shocked than at the
first discovery of her badness, and sometimes I was conscious of a
temptation (so weak we are) to imitate. I claim no merit for not
telling lies, cheating, or stealing sugar and cake ; such mean
vices ; but to neglect my books, wardrobe, and person, spend my
time in looking at myself in the glass, or reading the novels Henrietta had surreptitiously procured, and, worst of all, to think when
alone of what she had said to me on topics which openly to her I
resented her mentioning—these things, Mr. Alban, sorely tried the
principle of a child to avoid."

" I tremble for you."

" At last :—it was on a day, or rather a night, of mid-winter ;
—a bitter night, when the door-handles in our fireless dormitories
blistered my little hands, and the crusty snow on the window-
panes made them half-dark in spite of the moon, after the candle
was put out. We had gone to bed, and Henrietta talked to me.
She was in one of her communicative moods, such as I had often
answered by flying into an impotent passion. That night, somehow, I had not the spirit to be angry. I had been thinking of my
desolate, half-orphan condition, and the difference between school
and home, and what care my own mother would have taken to
guard the innocence of my mind, of which I was being ruthlessly
robbed, and (I well remember) of the terrible school-future that
lay before me, when perhaps I should get to be as bad as this cor-

rupt companion,—and even at the moment I was assailed by the dreadful suggestions of curiosity to know how I should feel if I were wicked like her. So while she talked, I lay silent, weeping and struggling with myself—oh, it was horrible!" cried Mary De Groot, half turning away from her companion, and hiding her face in the sable of her muff.

"Poor child!" said Alban, in a tone of deep commiseration, "I enter into your feelings perfectly. It is a pitiable tale."

She walked on a little way, looking down, but never withdrew her hand from his arm.

"I never dreamed of being carried away to tell so much—but now I *must* finish."—She resumed in a steady voice.—"I was always sensitive about being touched. It was one reason of my dislike to Henrietta, which amounted to perfect detestation; for she was very caressing. Me she generally left alone; for the contrary was sure to provoke a storm. I believe I was terribly quick-tempered. Well, this night, when she found I did not reply to her as usual, she got up, and making a plea of the cold, proposed to get into my cot. I flamed up in a moment. I said she shouldn't; I resisted; I struck her. She got angry, too, and said she *would* in spite of me. I soon found that she was a great deal the strongest, as well she might be. She overpowered me, and then I experienced the most piercing temptation of my life, before or since, which was to abandon that inward resistance which I had hitherto opposed to her corrupting influence—for it wearied my life—and henceforth be even like the companion to whom Providence seemed to have abandoned my orphan youth. I believe it was the thought of my mother that saved me. My despair changed to fury. I fastened my teeth suddenly in Henrietta's arm, and she let me go with a scream. I sprang up and ran just as I was, and as fast as I could, through the hall and down stairs, to the room of the principal, where I burst in and threw myself at her feet. Fancy her astonishment. I recounted with sobs the insult I had received, exposed Henrietta in all respects, and implored Madam —— to let me have a room by myself.

" How well I remember her conducting me, barefoot and in my little night-dress, up a moon-lit stair and into a large, carpeted room, where was indeed a single cot, but occupied. The young lady occupying it started up, and the principal, having told my story with brevity, said to her, ' Will you change beds for to-night with this child, Alexandrine, or will you take her into yours ?'— ' If she will come to me,' replied Alexandrine, ' I will take her into mine.' The next day at her earnest petition I was placed with her, and Henrietta was sent away—packed off home ! Nobody ever knew why, except Madam ——, Alexandrine, and myself; and *that* caused me a great deal of suffering ; for I passed for a tell-tale (Henrietta gave me the name ere she quitted the house) until I left the school. Quick as my temper was, I had been the universal favorite before ; and after it, although I was respected, I was never popular again. I don't think any of my female friends.now love me much."

" Did not Alexandrine love you ?"

" Did Alexandrine love me, Mr. Alban ! Oh, never shall I forget the tenderness with which she folded me to her bosom that first night that I, little trembler, lay beside her like a frightened dove. How sweetly she talked to me, how wisely she instructed me, how earnestly she prayed for me ! She told me that Jesus was the lover of chastity and purity, and that when He became man for our sakes He chose to reside first in the bosom of a spot-less virgin, probably at that time not a great deal older than I was. Then when I cried and confessed to her in what respects I had not been so good as she thought, she begged me never to think or speak of it again as long as I lived.—' These are almost involuntary stains, dear Mary,' she said, ' which your brave and lovely behavior of to-night has, I am sure, entirely effaced. Except our immaculate Lady, perhaps no mortal tempted as you were, was ever entirely free from such.'—' Did I do right to bite Henrietta ?' I asked.—' A thousand times right !' exclaimed Alex-andrine, in a way that made me love her so dearly ! ' You would have done right to bite her head off, if you could, sooner than risk

consenting to a mortal sin !"—Ah, Mr. Alban,·you are as gentle
as a girl, and it makes me forget who you are."

  " Still you have not told me your dream."

  " It was just four weeks after that. I had fallen asleep in my
cot with my hands crossed on my breast as Alexandrine had taught
me, and I knew that I was dreaming of the room being full of
angels. Alexandrine had told me about our guardian angels. At
last I became sensible that one approached my bed, and by degrees
all the rest faded away. It was not winged, as we see angels
represented in pictures. Its face was beautiful, and its golden hair
was full of light, by which the rest of the appearance seemed visible. Its garments were simple and white, girt under the breast
with a golden girdle, and its sparkling hands were crossed on its
bosom. Its eyes, radiant and full of love, were fastened on me."

  " Well ?"

  " It spoke to me. You can form no idea of the mortal fear I
was in. It was not like dreaming of one speaking to you ; but if
you saw some one in your room and supposed you were dreaming,
and the person were suddenly to speak, you know how it would
startle you.—' Mary,' it said,—but I need not repeat the very
words ;—they intimated that it was the spirit of my mother, and
warned me just in the simple way that a living mother might,
against three things—pride, love of dress, and whatever could sully
a maiden's purity ; ' for in three years,' concluded the vision, ' you
will be married and buried in one day.'—You will say, Mr. Alban,
that this singular admonition is easily accounted for, like the vision
itself, by the strong impression made on my mind by recent occurrences. I leave you to settle that as you like. I only know that
Alexandrine said I shrieked, and that springing up to waken me,
she found me cold and insensible, not asleep, but having fainted
quite away. The next year, when I had some expectation of
dreaming again, nothing happened that is worth mentioning ;
but on the second anniversary Alexandrine died, and she declared
a little while before she expired, being supported at the time in my
arms, that the same bright visitant whom I had described came

into the room, (she was sleeping, and told me this when she awoke,) approached and touched her, and that the soft, sparkling hand sent a coldness like ice to her heart."

"Strange! What is the day thus marked?"

"Next Saturday is the anniversary."

"Did you tell any one your dream at the time?"

"Oh, yes, I told it to Alexandrine herself, and to several girls who were intimate with us. They all said 'Well, Mary, you must take care not to marry till the time fixed by the vision is gone by. But I don't know, Mr. Alban, if it is possible so to disappoint a real prophecy, which always comes true by some combination that we do not foresee. As the time approaches I cannot help thinking of it a good deal. It is one reason why I am anxious to be baptized. If I were baptized, I should be willing to die next Saturday, wedded or unwedded : and as I was saying to you, Mr. Alban, such is the picture that closes *my* day-dreams,—myself vested as a bride with orange flowers and veil, but white as they, and stiff, laid out with bloodless hands crossed and tied on my girlish breast, ready for the pure and passionless grave."

"Dreadful!"

The Fanny was got alongside the wharf by cables and backing water, with hoarse vociferations of the captain from the wheel deck. The plank was thrown across the gangway in the midst of a flock of drivers flourishing their whips, very much as at the present day. Mr. De Groot's carriage was waiting on the wharf. He offered Alban a seat, which our hero declined, but accepted an invitation to call very soon at Mr. De Groot's residence up town. In New York the snow was pretty much confined to the dirty heaps shovelled up on the sides of the streets. Alban had soon passed all the familiar corners, and was set down by his hackney-coach at the old house in Grey-street. Embraced with pride and affection by his father and mother, and sitting between them on the old-fashioned chintz settee, he felt that their hearth was the warmest, brightest spot in the world.

BOOK IV.

A Vacation. The Entire Front of the Building.

CHAPTER I.

" CALL on Mr. De Groot ? Of course you must, my son, since he asked you. Why, what a proud fellow you are !" said Mr. Atherton.

It was in a sunny back parlor, snug and old fashioned, with the wood fire blazing cheerily on tall brass andirons, and a bright copper kettle singing on a chafing-dish inside the fender. For the Athertons were at breakfast, and a tidy girl brought in from time to time, a hot plateful of that Knickerbocker delicacy—buckwheat cakes.

The gilt pendulum of an old-fashioned French clock on the handsome mantel, swung and ticked between white marble columns, and the hands pointed to the quarter before nine. The apartment was pretty enough altogether. A massive sideboard of golden mahogany, that shone like a mirror from constant waxing and rubbing, with its bright ring handles dependent from gilt lion-heads, and an escritoire book-case to match, had been stylish in our grandmothers' day, while the light chintz-curtained chairs and settee, painted in green and gold of the Greek pattern, bespoke a later date and newer country. The chimney was adorned with miniatures, the walls with portraits—Mr. Atherton, senior, in a red-backed chair, and the same boy-face in gown and bands, which we have seen once before at the old Atherton house in Yanmouth ; both mellow, broad, old-masterish, but plain, unaffected pictures ; and at the end of the room, on either side of the folding doors, hung a water-color of no great merit, but both immense favorites with Mrs. Atherton, having been executed by Rachel one winter that she spent with her aunt in the metropolis. To complete this interior, we should not omit the Indian chintz window-curtains, and the green crumb-cloth under the table, to save the ingrain carpet, the formal squares of which our hero had measured to and fro in the reveries of many a dreamy vacation.

" But you say that he is one of the richest men in New York, sir."

" Undoubtedly. And a great aristocrat, like all them old patroons," said Mr. Atherton, whose early education, owing to his father's death, had been left pretty much to chance. Mr. Atherton laughed heartily at the idea of any one being an aristocrat in these times, and proceeded. " I remember when his father was not so rich, but extremely proud of being the Patroon of Wallahook. Thirty years ago he offered me the old De Groot farm up town—it was out of town then—for a mere trifle. I wish I had bought it and retired from business ; but I had no idea that real estate would rise so immensely in New York. The property is worth a million now at the least calculation, and by building judiciously he may treble it in ten years. You must call on him, Alban. I dare say he will show you his pictures and books. Perhaps not. He is shy of letting people see his things. He *may* receive you in his office."

" It is likely that Alban will see Miss De Groot, since he is so well acquainted with her," observed Mrs. Atherton, with a slight warmth. " I should think it was very strange if he didn't, after she had asked him to take charge of her on the boat."

" Mr. De Groot is a very proud man, my dear," said Mr. Atherton, laughing and drumming on the table, for his breakfast was finished.

" I shall feel awkwardly in calling," said Alban.

"I don't see why," replied his mother. "I don't see why you should feel awkward about calling on any body."

"I don't think Mary is at all proud," continued Alban.

"I should call upon her just the same, whether she is proud or not," said his mother.

"Undoubtedly," said his father. "That should make no difference. If you meet with a cool reception, you need'nt be in a hurry to pay a second visit; that's all."

"A cool reception!" said Alban, musingly.

"Oh, Mr. De Groot will be very polite to you," said his father.

"Pity if he were not, in his own house!" observed Mrs. Atherton.

"You will ask for Mr. De Groot, you know," said his father. "Afterwards make inquiries for Miss De Groot. I dare say, (since your mother seems to think so,) she will come down and make you a curtsey before you go."

"If I don't see more of Miss Mary than that, I shan't call again in a hurry," said Alban.

"Mr. De Groot does not live in Greenwich-street now," pursued his father. "He has built a new house on his up-town property—in the Fifth Avenue, I think they call it. You had better take the omnibus as far as Washington Place. It is the nearest point. You go on about a quarter of a mile beyond the new houses on Washington Parade-ground. Mr. De Groot's is a large house of brown stone standing by itself. You can't miss it."

Before departing for Wall-street, Mr. Atherton, who knew what young men want, drew his son a check, and bade him order a new suit and a fashionable cloak of a Broadway tailor.

CHAPTER II.

" A LARGE house of brown stone !"

It were not a very clear direction now to a house on the Fifth Avenue, but it sufficed sixteen years ago. Passing the " new houses" on Washington Square, the mansion thus described became visible at a distance, with fruit-trees and the glazed apex of a conservatory rising above its garden wall. Arriving at the square on which it stood, Alban beheld the front and lateral perspective of something like a palace. A lofty rustic basement of great beauty and solidity, crowned by a massive, projecting balcony, had in the centre a nobly-arched portal.

The vestibule was hospitably open, showing a pavement of tesselated marble, a rich hanging lamp, and an inner folding-door of carved and polished black walnut, with plate glass lights curtained with French embroidery. Alban timidly pulled a silver bell-handle, and one of the *battants* was instantly flung open by a blue-liveried porter of foreign aspect.

" Is it on business ?"

" No," said Alban, foolishly coloring, " I merely called to see Mr. De Groot."

" Oh !" said the porter, with a glance that took in our hero, faded purple camlet and all, but admitting him. " What name shall I say, sir ?"

Alban found himself in an imposing hall of great length, paved with white and green marble and adorned with busts and bronzes ; but the porter rather insisted on his entering a sort of waiting-room, an oil-cloth'd apartment hung with engravings from Trumbull's pictures, and having high-backed walnut chairs stiffly ranged against the walls. Our hero rallied at the print of the Declaration ; the head of his ancestor among the Signers,

18

inspiring a feeling akin to that with which a scion of English no-
bility might have seen his on the tapestry of the Lords.   The servant who had taken his card returned, took the purple camlet
with a grimace of respect, and showed him up an imposing
staircase to the drawing-rooms.

Three spacious saloons *en suite* extended in a vista of hitherto
unimagined splendor, carpeted from French looms, ceiled by Italian painters, the walls covered with the delicate papers invented
by Parisian taste, and hung with endless pictures in elaborate
frames of massive gilding.   Ideal busts of lovely female person-
ifications, placed on pedestals of buhl or precious marble, flanked
the doors ; statues sparkled like snow in front of the lofty mirrors.
Tables of buhl and pietra dura, cabinets of inlaid work, and
etagères of rosewood or ebony, supported vases and other curious
objects ; here gleaming solitary, as if too rare to be otherwise ;
there grouped in orderly confusion ; of porcelain, of Etruscan pot-
tery, of half-gems, even of gold and silver.   The wilderness of
sumptuous seats astonished him.   The corresponding richness of
the window-curtains was enhanced by the style of the shutter-
panelling in dark wood, and by the massive stone balconies seen
between.   A line of rich chandeliers consummated an effect
which was not of mere splendor, for besides the grand effect of
space, a certain simplicity presided over all.

The rooms were all well-warmed, but in one only a sea-coal
fire was burning brightly in a mantel-piece of sculpture in Carrara
marble.   The shelf, sustained by elegant Caryatides, was orna-
mented by an Italian clock of bronze,—Phœbus and the Hours ;
supported on one side by a magnificent bacchanal cup of the same
material, with a lip of gold, and on the other by a funeral-urn,
with candelabra, and so forth,—beautiful and heathenish.   While
Alban yet stood admiring it (for he was afraid to sit on the
rich chairs) the soft rustle of female garments made him turn.
It was Mary's simple garb, and the same beautiful, ingenuous
face, bright with friendship.

" Do these rooms make as awful an impression on you, Mr.

Alban, as they did on me when I first came here from school, I
wonder."

" I am quite overpowered."

" You will soon get over that feeling—wonderfully soon."

She made him sit on one of the richest sofas, while she placed
herself near him in a light chair of gilding and brocade. She inquired if he had found his parents in good health, and told him
that papa had requested her to show him the house and pictures.

" At least," thought Alban, " it is not the reception which
my father led me to anticipate."

The pictures in the drawing-rooms were chiefly by such American artists as were then known to fame. Allston contributed a fiery
Prophet and a pair of love-lyrics ; Cole, two romance-landscapes.
Stuart was represented by a lovely female head. A conspicuous
portrait by Ingham, finished like a miniature, represented a beautiful, fair woman, in a well-fitting muslin robe and silk shawl,
more natural than reality itself, which pleased our hero's undeveloped taste. " My stepmother !" said Mary.

There was a child's head by Sully, with the shoulders bare
to the waist ; the flesh crude ; the slight drapery merely indicated ; but the dark, living eyes a miracle.

" That's me at seven," said Mary, with a blush.

Adjacent to the third saloon of the suite was a cabinet, or
rather boudoir, in which one wall was occupied by a large paint-
ing covered with red silk. The young lady with a slight hesitation drew aside the curtain.

It was the Ariadne of Vanderlyn—world-renowned for that
one picture, but doubly a favorite with Mr. De Groot on account
of his descent. The enchantress is represented at the moment
when Theseus deserts her in her sleep. She lies on a bank of
grass and sand, backed by trees. Her drapery—purple and linen
—is beneath her, an extremity of the latter slightly covering the
groin. The arms being raised over the head in a natural attitude
of slumber, the hands freely grasp the black, goddess-like, waving
and dishevelled tresses. The flesh, upon the whole, is sweetly col-

ored, especially in the face, the light broad and simple, the outline elegant. The greatest beauty of the picture, however, is the background—a deep, olive-tinted landscape, with mighty trees and broad leaves overshadowing the repose of Ariadne, while in the distance is seen the Mediterranean, with the bark of the treacherous Theseus. The smoke of his parting sacrifice ascends from the shore, and a rosy, volcanic peak rises beyond the blue waves.

While Alban was looking at it he found that Mary had disappeared, and perceiving that the Venetian window of the cabinet was open into a conservatory, he went out presently, and discovered her making a nosegay. An amphitheatre of beautiful plants, with orange, lemon, and magnolia trees, surrounded a fountain. Going round it (after she had given him the bouquet) they came to a flight of steps, and a door in a blank wall. It admitted them into a lofty gallery lighted from the roof. Here was the bulk of her father's collection—Reynolds, Wilkie, Newton, Leslie—names that awed Alban—a reputed Titian, some fine Italian pictures by less known masters, some Flemish interiors of churches, and Dutch market scenes. The floor was parqueted and spread at intervals with small Turkey carpets, on which antique oaken chairs were placed for the view. There were also huge stands filled with portfolios, and solid oaken tables for the inspection of engravings ;—" But these," said Mary De Groot, " we will keep for the next time, Mr. Alban."

They spent more than an hour in the gallery, time passing away quickly where was so much to interest ; and Mary was never weary of those interiors of churches, where in one a priest was saying mass at an early hour, with a devout congregation of peasants, in another a stately procession bore some holy relic to its shrine. Except the little chapel at New Haven these were the only Catholic churches she knew. She entertained Alban meanwhile with her lively and natural gossip. When they had looked enough, she took him back by the conservatory, and the Venetian window of the Vanderlyn cabinet. Mary drew the curtain before the Ariadne, and then led him on to a room beyond.

"This is the dining-room, Mr. Alban. I have kept it for the last."

Alban was not surprised at her doing so as he gazed around the apartment. It was wainscoted to a certain height with old dark oak, carved with fruit, flowers, satyrs, bacchantes, and leopards' heads. Superiorly the walls were covered with red-figured velvet and adorned with genuine family pieces of the Dutch and Flemish schools, brought by the ancestor of Mr. De Groot from Holland. In splendor of tone and purity of carnations these surpassed all the rest of his collection. Alban had no idea that New York possessed such treasures. "A good many old Dutch families," said Mary, with pride, "possess such heir-looms; but none so untouched as ours, or so valuable. The carved oak papa got from Belgium."

Alban slightly smiled, but he felt a strong sympathy. The furniture of the banqueting-room corresponded to the walls—dark carved oak and red velvet. Massive silver sconces holding wax candles were fixed to the wainscotting at suitable intervals, and at the upper end of the room, a lofty oaken cupboard in the same style, with its carved doors thrown open, displayed a range of shelves that glittered with ancient plate and porcelain. The room was lighted by a single large window, the lower half of which was filled with stained glass that probably had once lighted a refectory, for the subject was from Scripture—the Lord entertained by the Pharisee.

When our hero had admired all this sufficiently in the estimation of his young cicerone, she opened one of the knopped and flowered oaken doors, and preceded him into a dim, secluded, wainscoted lobby, lighted by an oriel of stained glass. She showed him that this passage communicated both with the hall, and with a private stair, by separate doors concealed in the panelling.

"What a place for lovers! I must be a little witch at heart, for I declare I never pass here without that thought popping into my head. Can't you fancy a midnight meeting at the foot of that secret stair, Mr. Alban, or a stolen kiss by day in one of these shadowy corners?"

18*

The instant these words had passed her lips, Mary became scarlet, and tripping away to a door in a deep recess, set it wide open and invited her student friend to pass. As he approached she leaned back against the wainscot, and her face was laid like a rosy cameo against the dark panel. Alban would as soon have dared strike that red cheek as kiss it, and the picture lasted but a moment. She whispered " Papa !" He glanced into the next room and saw that it was the library, where, about half-way down, Mr. De Groot was reading by the fire. He moved on therefore, but when he looked back for his fair guide, she made a graceful obeisance and closed the door on him.

Although our pen is almost weary of description, we cannot quite pass over a locale so celebrated and yet so inaccessible as Mr. De Groot's library. It was a room at least twice as lofty as any of those Alban had seen, except the gallery, and was lined to the ceiling with glazed bookcases of black unpolished walnut. The ceiling was coved, and admitted the light by a lantern dome. There was also one high, dim, square, mullioned window of stained glass. A solid gallery, of the same material as the bookshelves, ran round the room about midway up. The white vellum and other rich old bindings, and the vast number of folios, promised well for the collection. At regular intervals round the lower room, in walnut niches, were placed busts of philosophers and founders of sects. Over the mantel hung a beautiful youthful portrait of Dr. Channing. The book tables and study chairs were of black walnut, and the latter had cushions of dark green leather. The soft light from the dome produced a beautiful effect on this sober and scholastic interior, into which Alban advanced slowly, and at first unnoticed.

CHAPTER III.

ALBAN was received by the owner of this magnificent house with the appearance of perfect cordiality. Mr. De Groot inquired particularly how he had liked the pictures, and made him specify which he had preferred. Every thing that Alban said suggested some striking remark on the part of his entertainer. The Ariadne was alluded to.

" In persons unaccustomed to Art," said Mr. De Groot, " there is a kind of susceptibility which compares with real modesty as the liability to take certain infections on the part of those who have never been exposed to them, does with health. Our country-women have a great deal of this. The purity of a work of Art does not depend on its being draped or the reverse. There are draped representations which are immoral, and there are nude ones which are pure as new-fallen snow. I don't say the Ariadne is quite one of these. The motives of Correggio, who was Vanderlyn's master, were not of the highest kind, although he has succeeded in investing the most repulsive subjects—the Danaë, for example—with a haze of luminous execution, that prevents the dazzled eye from seeing their indelicacy. The nude, purely treated, blunts curiosity, and in that point of view has a moral utility."

Alban listened with interest.

" I remember," continued Mr. De Groot, " a picture of Titian's, called *Sacred and Profane Love*. By the by I never saw a true criticism of it yet. The background is one of Titian's noble landscapes, with deep blue hills. A clump of brown trees divides the distance, on one side of which is seen a castle, representing the secular life, and on the other a convent, or the life of religion. In the foreground sits a young lady completely attired and coiffed, in the mode of Titian's time. She is debating between Sacred and Profane Love—the world and the cloister. Directly in front, on the edge of a fine yellowish-white sarcophagus, sits another female figure, entirely nude, except a crimson drapery just falling from her shoulder, and against which her elegant form is defined : she regards the other with a face full of tenderness, and extending one pure arm, lifts on high a burning lamp :—this is *Sacred Love.* Imagine the sweetness and purity of color and outline in this sitting figure, with its innocent nakedness and modest candor of attitude, in contrast to that modish damsel, clothed to her finger tips ! You feel at once, that drapery would impair its spirituality and destroy its chastity. What ardor in the action of the pectoral muscles sustaining the lifted arm—what modesty in the close union of the limbs and bend of the knee—would be lost ! Behind the sarcophagus, and stooping over the edge to gather the flowers within it, is a Cupid, nude and winged boy—*Profane Love.* Thus Profane Love gropes in a sarcophagus for flowers—the perishable offspring of earth ; Sacred Love lifts above the tomb itself a flaming lamp—type of the soul and immortality, and the aspirations that ascend to Heaven."

" Beautiful !" exclaimed Alban.

Our hero's eye had often rested during this conversation on a low desk and stool near the fire. The desk had upon it an open volume in black letter with richly illuminated margins, and a lady's pocket-handkerchief.

" A manuscript missal on vellum," said Mr. De Groot, fastening his dark eyes on the volume, but not offering to show it. " The illuminations are not in the highest style of art. I will show you some one day, that I am really proud of. I am glad you have a taste for these things. I often think what will become of my treasures when I am gone and Mary is married." Mr. De Groot cast a jealous glance around the stately book-chamber. "A fellow, for example, whom I would not willingly let peep under the covers of my favorites, how could I bear the idea of his being their master !"

" It is to be hoped that Miss De Groot will take a fancy to some one capable of appreciating your fine collection, sir."

"What profession do you intend to follow, Mr. Atherton?" inquired Mr. De Groot, rather sharply, after a moment's pause.

Alban was undecided. In his pious days he had looked forward to the ministry. Lately he had thought of Law and Medicine, of Literature and the Army. He had in fact a hundred wild ideas in regard to his future career.

"A medical education will do you no hurt," said Mr. De Groot, in his oracular way. "All knowledge is good. But as a pursuit it would leave some of your finest faculties unemployed. The pulpit offers a field to a man of first-rate organization," glancing at the portrait of Channing—"but it requires too great a sacrifice to consecrated prejudices in order to win or retain the popular approval. The Protestant preacher, however superior he may be, is obliged to cede as much as the Catholic, to the tyranny of his sect, without having the comfort of believing his guide infallible. Law is a hard, dry pursuit, but it will give you independence. Then with us the forum leads to the senate. Your grandfather was a lawyer, and rose by his own abilities from a carpenter's apprentice to be President of Congress."

"My paternal grandfather," said Alban.

"Hem! Your *maternal* grandfather was a soldier. He got rank because he was rich and well-connected, but I don't remember that he distinguished himself particularly. A conscientious, dependable man, and the confidential friend of Washington; but that was all?"

"I believe so."

"Oh, you can go farther back—if that's what you mean," said Mr. De Groot, with a dry smile. "You came of English squirearchs—*armigeri* at least. Your Puritan ancestor, who fled to New England from Laud and the pillory, or the branding-iron, or some other mild argument for Episcopacy, had a brother who was a rattling cavalier and a captain in the life-guard of Charles I. himself. I know something, you see, of your antecedents. Well, I don't see why you shouldn't follow the *noble* profession of arms, if you have a leaning thereto. In popular states a successful general will step up before all the orators and statesmen in existence into the seat of power. We shall have wars. There will be opportunities enow. But think of spending the best years of your life in garrisons and frontier forts, and perhaps dying at last in your first battle without any kind of distinction, or the peculiar usefulness of which distinction is the token. In another career you may *command* it."

"That is why I turn to literature with such predilection," said the young man, greatly excited by Mr. De Groot's way of talking.

"Letters," resumed Mr. De Groot, after a long glance around his endless book-shelves, "are a pursuit that surpasses every other in enjoyment, and nearly every other in dignity. We must have our own literary men. We can't afford to let other nations write our books for us. That were worse than the policy which would hire them to fight our battles. There is a thought and there is a sentiment which belongs to *us*, and which we are in a manner bound to elicit. But—I am sorry to interpose so many *buts*, young sir—you are to consider that you must live. You cannot live by literature. It is difficult anywhere, but in this country it is impossible. As pride distinguishes the Spaniard, revenge the Italian, lust the Saxon, and sanguinary violence (they say) the Celt, so pecuniary injustice is our national trait. We steal the author's right in every book we publish, native or foreign. Now, Atherton, you can't live by a craft where people hold themselves at liberty to *steal* what you have produced."

"You are very kind, sir, to give me all this advice," said Atherton, sincerely.

"We are a rich people," pursued Mr. De Groot. "A virgin soil—the untouched mould of centuries—yields us—fortunate proprietors—its overflowing returns, and yet we are mean enough to be willing to enjoy the fruit of others' labor without paying for it : —and who are those others ? our brethren, whom nature distributing the faculties and inspiring the tendencies of men according to a law not to be violated with impunity, has compelled to construct out of meditation and passion through the divine art of language, our mental habitations, and whom we are not ashamed to compel to find straw as well as brick, and to rob of their just wages. It is a thief's mistake to suppose that we derive any benefit, except of the most temporary and illusive kind, from the cheapness of our pirated literature. No doubt we have a selfish pleasure in getting something for nothing, but it is a pleasure which pollutes and degrades. We are such a reading people, forsooth! Yes! it is one of our vices: for the endless reading of cheap books is a vice. I am an old Knickerbocker—a plain Dutchman, not sharp, perhaps, but honest, and I detest (excuse me. Atherton) these Yankee notions of property. I thank Heaven I am pure in this matter. I can look round these walls without a reproving conscience. There is not an American reprint in my whole library. No poor devil of an author, starving in a garret, while I weep over his pathos or smile at his wit, curses me over my shoulder with his spectre face."

"I give up authorship," said Alban. "I think it must be law for me."

"If I were you I would enter myself in a lawyer's office at once," replied the patroon. "Those handy octavos in tawny sheepskin will be better reading for you than illuminated missals."

Alban confessed that this was probably true enough. Mr. De Groot mused, and then adverted to the subject of his daughter. She was very young. He felt bound to watch over the formation of her friendships, especially with persons of her own age and another sex.

"If parents were not proverbially blind," he said with a smile, "it would be strange that in sending my daughter to visit some old friends at New Haven, the possibility of her forming some intimacy that I might not approve in a place like that, never occurred to me. When I told her at parting not to fall in love with any of the College boys, it was certainly not because I apprehended such a thing, and I believe she deemed the idea quite beneath her dignity. I was completely taken by surprise, therefore, Mr.

Atherton, to hear from her in á letter of characteristic frankness, that the conversation of a 'distinguished' member of the Senior class whom she thought I would *like*, had unsettled her Unitarianism. I went to New Haven express. I found her, as you remember, out walking with you on a Sunday afternoon. She had also accepted your escort down to New York. I confess I was more annoyed than a little, although I saw that you were not an ordinary youth. Perhaps you will not blame me for overhearing your conversation with her on the boat yesterday—at least enough of it to give me a pretty good notion of your character."

"Certainly not," said Alban, who had blushed during this address.

"Let it suffice that I was convinced by it that you would be a safe friend for my little girl. I perceived, Mr. Atherton, that it was really friendship, a point in regard to which I was at first skeptical," said Mr. De Groot.

"I was going to say," eagerly interrupted Alban, "that I have never breathed a syllable to Miss De Groot that could bear any other interpretation."

"Well, all I ask is, that you will avoid the delicate ground of religion with your young *friend* as much as possible. Her youth and her sex alike unfit her to consider such questions with profit. I have imposed the same condition on her. I hope you will consent to it as she has."

"Of course," said Alban.

"I suppose Mary did not take you over the chambers," pursued his host. "Would you like to see them? To one who has not been in Europe they may be curious."

Alban would have preferred to look over the library, but he assented of course to what Mr. De Groot proposed. The latter made him admire the great staircase on the side of the hall, with its massive oak-grained balustrade, its broad leisurely flights, the bronzes which sustained the lamps at the landings. They reached the corridor of the chambers, hung in its whole length with colored prints and drawings, following which you might make the tour of Europe without missing one of its celebrated sites or monuments. Then through room after room in which, although everything was really sumptuous and nothing wanting, yet all seemed simple. Alban admired the bath-rooms, (the Croton had not yet rendered this luxury familiar,) where hot and cold water was supplied to marble basins by silver cocks. In one stately chamber, with dressing-rooms attached, and separate baths, two elegant couches stood side by side under the same canopy of blue satin, and veiled in clouds of embroidered muslin.

"Mrs. De Groot's room," remarked his host. "We became accustomed to separate beds when abroad, and now we prefer it."

The last room which Mr. De Groot showed our hero was somewhat different from the rest. In lieu of the French bedsteads and silken draperies elsewhere seen, it had an old-fashioned four-poster of old mahogany, almost as black as ebony, with curtains of Indian chintz. The rest of the furniture was of the same style and date. The toilet-glass—placed in front of the large, deeply-recessed window—had a frame of silver, with sconces. But a more interesting object was an antiquated *prie dieu*, or kneeling desk, supplied with sconces matching those of the mirror, and a massive silver crucifix. The room had an air of occupation, a wood-fire burning on the hearth. Over the mantel hung a portrait—of whom it was easy for Alban to divine ;—a beautiful woman in a dress of dark gray cloth falling softly over a figure of unusual elegance, and confined at the waist by a simple cord of the same sombre hue. In her finely-shaped hand she held a common black rosary. Yet it was not a nun ; for her raven hair, arranged as Mary De Groot always wore hers, was profuse in quantity. The only ornament of any kind upon this striking and noble pictured personage was the tiny circle of gold on the ring-finger of her left hand.

"My daughter's taste," said Mr. De Groot, standing on the threshold and looking at the portrait. "Perhaps I should not have shown her room. Do not mention that you have seen it."

The basement of the mansion was like another house, and here, in one of its lofty, sunny parlors, portrait-hung and of domestic aspect, a white-haired negro—the type of an old family servant—was getting luncheon ready. Here Mary De Groot was again found, sitting, or rather half-reclining, in a red Boston rocking-chair, with her tiptoes just touching the carpet, a position which she quitted when the gentlemen entered. And here was also a lady whom Alban, by the resemblance to Ingham's portrait, knew to be Mrs. De Groot. She was nearly as handsome as her picture, and quite as handsomely dressed. A robe of rich shot silk, fitting very, very tight, (for the figure was redundant,) a costly lace cape, and a delicate coif to match, made an imposing drawing-room lady. She received Alban with great cordiality of manner, accompanied by the warm pressure of a plump, white hand sparkling with rings.

"Are you not a nephew of the late Rev. Jonathan Atherton? Delighted to see you! Mary has been telling me about you. Your uncle was *instrumental*, Mr. Atherton—but you understand me. Where does your mother live? I must really take the liberty of calling on her immediately to tell her how much I loved her brother, and also to congratulate her on the possession of such a son."

CHAPTER IV.

" I AM afraid you have given up reading your Bible, Alby ?" said his mother, with a grieved but tender look. We may understand from this expression that Alban had been making his mother a confidant of his religious difficulties.

" The more I read the Bible the more I am filled with doubt."

" You must not consult your own reason—but look to Heaven for light," said his mother.

" The more I pray the mightier are my perplexities."

" It is a trial of your faith ; you must persist in reading and praying," said his mother.

" But what can I do with such a passage as this of St. Matthew ?" said Alban, with a sort of irritation : " *That it might be fulfilled which was spoken of the Lord by the prophet, saying, Out of Egypt have I called my Son.* I turn to the prophecy referred to and find it thus, *When Israel was a child then I loved him, and called my son out of Egypt ;* referring, as the context plainly shows, to the departure of the Israelites out of Egypt under Moses ! Such were the arguments of the Apostles ! The dexterous application of the words of an ancient Jewish prophet, so as to tally with some real or supposed event in the life of JESUS, sufficed to produce faith in their credulous hearers."

" You shock me, Alban."

" Nay, mother, I only adduce it to show you how things strike me as I read the Bible even on my knees. I could multiply such instances in the New Testament : *He shall be called a Nazarene ; A Virgin shall conceive ; A bone of him shall not be broken ;* or Peter's argument from the words of David, *Thou wilt not suffer thy holy one to see corruption.* All fall under the same category. In fact, the reasonings of our Lord Himself with the Jews are open to the same objection. How inconsequent is it to infer the *resur-*

rection of the body from the words *I am the God of Abraham, Isaac, and Jacob*, since it is manifest that in the ordinary use of language this expression need mean no more than that *I am the God whom Abraham, Isaac, and Jacob worshipped when alive!* Just so," continued Alban, waxing warm, " of our Lord's celebrated question which silenced the Pharisees :— *The Lord said unto my Lord, Sit on my right hand.—David therefore in spirit calleth Him Lord, how is he then his Son?* Whereas, if the Pharisees had understood the simplest figures of rhetoric, they would have answered, that although David may have been the composer of the psalm in question, he need not be supposed to speak always *in his own person*."

" You must put such thoughts away ; they are suggestions of Satan," said his mother.

" Why, it is precisely thus that Roman Catholics reason from the words of Christ Himself. Why does not *This is my Body* prove Transubstantiation, as they say ?"

" Because, my dear Alban," said his mother, impatiently, "that only means that the Bread *signifies* Christ's Body."

" Ah ! there it is. That is all it *need* mean, and the same might have been said by the Sadducees in answer to the passage adduced by our Lord for the resurrection."

" But Transubstantiation is an absurdity, Alban," cried his mother, quickly, " and therefore *cannot* be the meaning of our Saviour."

" And pray what is the resurrection of the bodies of the infinite myriads of men since the world began, after they have been scattered to the four winds, and dissolved into dust and gas ? And what is to be done in the case of cannibals, my dear mother ?"

" The power of God, my dear Alban ! You don't pretend to limit omnipotence," retorted his mother.

" No, *I* do not pretend to limit it," replied Alban, with a slight smile at himself for getting drawn into such an argument. " I only spoke because I craved sympathy, my dear mother. Nobody understands my difficulties."

Mrs. Atherton was silent. A syllogism is pretty much lost on a woman, but she feels the faintest appeal to her heart.

"I am glad you have told me your difficulties, Alby," she said at length. "I should be very sorry if you were afraid or unwilling to confide them to *me*. I dare say now you've relieved your mind, it will be easier."

"There are things in the *Old* Testament I can't get over, or get round," resumed her son, who was sitting on the settee with the family Bible open on a stand before him,—his mother's work-stand, the remainder of which was taken up with the etceteras of her plain sewing. "For instance, the history of Moses, the providential circumstances attending his birth and education, the appearance of God to him in a bush, the miracles by which he is said to have brought out his twelve tribes from the land of bondage, the wonderful passage of the Red Sea, the manna and miraculous water in the desert :—all to usher in what? The giving of the Ten precepts of the Moral Law on a desert mountain to this camp of fugitive herdsmen and bricklayers! I do not think it possible that such a history, with such a finale, could have been imagined or invented by mortal man. If God ever took out a people for himself out of another people, as Moses says, with signs and wonders and an outstretched arm, it must have been, it would have been, to announce such a code, which contains the essence of all religious and social rules, the great foundation-stones of the primary duties, stripped of all extraneous matter, simplified, methodically placed, and laid firm in the authority of the Creator Himself. The history of the Jews ever since just comes in as a proof that this view of the transaction is no flight of fancy. The Jews are a fact. *I am sure that God spake by Moses!*"

"And not by Jesus Christ?" inquired his mother. "Surely you must be blind, Alban."

"I can find nothing worthy of God in Christianity as it has been taught me, mother," replied her son, sternly. "Forgive me for saying so. I don't mean to reflect on your teaching. I speak of what is current. Justification by faith and this new heart, seem to me mere baby-talk. It is worse than that, for it is talk that undermines the first principles of morals. I see it theoretically, and I have experienced it practically, and I have done with it for ever."

"This comes of New Haven divinity," said his mother, tears running down her pale, delicate cheek, and falling on the shirt she was making for her son.

The sound of wheels was heard in the quiet street, and ceased at Mrs. Atherton's door. The bell was rung with a jerk. Mary Anne, the maid of all work, was cleaning her knives. You could hear her in the kitchen entry. But the sound instantly ceased, while the girl hastily washed her hands and tied on a clean apron before running to the street-door, which she would be sure to open, out of breath, and with a face as red as a peony. Alban observed that it was the De Groots, and half wished a fire had been lit in the front parlor : but it was too late to wish it, for the lady visitors came sailing in like two angels fresh from Paris.

Not to describe Mrs. De Groot's costume would be to omit her almost entirely. She was nothing apart from her clothes, and with them she appeared to be a great deal. Her large, white velvet hat (*Anglicé*, bonnet) and its drooping plume, the long, starry veil, trailing cashmere of Ind, and flounced amethyst silk, seemed, as they spread in a glory of shooting iris hues and snow over the chintz settee, to look Mrs. Atherton's modest parlor out of countenance. As for Mary, she appeared to have caught a light from her mother's effulgence of fashion. No more of that charming plainness which had marked her at New Haven. A great bonnet of Mazarin blue silk surrounded her lovely face, and a cloak and robe of the same material and of the newest fashion invested her form. She looked surprisingly larger and older, and Alban realized that she had grown since he first saw her. She was so wonderfully easy, too, sat with such a careless grace in her corner of the settee, her neatly shod feet playing hide-and-go-seek with each other, for the robes were short in those days, and betrayed the white stockings and morocco slippers neatly cross-laced around an ankle straight and fine. Alban introduced the visitors to his mother, who quietly laid aside, but did not put out of sight, her homely work. Mrs. De Groot glanced at the portrait of the clerical uncle, and began at once on that subject.

It soon appeared what Mrs. De Groot's idea of our hero was, nor was it unnatural. Mary had truly said that Alban's conversation had first set her to thinking, which had ended, as Mrs. De Groot expressed it, in her abjuring her father's shocking opinions —so far a great triumph for Mrs. De Groot. In answer to her stepmother's further inquiries, she had stated that Mr. Atherton was a member of the College Church, reputed very pious, eminently pure and irreproachable in morals, &c. Of course she could say nothing about Alban's skepticism, which he had acknowledged to her in confidence. Moreover, Mary herself believed it to be but a temporary perplexity, natural and inevitable in a thoughtful Protestant, (the child already begins to talk in that way,) and rather to be approved as disposing him to seek a better faith, which she was sanguine he would. Mrs. De Groot, therefore, had really formed the most exalted opinion of our hero, and as women generally forestall a conclusion, above all where young marriageable people are concerned, she considered him already as good as a son-in-law. Nor was this an ill-founded or rash opinion ; for both parents naturally regarded their daughter as being in love, and had discussed the affair in that point of view. If Mary should *marry* an orthodox Presbyterian—particularly a " nephew of Mr. Atherton's,"—really Mrs. De Groot had not expected any thing half so good. Her father thought—but *his* motives are not so easily fathomed : at all events he told his wife that he had determined to let things " take their course." He thought Atherton was a conceited puppy, and Mary might do a great deal better, and she might also do a great deal worse. " He's as poor as Job's turkey," he concluded ; and this again rather pleased Mrs. De Groot, who liked to feel herself in a position of patronage towards the future connections. The origin and past of the Athertons were such as to make this peculiarly gratifying to Mary's stepmother, who had not always enjoyed so eminent a station as at present. One might have supposed, to hear her talk to Mrs. Atherton about her brother, that she had been in a situation to patronize her minister extensively, in the days of which she spoke, but the fact was, that only her " interesting state of mind" had ever obtained his notice. Let us do Mrs. De Groot justice, however. We believe there is always a heart—seat of amiable weakness—under the tightest silk bodice ever held by hooks and eyes. In those days, before Mary was born, or Alban either, when that heart was eighteen years old, and beat in a maiden bosom, she had loved the clerical boy-face whose likeness hung over Mrs. Atherton's bright sideboard. The Rev. Mr. Atherton never dreamed of it, and soon scattered many such hopes to the wind by bringing from his former parish in the country a beautiful, pious, clever creature, to fill the important and envied station of minister's wife : and now a nephew of whom he knew nothing, reaped a benefit from his unconscious conquest.

Meanwhile the young people conversed separately.

"What a dear home-like home you have got, Mr. Alban," said Mary, with a smile.

"You think so ?" said Alban, looking round.

"And what a dear gentle mother ! I love her already."— With a blush, and in a whisper.—" I wonder if she would like to have me come and read to her. I should enjoy it so much."

"She would be charmed," said Alban, with a gratified look, yet a little embarrassed ; for he had not Mary's openness.

"I am ashamed to admire every thing," said she, " but really what a pretty fire-screen that is of your mother's. Did she embroider it herself ? Oh, I wish she would teach me. Of all things I want to learn to embroider."

"Mother—"

"Oh, don't, Mr. Alban—"

"Miss De Groot wishes you to teach her to embroider—a fire-screen, Miss Mary ?"

"Not precisely, Mr. Alban."

"Where *did* you learn to work so beautifully, Mrs. Atherton?" asked Mrs. De Groot.

"At Bethlehem," replied Alban's mother.

"What, where our blessed Saviour was born!" exclaimed Mary, innocently.

But Bethlehem was a celebrated Moravian school in Mrs Atherton's girlhood. The conversation turned on it. Mrs. Atherton described the customs of Bethlehem in a lively manner, with many a characteristic New England turn of expression and accent, refined, as all national peculiarities are in cultivated women. Mary listened with tears of delight in her joyful dark eyes, and a vivid blush on her rich cheek. Mrs. De Groot shrugged her shoulders at the Easter processions, white robes, and lighted tapers of the Moravians. After that, the call terminated by Mrs. De Groot inviting Mrs. Atherton with her son and husband to dinner the next day to meet the Rev. Dr. Fluent, Mrs. De Groot's pastor.

"You were reading the Bible when we came in?" said Mary, glancing, as she rose, at the sacred volume still open on the workstand. She smiled and hesitated.—"I suppose I may ask how you get on, Mr. Alban?"

"I have got so far as to believe in Moses," replied the young man, remembering his promise to her father.

"Moses!" said Mary, curiously.

"Exactly," said Alban, smiling. "You are going to turn Roman Catholic, Miss Mary. I may perhaps be forced to embrace a faith yet more ancient, and become a Jew."

"Christians," Mrs. De Groot was saying to Mrs. Atherton, "should maintain a closer intercourse. In future, I trust it will be so with us."

"We shan't keep up much intercourse with Infidels and Jews, I hope," said Mary, aside, with a flash of the old haughtiness.

"I shall follow my convictions," returned the young man in the same tone, "even if they lead me to the Synagogue."

"Well, don't ask me to be present at the ceremony of your reception—that's all" cried the young lady, turning away to follow her stepmother out of the room. She came back, quite scarlet, to shake hands with Mrs. Atherton, but did not salute Alban at all. He conducted them to the carriage, but she never looked back, and sprang in without touching his offered hand.

" People will treat you so, one day."

Having picked up her muff, which she seemed to have knocked purposely off the seat, as she raised herself with a countenance still brightly tinged, she answered to her mother's evident horror—

" You read the Bible too much, Mr. Alban. That is not the way to find out the truth, but to become an infidel, a heretic, and an apostate. Oh, Mr. Alban, I hope you will never be an apostate !"

"Did you ever !" exclaimed Mrs. De Groot.

" Miss De Groot means that we cannot hope to understand the Scriptures without the light of faith," said Alban.

" Yes, the faith of the Church," said Mary.

" Well, I concede that," replied Alban ; " but you must let me search till I find the *true* Church."

She extended her hand frankly, and pressed his with a freedom unusual to her.—" I shall pray for you," she said.

" Do come to see us often," said Mrs. De Groot, as he bowed himself away.

Our hero's aberration seems at present grievous indeed. How he will get out of this scrape is more than we undertake to answer for. We shan't have recourse to a miracle to open his eyes. He has Moses and the Prophets, and to them he has appealed : by them he must be taught, if at all. As ceremonies—next to costumes—are allowed to be our *forte*, the reader must not be surprised if we have presently to describe that of our hero's circumcision. We engage to do it with the most perfect delicacy, and meanwhile must accompany him to a scene which certainly looks that way.

In the afternoon Alban dressed himself in his new clothes, just sent home from the tailor's. In pumps and tights, and an embroidered waistcoat, his own mother would scarcely know her son. He throws the new Spanish cloak gracefully over one shoulder, and enters a hackney-coach.

It rolled slowly down Greenwich-street, entered State-street, while the waters of the chilly bay still gleamed with the dull red of the Western sky, and stopped before a large irregular house, following the curve of the street, with a deep balcony-portico, and white marble steps. It was in this mansion—once his father's —that our hero was born, and it was one of the homes of his childhood.   The door-plate now bears, simply " SEIXAS."   A servant of peculiar physiognomy admits him, and asking " Mishter Atherton ?" admits him into a drawing-room, around which he throws a glance of curiosity.

On a yellow satin divan, extending the whole length of the room, on the side opposite the door and old-fashioned chimney, re-clined a man in the prime of life.   His waistcoat was finer than Alban's, and a mass of brilliants glittered on his bosom like a star. He had gentle black eyes, black pencilled eyebrows, jet curls, and beard, fringing fine, but characteristic features.   He was lion-chested and narrow-hipped, but stooped slightly in the shoulders.

" The salutation of peace," said he, smiling, as he sprang up, and took Atherton's hand. " You are in good time.   We will order dinner at once, that we may discuss it at our leisure, since we are going to the Opera afterwards.   I am sorry that Mrs. Seixas cannot appear, but my sister will play hostess in her stead.—Miriam !"

The place of the folding-door—between white Corinthian columns—was hung with a crimson velvet curtain looped up with a cord and heavy tassel of gold bullion.   At the call of Mr. Seixas a young lady presented herself beneath this rich drapery.   She was apparently a year or two younger than Alban, tall, elegantly formed, and perfectly beautiful, although in a very peculiar style. What Alban first noticed, however, was her garb, which was different from the fashion of the day.   It was a light green bro-cade of India, the gold pattern predominating so as almost to hide the ground, and fitting closely to the shape to the lowest point of

the natural waist. The neck was cut in an indescribable curve,
to uncover just so much of the bust as was beautiful to show
without any immodesty, and the short loose sleeves were looped
over gems upon each polished shoulder. For the lady's figure,
notwithstanding her manifest youth, was the deep-breasted, uni-
versally-undulating beauty of the Orient. Her hair—purple
black—was in plain bands, without a single ringlet, secured by a
gold comb, from which a white lace veil fell nearly to her feet.
And she bore a jewelled fan. Her face must be imagined ; it
was on the softest Jewish model, and of a rich golden paleness.
Never were seen such long, long-eye-lashed black eyes, liquid in
their glance, yet virginal and calm. Alban had never felt so sudden and vivid an admiration for one of her sex before. He had
heard of love at first sight, and now he experienced it.

CHAPTER V.

WE must retrace our steps a little, and as the way our hero is going on does not please us, turn our attention to the more interesting course of Mary De Groot.

We take her, then, on the first day after her return home, at the hour between luncheon and dinner, when Alban, having concluded his long call, had left the house. It is a beautiful afternoon, she dons her Broadway walking gear, and in the accustomed liberty of a young New York lady, sallies forth alone for a walk.

She proceeded down the Avenue towards Washington Square —then an almost naked rectangle. There were no churches on the Fifth Avenue or near it, where now so many cluster. There were none on the Square, nor had the white marble turrets of the University yet risen, nor did its chapel window glimmer through trees. She turned into Broadway and walked down one or two squares. There was a church on the corner ; a Gothic church of gray rough stone, flanked by grim towers. The ways of New York were then simpler than now, and Broadway "so high up" as Houston was quiet in a way that cannot now be imagined. Mary stopped at the iron railing and gave a wistful glance to the stern church front. Usually an inscription tells to what faith the edifice is dedicated, but here was none.

"I see no cross on the gable-peak. And if it were a Catholic church I guess there would be images of saints in the niches. I bet any thing it is Episcopal."

Good reasoning in '35, but it would not serve in '51. A cross on a gable is no more a safe guide, nor yet a marble saint looking down from the niche of a medieval tower. We do not say that there is not yet a physiognomy by which the pinchbeck religion that takes so with our fashionables, may be detected even at first sight, and distinguished from the faith it imitates.

20

Our young friend might have consulted a directory, but she forgot there was such a thing, or she might have asked one of her father's Irish servants, if she had not been restrained by a feeling of delicacy. She thought of inquiring in a shop, or of some passer-by, for the nearest Catholic church, and then again an invincible timidity prevented her. She began to reflect. The Catholics were poor—foreigners—Irish—were they not? Their churches were not to be looked for in Broadway, but in some obscure district. Mary had an idea that such a region lay on the east of Broadway, but she had a fear of wandering in that direction. It was a *terra incognita* to the young Knickerbocker, and contained, she knew, some dreadful places where a modest girl's foot could not pass without danger. And yet surely it was safe so high up. Lafayette Place was east of Broadway; so was Bond-street. She had friends living in both; they were fashionable streets. From Bond to Houston, on the corner of which she stood, was only two squares; she would venture to walk a little way down Houston-street, east.

Indeed, it was rather a nice street; a stable in the first "block," but that was common in cross streets. At the first corner she stops, and looks up and down Crosby. She sees no church, but the High School, and troops of boys (for it is just three P. M.) running and shouting. She has a mind to retreat, but they are only boys, and she crosses Crosby and boldly pushes forward to the next corner.

What sees she? Not the great silver door-plate of St. Catharine's Convent of the Sisters of Mercy, (for neither Convent nor Institution yet existed,) but on the lower corner of the opposite square in Mulberry, in a walled churchyard, she saw the rear gable of a Gothic edifice. It was of stone, plain and high, but faced below by a wooden lean-to of octagon shape, with a wooden porch and steps. The body of the church was hidden by the houses in Mulberry-street, but over the roof-line of the latter rose a nondescript wooden steeple, or pinnacle, surmounted by a great gilt cross. The sign of salvation, glittering in the afternoon sun which smote the roof and upper portion of the church, extended its arms brightly and boldly against the blue sky.

So Mary turned into Mulberry-street and walked slowly down the square, looking at the church and its lofty, glittering cross.

"How impossible to mistake it!" she thought. "I need no one to tell me that this is one of the homes of our mother—*sancta mater ecclesia*—humble, yet exalted in the eyes of her God. Surely an angel guided my steps."

A man in a long surtout came out of Prince-street and crossed Mulberry in front of her. He turned into Mulberry, walked rapidly along the church-yard wall to the back entrance of the cathedral, ascended the wooden steps, and disappeared in the porch.

The steps were shackling and creaked under Mary's light foot. The outer door of the hurricane porch (as it is called) was closed by a pulley. The inner one was heavy, but yielded to a resolute push, and she found herself in a small chapel. The first object that struck her eye was a wooden Baptismal Font against the wall. At the altar end of the chapel was a door that stood ajar. Seeing no one, she proceeded thither and tapped. No answer; and she ventured to push the door open, and then to enter. It was a carpeted room with a fire. It contained some large wardrobes, as they seemed, of dark wood, a crucifix against the wall, and a confessional in a corner. Then she knew that it was a place where women might come. Father Smith and the New Haven sacristy recurred to her mind. Next she perceived another door which she knew must lead into the body of the church; but as the adventurous young girl approached to try it, it opened and the man in the long surtout appeared. His face, now that she saw him uncovered, gave her a great surprise: it was the New Haven missionary.

"Father Smith," she joyfully exclaimed.

The priest did not remember Mary, and intimated as much with great courtesy. She reminded him of his third mass on Christmas Day.

"Ah, it is the young New Haven convert," said the missionary. "I should not have known you had not you spoken first, my young lady. So you have come to New York. I suppose you have been received into the Church."

"No, sir, I am waiting a month as you directed me, studying my catechism and other books."

"You have seen no clergyman here then?"

"We arrived from New Haven but yesterday."

"You had better see the Bishop or the Vicar General. I suppose you are in the cathedral parish."

"Whatever you tell me, Father Smith, I will do."

"I was just going to call on the Bishop. I will mention your case to him. What is your name, my dear young lady?"

He took down her name, age, and place of abode.

"Go into the church and say your prayers," said the missionary, "while I see the Bishop. In a short time I will bring or send you word."

At present the cathedral extends back to Mulberry-street, and the lean-to chapel no longer exists. The space thus gained affords a deep and spacious sanctuary; but at that time the sanctuary was miserably contracted, and the pews were pushed to the very rails. Mary found the church empty, and most of the pews locked. She discovered at last one that was open, and entering, placed herself gladly on her knees. This cathedral was very unlike those beautiful Flemish interiors in her father's gallery from which she had drawn her principal notion of a Catholic church. Over the altar was a painted perspective that carried the church back like a deep choir, closed by a calvary. If this did not please our young friend's refined taste, it did not long arrest her attention, caught by a reality which makes us forget all outward tawdriness, all poverty. A lamp hung burning in the empty church before the tabernacle, and Mary now knew what that meant. The thought of that heavenly presence had not occurred to her before. She put down her head and adored. So low, however, was then the tone of Catholic feeling, (to borrow a phrase from a recent sect-movement,) or so great the poverty of Catholics in New York, that there was nothing else in the church to excite either interest or devotion—not even a picture of our Lady. But the young convert drew from her bosom her mother's rosary and began to say her beads. She was just finishing the "Sorrowful Mysteries," with her eye fixed on the calvary, when the sacristy door opened, and a female came out attired in deep black—as one might fancy a Quakeress in mourning. As soon as her eye rested on Miss De Groot she came forward. In passing before the altar this dark-robed person turned and sank on one knee. She uttered Mary's name, and receiving a word of assent, with a look and tone of sweet courtesy invited her to come to the sacristy. Trembling, though glad, Mary followed her dark-stoled guide, who, as they went before the altar again, again bent the knee to the earth. Mary followed her example, for she was not ignorant why it was done. Her new companion made her sit by the sacristy fire. They were alone.

"You desire baptism, Miss De Groot?" inquired the dark-habited lady, with a glance that habitually, it would seem, sought the ground.

"I do," replied Mary, fastening her earnest eyes on the face of the questioner.

"You are sure you were never baptized?"

"I have always been told so."

"I suppose you can say the Creed, the Lord's Prayer, the Hail Mary, the Commandments, and the *Confiteor*."

Mary answered like a little girl, by reciting each formulary as it was named. The Sister smiled, and asked how many sacraments there were, whether all the seven were instituted by Jesus Christ, and how that was proved from Scripture. Mary recited the texts.

"As you have been bred a Protestant, I suppose you are very familiar with the Scriptures?" said the Sister.

"O dear, yes! I know the greater part of the Bible almost by heart."

"That's more than I do," answered the Sister, smiling. "Was

it in the perusal of the Scriptures, Miss De Groot, that you became
convinced of the truth of the Catholic religion ?"

"O no, indeed !"

"Well I think that without the lamp of faith the sacred
volume must be a labyrinth to the inquirer," said the Sister, looking up with a bright intelligence, but immediately withdrawing
her glance.   "Whence do you obtain faith, Miss De Groot?"

"From the Church," said Mary.

"What is the Church ?"

"The society of the faithful under legitimate pastors," responded the catechumen, following her catechism.

"Then from what part of the Church do you obtain faith ?"
"From the pastors."—"Right.   *Faith cometh by hearing ; and
how shall they hear without a preacher ? And how shall they
preach unless they be sent ?*   What is not proposed to us to believe by an authority appointed by God, and secured from error by
His promise, can never be the object of faith.   Hence we Catholics say and prove that Protestants, so far as they are such, can
have no faith, but only opinion.   However, the grace to believe
what the Church teaches—whence comes it ?"—"From God
alone."—"Right again.   And by what means do we obtain it
from God ?"—"By prayer and the sacraments."—"Right.   By
the sacrament of baptism more particularly.   For though none
but believers are to be baptized, the sacrament infuses the *habit*
of faith, which before was only a precarious act.   *You* believe,
but you have in a manner no right to faith, and except in virtue
of the sacrament you cannot retain faith."

The Sister of Charity had a pleasant face, though not beautiful.
Her complexion had that peculiar brilliancy which is so often seen
under the veil of the Virgins of the Church.   Her eyes, as we have
said, were habitually downcast, yet with an occasional glance of
singular penetration.   Her manner was refined, her voice sweet,
the accent slightly foreign :—it might be French or the high Irish,
which is the most pleasing and thorough-bred in the world.   She
touched the rosary which hung at her girdle.—"You know what

this is ? And how to use it ? Oh, you say the beads daily, do you ?" She regarded Mary with an expression of great tenderness, which, however, she immediately checked. " It would be a sin," she continued, " to keep you from baptism. Father Smith mentioned that you had no Catholic friends. Should it be necessary I would present you at the font, although it is against our rules."

Mary gently hid her face in her hands.

" The Bishop has requested Father Smith to receive you as soon as he finds you prepared," added the Sister. " But here comes the good father himself."—Father Smith entered.—" She knows her catechism, father. Her faith is rational as well as firm, and she prays, above all."

" Have you a great desire for baptism ?" inquired the priest, standing by the fire, and looking down upon her tranquilly. " I desire it," replied Mary, in tears, " more than any thing else in the world."

" Why do you ?"

Mary looked up.—" Because unless we are *born of water and the Holy Ghost* we *cannot enter the kingdom of God.*"

" You are then formally a postulant for salvation—" glancing from her to the Sister. " We cannot refuse you what you ask. God would require your soul at our hands."

He inquired about her father. Mary frankly stated that her father knew and strongly disapproved her intention of becoming a Catholic, that she believed he would absolutely refuse his consent to her being baptized, and that she would prefer not to ask it. When it was done, and could not be undone, she meant to tell him at once, and did not doubt to obtain his forgiveness. The missionary sat down and questioned her on the nature of the sacrament she was about to receive, but rather in the way of instruction than to elicit her knowledge.

Did she understand why she needed baptism at all ? He asked because it was an error of the sect in which she had been bred, to suppose that the human being was born innocent.

" Your soul was created by God, and you may say that it came pure and good from the hands of its Creator ; but that which is born of the flesh is flesh. Child of Adam, you did not receive at the moment of your conception that which is the complement of a moral creature, the divine life of grace. Naked and stripped of original justice and sanctity you were born ; and hence, ignorant of God, perverse in will, weak in virtue, a captive to the desires of the flesh and fleshly mind, a seeker of pleasure and transitory good : which is concupiscence. Humiliating as this fact is, it is true ; and up to this date you have done nothing, nor can you ever do any thing, to merit that God should bestow upon you the grace which in a moment can efface it all. If you had died in infancy or in youth, while yet unconscious of this misery, you could never have seen God ; and if old enough to have committed actual sins, you must have endured for ever their punishment, according to the greatness of their demerit. Now then you see why you need baptism. It is the womb of a new birth, wherein that which was born of Adam may be born again of Christ, and the soul united to sinful flesh may receive its true life—the Holy Spirit which Adam forfeited."

To this the young lady listened with an air of quiet assent and pious interest.

Did she understand, then, pursued the missionary, with deliberation, that in baptism, provided she received it with suitable dispositions, all the sins of her past life would be entirely washed away, together with that sin in which she had been conceived— the original defect and guilt of her human nature—so that she would become in an instant perfectly pure and holy, and if she were to die that moment, would go immediately to heaven, and see God eternally as he is, by the sole merit of faith ; God, that is, crowning his own free gift by a free and infinite reward ? Did she understand this ?

" I understand it," said Mary, tremulously.

Did she understand, moreover, that this sacrament, thus worthily received, (for that was a condition,) would change her in an instant from a child of wrath into a child of grace, infuse into her soul the justice of God, (that, namely, whereby He makes us inwardly and truly just,) illuminate it by His light, inflame it with His charity, implanting the habit of all virtues ; that her very body would become the temple of God, her members the limbs and members of Christ the Incarnate Son, the same Spirit inhabiting her mortal frame and taking possession of the interior recesses of her heart, which dwelt in and quickened, sanctified and united to the person of the Word, the adorable Humanity of the Son of God ?

"The Holy Trinity will come and dwell with you : do you understand that ?" demanded the priest.

"Yes," murmured the catechumen.

Did she also know—the priest's voice lowered a little—that the sacrament which thus effaced all sin and replenished the soul with the Author of sanctity Himself, would leave *concupiscence* within her, wounded but not destroyed ; whence must spring a daily, hourly conflict—a conflict in which she would be liable to fall, but in which if she overcame she would be *crowned ?* This was serious : let her think of it well.

Mary wept.

"In what degree the sacrament of baptism may diminish concupiscence, depends in part on the dispositions more or less perfect with which you receive it, on the fervor of your prayers, and the simplicity of your intention before and after. The sevenfold grace which the Holy Ghost inspires in confirmation is a sevenfold panoply against this enemy as well as every other. The daily, supersubstantial bread of the Divine Eucharist will be a remedy for infirmity as well as a perennial source of life ; and finally, even a fall will not be hopeless, for the Sacrament of Penance remains. Still I must tell you that none of these things will change your nature, my dear child, nor your acquired habits ; but they will give you a life and a strength above nature, by virtue of which, if you will, you may, while in the flesh, live not after the flesh but after the Spirit. But to do so is not easy. It will cost you much suffering—internal and external, many a hard battle with yourself; nor must you count on a single day's remission of the struggle while you live. It is a narrow way : you may easily miss it. It is a rough way : you may easily be discouraged by it. It is the only way : you must persevere in it till the soul and body are parted by death, or both are lost for ever. I rejoice, and yet I tremble, when I see one like you who has been nursed in the lap of luxury, and before whom the world spreads a thousand fascinations, called—mysteriously called, as few of the rich and noble are —to enter upon this rugged path, which leads indeed—but through much tribulation—to the kingdom of God."

"I *am* called, father : let me enter it," said Mary, sinking on her knees by the side of her chair.

"You must spend some days, my daughter, as our holy mother the Church enjoins, in exercises of piety, viz., fasting, alms-giving, and prayers, which you know from your catechism are the three eminent good works. It was by these that Cornelius the centurion, while yet a heathen, gained such favor with God that an angel appeared to him by whom he was directed to Peter to learn the terms of salvation. At your age fasting must be practised with great moderation. Sister Theresa will suggest to you what is prudent ; if you can deny yourself some delicacy which you would buy from your own purse, so as to give the money to the poor, it will be very acceptable to God. It is probable you have not many grievous sins to charge yourself with, but you must call them to mind, whatever they are, and be very penitent for them. Resolve, by the aid of God's grace, never to offend him deliberately again as long as you live, and remember constantly what you are about to do—to renounce Satan with all his works and pomps. Your own will, the world's vanities, the desires of the mind and the flesh, are no more to be your rule ; but you are to mortify your passions, to imitate the humility of your Saviour, and, like Him, live only to do the will of God. Will you endeavor in this way to dispose yourself to receive the grace of baptism ?"

"I will, father," said Mary, still humbly kneeling.

The priest made the sign of blessing over her, and gently bade her rise.

"There is a mass at the cathedral every morning at half-past six, another at seven, and by the mercy of God I shall say one here every day this week at half-past seven. Now you can do as your piety and your circumstances allow as regards coming on the intermediate days, but on Saturday morning, if you will be here as early as seven, with any of your friends, or alone, Sister Theresa, if no one else can be thought of in the mean time, will be your godmother, and I will baptize you. Probably the Bishop will give you confirmation immediately after. At all events you will stay to hear mass, and make your first communion. And would, my child, that I were in your place."

Sister Theresa led away Miss De Groot. They pause and converse in the chapel. It is growing dusk, and a little lamp, which Mary observed not before, gleams out upon the almost naked altar. Above the low, plain tabernacle is an image, carved in wood, of the Mother of God. The meek brow, on which the altar lamp at her feet casts upward an effect of light like life, is crowned with white roses. The two females implore the protection of the Queen of Saints. The young convert indeed felt a thrill of indescribable joy for the first time to see Mary thus publicly honored. But her father's dinner hour was close at hand. It was important not to be called upon to explain where she had been. So she kissed the Sister of Charity, and sped away, light of foot and rejoicing in heart.

No one insulted by word or look the beautiful and well-attired young lady, threading so rapidly and fearlessly the half-twilight, half-lamp lit streets. It was a familiar sight in New York, and by no means an unfamiliar circumstance to herself. But the last lonely quarter of a mile after she had left the houses behind, was more nervous, and our dear heroine almost ran over this part of the way, till she set her foot, reassured, on the broad pavement before her father's stately mansion.

CHAPTER VI.

It was a cold, stormy morn of mid-winter, when, at about a quarter past six, the young convert stole down the private stair and let herself out of the house by a side-door. There she paused. The street was dark. The line of lamps down the lonely Avenue rendered it more gloomy. The young lady was afraid to venture forth.

A man passed, going towards the city, and walking fast. He was attired as a laborer, and heeded not, if he perceived, the female form in the basement doorway of the great house. Then a milk-cart rattled by. Not being given to foolish fears, Mary began to accuse herself of timidity. She stepped forth and walked on quite bravely. But she sees a man approaching in the opposite direction, she becomes nervous and retreats to her doorway. The individual approached. His appearance, as he passed under the street-lamp, was that of a gentleman, and he slackened his pace on seeing a girl in a doorway at that hour. He stopped at the court-yard and spoke to her, whereupon Mary hastily retired into the house, nervously bolting the door. The stranger impudently whistled a tune and sauntered on. The young lady opened the door ajar, but dared not come out again from her place of security, until she distinguished the voices of some women. They were approaching rapidly, and speaking in an unmistakable national accent. She went out to them as far as the gate. They were hurrying past.

"How far are you going, ma'am, please?" said Mary, with quickness.

"Sure we're goin' down the street a piece, ma'am."

"May I keep along with you?" asked Mary, hoping it might prove a good piece. "I am afraid to go alone."

"Ye're entirely welcome, and any way the street is free. But it's late we are this minute."

They strode on as fast as she could well walk, though active of limb.

"It's mighty discreet ye are to want company," said the woman who had answered her. "I suppose ye work for a milliner?"

"Not exactly," said Mary. "I am not going to my work."

"May be ye've a place in yon great house?"

"Yes, I have a place there at present."

"But ye're afraid of losing it. Well, there's always more to be had in this counthry, they say. But they're not all good places by a great dale. Here's me daughter has jist lift one where she got siven dollars a month, becase she thought better to lose a place than her sowl, let alone her body into the bargain. The thrials a poor girl has to go through in most rispictable families from them as should know better is dreadful. Lord have mercy on us!" sighing. "'Tis a wicked city, as Father Murphy tould *her* at confession, jist to encourage her like, and the poor Irish servant girls, says he, is what saves it from bein' burrent by a shower of fire and brimstone like Sodom and Gomorrhay."

"I dare say he spoke truth there," observed Mary.

"Och!" sighing again, "it's likely enough ye know the thruth of it as well as us or better, if ye live in yon fine house. Ye seem a purty gintale little body, and a sweet voice ye've got any way: I wish ye mayn't know the thruth of what I've been sayin', too well. Ye've not the honor and advantage of bein' a Catholic, I suppose; but keep y'r innocence, and may be it's yourself that will be one before ye die."

"I dare say you are going to the cathedral to hear mass," said Mary.

"Indeed, ma'am, ye niver spoke a truer word in y'r life. It's jist to the cathaydral we're goin'."

"I am going there too for the same purpose," said Mary. "I call myself a Catholic."

"And is it a *Roman* Catholic that you mane?" returned her new acquaintance, with characteristic caution.

" Yes, a Roman Catholic, or what should I be going to mass
for ?"

" Indeed, and that's true, but there's people that wants us to
take their little books and says they ' call themselves Catholics,' but
the Lord knows that nobody else iver called them so," said Mrs.
Dolman, whose acute ear had noticed both the unfamiliar expression and the young lady's accent.

The discovery somewhat altered her companions' notion of her.
If she was a Catholic and going to mass, her being in the street at
that early hour was not so positive proof of belonging to their own
class or one not much above it.   It was now clear twilight.   Ten
or fifteen minutes had made a great difference.   The Irish mother
and daughter regarded the young lady with curiosity.   Mary's
courage and dignity came back with the first ray of the ever protecting light.   She asked her companions where they lived, and
learned that it was in a shanty on the Avenue, near her father's
freestone palace, and that they went to mass at that hour every
morning.   She engaged them to stop for her.   The old woman
began to apologize for speaking too freely to the young lady, but
Mary cut her short.   They reached the cathedral, which was
crowded—at least in the aisles ;—for it was a day of obligation—
the great feast of Epiphany.   With some difficulty Mary made her
way to a pew, one of the few open so early.

The seven-o'clock mass was said by an old ecclesiastic, who
entered in a trailing purple cassock and rochet of very rich lace,
and who put on the vestments for mass at the altar itself.   It was
the first low mass Mary had heard ; it seemed to her very rapid.
A considerable number of persons received communion, and among
them one of her new Irish friends—the daughter.   Mary could not
help noticing this girl's absorbed attention, kneeling on the floor of
the aisle just before her.   The mother, except at the gospels and
creed, remained nearly prostrate on the floor, and when her daughter
went up to the rail, sobbed aloud.   Mary observed how wretchedly
they both were clad.

" The life that dwells in those poor creatures," thought she "is the very life of my Lord : when shall it dwell in me ! The Star which I saw in the East, has again appeared. I rejoice with the Magi. I have found the young Child with Mary His mother, in the House of Bread. But come and inhabit my heart, O divine Babe ! Expectation of the Gentiles, I expect thee. Messiah, King of Israel ! I long for thee, as wanderers long for the morning light. O Sun of Justice, arise on my soul !"

She was full of ardent desires : the mass intensely excited them. She would gladly have waited for another; indeed, it seemed to her that she could hear mass for ever,—never quit her knees before the Tabernacle. She dared not stay, however, but while the purple-stoled ecclesiastic was unvesting at the altar, went by lowly genuflecting, openly and yet unnoticed, with deep and safe feeling shared by many and deemed natural by all, and so passed out by the chapel, leaving her humble friends, one at her thanksgiving, the other at her beads. The city, adorer of Mammon, is now awake.

Miss De Groot's morning excursion attracted no notice at home ; for she had been accustomed to walk before breakfast in the autumn, after she came from boarding-school to reside with her parents in their new house. Sometimes it would be on Washington Square, then not very inviting ; sometimes down a cross street to the still beautiful river-side ; or again, beyond Broadway, where at that time a winding road passed by gray rocks and golden groves. To have gone forth a half hour or so earlier, to attend church with some hundreds of poor people, did not constitute a very grievous offence, and the father whose daughter is guilty of no greater indiscretion, may congratulate himself.

Mary was a sensible girl, in spite of her popish flights. She was aware that no act of piety she could perform would be so distasteful to her parents as fasting. Much, therefore, as she desired to fast on the days preceding her baptism, she resolved to do nothing that could attract their attention. Nevertheless, by a holy artifice which saints have practised, she contrived to go without her breakfast every morning. One day she had it sent

to her room ; another she amused herself during the entire meal
with reading the newspaper aloud ; the last day, which was Friday, she had no need to dissemble the matter.   As for luncheon,
she could make it as sparing as she liked, and confined herself
to bread and water for the quality, which cost her much faintness
and headache.   At dinner she made amends, (for a growing girl
must eat,) but (except one day) on fish and vegetables ; flatulent,
unsatisfying food she found it.   Altogether, the flesh suffered,
and it is to be hoped that the spirit profited.

    After breakfast on Wednesday morning, Mary tied on her
bonnet, and visited the shanty of her Irish friends—a low cabin
of boards, ten feet by twelve, with one small window, through
a pane of which the stove-pipe made its exit.   Like Mr. De
Groot's freestone mansion, it occupied an entire square ; but in
lieu of the high-walled garden planted with fruit-trees, and
traversed by lines of box, the circling court-yard with its shrubs
and frequent evergreens, making even winter cheerful, and the
conservatory glowing with red cactus, and a hundred other
bright-flowered plants, and exhaling on a sunny noon the fragrance
of the myrtle, the rose, and the orange-tree—around the widow
Dolman's shanty extended a bare stony lot, fenceless and rude,
where not a blade of grass would grow even in summer, the soil,
and many a foot more of the old earth, having been carted away
in grading the Avenue.

    The widow Dolman had six children, of whom Margaret, the
girl who had received at mass, was the eldest, and about seventeen.
Three more were of the same sex, with a good leap from Margaret
to the next sister, and the two boys were quite little.   They were a
bare-footed, ragged set, not over clean, with long uncombed hair
flying loose on the shoulders of the girls ; but all had good features,
though wild ; and Margaret was pretty ; her poor calico frock, and
the scant under-clothing which made it hang like a rag about her,
betrayed a rounded, healthy shape.   The shanty contained neither
table nor chairs, nor yet a bedstead.   The beds were miserably
huddled into a corner, and the younger children sat upon them.

To Miss De Groot they offered a trunk. Yet there was a cradle where the baby nestled, (a child under two years,) and with it the youngest girl, a poor little creature barely four, white as chalk with chronic dysentery. And yet this family, poor as they were, had taken in out of charity a woman poorer still, a common street beggar who sought cold victuals from door to door, and who with her child of seven, both in the unequivocal garb of beggary, with their mop hair and dirt-brown garments, the child's dark skin showing through her rags, cowered over their bag of broken meat in a corner of the shanty. The young visitor was shocked at the all but nakedness of the girls.

"How you must have suffered this cold weather! And you, Margaret, are hardly decent."

Margaret began to cry.

"And indeed, miss, I would keep meself dacent if I could."

"Och, and I must tell ye the thruth," said Mrs. Dolman, "Margaret has gone and pawned her petticoats (beggin' ye'r pardon for mentionin' them,) to pay for doctor's stuff for this one," pointing to the pallid little creature in the cradle. "And I've been tryin' to get some lady to take her sisters there, for it's too hard upon meself to fill so many mouths."

"How can you expect a lady to take such dirty little girls?" demanded Mary, with quickness. "Even if they must go in rags, and without petticoats, Mrs. Dolman, their faces might be washed and their hair combed."

"And indeed, miss, we've niver a comb lift, for we've been sellin' and pawnin' these three months, and I not able to get work. And it is of washin' ye were spakin'? Sure there's nothin' lift to hold water, barrin' the one mug, and the pot to boil the pratees in."

"And the pratees—you have enough of them at least?"

"Troth, miss, there's niver been the day yet but we've had some, let alone that we mightn't always have what we wanted. But thank God for not littin' us starve either with cowld or hunger."

21*

And how had they been reduced to these straits was what the
visitor wanted to know : for it seemed to her almost incredible
that such destitution existed. The thing began about six months
before, when the father was brought home on a shutter, killed by
the falling in of a bank :—an Irish laborer, honest, industrious, and
thoughtless; a trifle fond of the whiskey, and ready, under such
circumstances, for a row ; given to hearing mass outside the
church when he might as well have gone in, negligent about his
" duty," but chaste from infancy to manhood, and most happy in
having made his Easter only a fortnight before his unexpected
death. For the first three months after this bereavement they got
on pretty well, for Margaret had a place, and a good share of her
earnings went to support the shanty establishment. Mrs. Dolman
got some chores, and they trusted in God. Then Margaret, who
like her more favored visitor, was just budding into womanhood,
began to be tried. She did not mind the impertinence of the
young gentlemen in the family ; she told her mistress, who put a
stop to it, at least to what could not be endured. But to go to
mass on Sunday morning she staid at home all the Sunday after-
noons ;—the time that girls at service generally prefer going out,
for it is a time of visiting, walking with beaux, &c. Thus she
was left alone in the kitchen, and her master, feigning an excuse
for not accompanying his wife and daughters to church, used to
come down and attempt to corrupt the innocence of this young
maid-servant. He offered her money and presents of finery, such
as other girls of her rank wore, but which she could not afford,
(for he knew where the wages went,) and offered to clothe her
sisters and get them places, and all that ; while Margaret, as appeared from her own artless story, resisted in the most feminine
and gentle way, weeping, and representing to him the wickedness
of his conduct. Finally, after telling her story to Father Murphy
one Saturday afternoon, she left her place, giving so short notice
that her mistress refused her a character and kept back part of
her wages. Since then, she had been an inmate of the crowded
and dirty shanty, and a full sharer of its privations.

Our delicate Broadway promenaders will of course laugh at Mary De Groot for parting with one of her petticoats to Margaret on the spot, in a fervor of charity. The next thing was to get the poor girl's clothes out of pawn, and provide the whole family with the means of cleanliness at least. Mary's pocket money was nearly exhausted, when all was accomplished which she deemed absolutely necessary. To put the girls in such decent trim that they could reasonably hope for admission into proper families, seemed the wisest outlay she could make for them. The grateful Margaret accompanied the young lady home to receive some additional presents of cast-off clothing. Mrs. De Groot's carriage was at the door, it being the day and nearly the hour when Mary and her stepmother called on Mrs. Atherton. The astonished Irish girl followed her young benefactress to her apartment. Strange contrast to the board shanty, that marble hall and broad staircase; nor less the young lady's own room, with its rich old furniture, its bath-closet open, streams of hot and cold water steaming and dashing into the marble basin; the tall mahogany wardrobe agape, and the well-stocked, nicely-arranged drawers; the toilet's elegant apparatus displayed:—for Mary had to dress in haste, while Margaret Dolman, staring around, ate up her luncheon with an avidity painful to see.

CHAPTER VII.

OUR hero and his parents appeared punctually at five on Thursday, at the mansion in the Avenue.   A bright sea-coal fire illumined the innermost saloon, and the Rev. Dr. Fluent, whom they were invited to meet, was already there, sitting bolt upright on a sofa of silver brocade.   He was a gentleman of striking physiognomy and high-bred air, and his black, erect form, relieved against the throne-like seat he had taken, was quite imposing.   Mrs. Fluent was nooked with their hostess in the corner of another, a retiring woman, remarkably pretty withal, as your ministers' wives generally are, and no wonder, since the ministers, if at all popular, usually have their pick among the young lambs—we mean the young ladies—of their flocks.   At first there was no one else present, and the conversation ran very orthodoxly, the reverend doctor pretty much engrossing it.   He spoke *en passant*, but with unction, of a revival in which he had been engaged ; and Alban, who knew what revivals were, hardly listened, till the doctor diverged to a paper conflict into which he had been drawn with a high-church bishop, wherein, from his own account, confirmed by Mrs. De Groot, our hero would have supposed the former to have been completely victorious, and to have demolished for ever the figment of Apostolic Succession, if he had not that very morning heard the very contrary asserted by his cousins the Greys. Then the doctor spoke of Old School and New School, (or " Tweedledum and Tweedledee," as he termed them ;) of Low Calvinism and High Calvinism ; and of the Hopkinsian tenet once popular in New England, or that it was necessary to be willing to be damned for the glory of God, which he entirely exploded.   This led him to discuss a famous text of the Hopkinsians, which the doctor slipped through finely, by dint of grammar and rhetoric, and thence, to defend his position, his genius and his memory leading him on, plunged into an ocean of quotation, passage after passage heaving up *ore rotundo,* like waves breaking in foam. It was a novel exhibition to Alban, who was equally surprised and entertained.

The De Groots, however, had invited others. A Mr. Clinton came first—a retired merchant, with his fashionable wife and daughter, people of particularly easy manners, whose arrival entirely changed the tone of the conversation from religion to the chit-chat of the day. Next entered a Mr. Livingston Van Brugh (so announced) a tall, broad-shouldered young man of some five-and-twenty, appertaining to Mr. De Groot's own class, his father being a manorial proprietor on the Hudson. After him entered the patroon himself, who alone of all the manor-lords disputed Mr. Van Rensselaer's exclusive claim to that title, and, leaning on his arm, a friend—the Rev. Mr. Warens, minister of the Unitarian church, or chapel, in which Mr. De Groot was a pew-holder. Last of all glided in the daughter of the house, in virgin white, and a trifle pale.

Mary was saluted by Mrs. and Miss Clinton with a kiss on both cheeks ; to the remainder of the guests she made her wonted graceful obeisance, except Mr. Warens, to whom she went up, and shook him cordially by the hand as an old friend. White-haired Scip announced dinner, and the party filed off through the Vanderlyn cabinet into the dining-room.

An effective scene of domestic splendor presented itself to them as they entered. The table was round, lighted with branches of silver gilt, and in the centre an ancient salt-cellar of the same, terminating in a quaint, spreading flower-vase. The sconces on the walls were filled with lighted tapers, and the old Dutch pictures, the carved oak wainscot and chairs, the sparkling cupboard, the high and broad oak-shuttered window, the rich festive board, the soft abundant light, completed a picture rarely seen on this side the Atlantic. Nor were the guests unworthy of it, at least in outward appearance. Mr. Clinton, notwithstanding his aristocratic name, had been a poor boy and the architect of his own fortune ; but he had rather the air of an old noble gracefully decaying after a youth of splendid excess. It was the more remarkable, as he was not an American but a native of the Green Isle. His wife was a New Yorker, of a fashionable family— Grace church people : all the world knows what that signifies. Their daughter was highly distinguished, brilliantly fair, with a profusion of light brown ringlets, very fine teeth, and a delicate though sensual physiognomy. Next to Miss Clinton sat Van Brugh, who had a gentlemanlike countenance, a little marred by dissipation. Mr. Warens was short, thin, and dark, with a bald forehead and penetrating black eye, somewhat restless. The head of Alban's father had become grand and historical as he advanced in years ; but slight, pale, irregular in features and plainly attired as she was, nature and breeding had written *lady* on the face and mien of Mrs. Atherton, more unequivocally than on those of any other woman present. The time we have occupied in noting this would scarcely have sufficed for Dr. Fluent's eloquent grace, in which he thanked God for every thing but the dinner, and asked every blessing except a blessing on the food.

" The reverend gentleman must have forgot to say his prayers this morning by his taking this opportunity for it," whispered Mr. Clinton to Mary De Groot, while she took off her gloves.

" We must say grace for ourselves if we don't like what is said for us," replied the young lady.

" I observed you ' blessing' yourself. Is that anywhere a custom of Protestants ?"

" Blessing myself ? What is that ?"

" Making the sign of the cross. We call it so in Ireland."

" Oh, indeed !"

" You seem hungry, Miss Mary."—She had attacked her bread. " Be patient and your turn will come for soup."

" My fingers were restless, Mr. Clinton."

" No, I see real hunger sparkling in your eyes. The sharpness of famine is in your youthful face. You have been fasting. This is wrong. Even in the Roman Catholic Church boys and girls under age are not obliged, and generally not permitted, to fast."

· "What do you know about that ?"

"Living so long as I have, one picks up a deal of miscellaneous information."

We are thinking whether it would not be something in our way to describe the dinner, course by course, as was the method of the old romancers and poets, beginning with Homer. A first-rate Knickerbocker dinner is a peculiar, a national thing. We may pass over the inevitable fish and boiled, with a gentle reference to the oysters, which do not taste as if they had been stewed with an equal quantity of old ha'pennies, as oysters always do in Europe, (but we learned to like that coppery flavor,) and to those innocent apples of the earth (let us have refinement in phraseology before all things !) crumbling like pollen, white as lilies, and hot as—don't burn your mouth with them at least. But we can't help a sensation, however we may try to look calm, when that huge saddle of underdone wild venison appears, with a bright array of silver heaters to cook the slices on the table according to the taste of each several guest. This is our real dinner—a meal which London or Paris, or the ancient Baiæ, never knew—of which, and of some of the endless American legumes, our innocent and refined predilection, all partake : and we will not spoil it, although a course of small game tempts us not altogether in vain by the bounteous choice it offers—partridges from the mountains, grouse from the plains, canvass backs from the rivers, and flocks of nameless smaller birds. What Muse that neither soars too high nor sinks too low, shall aid us to present the delicacies of the dessert (general cisatlantic name for things separately classed abroad) so refreshing alike to the eye and the palate. Snowy ice creams—as glaciers descend to the border of flowery valleys—precede by a moment the rich tropical and native fruit and flowers intermingled, that finally stand, with the wines and colored glasses, on the polished black oaken table. The patroon though a philosopher, being also a true Knickerbocker, was proud of his wines. The choicest vintages of France and the Rhine made his cellars almost poetical, and he invited you to try some Madeira which had mellowed for a third of a century in his garret storeroom under the suns of American summers, with as high and fine a feeling of dignity, almost, as that with which he had received Alban in his magnificent library.

When the weather had been spoken of, and all had agreed that December had been a very cold month, but not so cold as the year previous, that we were now having the January thaw, but that we might expect something severe in February and March, Mrs. Clinton mentioned the new Opera House in Church-street, and as this topic was taken up rather timidly at first, owing perhaps to the presence of the reverend clergy, the conversation ran in a general, abstract way on the practicability of establishing this musical luxury in America.

" It can be introduced, but not yet," said Mr. Clinton, who was generally right.

" Never in this country," said Mr. Atherton, senior, with positiveness. " We don't want to pay so much money to hear Italian singing."

Mr. De Groot differed from his guest. " The opera," said he, " has produced some of the sublimest works of human genius. Without it a chasm would exist in the works of the imagination which ought not to exist there any more than in nature."

" The grander it is as a work of art, the more I object to it," said Dr. Fluent, looking round and sitting up. " Yes : for that but renders it of all theatrical amusements (which I condemn *in toto*) the most perfect masterpiece of sensual and secular seduction." Dr. Fluent rounded off his periods with an oratorical flourish. " With the opera," he continued, " is necessarily connected the ballet, and the defence so ingeniously set up for the one by our accomplished host, is equally applicable, *mutatis mutandis*, to the other. Without the ballet—the laws of beauty and rythmical expression applied to the movements of the human (and particularly of the female) body—" the doctor was somewhat too

scientific here for the ladies—"there would be a chasm in the
works of the imagination.   This is a *reductio ad absurdum ;* for
the immorality of the ballet, I hope, will be admitted."   The
reverend gentleman finished with a long quotation from a Latin
satirist that threw the few hackneyed phrases which he had already
from habit employed completely into the background.   He first
recited the original with great effect and then edified the company
with an elegant extempore paraphrase.   With all his pretension
and extravagance Dr. Fluent possessed a scholarship and taste that
carried him through.   The finest actor could not have done it better ; it told admirably ; and Mr. Clinton ironically applauded with
his two index fingers.

"I still must think the opera moral," said Mr. De Groot, with
a smile.   "I can never forget the effect of the Freischutz at Dres-
den, performed by Weber's own choir.   That opera, and Don
Giovanni, are as edifying to me as High Mass to a devout Catholic
like Mary, or one of Dr. Fluent's eloquent discourses to a pious
Presbyterian like her mother."

This caused some gentle laughter ; but Mrs. Atherton looked
shocked, and Mary De Groot blushed.   Miss Clinton turned quickly
to the latter, and leaning somewhat familiarly past Alban, who sat
between them, half-whispered "Is that true, Mary ?   Have you
become— ?   Well, I always thought you would, you know."

Miss Clinton's attention was principally occupied by her other
neighbor, Mr. Van Brugh, but she occasionally spared a soft question or two for Alban, looking into his dark blue eyes while he
responded, and if any thing was said that excited a general smile,
like Dr. Fluent's display, she generally bestowed hers sympatheti-
cally upon him, showing her double string of pearls set between a
pair of rose-leaved lips.   But now our hero found himself appealed
to most unexpectedly by his host.

"What is your opinion on this subject, Mr. President ?—I heard
at New Haven that your son's decisions," addressing Mr. Atherton
—"were famous in the Brothers'."

"Were you President of the Brothers in Unity ?" inquired Dr.

22

Fluent, with obvious deference. " Pray let us hear your decision. You have heard the argument on both sides."

" A decision from the President of the Brothers' Society !" said Mr. De Groot, in a low voice and looking round.

"Speak up, Mr. Alban," whispered Mary De Groot, addressing him almost for the first time.

" The question is the Italian Opera :—can it, and ought it, to be introduced in America ?" put in Mr. Warens, neatly.

" *Can* it ?" said Alban, plucking up courage, " has been answered by Mr. Clinton. I think we are Europeans still, after all. We have changed our sky but not our minds."

" Hear, hear !" said Mr. Clinton.

" Black Care behind the horseman sits," quoted Dr. Fluent, (he quoted it in Latin, however,) " and you think, Mr.—Pres-i-dent, that something blacker yet sits at the poop of ships bound from the old world, *novas quærere sedes.*" Dr. Fluent pronounced the Latin so distinctly that even the ladies fancied they understood it.

" I don't know," replied Alban. " I saw the Opera last night for the first time—"

" Did you ?" exclaimed his mother.

" And I certainly felt what Mr. De Groot has said so much better than I can, that it was one of the foreordained achievements of the imagination."

The patroon nodded approbation.

" But whether Christianity would not class such creations of genius among the pomps of this wicked world—"

" Well, I *thought*," said his mother, exchanging a glance of satisfaction with Mrs. De Groot.

" Is a question,"·continued Alban, " upon which I cannot be so presumptuous as to offer an opinion in the presence of the reverend clergy."—Bowing to Dr. Fluent and Mr. Warens.

" Very well done, Mr. Alban !" said Mary in a whisper, and with a smile of triumph.

" Alban dined with Seixas yesterday," observed Mr. Atherton, senior, by way of explanation.   "He invited you to go to the opera with him afterwards, I suppose."

"Exactly so, sir. And he told me what I was surprised to learn, that all the great operatic composers, as well as singers, were Jews."

"I had a dispute on that point with Seixas the other day," said Mr. Clinton. "I maintained that the greatest composers were Catholics in religion, and not even Jews by birth. I wonder if Mozart and Weber were Jews. And even —— and ——, the new composers, and the greatest of all, if they are Hebrews by origin, are Catholics in faith."

"Catholics or Jews—it amounts to the same thing, I suppose," observed Mr. Atherton, senior, with a look of humor.   "At least I never could see any difference."

Mr. Clinton reddened, and Mary De Groot opened her candid mouth in a half-scornful surprise ; but every body else smiled except Dr. Fluent, who seemed to think that some slight was intended to religion in general.   Miss Clinton, with the blended forwardness and tact of an American girl, turned the conversation to Mr. Seixas's liberal support of the Opera, which led to a discussion of his wealth.   Miss Clinton was enthusiastic on the subject of his beauty.   She thought he was the handsomest man in New York. Alban observed that Miss Seixas was very beautiful—a real Rebecca.

"What jewels she wears !" said Miss Clinton, turning to him. "If she were not a Jewess it would hardly be in good taste for a *demoiselle*—would it ?"—Miss Clinton herself was simple as a white rose, yet one of her taper indexes sparkled with a little hoop of brilliants.   "And Mrs. Seixas ! since the last *bal* we were at at the Tuileries, I have seen nothing to compare with her stomacher."

"I have not seen Mrs. Seixas yet," said Alban.

When Miss Clinton turned again to her other supporter, Mary addressed Alban in a slight tone of pique.

"So you have found some Jewish friends ?"

"Very interesting ones."

" I have found some Catholic friends who interest me.   One is a young girl—about my age—who possesses finer jewels than Miss Seixas, I dare say."

" You mean virtues ?"

" Yes, humility, resignation, devotion, purity, charity, self-denying love, and unspotted chastity," said Miss De Groot, with a slight flush and speaking quick.

" The last," replied Alban innocently, " is a virtue, as Mr. Seixas told me, which is most conspicuous in Jewish females. Their notions of delicacy, he says, are strict to a degree unknown among Christians, and as for a Jewish lady's slipping, it is unheard-of.   I did not quite appreciate his remark," continued Alban, " for I told him I thought *all* ladies naturally detested every thing of that sort.   With rare exceptions, of course, like your friend—"

Miss De Groot turned to him quickly and pressed his arm, although Alban had unconsciously lowered his voice.

" Hush !" she whispered.

Mr. Clinton, listening, smiled.

" It is very true, Mr. Alban," said Mary gravely, and yet with a glance almost of tenderness.   " In us—as in Jewesses—it is a virtue in the natural order, but in Catholics it is a grace."

" You are a zealous convert," replied Alban, while Mr. Clinton listened with a peculiar look.

" My poor Margaret Dolman," she continued, " is nothing but an Irish servant girl—careless and slipshod as any you will meet ; no one has ever taught her how to be otherwise ;—but such whiteness of soul !   *I* could not have acted as she did.   I could not have united such meekness under insult with such firmness in not doing the slightest wrong.   *My* virtue would have been half pride, but *hers* was supported by the single fear of offending her Creator :— 'You know, miss,' she said, 'it would be better to die a thousand deaths than offend Almighty God once !'   What a beautiful motive, and so holy !   It could never fail, but pride might, as I have often feared, Mr. Alban, and Alexandrine used to warn me."

Mary raised her voice a little in uttering the concluding sentence, and Miss Clinton gave a start. Mr. Clinton fell into so deep a revery that he forgot to rise when the ladies left the table.

Cigars, and wreaths of smoke curling among the candles! Livingston Van Brugh was now at home. He asked for some brandy and water. Old Scip brought in a boiling tea-kettle and a silver punch-bowl. All smoked except our hero and Mr. Warens. The latter drew up to Alban and asked about New Haven. He was evidently surprised to meet a young man of untrammelled mind from the orthodox university. Mr. Warens spoke of the want of moral culture among the orthodox.

"They substitute for it," observed Alban, "the spasmodic stimulus of revivals. A young New Englander, instead of regarding the whole of life as a continuous probation, from the dawn of reason to the grave, considers that all depends on being truly converted once. Hence, before conversion, he makes no conscience of his actions, for he is not a Christian. After it, he is careless of committing private sins, provided he can retain the belief that his conversion is genuine. If this proves too difficult, the remedy is to give up the old hope and get another. A fresh delusion thus succeeds, and so on, till shame forbids the repetition of the process, or a hardened insensibility is content to dispense with it."

Dr. Fluent had pricked up his ears at this conversation, and now regarded the wainscoted walls with a wild stern look.

"These are the majority," said Mr. Warens, laughing at Alban's picture. "But all are not such."

"Oh, there are good people among us," said Alban,—"a sort of spoiled angels! They disdain, you know, to do good works to merit heaven, which they consider already secured to them by God's special favor; but they will do something for the Almighty in return, purely out of gratitude. It is impossible to give an idea of the intense spiritual pride fostered by such a system."

"You must get acquainted with liberal Christianity," said Mr. Warens.

"How can revealed religion be liberal?" replied Alban, thoughtfully. "If you deny the faith in one point you cannot be saved."

"That is Roman Catholicism."

"And Judaism. What religion was ever more intolerant than that of Moses? A liberal Judaism was punished with death."

"Christ has done away with that."

"Yes! the alternative HE offered was faith or damnation."

"You ought to be a Roman Catholic," repeated Mr. Warens, with a slight asperity, while Dr. Fluent, with his massive chin in the air, smiled grimly at the carved Bacchantes of the wainscoting.

"Or a Jewish proselyte of the gate," said Alban.

"Then you do not accept Christianity at all," returned Mr. Warens, stiffly.

"I believe God spoke by Moses," said Alban, "because the existence of the Jews at this day proves it. I know what Judaism is, and my heart bows before a system of morals evidently divine. 'The Law of the Lord is perfect, converting the soul; the commandment of the Lord is pure, enlightening the eyes,'" added Alban, with a certain fervor. "Let Christianity present me similar credentials. Let it show me a people—a polity—built upon it, and witnessing to it, and gifted with like permanence. Let its doctrine seem worthy of God and wholesome for man. Let some one at least tell me what that doctrine is, for after all my inquiries I am still in the dark on that point."

Mr. Clinton had been puffing out volumes of smoke from his nostrils (for he inhaled the weed) and apparently not listening. He broke in with unexpected effect.

"You want a people—a polity, Mr. Atherton,"—Mr. Clinton spoke with a rich, unusual brogue, from which he was generally quite free—"a polity built on Christianity, or rather built by its Founder, sir, to bear witness to it, and existing immutably, like the Jews, in spite of all changes. Sir, the Catholic Church is such a polity. She can tell you, sir, what Christianity is, and you will find it worthy of God and wholesome for man. You are nearer faith, Mr. Atherton, than either of these learned divines. I declare it is strange to see a man in a fog, seeking for what is close at his hand.   Any poor Irish servant girl who knows her catechism could teach you more about Christianity, gentlemen, in five minutes, than you have all learned in your great universities in all your lives."

This outburst was received in silent astonishment, not less than if Mr. Clinton had suddenly given signs of lunacy.   Meanwhile the apparent, because louder, stream of conversation had run in a political channel, whither, by an abrupt defection of Mr. Warens, the whole current now flowed.   Nullification, the great speeches of Webster, the policy of Clay, the craft of Van Buren, the rude but patriotic energy of Jackson, were successively discussed.   Alban listened in a fever of ambition, and was sorry when Scip brought a message from the ladies that the gentlemen would please come and take some coffee.

CHAPTER VIII.

In the drawing-room the ladies had divided into pairs. Mrs. De Groot took Mrs. Atherton into a corner to tell her (she could keep it no longer) the story of her stepdaughter's sad perversion, to which Alban's mother listened with astonishment, and considerable alarm for her unsettled son. She felt that so eccentric a pair of young people had better have as little intercourse as possible, and when Mrs. De Groot, fearing that Mrs. Atherton might be alarmed for Alban, proceeded to say how much she hoped from his pious influence over Mary, Mrs. Atherton thought herself obliged to let Mrs. De Groot know how much she was mistaken. It was now Mrs. De Groot's turn to be astonished, and to perceive, moreover, that she had been regularly *sold* by her husband in this transaction, having been allowed to suppose that Mary was attached to a pious and orthodox young collegian, when all the while it was an audacious speculator like Mr. De Groot himself— " one of his own kidney"—as she somewhat hastily expressed herself,—an infidel, a moralist, and perhaps a Jew ! Mary, too, had deceived her, like a Roman Catholic as she was. In her agitation Mrs. De Groot nearly suffocated, being, as we have said, inclined to flesh, and tightly laced. Meanwhile the easy Mrs. Clinton entertained Mrs. Fluent (who was naturally an accomplished listener) with an account of the splendors of their last winter in Paris ; and Paris was the theme on which Miss Clinton expatiated with Mary De Groot.

Miss Clinton, whose companion listened with a singular smile, and made half-sarcastic replies, could tell of balls, operas, and carriage-promenades in the Bois de Boulogne, and of the court at the Tuileries. She was enthusiastic about the young French princes, and had danced with the Duc de Nemours. She thought American society so unexciting—no dukes and duchesses, no princes and courts. Mary ought to go abroad. With her beauty and fortune, and aristocratic position, she would have the *entrée* everywhere, and might marry a duke.

"Thank you," said Mary, with a flash of that pride of provincial noblesse of which she was very sensible; "the duke who marries me will have to come to the Manor to woo me. I shan't cross the water for a husband, I promise you."

"Your being a Catholic would add to your currency in the high French circles," observed Miss Clinton, after answering a question of Mary's respecting the churches in Paris.

"I wonder you didn't become a Catholic, Henrietta!"

The gentlemen approached from the Vanderlyn room where the Ariadne was now unveiled, the ladies having been looking at the pictures. Mr. Warens and Mary's father threw themselves on a sofa together to take their coffee.

"How do you like the youth, Warens?"

"A brilliant fellow, but eccentric. Says he's a Jew."

"Ha, ha! Better a Jew than a Papist. The Jews are Unitarians, Warens."

"And Romanists are Christians. I am sorry to see you so bitter."

"Look at those girls, Warens, with Van Brugh and young Atherton doing the agreeable to both. Do you see how Henrietta Clinton's eyes turn sparkling from one to the other? What a sympathetic smile! Livingston, you see, is a trifle too familiar —he has taken punch enough to stir his Dutch blood—and she laughs and edges off from him. How quiet, on the contrary, is Mary De Groot. She has color since dinner, but her eyes are fastened on the magnificent head of old Atherton as he bends over that table of miniatures."

"Like the virtuous Moabitess, she follows not young men, whether poor or rich."

"I would rather," said Mr. De Groot, with irritation, "see her voluptuously flirting like Henrietta Clinton, than hiding filial disloyalty under that modest show."

"You shock me."

"I have had experience. The moment your wife or daughter embraces this religion—adieu to confidence! I adored her mother, who was purity itself. When we were first wedded I could with difficulty make her undefiled fancy comprehend my rights. In twenty maiden years her thoughts had never strayed, although I received her not from the cloister where she was educated, but from the midst of a court. And yet the thought was ever between us, that unless I adopted her faith, I was the future companion of devils—the food of Hell, body and soul!"—Mr. De Groot frowned terribly. "Is it nothing to me that my daughter adopts these dogmas?"

Mr. Warens soon after quitted his friend and drew Mary aside. She blushed a good deal while he talked to her, answered with animation, and when he left her, dashed away a tear, Van Brugh and Miss Clinton being now at the piano, she joined Alban again.

"Are you really going to turn Jew?" she asked, with vexation.

"The Jews do not admit proselytes now," replied he, smiling. "Nevertheless, I am going to the Synagogue on Saturday to witness the ancient worship."

"On Saturday! to the Synagogue!" said Mary.

"Will you go? Females, you know, sit in a gallery by themselves, but I will introduce you to Miss Seixas."

"*I* go to the Synagogue on Saturday!" exclaimed Mary.

"I remember—it is your anniversary."

"If I engage to go, you will say nothing to any one of my intention?"

"It shall be a profound secret."

"Will you come for me in a carriage?"

"Of course. It is going to be quite a mysterious adventure."

"At such an hour as I shall designate?" she continued. "On your honor?"

"Command me, Lady Mary," said Alban, gallantly bending, as if to kiss her fingers. "The Synagogue service lasts from eight to twelve."

"I will let you know what hour will suit me when I know it myself. I count upon you on Saturday, remember."

"You may do so with confidence," said Alban, gravely and significantly.

And now by twos and threes, white-necked young ladies and white-waistcoated, or at least white-gloved young gentlemen dropped in. A rattling fire of small talk ran along the intricate battle line of silken seats. The piano, which had merely motived a desperate flirtation between Van Brugh and Miss Clinton, awoke into life. There was a heavy cannonade of instrumentation, and a brilliant charge or so of songs. Some of the newcomers clustered round the beautiful daughter of the house, whose return home seemed the occasion of this reunion, others swarmed round the piano and music-racks, ferreting out the most approved pieces. These were not the charming negro melodies since so popular, nor the noble German airs, but some Italian opera-bits, Mrs. Hemans' romantic ballads, "The Sea," "The night was dark," and other old favorites now forgotten. Accustomed to a society with a deal more whalebone in it, Alban was equally surprised and gratified by the facility with which he got acquainted with Mary De Groot's friends. A most unusual sympathy and mutual kindness appeared to exist between these young people, as well as a spirit of frank enjoyment which he had not elsewhere observed. In the surnames of those to whom he was introduced, he perceived one cause of this difference. It was a set of Stuyvesants and Brevoorts, Gansevoorts and Van Rensselaers, Van Brughs and Livingstons, De Witts and De Lanceys. As the evening advanced a marked disposition to romp developed itself in this very well-dressed but very inartificial circle. Dancing, which they tried first, did not appear sufficient for their spirits. Different plays were proposed. Mary De Groot objected to several, and finally blind-man's-buff was carried by acclamation.

"Oh, really!" said Alban, "are these grown-up young ladies and gentlemen going to play blind-man's-buff in your father's beautiful rooms?"

"As sure as fate," replied Mary, laughing and spinning away from him in a dancing step, with her drapery spread and whirling around her.

In short, they were soon all racing through the saloons like children, dodging behind chairs and tables, springing over divans, hiding in corners. There was much laughter, now and then a scream, and the young gentlemen who were blindfolded handled the young ladies when they caught them, rather freely. Alban could not help suspecting that this was half the charm of so rude a game. Van Brugh really carried it quite too far, particularly with Henrietta Clinton, who was several times caught. The last time she caught Alban. He was so modest that he would never have detected those who suffered themselves to be apprehended, particularly as he was not yet well acquainted, and he invariably called the names wrong, amid bursts of laughter. He began to feel annoyed. He had observed that Mary, while she entered into the amusement with spirit, running like a little deer, and perfectly wild with fun, always contrived, in whatever position her sportive fancy involved her, to escape without being caught. Livingston, with one eye (as all believed) unblinded, pursued her once with pertinacity, but he might as well have chased a ray of light. Now our hero had perceived some one hovering near himself, evidently of the long-robed sex, who evaded his pursuit with a similar dexterity. At last she stood on the opposite side of a gigantic vase; they went round it once or twice; suddenly, whether accidentally or purposely, her hand rested on his, and with a quick motion he caught it. There was a laugh. He drew her into the middle of the room. Was it Mary or was it not? The manner of play was like her, but would Mary have touched his hand? He could have decided the question in a trice by feeling her temples, for no other girl present had the hair similarly arranged. It was a liberty (not to speak of others) which the young men had taken with their prizes without ceremony. While he stood considering, the hand at first passively resigned in his, made a slight effort to withdraw itself.

" It is Mary De Groot.

The young lady removed the bandage from his eyes amid a general silence. All the youths and maidens were gathered in a close circle round them, looking over each others' shoulders. Then they all laughed, and the young ladies demanded, " How did you know ?"—others exclaimed, " You saw !" and one, " There's some freemasonry here !" Henrietta Clinton said, " It is magnetism." But Alban, tying the handkerchief over Mary De Groot's eyes, said, " There are moral as well as physical signs of individuality." Mary said nothing, and darting off, in a minute or two had caught and named quite a little girl—the youngest of the party, whose eager flight and vexation at being captured were extremely amusing.

The company were gone. The father and daughter were alone in the library. The walls piled with bookcases, and the gloomy circling gallery frowned around them. Mr. De Groot placed himself in his study-chair and motioned Mary to her stool. The fire was expiring in the grate, and a solitary burner in a chandelier of Berlin iron, which represented a mass of shields, swords, spears, and other weapons, offensive and defensive, cast a cold light upon her virgin drapery. The meaning of this was that her father had first observed her abstinences, then suspected that she went to mass, next had watched to see, and that morning from his window had perceived her exit, (being too late to prevent it) observing her come out of the side-door, join her humble friends under the street-lamp, and hie away.

" You are treacherous, ungrateful, and unfilial," said her father, after stating these circumstances. " After all my indulgence— my readiness to gratify your least whim ! You asked to come home that you might learn, forsooth, to fulfil your duty as a daughter, and the first thing in which you are detected is stealing away before light to attend the mummeries of the mass, disapproved and detested by both your parents. I can characterize such conduct but by one word—hypocrisy ! It is of a piece, indeed, with the maxims of Romanists."

"I am no hypocrite, papa," replied Mary. "You knew that I had embraced the religion of my mother, and you might infer that I would practise it."

"You have embraced a religion! A chit of sixteen! a child just out of school, and taken out too soon. Your religion is to listen to the advice of your living parents and to obey their commands," said her father, with some violence.

"I am sixteen and six months," replied Mary, "and Sister Theresa says that St. Catherine and St. Agnes were only thirteen when they were martyred. Father Smith says the Church has decided that when children are old enough to have faith, they are bound to embrace the true religion whether their parents consent to it or not. It is plain, papa, that I have a right to be baptized," she continued, with a bright and sparkling courage; "and to whom shall I apply for baptism? Not to mamma's pastor, surely: he would not baptize me, because he would say I had never been converted. Not to Mr. Warens, certainly, since he does not believe in the Trinity. Oh, I must go to the Church, of course—there is no other way for me. And *soon*, papa,—or else I may die, young as I am, and lose Heaven. And *secretly*, papa,"—with increasing spirit,—"for you know you would try to prevent it, and why should you and I have a fight about that?"

Mr. De Groot stared at her with mingled astonishment and wrath. He grew almost livid, so that Mary began to be frightened. He started up and seized her wrist. His lip was flecked with a slight foam.

"You defy me, do you? What hinders me, insolent girl, from inflicting the summary chastisement such language to your father merits?"

Mary now held her tongue. Courageous as she was, she quailed. Physical pain and fear subdued her partly, and partly the moral agony of incurring what is intolerable to a woman's feelings, particularly to one who had never, even in childhood, known what it was to be so much as threatened with corporeal punishment. Her spirit rose again with a rebound.

"It is the first time, papa, you have ever threatened to whip me—now that I am a woman!"

He flung her arm from him as by a violent effort at self-control, and resumed his seat. She glanced at her empurpled wrist. This violence was strangely contrasted with her graceful mien in her party dress, a white rose at her bosom, and buds of the same with rich green leaves, in her raven hair. Haply this modest elegance pled for her. Reproaches are sometimes excuses in disguise.

"Your conduct, Mary, whatever you may think, is a treason to that love which once bound us together as father and only child. You have wounded me in the tenderest point—robbed me of the hope of years. From the daughter and friend you have voluntarily sunk into a slave, doing things by stealth, abusing confidence reposed in you. You can no longer be trusted. Generous, delicate treatment is become inapplicable to you. Harshness, strict surveillance, and physical restraint must take their place."

"Papa, you wrong me indeed," replied his daughter, in a heart-broken tone. "Last fall you refused to let me be baptized by Mr. Warens. I thought it was a shame for such a great girl to be unbaptized, but I submitted. Now I *must* receive baptism. I believe it to be necessary to salvation. I may die very soon. I have some reason to think that the day of my death is at hand."

"What stuff!" said her father.

"Nay, sir, hear my reasons," continued Mary. "They may be silly, but you shall not accuse me any more of want of openness."

She told the story of her dream plainly and without a blush.

"And to whom do you expect to be married next Saturday?" demanded her father.

"I leave that to Heaven, and you, sir. It matters little, if I am to die immediately afterwards," replied Mary, innocently.

"I am to conclude, then, that in anticipation of dying next Saturday you have been baptized? or is that still future?"

"Nay, papa, I am not so weak as to be governed in my conduct by a dream. You may be sure I have not, when I tell you that Saturday has been appointed for my baptism, and that I would not yield to a superstitious feeling so far as to ask for an earlier day."

These ingenuous avowals had not the effect which might have been expected. Mr. De Groot surveyed his daughter with a look of stone. What he said partook, nevertheless, of his characteristic composure, though broken by more than one sudden burst of almost inexplicable passion.

"When you were born at the Manor," said he, "there was no Romish priest to be had short of New York. Your mother, though the least ailment incident to infancy excited her anxiety for your salvation, was willing to postpone the great remedy for the guilt you had incurred by being born, until it could be administered with all the ceremonies. From your birth till her death I resided constantly at the Manor for this very reason. Once a year a priest came up that she might fulfil the obligations of her religion, and then I had to undergo a species of martyrdom to prevent your being subjected to this magical rite which was to make your Maker cease hating you. I was determined to allow no incantations over my innocent child! I had to tell your mother," said Mr. De Groot, with vehemence, "that a priest should never cross my threshold, for such a purpose, unless over my dead body." He rose and repeated it, as if the words called up the scene, and looking at Mary as if she were his departed wife, struck his hand violently upon the table, saying again,—" never—unless over my dead body!" He was white as a sheet, and stared as if he saw a ghost. Again he struck the table violently. "Never shall a popish priest enter my house for such a purpose—unless over my dead BODY!"

"Papa!" said Mary.

He looked at her wildly, and sat down again, glaring still; his hand trembling and clenching itself. He passed it through his hair and resumed.

"When she was dying I had a priest sent for, to save her from the horror of leaving the world without the sacraments—a horror which caused me horror. At that time I had a last contest with her on this point. She said—but no matter for that! Do you think that after having been deaf to her entreaties and wild, absurd threats, under such circumstances, I shall yield now to your wilful fantasies ? Do you think it ?" said her father, rising again, and glaring at her. He resumed his seat. " I shall take care of you for a few days, as I would if you were out of your senses. You fancy something supernatural has occurred to you ! At your time of life girls are subject to these illusions. I shall contrive it so that you get over next Saturday without either wedlock, or burial, or baptism. After that I will talk to you again. Be sure that I shall not permit you, at your inexperienced age, to be inveigled"— Mr. De Groot again (apparently because he could not help it) struck the table forcibly with his hand—" *inveigled* by the arts of Romish priests or nuns, into committing yourself to a system of vile trumpery and imposture"—again his manner became violent—" of vile trumpery and imposture. Entice a girl of sixteen—without the knowledge of her parents—to throw herself into their detested sect ! A young lady of fortune—an heiress ! Never was any thing more base. But they will find in me an older and more determined opponent than they dream of."

A chasm had suddenly gaped at the daughter's feet ! In the father she still loved next to God, what new revelation of insane violence and hate ! what a drear change in their mutual relations —drear and scarce credible ! As soon as Mary really understood it, she behaved in a quite feminine and filial way, threw herself at once at her father's feet and implored his forgiveness, if she had forgotten the respect she owed him. He bade her rise, and desired her to go to her room, accepting with coldness her kiss of good-night.

In the hall Mary paused a moment, hesitating whether even yet she ought not to return and humiliate herself still more, but she glanced at the arm which bore the mark of her father's fingers, and catching up her robe with feminine spirit, flew up to her own apartment. Here the crucifix recalled her quickly to humble and patient thoughts. Her humiliations, however, were not ended. While she was yet kneeling at her mother's *prie-dieu*, praying and meditating on the silent sufferings of the Lamb of God, her stepmother entered unbidden. Our heroine's rapt expression, her large dark eyes fastened on the crucifix, her lips just moving, the beads dropping between her slightly clasped fingers, were a picture of devotion, which, unconscious as it was, excited the instinctive disgust of Mrs. De Groot. Had any convenient weapon of destruction been at hand she would have dashed in pieces the image which appeared to her the object of this worship, in a transport of iconoclastic rage. "Idolatress!" was the only word she could at first utter. Mary rose, a little astonished at this new style, and crossing her hands meekly on her breast, listened in silence to such a reproof as the indulged child had never received before. Finally Mrs. De Groot directed her daughter in a severe tone to read before retiring, the eleventh chapter of Hebrews, and withdrew, locking the young lady in. The philosophy of sixteen could not repress some tears, but it was some consolation obediently to read the chapter assigned her, where she learned that the Patriarch Jacob when dying, prescient of the wood of the cross on which the World's Salvation was to hang, "adored the top of his rod."

CHAPTER IX.

An Irish girl came out of the garden gate of the great house with a bonnetless head and a pail of dirty water. Another girl was passing and repassing, and watching from a distance. The latter drew near, and the two recognized each other.—"What, Ann Murphy ! is that you ?"—"The Lord save you ! is it Margaret Dolman ?"—so they stopped and chatted.

"And sure it was a dreadful sin to keep Miss from bein' a Christian," said Ann. "And there's Catharine—that's the chambermaid—she towld us this morning that Miss was locked up, and there was a talk among the servants that she was wantin' to run away with a young gintleman that was here to see her the day after she came home—a young college gintleman he was— but niver a sowl of us suspicted it was because Miss was going to be a Catholic like her mother. And sure this very morning when I set her room to rights, the cross and beads was gone. And it's no wonder Miss looked as if she'd niver a friend lift in the worrld."

"I don't believe she'd be for mindin' any thing at all, if she was only baptized," said Margaret. "And to-morrow morning it was to be. Pity it was not yesterday, and the divil himsilf couldn't help it now."

"Troth, but its cruel. To think there'd be such heathens," replied Ann. "And I would have me clothes torn off me back for Miss Mary any day, but what can *I* do, Margaret dear ?"

Here a loud cry of " Ann ! Ann !" from the kitchen windows, separated the two girls in haste.

We have mentioned that Alban called upon his cousin Greys. This he did in all his vacations. They lived in a sort of clerical street near old King's College—such a street as nowhere exists in New York now. Low half-blinds softened the light in the southern parlor and excluded the gaze of passers-by. The walls were

hung with prints of British battles, encircled at this festive season
with rich green wreaths. The Greys were kind to Alban, and a
good deal pleasanter than his Presbyterian friends in his then turn
of mind. They were great laughers. They laughed about Pres-
byterianism, and prophesied that he would be a Churchman.
They advised him, laughingly, to attend Wednesday and Friday
prayers. It impressed him so favorably, that the next morning, at
eleven o'clock, he sauntered into St. Paul's chapel.

A few High Church old ladies, mostly in weeds, one elderly
gentleman, a young man looking forward to the Episcopal ministry, who responded very loud, and the sexton, whose loud parish-
clerk tone was heard in the gallery, constituted with our hero the
congregation. The small number present scarcely diminished the
impressiveness of the service, and rendered it perhaps more soothing. The fine old chapel, with its beautiful Corinthian columns
and nobly recessed chancel, the numerous mural tablets, the high
pews, the lofty white pile of the reading-desk, pulpit, and sounding
board, all handsomely carved, contributed to the effect. The peculiar, deliberate sing-song of the rector, whose locks were already
prematurely sprinkled with gray, his quiet, yet interested air in
going through the service, and even the soft, regular, impressive
gesture of his hand, that reposed on the cushion of the desk in
reading the lessons, were singularly in harmony with all the rest.

"We have here," thought Alban, "a venerable Church, a beautiful Liturgy, decorous forms, a sober piety, equally removed from
the extravagances of Puritanism and the superstitions of Rome.
I like this notion of a week-day service. Even if ill-attended, it
is an impressive witness to the duty of worship; and to the few
who gather here, how consoling!"

At that period Morning Prayer was read in Trinity, and its
two chapels, on Litany days, at the hour which we have already
mentioned. This was all the week-day service of a regular kind
in about twelve large city parishes of the Episcopal Church. This,
however, was an inestimable consolation, as Alban observed, to
those who knew how to appreciate it. The mutual reciting of

psalms, the reading of Scripture lessons, the beautiful suffrages of the Litany, made an hour of ancient calm in the vulgar hurry and noise of the commercial emporium. Since '35, there has been a great development in the Episcopal Church, in the way of week-day services. We find by the Churchman of the present date that seven churches of that denomination in the city of New York have daily Morning-Prayer, and four of these the Evening service also. In one there is a weekly celebration of the Lord's Supper. This may seem little, considering that the whole number of their churches in the city is between thirty and forty, and of clergy about seventy, but still it is an increase. The week-day congregations also are larger than they used to be in the old times, and we are sorry to add (for this thing ought to be encouraged) that for some two or three years the movement has been stationary.

It is hardly fair to Episcopalians, but to excite them to emulation, we may compare with this the week-day worship of the Catholics in the same city. In '35 there were but four Catholic churches, but two masses, at least, were said daily in each, eight or nine in all, or one-third (perhaps one-half) more services in a *day* than the thrice as numerous and vastly richer Episcopal congregations sustained in a *week*. We have not yet overtaken our friends in the number of churches or of clergy. Of the former there are only nineteen in New York, and four convent chapels; but the number of daily masses in this city cannot be less than fifty, at a considerable majority of which, if our observation holds, there are communions. On Sundays and Festivals the communions are large; on ordinary days, of course, they are smaller. Sometimes you will see one poor laborer go up to the altar, or a single poor woman. Some—particularly servants, who cannot go out at an early hour—communicate on Sundays at High mass, although it obliges them to be fasting till past noon. But be it one or more, rich or poor, High mass or low, the rite is suspended, the white linen is turned over the rail, the confession is said, the tabernacle is opened, and the people kneel. The things that are said are said softly, although they are so beautiful that in a Protestant Church they would be proclaimed as with a trumpet. He comes and departs almost in silence, as of old :—*He shall come down like rain upon the fleece, and as showers falling gently upon the earth.* Who thinks of that unfailing early, and that latter, rain which descends on the mountains of Israel ? Who thinks of the fragrance that ascends unceasingly from its humble valleys ?

If Alban had thought of it at all, he would have deemed the murmur of the mass a blank and little edifying substitute for the intelligible Common Prayer. But *Moses hath in every city them that preach him, being read in the synagogues every Sabbath day.* As Mary told him, what doth it avail to read or hear the word written, while the veil is on your heart ?

Our hero came out of St. Paul's into the thronged Broadway. Sights of this world assail him : a theatre, a museum, a Hotel de Ville, and "stores" without end : hat-stores, dry-goods-stores, book-stores, any kind of store you like ! On the sidewalks are ladies in silken walking-dresses and gay winter-bonnets, rich shawls and splendid cloaks—the gayest promenade in civilization. They are shopping—shopping in the Broadway stores. It ought to be " storing," or else the stores should be shops. Omnibuses, there are not many yet, but carriages and cabs not a few. A line of handsome ones extends along the north side of St. Paul's : in London you would suppose they were private equipages. Then in front of the church, under the protecting image of the great Apostle in the pediment of the portico, are ranged the contradictions (in terms) of which Miss Sedgwick took notice—the Catholic orangemen with their rich brogue and baskets of golden fruit. These are things which have passed away already, *i. e.*, the cabs and the orangemen : for a few years on this side of the Atlantic, make antiquity and give us a right to remember. But we dilly-dally here in Broadway, among the free and loitering crowd, whilst Mary De Groot is a prisoner in her father's freestone palace : she whose graceful step has made this vulgar flagging poetical. Not a square inch on these sidewalks but may have been pressed by her light foot; not a stone on that half-dry crossing on which she may not have stepped. Even Alban, with conscious thoughts of a very different kind about others, so far worshipped his beautiful and innocent mistress as to feel thus about the places where she had been.

An elegant chariot stopped before Marquand's as Alban approached that famous shop, and two ladies got out. One of them arrested her tripping step, and saluted him. It was Miss Clinton.

"Are you buying jewelry this morning?"

"Merely going to have a cameo set. Come in and look at it, Mr. Atherton. It is one I bought in Rome."

Alban went into the jeweller's accordingly: Miss Clinton produced the cameo, which was large, classic, and admirably cut after an ancient terra-cotta. The subject was the Flight of Helen. The lovers were in a Greek chariot drawn by four spirited steeds. Paris was driving, nude; Helen, graciously draped.

"It is exceedingly admired," said Miss Clinton.

Our hero admired it, although he thought it required some hardihood for a young lady to wear it on her bosom. Miss Clinton told him that her father was going to build on the Avenue, on the square next to Mr. De Groot. Mrs. Clinton invited him to visit them in Broadway, and after some further chat, at the instance of the young lady he promised to call that very evening. Having handed them into their carriage again, giving his circle cloak a cavalier sweep, he pursued his walk towards State-street. As he went along, he drew a comparison between the young lady he had just left and his friend Miss Ellsworth, and this brought to mind his conversation with Mary De Groot on the Sound, and the story of her school-days, which again, by an association of ideas, recalled Henrietta Clinton. In such a revery, he arrived at Mr. Seixas' door, and after feeling for a moment that he had a right to enter here without notice, rang the bell, and the sound of a piano and female voice, which he had previously heard, immediately ceased.

Miriam Seixas rose from the instrument at his entrance, and

saluted him with grace. She motioned him to the yellow divan, and, after ringing the bell, took a seat opposite him upon an ottoman. A moment after, a maiden of inferior aspect, but neatly attired, entered the room, and placed herself in a corner where she remained, silent, and almost unnoticed, during Alban's stay.

Notwithstanding this etiquette, Miss Seixas was full of affability. She was even a voluble talker. She was a musical enthusiast. The opera was her chief passion, nor did she scorn the ballet. She was a proficient in both arts. She sang for Alban some beautiful Spanish songs; she danced Spanish and Moorish dances for his amusement in the most obliging manner. Nothing more oriental, even in a New York drawing-room, than Miriam Seixas with the castanets. The virginal freedom of her movements partook of the heroic, revealing her noble figure in outlines so grand and flowing as to blend rather with feelings of religious awe or patriotic ardor than of voluptuousness. She might have danced with her ancestress and namesake on the sands of the Red Sea, or in the procession of the virgins of Zion, before the triumphant returning Ark.

Nor was she without serious thoughts, such as were not unworthy of her origin, and her frankness was unlike any thing he had known. She told Alban that there were children of the Most High (blessed be He) among all nations, and in every faith which acknowledged His unity, but Israel, though degraded and despised, was his chosen people. She herself was not without hope of being at least the ancestress of Messiah, and would deem it a misfortune, if not a reproach, to die unmarried or childless. She was espoused to her cousin, a Hebrew of pure blood, whom she had not seen since she was twelve years old. Alban had got upon this ground by asking Miss Seixas if she would be courteous on the morrow to a young Christian lady whom he was to bring with him to witness the synagogue worship. Miriam readily promised to pay her every attention. The young Jewess spoke English with perfect purity, but with a foreign accent.

"It is a high order of character," thought Alban, returning home, " but peculiar."

There was a naïve earthliness about the beautiful Miriam that reminded our hero of the old Greek spirit. She seemed not to look beyond the grave. Her idea of her own sex partook of the ancient depreciating estimate. She was the handmaid of man, and aspired to no higher destiny than that which nature had written in such exquisite characters on her very form. The chastity which breathed like a natural fragrance in all the language and manners of the young Jewess seemed to Alban quite different from the same quality in the purest Christian maidens whom he had known. It was not the pride which in his Puritan kinswomen scorned to defile an imagined sanctity ; still less the humble vigilance with which Mary De Groot watched over what she seemed to regard as a sacred, though scarce understood, deposit intrusted to her care ; but simply the native reserve of her sex, which the culture of a law extending to the minutest points of female conduct had developed into a moral habit. Her openness again was different from Mary's, being a matter of familiarity, while the latter's sprang from ignorance : for Mary's child-like candor (it required little penetration to see) arose from her comprehending, indeed very well, what was the virtue which she practised, but not having the least idea wherein consisted the vice which she abhorred. Thus our hero felt that something was wanting—a trait of spiritual beauty—in what was else so worthy of admiration. Alban could not divest himself of his Christianity, do what he would. The character which baptism had impressed was not to be effaced.

But the passion which the first sight of Miriam had awakened, was strengthened by all that he observed at this interview ; and even her betrothal to a distant, scarce known cousin, was a circumstance which inflamed it, by means of the jealous anxiety which it excited.

After quitting Miss Seixas, Alban returned home to dinner, and it happened that on that day his mother's uncle, Bishop Grey, whom we met some dozen years before at Yarmouth, was his

father's guest.   The bishop had become a most venerable florid old
gentleman, adhering to his knee-buckles, &c., and with long silver
locks streaming down upon his shoulders.

Bishop Grey partook of some boiled bass and oysters, and afterwards was helped twice to roast turkey, which some may deem a
luxurious Friday dinner for a bishop ; but " the measure of abstinence especially suited to extraordinary acts and exercises of devotion" (as the prayer-book luminously expresses it) may vary
greatly in individuals.   Dr. Grey was a fervent evangelical, and
conversed with unction on the subject of personal religion with
Mrs. Atherton.   At the same time he was a great enemy of Calvinism, and defended Baptismal regeneration, although in a timid
way, as conscious of the unpopularity of the tenet.   The good
bishop in fact had a High Church head and a Low Church heart,
and that we take to be the perfection of an Episcopal clergyman.
When the table-cloth had been removed, with some old Madeira,
and a decanter of fine port before him, he became witty and con-
versational, told anecdotes of the Revolution strongly smacking
of Toryism, and gently dissected the Puritans, to Alban's great
delight and the hearty amusement of his father, who had small
sympathy for religionists of any creed.   There was a keen yet
calm fire in the old prelate's eye, as he delivered himself of the well-
arranged and sweet-toned sentences, not unconscious of his own
witty facility.   Tea was over before Alban remembered his
promise to call on the Clintons, as well as the necessity of learning
from Mary De Groot at what hour next morning it would please
her that he should come with a carriage to take her to the Synagogue.

The hand of Providence was quietly guiding our hero along.
He found the ladies of Mr. Clinton's family in a state of affliction
for which he was not prepared.   Mother and daughter were both
in tears, and could not disguise their distress from the young
visitor.   He feared to ask the cause.   Bankruptcy or a death
could alone account for such visible grief.   He rather insinuated
than openly addressed an inquiry to Miss Clinton.

"Would you believe, Mr. Atherton," cried Henrietta, "that papa has declared himself a Catholic! He has been one all along, without our knowing it. It has come upon us now like a thunderbolt."

"Well," thought Alban, "I could have told you this morning."

"He has been Jesuitically concealing his sentiments from me ever since we were married," exclaimed Mrs. Clinton. "But they think deception is right, you know."

It appeared on further inquiry that when Mrs. Clinton was married she supposed her husband to be indifferent to all religion, "like most men of the world." He had taken a pew in Trinity, and subsequently in Grace church, and had even been talked of for vestryman. It was an aggravated case.

"Papa expresses a great deal of sorrow for having deceived us," said Henrietta, (a curious expression on her part,) "but what reparation is that now?"

"After all," observed Alban, consolingly, and taking his usual high religious tone, "is it not better that Mr. Clinton should be a good Catholic than nothing at all?"

"You do not understand it, Mr. Atherton. Papa is going to take the children (not *me*, be sure,) away from Grace church— from among people of our own class—to that horrid St. Patrick's, crowded by all the low Irish!"

"To think of my girls being taken to confession! And Mr. Clinton says they must be brought up Catholics from this day forward."

"*I* will never go to confession," cried Henrietta, with spirit, "to be asked insulting questions by an unmarried man!"

"Is that the case?" inquired Alban, thinking immediately of Mary.

"Indeed, Mr. Atherton, if you have any influence, as is generally supposed, with an amiable young friend of ours," said Mrs. Clinton, "I do hope you will use it to prevent her from exposing herself to what must be so shocking to female delicacy. The books which are put into the hands of young ladies to read in preparing for confession (for I have read them myself) are not fit for the eye of any virtuous and innocent young person. And it is upon these delicate subjects that they must communicate in private with priests, who, as Henrietta says, are not married, and it is not uncharitable to suppose, few of them correct."

"It is a sad thing," said Alban, warmly. "Have you placed the matter in that light before Mr. Clinton, ma'am?"

"You might as well talk to the wind," said Mrs. Clinton.

"To the wind!" echoed Henrietta.

Alban remembered his appointment with Mary De Groot. He must keep it, and yet he must endeavor to remonstrate with her, if, as he suspected, this morning expedition of hers tended to something very different from the Synagogue. Mrs. Clinton and her daughter both thanked him warmly for his sympathy, and begged him to call again very soon. He was hurrying through the basement hall, when a servant advanced and requested him to step for a moment into his master's study. Although annoyed at this detention, he could not well refuse. It was the back basement room, neatly furnished with bookcases, a study-table, study-lamp, and cheerful fire. Mr. Clinton had a happy look, although his manner was more grave than ordinary. He did not keep his visitor long in suspense. Not to keep the reader in suspense either, it was about Mary De Groot's intention of baptism that Mr. Clinton wished to speak. Alban had not heard of it, which a little surprised him. *He* had heard it from the bishop, who had asked if he knew the family. It seemed that Miss De Groot was not at church as usual in the morning, and a suspicion was entertained that her intentions had either been discovered by her parents, or voluntarily communicated to them, and that she was consequently under restraint.

"Ah?" said Alban, in a tone that implied, "What business is it of mine?"

"I have no right to interfere, of course," pursued Mr. Clinton. "Mr. De Groot would brook my meddling in his family concerns as little as I would his in mine. At the same time, I thought it my duty to do what I could, and, if possible, induce you to use your influence, which is considerable in a certain quarter, I have reason to think, to obtain for our estimable young friend the free exercise of her religion."

"Miss De Groot has a right to be baptized," said Alban. "That is incontestable; and I should regard it as a manifest wrong in any one to attempt to prevent her. At the same time, Mr. Clinton, I must say, that I should not be inclined, even if I had the power, to further a step which, in the way she means to take it, is to commit her so early in life to the system of your Church, objectionable as I fear it is in ways of which she probably has no idea. Pardon my frankness."

Mr. Clinton bowed, disappointed, but giving the matter up.

"I do not mean that I consider the Church of Rome anti-Christian or idolatrous," pursued Alban, rising. "I have none of those bigoted notions, Mr. Clinton. My objection is a practical one altogether, founded on what appears the necessarily evil influence of the confessional, and its degrading danger to a young and innocent *woman*—and on what is said with apparent probability of the personal character of the Roman priesthood, with whom this institution brings every member of your Church into so close intercourse. Pardon me again."

"Stay a moment," said Mr. Clinton. "If I could convince you, Mr. Atherton, that these objections are utterly without foundation—would you use your influence in favor of your young friend's liberty of conscience?"

"I have little time to spare at present," said Alban.

"A quarter of an hour is all I ask," responded Mr. Clinton.

Alban could not refuse a quarter of an hour to be convinced of so much.

"Perhaps you will be disappointed by what I have to say. It is only to state facts observed by myself. If the confessional be what Protestants suppose, how is it that Catholic females of all classes of society, married women and single, mothers and young maidens in the bloom of modesty, but especially those who excel

in piety, Mr. Atherton, consider it as the greatest means of sanctification, and the greatest security for an unblemished life ? Do
you suppose that all these Catholic women and ladies are corrupt,
tolerant of insult, and devoid of self-respect ?"

"There is great force in that," replied Alban, with his wonted
candor.

"How is it that Catholic women always entertain an exalted
opinion of the goodness, and very frequently of the sanctity, of their
own confessor ? For it is a fact that they do. I have heard priests
accused by their female penitents of severity, of impatience in
listening to confessions, which are often of a tiresome and useless
character, or of being prosy themselves, but never once did I hear
a complaint of being rudely or improperly questioned. Priests are
generally prudent men, to say the least, with a perfect knowledge
of what is expected of them. The morals of the confessional, and
its proprieties, are well understood, and are rigidly enforced by the
law of the Church. And what is more, Mr. Atherton, a considerable number of our clergy—quite enough to raise the tone of
the whole body—are saint-like men, whose whole lives are passed
in the presence of God. It is such who are always sought after
as confessors."

"I can understand," said Alban, "that it must be as you say."

"I am not willing to stop there," continued Mr. Clinton, flushing slightly, although his manner was calm. "I am *certain* that
the confessional is an immense safeguard to the purity of both
sexes. You must bear in mind, Mr. Atherton, at what age children begin confession. It is at about eight or nine years. Now
every body must see that a child of that age could only be bene-
fited by being questioned prudently and in private by a grave and
perhaps aged clergyman, on the subject of any sins into which it
may be liable to fall. Imagine an experienced pastor, who is
familiar with the heart, hearing the sincere confessions of two or
three hundred boys and girls of that age. Of course he will know
how to ascertain whether they are conscious of any offence against
modesty, in act or word, without suggesting to their minds any

thing of which they are happily ignorant. You know better than
I do, in what ways Protestant children of both sexes corrupt
themselves and each other at so early a period of life. But suppose they knew they must tell every immodest word or action
they say or commit to the *minister !*"

"Ah," exclaimed Alban, "would that I had felt such a restraint pressing upon me when a boy !"

"There it is ! Catholic boys, and, above all, Catholic girls,
learn at a very early age to avoid such things. The shame of
confessing them is too great. Hence, as they get older, they are
able to resist in the same way the first beginnings of more serious
sins against purity. The vile secret habits from which, I am
credibly informed, not one Protestant boy in a hundred is free, are
comparatively unknown among Catholic youth."

"Are they indeed ?"

Mr. Clinton told several stories illustrative of the singular innocence of Irish Catholics of both sexes, even at mature age.
Whatever else they proved, they proved that the confessional had
not tainted such people's minds with premature knowledge.

"Why, it is the complaint of our old Irish people that the
children in this country know what married people hardly know
in Ireland. A young man of twenty-five, butler in a wealthy
family, left his place because his young mistress offered him a kiss.
No mortal would ever have known it, if he had not told his priest.
What compelled this Hibernian Joseph to act thus ? *Faith*, Mr.
Atherton, and the fear of committing mortal sin :—the last instilled
by the peculiar and silent operation of the confessional. A beautiful young woman of twenty (I knew this case personally) a
daughter of the people, but intelligent beyond her class, for she
had been instructed in the day-school of the Sisters of Mercy in
Cork, a gay, affectionate creature, married a Protestant in this
country, away from her mother. She had been in the habit of
going weekly to confession, and twice a week to communion ; she
had once made a sort of resolution never to marry ; you would
not suspect *her* of not knowing what her new duties were ; yet

so it was : and distrusting her bridegroom's representations, after a painful struggle with herself, her love of purity and resolution to maintain it being stronger than virgin shame, she flies to her priest—an aged man—and tells him all."

"Beautiful!" said Alban.   "I should like to have been corrupted in the same way myself."

"There have been bad priests, and the tribunal of penance has been abused, like every thing good," said the Catholic layman, "but that does not prevent, Mr. Atherton, that one great motive of my return to the Church, is my desire to secure its advantages for my young sons and daughters.   And one thing you may depend upon, that if any thing can arrest the torrent of licentiousness which threatens to undermine the whole fabric of society in this country, it is this very institution.   I was tossed about a great deal in my youth, and have consequently seen a great many countries, and I know that in every land where the confessional has been laid aside, the common people are fearfully corrupt.   Want of chastity is the shameful mark of Protestant nations as compared with Catholic.   North Germany and Sweden, in this respect, are infinitely below Italy and Austria.   England and Scotland are not fit to be mentioned in the same breath with poor, ignorant, down-trodden and degraded Ireland.   As for America," added Mr. Clinton, "they say (you know best) that there is great purity of morals in New England."

"We will discuss that on another occasion," said Alban, rising, "but now I must really go."

"I have said nothing yet," exclaimed Mr. Clinton.   "I have not told you, for instance, how edifying confession is ; how advice comes home in that sanctuary of conscience, where your adviser knows what you are, for your own good, and brings a vast experience, and the rules of a science perfected by saints, to bear upon your precise case.   Let me tell you, Mr. Atherton, since you seem so sincere, that to one who knows the comfort and solidity of this system, Protestant religion seems the most dreary sham."

Alban hurried away to the Fifth Avenue.   It was past nine

o'clock, but, luckily, the distance was not great. The interview with Mr. Clinton had produced a complete revolution in his mind, but one which had been for some time preparing. Pledged already to aid Mary on the morrow, he now resolved, or rather, he was anxious, to do so in the most effectual manner.

Our heroine, still a prisoner in her room, was agreeably interrupted in her reading by her stepmother's entering and bidding her come down stairs. Mr. Atherton was there, and had asked for her.

The young lady appeared in the drawing-room cheerful and self-possessed as if she had been a domestic idol, and sat down with her work at the centre-table. The conversation ran pleasantly till ten o'clock. Young Atherton asked for some music, and Miss De Groot played and sang with gayety and spirit—

> " She's married the carl wi' a sack o' siller,
> And broken the heart o' the poor barley miller."

A servant brought in wine, cake, and fruit, and Atherton, declining the hospitality, rose to depart.

" What a short evening you make of it by coming so late, Mr. Alban. Pray, the next time you call on *me*, come at six o'clock instead of nine," said Miss De Groot, carelessly putting aside her work.

" I will be punctual to the minute, Miss Mary," replied the young man, with a patronizing smile. Mary was not given to shaking hands, but whenever she did go through that ceremony she did it honestly and cordially. Alban, on the contrary, had a timid, girlish way of giving the end of his fingers to a lady. It was a trait, like the satin softness of the palm and tips themselves. But he really had muscle under all that velvety surface, and Mary De Groot, saying " Good night, Mr. Alban," felt an iron grasp which almost made her cry out.

Alban, then, brave and faithful friend, would come for her in the morning, but how she was to leave her room was as great a mystery as ever, when her stepmother locked her in as on the preceding night. Still she prayed fervently without the crucifix and beads of which she had been vainly deprived, and undressed herself singing hymns. She was full of courage, for she had no will but the will of God. When she threw open the bedclothes, a dark object caught her eye. It was a key! Those Irish girls! She wept for joy.

CHAPTER X.

THE poor heathen father who was determined to keep his daughter from the arms of Christ, was a restless being that night. The devil who had possession of him tormented him grievously, and knowing that the believing maiden would else certainly escape, compelled him at last to rise from his bed, don his garments, and descend into the library to watch, lest his child should defy the polished bolts of her chamber doors, and come forth, according to her departed mother's prediction, to wed a heavenly bridegroom and be buried with *Him* in the waters where the old Adam expires. Eugene De Groot had a feeling that he was contending with the dead,—that the mother and he, who had once before struggled for the soul of their child, were now again antagonists. He swore that he would maintain his paternal rights against the grave itself. Yet he could not but fear his viewless and loving foe, one of whose prayers, perhaps, could crush him in an instant.

Mr. De Groot had a single candle, and he paced his library with both doors thrown open. One of these looked into the lobby of the private stair, the other into the hall near the foot of the great staircase. There was a couch in the library—a green leather couch, and, when he became fatigued, he lay down on it to think and listen. His eye fastened on the iron chandelier of trophies hanging black and flameless over his study table. Towards five o'clock he fell asleep, and dreamed that his daughter had eloped with young Atherton—not to be baptized, but married clandestinely. All the possible causes of such a step blended themselves confusedly in his dream, gathering vividness from reminiscences of his own wilful youth and Henrietta Clinton's indelicate behavior at school. He heard their carriage wheels rolling before him in the dark, while he himself, afoot, pursued the phantom fugitives.

He awoke. The sound of wheels was certainly in his ear. He rushed out into the hall, where a taper on a tripod gave a feeble light. There was the broad, oaken staircase, with its green bronzes and flameless lamps casting monstrous shadows on the wall, and he beheld, slowly descending the highest flight, a figure like a bride, veiled, and in white, which now passed behind the bronzes, and now came gleaming into view. Was it a bridal veil, or the garments of the grave ? Was it Mary from her bolted chamber, or Mary's mother from beneath the willow of the cathedral church-yard ?

Mr. De Groot had been laying plans all night against the very occurrence which had now taken place, yet the actual sight of his daughter escaped from a room where he believed her to be under lock and key, smote him with terror. Your skeptic is proverbially open to superstition. This rationalist believed that he saw the spirit of his Roman Catholic wife. Gliding down the last flight of the stair, Mary necessarily approached him ; her features revealed themselves distinctly ; and the eyes of the father and daughter met.

" Whither are you going, my child ?" said the patroon, whose knees knocked together.

" To church, my father."

" At this hour ! in this guise !"

" Mr. Alban Atherton waits with a carriage at the door."

So saying she offered her father a mantle, which lay across her arm, to place it on her shoulders. He mechanically complied. She drew the capuchin over her head. Her mien was full of womanly dignity, which seemed to rise higher under the outrages it had received. And the name of Alban at that moment was a powerful support, as Mary herself felt. It is one thing to be despotic with a daughter, and another to quarrel with a stranger to your hearth. Nothing bends a purpose, however violent, (if it be unjust, unbecoming, or violent,) like the certainty that it is to pass under the judgment of a person whose impartial and accurate estimate of conduct you know. The fairness of Alban's mind, his calm, sweet temper, and a certain solidity in his moral constitution, which gave this fine, smooth edge an irresistible force, protected Mary without his presence. Mr. De Groot had himself made young Atherton master of the situation ; he had exhausted the force of his own will during the night upon an impalpable obstacle, and now he was led, like the fierce Assyrian, " by a hook in the nose," to do the very thing which he had said a thousand times he would never suffer to be done. He accompanied his daughter down to the lower hall, took his hat and cloak from a hall-stand, composed of huge antlers of deer, and opened the vestibule doors. She fluttered down the broad stone steps to the gas-lit pavement. Directly in front at the curb-stone stood a carriage, and several persons. Young Atherton advanced a step or two, rather haughty and business-like. Mr. De Groot half expected to see the point of a rapier protruding beneath his young friend's Spanish cloak. But Mary tripped forward, as if she had been going to a party, and sprang into the carriage unassisted. With feminine promptitude she decided several questions which might have created difficulty.

" Get in, Margaret," she said, " and sit by me. Get in, Mr. Alban, and sit opposite me. Now, papa !"

The coachman closed the carriage-door and mounted the box. Mrs. Dolman was left standing on the sidewalk. Mary directed her to get up with the driver, and they set off.

Every minute or so a bright gas-light shone in at one or the other window, showing the faces of the party within the carriage to each other. Margaret Dolman's countenance, being that of a stranger, naturally attracted Mr. De Groot's attention. It possessed no rich physical beauty or fine intellectual traits—still less that rare combination of both which made his daughter bear off the palm even among the lovely ; but it was marked by the sweetness and purity peculiar to practical Catholics in that rank of life. It is the *mansuetudo Christi*, and often infuses its own gentleness into the heart of the beholder unawares. Some reflection of it speedily softened the sternness of Atherton's glance, which at first said very plainly that he had come to do a certain thing, and meant to do it, let what would betide. Mr. De Groot even yet wondered what that certain thing precisely was, and why Atherton had intervened. No one spake till the carriage stopped at the back entrance of the cathedral, when Miss De Groot let down the glass, and called for Mrs. Dolman. Neither of the gentlemen said aught, for neither knew what was to come next. The coachman—a Paddy—helped the good woman down with tender care.

"Go into the vestry, please, my good Mrs. Dolman," said Mary, sweetly, "and let Father Smith know that we are here." The old woman went up the creaking wooden steps and disappeared in the hurricane porch. Alban and Mr. De Groot successively bent forward and looked out of the carriage window at the church. Neither could fail to notice those singular adjuncts of the pile— the wooden lean-to, the boarded porch, and its rickety steps. All gave a notion of poverty and temporary shifts, which excited the contempt of the magnificent Anglo-Dutch patrician, but impressed Alban's imagination more than the elegance and ecclesiastical dignity of St. Paul's chapel. Was this the religion for the sake of which, long ages ago, in the dawn of its mysterious power, maidens of rank and wedded wives quitted before day the palaces of their consular fathers and husbands, to assist, in the dark recesses of the catacombs, at a rite universally execrated, yet pure and holy ?

Under no aspect could Alban regard the poor shabby cathedral with contempt. He could not look without emotions of inquisitive awe upon one of the local centres and radiating points of an influence pervading the earth which some thought divine and others diabolical, but which all admitted to be, in one sense or the other, supernatural. In this unsightly edifice was the throne of a Catholic bishop, one of a thousand similar seats of spiritual authority, so intimately united together that each became a representative of all, while the highest was but the bond and key-stone of a common supremacy. Alban had been taught to think, and, strange to say, the idea even now came over him with a mysterious horror, that such a church was one of Satan's visible seats, and the worship offered in it profane and impious. And truly if it were so, the Prince of this world had a powerful and consolidated empire, militant, by his profounder artifice, not under his own banner, but under that of Christ. What more signal triumph could Hell obtain over HIM who once conquered it by His death, than by converting His own appointed memorial of that death into a service of idolatry, so that at the very moment when His pretended ministers (but the ministers of Satan, in fact) are repeating the Saviour's words, "As often as ye do this, ye shall do it for a memory of me," His prostrate people adore a creature for Himself?—and they have done it well, for not an instant of time passes that a mass is not offered and the Host is not adored. Talk of an empire on which the sun never sets!—of the British *réveille* drum ever beating as our planet revolves on its axis, and day chases night round the globe!—what is that to the unending oblation of the Catholic Church?—what moment is not a priest's voice uttering, *Te, igitur, clementissime Pater!* in the low tone which is heard in another sphere!—What moment are not a priest's hands spread, dove-like, over the *oblata!*—What moment—what moment is not counted by the bell which announces the silent and invisible coming of their God to prostrate adorers in some quiet sanctuary, in Europe, or in Asia, or in America, in the Atlantic cities, or the woods of Oregon, in the Alps, or on the Andes, on the vast terra firma all along the meridians, or in the scattered islands of the sea!

It was into this vast fellowship, this society everywhere diffused and everywhere the same, (is not Popery everywhere the same?)—whether it were really the mystery of iniquity, the kingdom of Antichrist, the mystic Babylon, the harlot sitting on many nations, or the kingdom of the Son of God extending from the river to the ends of the earth, the rock become a mountain and filling the whole earth, the true Zion, the immaculate Spouse of the Lamb;—it was into this society, so mysterious, and whose character, like that of its Founder, is the problem of ages—that Mary De Groot, for her weal or her woe, came to be initiated.

Mrs. Dolman reappeared, and said that Father Smith would be ready in a few minutes. Then Sister Theresa came out, and approached the carriage window.

"Good morning, my dear Miss De Groot. Are you well? I feared you were not, from your non-appearance yesterday. Margaret is here too, I see! You adhere to your purpose? Well, Father Smith is now at the altar, my dear young friend, reciting the psalms of preparation."

Mary sank back in the carriage for a moment.

"I think you may come now," said the Sister.

Mary motioned to Alban to get out of the carriage. Her father followed. She herself, when she stood on the pavement, seemed overcome, and was as pale as if she were going to faint. She leaned on Margaret.

"Shall I fetch a glass of water?" said Alban.

"No, no. I must not drink."

The thought revived her. It was in great part physical weakness from her three days' fast, which had told on a youthful frame. Sister Theresa and Margaret were obliged to support her in ascending the steps. On the last step she looked round for her father, who had slowly followed them.

"Forgive me, papa."

He was silent, and Mary added, "God is too good to me in allowing you to be present."

Mr. De Groot suddenly advanced and took her hand. He was aware that the time was come—the last moment in which he could exercise his parental right of preventing by force the action which was about to take place. Once his daughter had crossed the threshold of the church, and physical coercion was no longer a resource. He held her hand firmly, and gazed sternly on the rest. The door of the porch was held open at that moment by Mrs. Dolman; that of the chapel was already open, and a procession with lights approached from within.

"You must return home," said Mr. De Groot, with a fierce calmness.

The Sister's mild countenance expressed surprise; Margaret exclaimed; and the old woman's dark skinny face, as the chapel lights fell upon it, was corrugated with indignation. Alban turned slightly away, when Mr. De Groot relinquished his daughter's hand as suddenly as he had seized it. His glance was directed to the door of the chapel, whither all instinctively turned. Somehow, in another minute all were collected within the porch, and the outer door had swung to upon them.

On the threshold of the chapel was a group composed as follows : On either side stood two young boys, with sweet, innocent countenances, robed in scarlet to the feet, over which they wore short, fine surplices, and each bearing a lighted candle. In the midst of these stood a priest. His short Roman surplice was fine as lace ; a magnificently-embroidered violet stole was laid over his shoulders, like a yoke of purple and gold, the beretta covered his head, a book was in his hand. His long black habit was confined at the waist by a sash. To Alban all this was utterly strange ; as a picture beautiful ; but with difficulty regarded as the serious garb of religion. The scarlet cassocks of the boys reminded him of the Woman in the Revelations. Mr. De Groot's eye was fastened with evident recognition on the priest's countenance. Both he and Alban involuntarily retired from Mary, who stood with Margaret, facing the clergyman. The Sister and Mrs. Dolman drew back on the opposite side. There was a moment's breathless silence, which was broken by the voice of the priest.

"What is thy name ?"

"Mary," was the reply, in a voice somewhat faltering.

"*Mary*, what dost thou seek of the Church of God ?"

"Faith."

"What doth faith give thee ?"

"Eternal life," answered the postulant, in a firmer voice.

"If thou wilt have eternal life," said the priest, "keep tne commandments. '*Thou shalt love the Lord thy God.*'

But *Faith* is," he added, after finishing the text, " that thou worship one God in Trinity and Trinity in Unity, neither confounding
the Persons, nor dividing the Substance.   For there is one Person
of the Father, another of the Son, another of the Holy Ghost ; but
of these three the Substance is one, and one the Godhead.   *Mary*,
dost thou renounce Satan ?"

    " I renounce him," said Mary, reading, in a firm voice.
    " And all his works ?"
    " I renounce them."
    " And all his pomps ?"
    " I renounce them."

    She gave the book to Margaret, as if no longer needing it.
The priest interrogated her on the Apostles' creed in a brief form,
dividing it into three parts, to each of which the answer was, " I
believe."   Then he seemed to blow in her face thrice, saying in
Latin and English, " Go out of her, unclean spirit, and give place
to the Holy Ghost, the Paraclete."   Beckoning her to approach,
he breathed in her face, in the form of a cross, saying, " *Mary*,
Receive by this insufflation the good spirit and the benediction of
God.   *Pax tibi*."

    " *Et cum spiritu tuo*," answered the boys with lights.   Their
young voices rung loud and clear, startlingly so.

    Alban had never before witnessed any Catholic rite, had never
stood even at the threshold of a Catholic church, or distinguished
a Catholic priest.   He naturally watched every movement, and
listened to every word with closest attention.   It would be giving
him altogether too great a superiority to the prejudices of education
to suppose that these insufflations and the accompanying words
did not appear to him superstitious.   Mary stood near the clergyman, and Margaret had put back the hood of her mantle.   He
signed her with the sign of the cross.

    "*Mary*, receive the sign of the cross as well in the forehead ✠
as in the breast ✠ : receive the faith of the heavenly precepts : be
such in manners that thou mayest now be the temple of God : and
entering the Church of God, joyfully acknowledge thyself to have

escaped the snares of death : abhor the Arian and Socinian per-
fidy ; worship God, the Father Almighty, and Jesus Christ, His
only Son, our Lord, who will come to judge the living and the
dead, and the world by fire."

The surpliced boys said, " Amen."

" Let us pray," said the priest. The prayer spoke of God's
handmaid Mary, (*famulam tuam Mariam,*) now wandering, uncertain and doubtful in the night of this world, and besought the
Holy Lord, the Almighty Father, the Eternal God, to show her
the way of truth and of the acknowledgment of Himself, that the
eyes of her heart being unsealed, she might recognize Him, one
God the Father in the Son, and the Son in the Father, with the
Holy Ghost, and reap the fruit of that confession both here and in
the world to come ; and Atherton perceived that Mary was considered as still unacquainted with God. But the rite rapidly proceeded.

The priest signed the candidate with the sign of the cross in
her forehead, and on several other places, saying,

" I sign thy forehead ✠ that thou mayest receive the cross of
the Lord.

" I sign thine ears ✠ that thou mayest hear the divine precepts.

" I sign thine eyes ✠ that thou mayest see the Brightness of
God.

" I sign thy nostrils ✠ that thou mayest perceive the odor of
the sweetness of Christ.

" I sign thy mouth ✠ that thou mayest speak the words of
life.

" I sign thy breast ✠ that thou mayest believe in God.

" I sign thy shoulders ✠ that thou mayest receive the yoke of
his service."

And as Mary, whose neck and shoulders Margaret had bared,
raised herself from bending before the priest after the last words,
he signed her whole body, but without touching her, saying,

" I sign thee all, in the name of the Father ✠, and of the

Son ✠, and of the Holy Ghost ✠, that thou mayest have eternal life, and live for ever and ever."

"Amen."

"*Oremus*" again—and the priest rapidly recited several Latin prayers, of which the purport was that this "Elect one, this hand-maid of God, might be kept by the power of the Lord's cross, and the efficacy of His mercy, so that from the rudiments of faith to which she had now been called, she might proceed day by day till she could fitly approach the grace of Baptism, arrive at the glory of regeneration, and what she could not obtain by nature, rejoice to have received by grace," always through Christ our Lord. And now followed a very superstitious part of this strange ceremony— the blessing and exorcism of salt, which one of the innocent-look-ing surpliced boys gravely presented in a silver vessel. The priest read a long Latin prayer, interspersed with ever so many crossings. We translate, that our readers, before they unawares adopt it, may see what a singular religion the Catholic is.

"I exorcise thee, creature of salt, in the name of God the Father ✠ Almighty, and in the charity of our Lord Jesus ✠ Christ, and in the virtue of the Holy ✠ Ghost. I exorcise thee by the liv-ing God ✠, by the holy God ✠, by the God ✠ who created thee for the safeguard of mankind, and commanded thee to be consecrated by his servants for the people coming to the simplicity of faith, that in the name of the Holy Trinity thou mayest be made a sal-utary sacrament to put the enemy to flight. Therefore we ask of thee, Lord our God, that sanctifying thou wouldst sanctify ✠, and blessing thou wouldst bless ✠, this creature of salt, that it may become to all who receive it a perfect medicine, abiding in their entrails, in the name of our Lord Jesus Christ, who shall come to judge the quick and the dead, and the world by fire."

And then the priest put some of the salt on the tongue of the young catechumen, adding, "*Mary*, receive the salt of wisdom : be it a propitiation to thee unto eternal life."—"*Amen.*"—"*Pax tibi.*"—"*Et cum spiritu tuo.*"—More Latin prayers followed, to the effect that the God of their fathers, the Author of all truth, would look upon His handmaid, *Mary*, and as she had "tasted that first food of salt, not permit her longer to thirst, but bring her to the laver of regeneration."

"Elect one, pray. Bend the knee, and say, *our Father*."

And Mary knelt before the priest and said the Lord's Prayer.

"Rise. Finish thy prayer and say, *Amen*."

"*Amen*," (*rising*.)

"Sign her," said the priest to Margaret, and to the young Elect he added—"Approach,"—and Margaret signed Mary on the forehead, completing the priest's sentence, "In the name of the Father, and of the Son, and of the Holy Ghost:"—an action and words which the priest immediately ratified by repeating. And then followed the strangest prayer of all, or rather, a series of prayers and adjurations, rising like the fearful note which shall prepare for the last regeneration. It was awful to hear in that poor porch. The priest lifted his hand over her head.

"God of Heaven, God of Earth, God of Angels, God of Archangels, God of Patriarchs, God of Prophets, God of Apostles, God of Martyrs, God of Confessors, God of Virgins, God of all that live well, God, to whom every tongue confesses, and every knee bends, of heavenly, earthly, and infernal beings: I invoke Thee, Lord, upon this Thy handmaid *Mary*, that Thou wouldst deign to keep her, and bring her to the grace of Thy baptism. Through Christ our Lord."

"*Amen*," was the voice of the young light-bearers.

"Therefore, cursed devil, recognize thy sentence, and give honor to the true and living God; give honor to Jesus Christ, His Son, and to the Holy Ghost; and depart from this handmaid of God, *Mary*; for God and our Lord Jesus Christ has deigned to call her to His holy grace and to the font of baptism, and this sign of the holy cross ►✝◄, which we give her in the forehead, do thou, cursed devil, never dare to violate. By the same Christ our Lord, who will come to judge the living and the dead, and the world by fire."

'*Amen*," they replied.

"Pray, Elect one. Bend the knee and say, *Our Father*."

And Mary knelt before the priest, and said the Lord's Prayer.

"Rise. Finish thy prayer and say, *Amen*."

"*Amen*," (*rising*.)

And the priest said to Margaret, "Sign her," and to the Elect, "Approach;" and Margaret signed her forehead, completing the invitation in the name of the Trinity, and the priest ratified it as before, by repeating both the action and words of the godmother. And the priest once more raised his hand over her head. It was a prayer to the "God of Abraham, Isaac, and Jacob, who appeared to Moses in Sinai, and brought the children of Israel out of Egypt, deputing to them the Angel of his pity to guard them day and night, that He would deign to send His holy Angel from Heaven to guard this His handmaid, *Mary*, and bring her to the grace of Baptism, through Christ our Lord."

And the light-bearers said, "*Amen*."

"Pray, Elect one. Bend the knee and say, *Our Father*."

And it was all done the third time. At the end, the priest, with his hand still lifted over her head, said,

"I exorcise thee, unclean spirit, by the Father ✠, and the Son ✠, and the Holy Ghost ✠, that thou mayest go out and depart from this handmaid of God, *Mary*. For HE commands thee, cursed, damned one, who opened the eyes of the born blind, and raised Lazarus on the fourth day from the tomb.

"Therefore, cursed devil, recognize thy sentence, and give honor to the true and living God, give honor to Jesus Christ His Son, and to the Holy Ghost, and depart from this handmaid of God, *Mary;* for God and our Lord Jesus Christ has deigned to call her to His holy grace and to the font of Baptism, and this sign of the holy cross ✠, which we place on her forehead, do thou, cursed devil, never dare to violate. By the same Christ our Lord, who will come to judge the quick and the dead, and the world by fire."

And the boys still answered, "*Amen*."

He raised his hand over the head of the catechumen once

more—yes, once more—and said, as she bowed before him, "Let us pray."

"I entreat thy eternal and most just pity, Holy Lord, Almighty Father, Eternal God, Author of light and truth, upon this thy handmaid, *Mary*, that thou wouldst vouchsafe to illuminate her with the light of the intelligence proceeding from thee : cleanse and sanctify her : give her the true science, that she may be made worthy to approach the grace of thy Baptism, hold a firm hope, a right counsel, a holy doctrine, that she may be fit to receive thy grace. Through Christ our Lord."

And those boys in scarlet and fine linen answered, as before, "*Amen.*"

He gave the end of the violet stole into her hand, and said, "*Mary*, enter into the holy Church of God, that thou mayest receive the heavenly benediction from the Lord Jesus Christ, and have part with Him and His saints."

And the boys answered, "*Amen.*"

Rapid in comparison was the remainder of the rite, of which the mere preparation had been so long, and, one may say, tedious. Many are the steps of the Temple, and its porch is many-columned and deep ; but once you have entered the gate—crossed the threshold—and the pure light shines, the cleansing water flows in a perennial stream. Holding the priest's stole, Mary entered the church, and, taught by the Sister, (for all accompanied her), fell upon her knees and adored, touching the chapel floor with her oft-signed brow. She rose and now recited with the priest the Apostles' creed, and Lord's prayer. He imposed or held his hand again over her head. It was another exorcism, but he signed her not again with the cross in pronouncing it. It reminded Satan of the day of judgment at hand, the day of everlasting punishment, the day which should come as a burning oven, in which everlasting destruction was prepared for him and all his angels. It bade him, therefore, "damned one, and to be damned hereafter," give honor, as before, to the living God, the eternal Trinity, in whose name and power he was commanded, whoever he was, impure spirit, "to go out and depart from this handmaid of God, *Mary*, whom to-day the same God and our Lord Jesus Christ had deigned to call by a gift, to His holy grace and benediction, and to the font of Baptism, that she might become His temple by the water of regeneration for the remission of sins;" concluding by the ever-recurring adjuration, "In the name of the same our Lord Jesus Christ, who will come to judge the living and the dead, and the world by fire."

With saliva from his tongue the priest touched her right and left ear, saying, "*Ephpheta*,—that is, be opened"—and her nostrils, "Unto the odor of sweetness; but thou, devil, fly, for the judgment of God is at hand."

Once more he demands, "What is thy name?"

"Mary," said the young Elect, pale and faint, in the midst of her friends, yet unsupported, though Margaret stood near.

"*Mary*, dost thou renounce Satan?"

"I renounce him."

"And all his works, and all his pomps?"

"I renounce them."

The holy oil of catechumens stood in a small vessel on a table, and the priest anointed her therewith on the breast and on the shoulders, as she bowed before him, temporarily unmantled.

"I anoint thee with the oil of salvation," he said, "in Christ Jesus our Lord, unto eternal life."

"*Amen*."

"Peace to thee."

"*Et cum spiritu tuo*," was the unwearied response.

"*Go out, impure spirit*," added the priest, drying with a napkin the places which he had anointed, "and give place to the living and true God. *Fly, impure spirit*, and give place to Jesus Christ, His Son. *Depart, impure spirit*, and give place to the Holy Ghost, the Paraclete."

And now they drew around the font itself, which was opened, and a silver vessel brought to receive the excess of the hallowed waters. The priest removed his violet stole, and assumed one of white silk, but richly embroidered, like the other. In laying aside the one, he kissed it ; he kissed the other in putting it on.

"What is thy name ?" he demanded once more of the trembling handmaid of the Lord.

"Mary."

The reply was low, but quite clear.

"*Mary*, dost thou believe in God the Father Almighty, Creator of Heaven and Earth ?"

"I believe."

"Dost thou believe in Jesus Christ, His only Son, our Lord, who was born and suffered ?"

"I believe."

"Dost thou believe also in the Holy Ghost, the holy Catholic Church, the communion of Saints, the remission of sins, the resurrection of the flesh, and life everlasting ?"

"I believe."

"*Mary*, what seekest thou ?"

"Baptism."

"Wilt thou be baptized ?"

"I will."

The veil was removed from her head, and the mantle from her shoulders, by the females. Mary bowed before the font, with head and neck and shoulders bare, her hands crossed on her bosom. Margaret held her arm ; and the priest, taking water in a silver vessel from the font, poured it on her head thrice, in the form of a cross, saying once,

"*Maria*, Ego te baptizo in nomine Patris ✠, et Filii ✠, et Spiritus ✠ Sancti."

No one said *amen*, but he touched his finger immediately in the sacred chrism which stood by the side of the oil of catechumens, and anointed her head in the form of a cross, saying,

"Almighty God, the Father of our Lord Jesus Christ, Who hath regenerated thee of water and the Holy Ghost, and Who

hath given thee remission of all sins, Himself anoint thee with
the chrism of salvation ✠, in the same Christ Jesus, our Lord,
unto eternal life."

"Amen."

"Peace be to thee."

"And with thy spirit."

He put on her head the white chrismal.

"Receive a garment white and spotless, which thou mayest
bear before the tribunal of our Lord Jesus Christ, that thou mayest have eternal life."

"*Amen.*"

He gave her a lighted candle of virgin wax, which was
brought by the dark-robed Sister. It was a noble-looking, gray-
haired man who gave it, and then drew back into shadow.

"Receive a burning lamp, and keep thy baptism without
reproach ; keep the commandments of God, that when the Lord
shall come to the marriage, thou mayest meet Him in the celestial mansion unto life eternal."

"*Amen.*"

"*Mary*, go in peace, and the Lord be with thee."

"*Amen.*"

The surpliced boys, with their candles and scarlet robes, turned
about to depart from the chapel, and the priest prepared to follow
them : but ere he departed, Father Smith, bending down, said to
her, in a low voice,—not the voice of a priest in the office, but his
own—"Pray for me." Margaret kissed her hand, which still held
the burning candle, and said, in a sobbing whisper, "Oh, pray for
me."—Sister Theresa approached in tears, and said, "Pray for me,
Mary," and kissed her. "Pray for me, I entreat you. Pray for
the sisters of our society." One or two old women, who had been
kneeling on the chapel floor, hobbled up and whispered, "Pray
for us." One said—"Oh that it was me, if I might die the next
minute !"

But there was another sacrament to be received. The Sister
took the candle from her ; the veil was thrown again over her

head. In a minute she was kneeling at the rails of the altar of the Virgin in the same chapel, where the candles were already lit, a little table stood prepared with the holy chrism : and the old ecclesiastic, whose mass she had heard every morning at seven, was sitting with a mitre on his head, and a priest for his assistant. In two or three minutes the bishop had confirmed her, had smitten her sinless cheek to teach her to bear hardship for Christ, and given her peace and a blessing. While she yet, lost and overpowered, thanked God for this second grace—the gift of the Holy Ghost Himself, and prayed for those who had asked her prayers, Sister Theresa put the candle again in her hand, and made her go into the church to hear mass. She knelt between the sister and Margaret, who offered their communion for her. Mary listened to the mass of the Epiphany, (for it was the octave,) familiar to her from having heard it already twice. The gospels, of course, were the same as at that Christmas mass when she was converted, although their relative position was reversed. She heard them now with the white veil of confirmation on her head, with the lighted candle of the neophyte in her hand. Again, as on Christmas morn, she adored with the wise men, but it was as one who had found the Saviour in the House of Bread; again she bent the knee in honor of the Word made Flesh, but it was as one who had received power to become the Child of God.

"*Ecce Agnus Dei ! Ecce qui tollit peccata mundi !*"

It came upon her before she was aware. The Author of sanctity reposed in a bosom made whiter than snow by His Blood. Love Incarnate sought and folded in Its divine embrace a creature purified by the divine love animating the creaturely heart, and effacing all its human stains. What joy, what peace, what purity on purity, and grace on grace, did He not impart in that kiss of communion ! in the touch though under a veil, of that life-giving and immaculate Flesh which has ascended to the Father !

" *Let Him kiss me with the kisses of His mouth, for thy breasts are better than wine.*"

Her father and Alban witnessed the communion from a pew

not far distant, where both patiently waited until the new received convert had finished her thanksgiving. The bishop was in the vestry when the party passed through, returning to their carriage. He wished to speak to the young convert, who knelt for his blessing.

" My dear *demoiselle*," said the purple-vested old man, mingling French words with English, and speaking the latter language with some accent, " you are fasting, you must be exhausted. Do not return home without some refreshment. Come into my poor house with your friends, and take a cup of coffee, I pray you."

" You are very good *monseigneur*," replied Mr. De Groot, speaking for his daughter, " but our carriage waits, as well as the breakfast at my house, and I therefore beg your lordship to excuse us."

" As you please, sir. I should be sorry if this young lady suffered any inconvenience. God bless you, my child. I thank Him for this auspicious day, in which He has been so good to you, and has consoled all our hearts by your faith. Pray for me."

The bishop and ecclesiastics made a courteous and very foreign reverence to the strangers, which Mr. De Groot, who was not to be outdone in politeness, returned in the most formal manner of the old court. When they got into the street Alban had some difficulty in realizing that he was in New York.

CHAPTER XI.

"WILL these Christians come, think you, señorita ?"

"The young man is not a Christian, Rebecca, and the young lady is one still less than he : for she believes not the divinity of the Notzry, and has never been baptized."

"I did not understand the young señor to say that precisely. That she had renounced the creed of her childhood was what he intimated ; from which I inferred, señorita, that she is now more a Christian than ever. At best, how can you be sure that she is purified to enter the sanctuary ?"

The young Jewess made no reply, though her brow indicated that the question troubled her. The mistress and maid stood in the porch of the synagogue, which was considerably elevated above the street. Many male Jews were loitering on the steps or about the doors, and the service within was already begun.

"I doubt they will not keep their engagement, señora, and I like not that you should wait here for them."

"I will wait," said her mistress, impatiently. "And see— here they are !"

A beautifully appointed chariot drew up, indeed, before the synagogue. A black coachman and footman, both bearded, cockaded, and arrayed in many-caped blue overcoats, sat together on the blue hammercloth, with a superb robe of fox-skins over their legs. A sympathetic smile, dashed with profound respect, was on their coal-black visages, when the fellow whose office it was, held the chariot door open for Miss De Groot and Alban to descend, and the face of the young lady was crimson as she set foot upon the pavement. She looked up at the two Jewesses with curiosity, being at no loss to distinguish Miriam by her richer dress, and particularly the lace that decked her ankles, and the immaculate purity of her white skirts, rendered visible by her elevated position. They ascended the steps of the synagogue, and Alban introduced the young ladies. After a brief colloquy, the latter withdrew to the women's gallery, and the young man entered, unquestioned, upon the floor of the Hebrew sanctuary.

The interior was fitted up with much taste. White columns in the palm-tree form supported the gallery ; columns of scagliola, with emblematically designed bronzed capitals, encircled the Ark, which had doors of fine woods, and curtains of silk. The holy scrolls, exposed to view during the greater part of the service, were wrapped in embroidered silk, and the silver rods on which they were rolled, terminated in glittering ornaments of silver bells and pomegranates, which tinkled when the sacred volumes in use were borne in procession to and from their place of repose. Before the ark burned the "Everlasting Lamp." There were also numerous candlesticks, containing huge candles of wax, but the latter were not lighted on this occasion. Upon an elevated square pulpit in the centre, trimmed with white damask silk, the service, consisting of the law, psalms, and prayers, was chanted with fine effect by Readers in white albes. The Oriental separation of the women, the men wearing their hats, their peculiar physiognomy and singular manner of worship, their long, white shawls, and see-sawing while they muttered Hebrew prayers, or joined in the harsh thunder of the response, were very impressive. At one point all present prostrated themselves with so much suddenness that our hero was startled.

"Such then," thought he, "is what remains of the worship of the sacred tribes—the worship in which our Saviour joined when on earth, and at which, after His ascension, the Apostles still occasionally assisted."

Alban had every disposition in the world to be pleased, and really the rite affected him deeply. The chanting, use of lights, vestments of the Readers, prostration, and other ceremonies, reminded him of the Temple. But where were the divine peculiarities of that celestially designed worship ? Where was the sacrifice, and Divine Presence, and the lamb for a burnt offering ?

From the steps of the Catholic altar, that morning, he had heard
a reply, which still rang in his ears,—" *Behold the Lamb of
God—behold Him who taketh away the sins of the world!*"
Despite himself, and as if by force, the conviction was wrung
from his mind—that not here, but there, was the continuation
of the Temple worship. It was an intuition above and beyond all argument. That everlasting lamp pointed to a local
sanctity, a divine inhabitation, which once existed. Had so
blessed a reality ceased these two thousand years? Impossible to
credit its non-existence if it ever existed at all. And the victims
which had ceased to bleed, the incense which no more curled
upward from under the hands of the Cohen! And the voice of
prophecy—the light and perfection of the High Priest's breast-
plate—the abiding oracles of God—the power which preserved
the line of Aaron, and inspired the lips even of Caiaphas—had it
all come to nothing, and vanished like the legends of a fabulous
age? Not if it was divine. Was the Babel of Protestantism
the successor of the Temple which was built without sound of
hammer; and where dwelt in visible glory the God Who maketh
men to be of one mind in a house? Was a system which left
all doubtful, and which substituted emotions for morality—a
debasing, inefficacious, no-creed—was this the heir of the prophets, and the antitype of the Law? He had answered that question before.

Alban opposed a vigorous resistance to these impressions. His
pride recoiled from seeming to follow Mary De Groot, and still
more from being forced by circumstances into the position of her
lover. It was her father who had sent them to the synagogue
together that morning, rather against both their wills, as matters
now stood, and sent them in his own carriage, which compromised
them both. If now he became a Catholic? And Miriam? His
heart beat as he glanced up at the gallery of the synagogue;
and her figure, as she stood on the steps, floated before him.
Then he beheld her dancing in her brother's drawing-room,
where he had played as a child. He saw her come bending for-

ward under the crimson drapery of the folding doors, and appear
in the sunset light, as at their first meeting. Then his imagination kindled, and he passed, in thought, to the East. Ambition
blended with passion. Adventure, conflict, triumph ! He was a
conqueror, a prince : he laid the reins on the neck of pride. This
was not the temper in which he could embrace the cross.

Meanwhile, Miriam and Miss De Groot were in the women's
gallery. Mary felt strangely out of place in it, and half-degraded.
Miss Seixas talked to her almost incessantly—chiefly about dress,
the opera, dancing, and her friend Mr. Atherton, topics more inconsistent with the sanctity of the place, if it had any, than the
ceremonial pollution which alone the young Jewess had seemed
to fear. Yet Miriam occasionally took part in the worship, and
prostrated herself with the rest, with great apparent devotion.
But she laughed the moment after, as she brushed the dust of the
floor from her silk dress.

Day after day of the vacation passed, and Alban became more
intimately acquainted with the persons he had met. Livingston
Van Brugh took a great fancy to him, and from a singular cause.
In a rencounter of young men one morning, at a chess-room, Van
Brugh avowed his unrestrained libertinism, expressing absolute
disbelief in the existence of virtue in either sex. Alban broke
out in such a hearty and contemptuous denunciation of these
principles, that most of the others expected Livingston to knock
him down. Instead of showing resentment, however, he immediately began to cultivate our hero's society—a flattery against
which Alban was not proof. Van Brugh laughingly said that he
wanted to find out to what sort of vice Atherton was accessible,
since that which contented young men generally, excited his disgust. So, with praise of his delicacy, and appeals to every latent
passion of youth, he worked to inspire, if possible, a craving for
forbidden pleasure. Van Brugh had too much tact ever to speak
of Miss De Groot, except in terms of highest respect. He
believed, he used to say, that if there was a virtuous girl living,
it was she. But to Miss Clinton he was not so indulgent.

On the other hand, Alban learned from Mr. Clinton that there was a discipline in existence designed to fortify man against himself, and a treasure of grace accessible to all ; by the aid of which, even youth, if it would, might perfectly triumph. Thus his bane and antidote were both before him. He used to see Mr. Clinton every day, for the latter never omitted to give him an excuse for calling again. And when Alban went away, Mr. Clinton would say, "Pray, go up to the drawing-room and see the ladies ; and if you have an opportunity of speaking to my daughter on these topics—since they interest you—I wish you would."

Thus Alban, who was ashamed to call in State-street as often as he wished, and who purposely stayed away from Mr. De Groot's, saw Miss Clinton daily, and sometimes alone. She was extremely agreeable—more so than Miss Ellsworth ; for she had seen so many things abroad that were interesting to Alban. Her temper was imperturbable, in which she had greatly the advantage of Mary De Groot ; and instead of treating our hero, like Miss Seixas, as a youth whom she was bound to amuse, she appeared to look up to him, listening with admiring respect to every thing he said, on the religious and moral topics on which he was stronger than on any other ; and, in fine, entered into Alban completely, just as he was—conforming herself exactly to him, not attempting to mould him to herself. Mary De Groot had an inward position of her own, from which there was no moving her. Her mind worked, and her heart glowed independently. Somehow, Alban did not like that altogether, even when the heart glowed towards him. Miriam seemed inapproachable in her race and her womanly loveliness—in her religion and her betrothal. But Henrietta floated right along with him, wherever he would. She merely undertook to improve his manners in some small particulars—reformed his French pronunciation, imparted to him several secrets of etiquette, and taught him how to tie his cravat.

We do not care to dwell on these things, but the interviews we speak of, coming upon the conversations of Van Brugh, and perhaps recalling associations with Miss Clinton's name, supported by much that he really could not help observing in her manners, threw a strange light into unsuspected hollows in Alban's heart. Strange images would rise up, and flit before his mental eye, like bats in the dusk. Not that they looked like bats to him. They had, on the contrary, a beauty from which he could with difficulty avert his gaze ; they had soft, seductive faces ; their flowing hair was like the hair of women ; their forms were female to the waist ; and the rest was lost in a drapery of fiery mist.

It must not be supposed that Alban did not visit the De Groots at all. He went there in the evening, when he was sure to see the parents as well as the daughter. Then they had a pleasant social time. You never would have supposed that of those four persons, one was a Pantheist, one a bigoted Presbyterian, one a devout convert to the Catholic Church, and one something between a Deist and a Jew. Religion was never mentioned, and if love was present, it was in a modest, quiet guise. The party generally played whist, after which Mary De Groot went to the piano. Her style was exactly suited to charm a domestic circle like that, patient yet flowing, and delightfully accurate, without too much vigor ; and her singing a full-breasted, smooth warble, negligent of petty ornament, and delighting in pure simple effects. Alban appeared very manly, and considerably recovered the good graces of Mrs. De Groot, to whom he was more attentive than to Mary. Twice he rode out with the latter and her father, and Mr. De Groot kindly placed a horse at his disposal, to use whenever he liked. Thus Saturday, Sunday, Monday, Tuesday, and Wednesday passed. Returning on Thursday afternoon, from his first solitary ride, and skirting the fine (but then leafless) woods, where the old Lorillard mansion (now the Convent of the *Sacré Cœur*) commands a view of both rivers, at the base of the hill he overtook a carriage containing two ladies. They were his Jewish friends. He had passed them going out, but at the New York trotting pace of a mile in two minutes and forty seconds, which certainly gave no time for recognition.

"You went by us like lightning. I was very much afraid for *you*," said Mrs. Seixas, in a foreign accent.

"When you go to the East, you will ride an Arab," said Miriam, eyeing with admiration the black, wild-eyed horse, with fiercely curving neck, which Alban rode.

"And wield a Damascus scimitar instead of this,"—waving his riding-whip.

"Exactly."

"We always rode donkeys at Smyrna," observed Mrs. Seixas. "They are safer, and none but Turks and Franks are allowed to ride horses in the East."

"Do you go to Mrs. Clinton's party to-night?" asked Miriam.

"Of course. Is not the whole world to be there?"

"I have heard so," replied Miriam, with a smile. "What is called the whole world in this corner of it."

"We shall be great people," said Mrs. Seixas—"I mean at Mrs. Clinton's party :—for we are to take with us a real Count, Mr. Atherton, who has brought letters of credit and introduction to my husband, from Baron Rothschild, at Vienna."

"I expect the Count to fall in love with your beautiful Miss De Groot," said Miriam : "for like her he is a Catholic."

CHAPTER XII.

THERE was something pleasant, and what is called aristocratic in
the way society was managed in New York sixteen years ago.
The wealthy families were fewer; the rooms were larger; the
parties not so large, but more select. It was possible to dance at
private balls, and even usual, and a young lady could attend one
without having her clothes torn off her back, which often happens
now-a-days. Mrs. Clinton, for instance, who was a leader then,
lived in a wide basement house, (as it is called,) the principal
drawing-room extending across the front, with three windows to
the floor. The back room was equally fine, though differently pro-
portioned, and there was an extensive back building with a dining-
room in the basement, and a billiard-room (Mr. Clinton was fond
of playing at home) on the first floor—a spacious, lofty apartment,
which, when Mrs. Clinton gave a party, the floor being prettily
chalked, was converted into a ball-room. What made this peculiarly convenient and agreeable was, that the windows of the
billiard-room looking south opened into the conservatory, which
ran the whole length of the back building, and was available on
a party night. The music was always placed here. Thus Mrs.
Clinton, who liked something of a crush at her parties, could
afford to issue three hundred cards of invitation.

By nine o'clock that part of Broadway was a regular lock of
carriages. The guests as they were set down ascended to the
bedrooms—gay with French upholstery and bright as day with
tapers—to lay aside their outer wrappings. In the room al-
lotted to the darker sex, Alban found Mr. De Groot, who immediately said—"You have no young lady with you, of course?
Well, you must take down Mary. Let us go into the hall as soon
as you are ready, and wait for them."

While they waited, Alban being extremely nervous, as it was

his first party, Miss Clinton, so beautifully dressed that he did not
know her, came out of the ladies' toilet-room, and after a glance
at the group of gentlemen, singled him out by name, saying,
" Mary wants you," and bade him follow her.   He did so, and she
re-entered the apartment whence she came, parting the fair throng
within.   Here a bevy of damsels were admiring their toilets
and figures in a psyche ; there one was adjusting her ringlets
before the toilet-glass ; in one corner, a prudent girl was exchanging the thicker chaussure with which it was deemed best to be
protected in stepping from the carriage to the door, for the satin
slippers appropriate for dancing ; and there was a slight movement
of apprehension and displeasure at the entrance of a young man ;
but it was to tie Miss De Groot's slipper—an office which the
young lady, already gloved, with her bouquet, tablets, and fan in
hand, seemed expecting from some one, but not from him, to
judge by her ready blush.   In a moment, however, at Miss Clinton's bidding he had knelt at her feet, thanking all his stars for
the happy chance which made that narrow ribbon come untied.
He was not used to tying ladies' slippers, his modesty was in his
way, and the beauty all around confused him ; he blundered,
and the young ladies tittered ; Mary, with angry promptitude, took
her foot upon her knee, turning away from him.   But Alban
looked so mortified that with a forced laugh she bade him try
again, directing him how to cross the ties, and inserting her finger (for the glove was already off) in the knot as he secured it.
When done, she dropped her foot and dress quickly, and took his
arm.

It was a trivial incident, but one of those which sometimes
are very important in the inner world, where our story mainly
flows.   It must be remembered that Alban's feeling towards our
heroine, up to this date, was principally characterized by esteem,
which had gradually increased until it amounted to absolute veneration.   The idea that her delicacy was in any way compromised in his regard, and that involuntarily, touched him deeply
There was nothing, however dear to his passions, which he would

not sacrifice, rather than it should be so, was his generous thought.

Mary hung on her friend's arm, while a brilliant mass of both sexes flowed and retired through the folding doors, like the moonlit tide through a water-gate. Her mien was embarrassed—not exactly because it was her first ball, for we have seen that she had, when she chose, a formed society manner, native as her graceful carriage, a matter of birth and early habit ; but she was an object of universal and inquisitive attention. People stared and people whispered. Some faces expressed pity ; some, horror ; some, contemptuous curiosity. It was a protection, even to the daughter and heiress of Mr. De Groot, to appear with such a beau as Atherton, under these circumstances ; and it was an additional relief that attention was soon diverted to her dress, although she was not arrayed in that pure white muslin, so effective and distinguishing, which your heroines always wear at the balls which are given in novels.

Father Smith had said, when the young convert had consulted him in reference to this party—" Go with the intention of pleasing them" (her parents) " and God ; but by all means, my dear child, be modestly dressed. A young lady who goes to a ball, as I am told they do now, more undressed than dressed, is an arrow of Satan, for the wounding of souls."

Mary was a determined character. She did not ask, when her dress came home, whether, after all, there could be any harm in being *decollettée* so slightly, at her age especially. She might be a dowdy, but she would not be an arrow in Satan's quiver. She had plenty of the stuff, fortunately, and with her own ready fingers—sitting up half one night for the purpose—somehow or other, she made what she was sure even Father Smith would allow to be a decent *corsage*. In those days young ladies did not wear the vapory tulles, and other gossamer robes, which are now the rage for dancing parties. A pink lutestring, changeable with white, which, in the evening, had a silvery sheen, extremely youthful and brilliant in effect, was the ball-dress of the wealthy patroon's daughter. The most modest of her school frocks had served Mary for a pattern ; but to give an elegant, and even *piquant* character to it, she had omitted the sleeves altogether, substituting a single ruffle of Brussels lace. It had the most ingenuous air possible.; and many a damsel, with a robe half off her shoulders, envied that innocent toilette. So much to convince our fair countrywomen that their costume is still a subject in which we are interested—as, in truth, it is one of great importance—and luckily, where we are now, every thing comes in play.

So does dancing, for instance.

Some Catholic ladies, the gayest people in town, had sought an introduction to Mary ; she was separated from Alban ; her spirit rose ; her beauty told upon the male portion of the company ; her modest garb inspired respect, for men are quick in observing those things ; and she herself determined to carry off her position bravely, By the time the quadrille was formed, she had more engagements on her tablets than the evening would have sufficed to fulfil. Alban's name was first. Mary laughed as they took their places.

" Dancing was a religious exercise among the Hebrews ; you, I take for granted, mean to practise it with devotion."

" Hang the Hebrews," thought he—" Miss Seixas is opposite us, by the by."

" And who is her partner ? How very distinguished he is !"

" By his decoration and yellow mustaches, the German Count, of whom they spoke to me."

" How incongruous for a Christian knight—all starred and crossed, and red-ribboned—to be dancing with a Jewess ! She and I ought to change partners, by rights."

It soon appeared, moreover, that the Count danced better than any body ; it made him more distinguished, even for a count. It was beautiful to see him—now with his partner, now with his *vis-à-vis*. Miriam's grand and plastic style has been described ; and a quadrille in those days admitted, though it

did not require, the display of it.   Mary De Groot—a girl
all over—danced as she sang, with faultless accuracy, which was
made beautiful by her gay manner, just checked by modesty,
bearing her head with a rose-like grace, and her arms, like
wreathed lilies, over or beside her silver drapery.   The Count,
attending to all her movements with foreign gravity, appreciated
her finely.   She praised, to her partner, his thorough-bred
respect, so natural and seemingly spontaneous—so unlike the untutored freedom which passed for ease with the native beaux.
They exchanged courteous French phrases as they touched their
gloved fingers.   Alban, on his part, flirted as much as he could
with Miss Seixas, who gave him every encouragement.

"He is just the proper person for you," said he to Mary, leading her into the conservatory to rest.   "You know he is of your
religion."

"Which is indispensable," she replied.

"Well, I think it ought to be in every case."

"You of course will make up to Miss Seixas."

"She is indeed charming," replied Alban.

"Oh, what a pretty waltz!"

The Count waltzed with the daughter of the house, the fair
Henrietta, and Alban, who had never seen waltzing before, looked
on, shocked but fascinated.   Henrietta's dress was a novelty—
white tulle, countless folds confined apparently by a silver girdle, over a rich white silk, and looped up with flowers.   It flew
behind her like a white cloud.   Then the Count took out Miss
Seixas.   This was less objectionable from the magic of art.   Miriam's slippers had no tie, nor even a heel—the fashion of Spain ;
it was wonderful how she kept them on by the mere muscular
action, her feet twinkling like moonbeams on waves.   Her rich
skirts did not fly like Henrietta's gossamer attire.   Waltzer after
waltzer joined the circling pairs, like birds rising from a copse.
Alban looked round for Miss De Groot, but she was gone.   He observed with a pang that Miriam accepted every invitation, and
after watching her for some time with strangely blended feelings,

upon Van Brugh's taking her out, he turned away and went in search of Mary. She was in a corner of one of the rooms, with the Count; Henrietta was retiring from them and looking back.

"I do not waltz, sir."

"You waltz not, mademoiselle? *Alors, il faut commencer.* But Miss Clinton assures me that you waltz extremely well."

"I have not waltzed since I left school, monsieur."

"*C'est à dire*—a week ago, mademoiselle, These are quite ideas *de pension*, I assure you."

He plead with so much grace and good humor that it seemed ridiculous to refuse him. Miss De Groot laughed. He even intimated that nothing could show off that charming classic style of costume but the attitude and movement of the waltz. He managed her as a gentle knight does a spirited but timid filly.

"I know some of the devoutest young ladies in Vienna who scruple not to waltz. There is Madame Washington Lynch waltzes, and she is a very good Catholic. I have waltzed with her myself, to-night, and she spoke of you in raptures. It is not a sin, I assure you, mademoiselle. You err to be so strict. At least suffer me to lead you back to the *salle* where they are dancing, and which your absence deprives of so great an ornament."

She took his arm and moved forward slowly, as if ashamed to persist in her refusal. Alban was so near as she passed that he could see the lace round her neck rise and fall. The hand which was free stole up to a spot where, doubtless, some memento was hidden. People made way for the Count; Alban followed; they got within the circle in the dancing-room; the waltzers swam round. Miss De Groot stood by the Count, with her hand on his arm, and in front of Alban, who, indeed, could not extricate himself from the position. In such a crowd, moreover, he did not feel himself a listener. Mary's eyes were steadily bent on the floor.

"I prevent your dancing, M. le Comte."

"Ah, one turn with you, mademoiselle, and I vow to you that I will waltz no more this evening."

"I certainly shall not waltz, monsieur, and if you please, I will not trust myself to look at the waltzing. I know, sir, that neither is a sin, but I have been advised that it is difficult to do either without sinning." She turned and perceived Alban, whose arm she almost instinctively took, relinquishing the Count's.

"Ah, I see that you are formed to be a saint, mademoiselle," said the latter. "I will not urge you further against your holy resolutions. More late in the evening I hope to have the honor of your hand in the quadrille. *Priez pour moi*," he added, bowing and smiling. But in a minute he was again among the waltzers.

It was with Miriam. Alban could not help trying to persuade Miss De Groot to look at this pair : the action of Miriam's feet was so beautiful. The room was now so crowded, especially about the doors, that it was nearly impossible to stir from the spot where they were ; it was somewhat difficult to keep from crowding in upon the dancers, and sometimes Mary, who persisted in not looking up, was pushed against her companion, by some sweeping couple. Alban was offended at this strictness, particularly that she would not look at the graceful Miriam. Not that he wanted Mary to waltz—far from it : he hardly knew what he wanted. Henrietta was now waltzing with Van Brugh, and her drapery brushed them as she went by.

"I must get into the other room, Mr. Alban : can't you manage it ?"

They ran across the waltzers. Alban penetrated resolutely the opposite mass towards the front drawing-room. He was obliged to put his arm fairly round Mary, which caused another of her perpetual blushes. At length they got through the folding doors, and found fresher air and iced punches circulating, while Mrs. Seixas was the object of attraction. She sat indolently on a divan—dark, but clear as amber, superbly embonpoint, and blazing with jewels like an Orient queen, or one of the diamond images of King Zeyn. Altogether these Jewesses outshone all the other women present. Yet some how a feeling had been awakened in Alban's heart, an idea (though repelled) had been presented to his mind, which made all the splendors of the world and seductions of sense seem dim and weak. In the midst of this scene so opposed to the cross in every shape, he had experienced one of those moments when Truth sends a piercing ray into the soul, and discovers to it the vanity of all earthly things, Was *he* the youth who that very day had dreamed of a flight to Syria with Miriam Seixas, and a passionate retirement with her in the desert or the mountains of that clime of the sun, preparatory to a fierce career of battle and empire.

At supper these sublime fancies received another shock. While our Mahomet was offering his Ayesha some oysters (which she of course refused) a careless youth ran against him, and made him spill some of the liquid on her dress. The individual who had caused this misfortune turned to apologize, and, in so doing, let nearly a plateful of the same mixture run over Mary De Groot's pink and silver skirt.

" Oh, my pretty dress," exclaimed she, in consternation, hastily wiping it with her handkerchief.—" How provoking ! I declare, Mr. Lynch, you deserve not to be invited to another dancing party this winter."—But she caught Alban's eye, and laughed,—" I will make him pay me for it, and put the money in the poor-box."

Miriam said not a word except to assure Mr. Atherton that it was of no earthly consequence, but she answered young Lynch's frightened apology with one look of her expressive Oriental face— a glance of her long Jewish eye—fit to have conveyed the tragic wrath of a Norma.

Mary De Groot would retire after supper with her parents, in spite of all remonstrances, although Alban offered to take her home, and her father rather encouraged the idea. In vain Henrietta called her a spoil-sport. The young lady was resolute, although very far from the appearance of moroseness. The brightness of her cheek, the sparkle of her eye, and beauty of her smile, rather indicated that the emotional nature was in a state of

effervescence. If the various incidents of the evening had affected her slightly one by one, the repetition had at length awakened
all her sensibility. But the voice of the spirit was clearly audible
amid all the tumult of the world and the flesh. She was not
forced to obey it, but she did without hesitation, humiliated by the
temptation—the love of pleasure and excitement which she experienced—but innocent of even exposing herself to it longer than
she could avoid. It was a great merit in one so young and so attractive, who could not but feel herself formed to be the ornament
of society. She would have persuaded Alban to come away too,
but he said it would not do for him—a young man and all that.

Returning to the ball, after handing Mary into her father's
carriage, he was caught in passing the supper-room by Van Brugh,
and compelled to come in and drink some more champagne.
Many other young men were lingering to eat partridges and toss
off champagne after their manner. Van Brugh assured him that
this wine was like so much water, which our hero, being unused
to it, partly believed. It was a gay party which sprang upstairs,
and encountered the Seixases also going away. Miss Clinton was
teasing Miriam to stay.

"This must be put a stop to, Atherton," cried Livingston.

Miss Seixas turned a deaf ear to Van Brugh's representations,
and listened to Miss Clinton's entreaties with an unmoved smile,
but when Alban chimed in, begging to dance with her, which he
had not been able to do all the evening, and offering to attend her
home, after a yielding glance at her brother, who offered no opposition to an arrangement then sufficiently common, she suffered
herself to be led triumphantly back to the dancing-room. They
were waltzing; Alban had never waltzed in his life, but wine
gave him courage for any thing, and having learned to dance at
an early age, before he was sent to that pious place, Babylon, he
caught the step from Miss Seixas directly. However, one does
not learn any thing perfectly at once. Mary De Groot had expressed a doubt of the possibility of waltzing without sin, that is,
as it seemed to him, without treading on his partner's toes : for

the agreeable sensations which he experienced in being taught by Miss Seixas, surely there was no sin in those. She bore his blunders with an almost Christian patience, and only laughed very much when once obliged to stop to recover her slipper.

Henrietta next offered herself to complete his education, and the difficulty of waltzing without sin was now very great, unless Alban had closed his eyes. Besides her extreme of fashionable undress, which had shocked our hero at the commencement of the evening, and was perilous indeed for her partner, Henrietta had adopted since supper a novel and spirited style of managing her drapery, instead of letting it stream cloud-like behind her, by taking it up on one side in a mass, and throwing the full skirts, fine as cobweb and white as spray, over her arm. What with the glancing arm buried in those innumerable folds of semi-transparent tissue, and the silver gleam of the under dress, it was irresistibly charming, and our poor Alban's bosom was soon all in a light blaze of concupiscence.

As the ships which approached the mountain of loadstone in the Arabian Tales had all the iron drawn out of them by the mighty magnet, and went to pieces, so it is with the souls which near this fatal coast. It is strewn with wrecks. Moreover, from the combined influence of the wine and the waltz, our hero's head began to swim, and his fine judgment to become not a little obscured. To vary our comparisons, he had arrived, unawares, in that region of inward illumination, where the moral sense is eclipsed, and man walks in the twilight, or rather the penumbra, of the irrational natures. In plain English, Alban was partly tipsy. Fortunately for him, habit is still a guide where reason ceases to be a light. Physically, Alban could no longer direct his steps—he made strange gyrations in dancing, and addressed his partner so strange observations, exemplifying the *in vino veritatem*, that Henrietta, for her own sake as well as for his, was glad to get him away from the company. Alban had began to talk about her school-days, evincing a knowledge more than he was fairly in possession of when in his sober senses, but which frightened her sufficiently. He was giving her maudlin good advice, and finally (for how far the unprincipled school-girl lived on in the dashing belle, or what startled Alban into a sense of his humiliating state, our story requires not to be said) he broke from her with a stern rebuke, such as perhaps only a Puritan, born and bred, would have had the heart to inflict upon a woman, whose fault, such as it was, he had shared. In truth, pride went for something in our hero's conduct ; but the main thing was the fear of hell ; for he had fallen so far, at least in his own estimate, that it seemed to him scarcely an additional humiliation to fall further, perhaps even less. But come what would—seem craven and spiritless as he might—he resolved to flee.

The ball-room was still full of light-hearted dancers ; the Count was indefatigably waltzing ; Miriam stood near a window listening, with a vacant air, to the compliments of Van Brugh. Alban approached, pale, but with a sparkling eye.

" One more waltz, beautiful Miriam."

" Spare my tip-toes," she answered, instantly breaking into a smile, and laying her hand on his shoulder. But he whirled her round the room without missing a step.

" Since you have really learned to waltz now, Mr. Atherton, suppose that we go home."

The distance that Alban and Miss Seixas had to accomplish was considerable, being nearly the whole length of Broadway. It was at about half-past two when the coach sluggishly stopped in State-street. Mr. Seixas himself came to the door to admit his sister, but instead of getting out, Miriam called to him from the coach window. He came down the old marble steps.

" Mr. Atherton has swooned in the carriage, my brother. We were obliged to stop to recover him, but he is not yet conscious."

Alban lay in the bottom of the carriage, with his head resting against the cushions.

" Why did you not take him home, Miriam ?"

" I knew not where that might be."

" This is the home of his childhood," said her brother, after some meditation, "we cannot deny him its hospitality. "You are strong, Miriam. Help me lift the boy out of the carriage."

Alban was soon laid upon the divan of the apartment where we first saw the Hebrew brother and sister. The scene was remarkable even for a metropolis which is the resort of all nations. Seixas was attired in an Oriental robe of scarlet and sables, having loose hanging sleeves. A high cap, in the same style, crowned his thick black curls. The jetty beard which fringed his colorless, peculiar visage, completed the ideal of his race. He regarded with a look tranquil as marble that pale face of the youth, on which an impassioned expression still lingered. The attitude and garb of Miriam, who, drawn up to her utmost height, looked down upon the insensible Alban with a strange regard, were not less striking than her brother's. The robe which Miriam had worn at the ball was of Eastern stuff, gold on a ground of blue, fitting closely to her flexible shape, but leaving bare the arms and superior portion of the fine amber bust, where it had a border of gems. Her waist tapered so exactly, her bosom swelled in such harmonious full waves, beneath this vesture, that nothing could be more admirable in female beauty. She lifted the skirt carelessly over one knee, the foot resting with graceful boldness on the yellow satin cushion of the divan where Alban lay, showing, what a deep slit up the side often exposed, an under-skirt or petticoat of cherry satin finely worked in silver. The barbaric splendor of this dress was relieved by the perfect simplicity of her black hair with its Spanish plait, and by the light effect of a veil of white lace which hung from her comb, and floated like a mist around her. An enormous taper of yellow wax burning on a lofty candelabrum of *rosso*, shed a soft light on this fine group.

"Was this sudden?" inquired Seixas.

"He had been saying to me beautiful but impossible things," answered Miriam, without taking her eyes off from Alban. "All at once he laid his hand on his heart, and went off thus."

"Were they ardent things, Miriam?" asked her brother.

"It may be. I never heard such before," replied the maiden, with haughty tranquillity.

"Were the lad's actions as strange to thee, Miriam, as his words?" continued Seixas, with a sudden flash of the eye, and turning towards her his astute Jewish countenance. "A freedom passes for naught with the colder females of this land, which a Spanish woman would resent as a deadly insult."

"Thyself, Manuel," replied his sister, rather slowly, but with her eyes still bent down on Atherton's form, "could'st not respect me more scrupulously, in the days of my separation, than this young Gentile to-night."

"A swoon from wine and emotional excitement is sometimes dangerous," said Manuel, meditatively. He stooped down and felt Alban's pulse, still looking fixedly in his face with those gleaming eyes. "Remain with the boy, Miriam, while I seek a remedy which may rouse him."

The countenance of the young Jewess underwent an instantaneous change when her brother had disappeared. She advanced a step and slipped down at the same time in a careless Eastern way, on the edge of the low divan. She took Atherton's hand into her lap; her soft, peculiar face, bent down to gaze on his, assumed an expression indescribably passionate. She remained thus, without motion almost, until her brother's step resounded again in the next apartment, when after a momentary sidelong glance of her eloquent eye, she bent down still further and imprinted a kiss on the youth's pallid lips. For a moment it seemed that she would fling herself upon his bosom, but when Manuel again drew aside the curtain between the rooms, Miriam had already resumed the position in which he had left her, and only the long swell of her respiration lifting the gold-wrought silk of her robe higher and more frequently than before, betrayed her recent passion.

"Go you, Miriam,—for 'tis not worth the pains of calling servants—and dispose the apartment over this to receive the young Atherton. He was born in it, I have heard him say, as were two generations of his maternal ancestors, merchants and exiles like ourselves."

"That chamber is next mine own, thou knowest," said the maiden, reservedly.

"There is no other where he can fitly be placed. Lock the door between thy chamber and his, if such a lad inspires thee with fear. Thou wilt do that at all events."

"Nay," said Miriam, "I shall do so, of course, though not from fear of him. But do thou take the key."

"If thy purity or my trust in thee needed such a precaution," replied Manuel, "neither were worth preserving. I might doubt him for a moment, for he is but a Christian after all; but my sister is above the very name of suspicion."

28

CHAPTER XIII.

AT about eleven o'clock, on Friday morning, our hero awoke and heard Trinity bells tolling. At first he supposed it was St. John's, thinking himself in Grey-street, till puzzled by the room and furniture, he sprang out of bed and ran to the window. The Battery, white with new-fallen snow—the wintry bay, and the tide dashing against the old sea-forts—the scene familiar to his childhood—told him where he was; and then he looked around and recognized the room which, in childhood, had been his. It all flashed on him—how he had drunk too much wine at a party, had unpardonably insulted one young lady, and betrayed to another the most ridiculous vanity conceivable. He divined that the Seixases had too well learned his condition, and had taken him in from pity; for his memory was here at fault. He could recall nothing later than a violent spasm at the heart, as he was talking in a most absurd way to Miriam Seixas, in the carriage. Hurrying to the glass, he perceived a pale, haggard face. Internally he felt an utter sickness and hollowness, a sense of misery and remorse. Glancing around the room, he perceived his clothes laid in order, with fresh linen, slippers, a chamber-robe, and a shower-bath, with its curtains open. He bathed and dressed as expeditiously as possible, hoping to escape from the house without notice.

While Alban was dressing, he adopted (as is usual on such occasions) several resolutions. First, he would write to Miss Clinton, retracting his unwarrantable observations, and imploring her forgiveness; although, indeed, it was manifest that he had said nothing but what was true. Then he must see Miriam, (he would rather enter the cage of a lioness,) and beg her to forget his folly—at least, not to mention it. And he must certainly tell the whole story, so far as it was proper to be told, to Mary De Groot.

He had implicated her (fool that he was) with Miss Clinton ; and besides, it was due to her that she should know his weakness—so true a friend as she was ! Otherwise, he should feel like a thief. But what should he say to his father and mother, in explanation of his staying out all night ? After involuntarily imagining fifty false statements, he adhered to the resolution of telling the exact truth. Perhaps Seixas had already told his father, and would not Henrietta avenge herself by telling every body that Mr. Atherton got tipsy at supper ? Had Miriam made herself merry that morning, with her sister-in-law, at his expense ? Would it be all over town ? Poor young man !

Recalling some of his impulses, and some points of his conduct, more exactly, he felt thankful for having been preserved, at any cost, from such sin as he had never learned to contemplate without horror. We have not dared, and certainly not wished, to paint Alban's temptation and Henrietta's want of virtue. He was sensible of little else but the degradation of having yielded at all, though no one but himself and God knew how far. Still their hearts had met in that polluting sympathy, and who could tell when the bond would be severed, or into what closer fellowship of sin—opportunity favoring—it might yet unite them ? He resolved, on his knees, and with tears, never to see her again if he could help it. So he finished dressing and went down, hoping to make his exit unobserved, and meaning to repair to Delmonico's for breakfast.

He was met at the foot of the stairs by Miss Seixas's personal attendant, who invited him with a sweet tone of arch respect into a room overlooking the Bay, and adorned with innumerable fine engravings, where a fire glowed cheerfully, and a table was spread. Tea, coffee, and cocoa were proffered him by the sprightly Rebecca, and a dumb waiter, at her touch, brought up every other luxury of a Knickerbocker breakfast—except ham and eggs. A beautiful bouquet lay beside his plate, and a note. The last was as follows :—

"DEAR ATHERTON,—To save your mother's anxiety I dispatched a line to Grey-street this morning, to say that you had kindly attended Miriam home last night at my request, and that on account of the lateness of the hour I had kept you. I added, that unless you had been sound asleep after so much dissipation, you would doubtless send your love. If I were you, I would not mention having been ill, as it might excite groundless apprehensions in regard to your health ; and I really think that your singular seizure was entirely owing to your stomach being disordered by that confounded bad champagne of Clinton's, which I have no doubt was made in New Jersey.

"Faithfully yours,

"SEIXAS."

The perusal of this note relieved our hero's mind considerably, and when a cup of coffee had dissipated his remaining headache, he was able to do his breakfast justice. He inquired cheerfully for the ladies, and learned from his dark-eyed, intelligent attendant, that Mrs. Seixas had not yet risen—a fresh consolation, although it confirmed an opinion he already entertained of her indolence—but that her more youthful mistress had been up a couple of hours, and that it was she who had selected the bouquet for Mr. Atherton from the conservatory, as soon as she knew that he was stirring.

Fascinating and reviving attentions ! Alban admired the fragrance and happy combination of roses and myrtle in the bouquet, and asked if he could see Miss Seixas, not doubting, though somewhat fearing, to receive an affirmative reply. But Rebecca, with a smile and arch toss responded, that at that early hour he could not expect a young lady to be presentable. Not that he must infer, continued she, quite in the style of an Abigail in Gil Blas, that her mistress was one of those fine ladies who in the morning, before being dressed for company, appear in a dirty and crumpled loose gown, and untidy hair, or flit from room to room in petticoat and stays, and stockings down to the heel, (the young Spanish

Jewess was evidently describing something very common ;)—no, it was only the perfect modesty and dignity of Donna Miriam that would prevent her receiving a young cavalier like Señor Atherton, in a wrapper, though white as snow. Alban let her run on, but when he had finished his last cup of tea, slipped into her hand, quite appropriately, a Spanish pillared dollar, and begged her to procure him a moment's interview with her young lady before he quitted the house.

"Why, you see, señor," replied Rebecca, dubiously, "what you ask is hard and easy. No one need know it if you spend an hour or two with Donna Miriam, for the Señora Seixas is asleep at this moment, and Moses has gone on an errand for my master to the upper part of the city, whence he will not return, I know, before three o'clock ; and there is nobody else in the house but the old black cook, who is so fat that she can't get upstairs, and Antonia, the Christian maid-servant, (for we must have one for the Sabbath, señor,) and she never by any possibility comes into this part of the house unless she is called to bring wood or water, or a fresh scuttle of this nasty coal ; and I need not tell you, Señor Atherton, who were born in the house, that Antonia has her back-stairs. But all these favorable circumstances, of which another would take advantage, are just what will prevent my young lady from acceding to your request."

"Well, well, Rebecca ; enough said," interrupted Alban impatiently ; "you can but deliver my message to your mistress. Say that I beg her to see me for a few minutes ; for I have—yes, I have an important favor to ask."

Rebecca retired with a shake of the head, which rather intimated her sense that no good would come of it, than any foreboding of the hopelessness of her errand. She was absent so long that Alban was beginning to despair, although, by a common contradiction, he was not sure whether he wished his request to be granted or not, when at last she returned with a grave, flushed face, and with an air of mystery bade him follow her. She led the way into the back drawing-room, which Alban had not entered since he had renewed his acquaintance with his childhood's home as the dwelling of these foreign Jews.

Rebecca closed and locked the white folding-doors between the two drawing-rooms, and let down the curtain already described, the solemn folds of which on that side were of dark purple, making an effective contrast with the old-fashioned white pillars and architrave of the doorway in which it hung. The walls of the room were adorned with Hebrew inscriptions in gold and color; the seats and furniture were of carved ebony, with draperies of purple velvet; and the means for lighting it at night consisted of silver lamps, ranged on tall stands or candelabra of ebony, and of antique silver branches on the mantel. A fire of hickory wood, laid on curious silver andirons, blazed in the chimney as in the time of Alban's mother. At one end of the room stood a harp, and near the fire a table whereon lay a casket of ebony mounted with silver. Rebecca turned the key in a door at the lower extremity of the room, which conducted, as Alban remembered, into the back hall and servants' stair. She also drew the window-curtains in such a manner that no one could see into the room from the garden. Alban wondered that the girl was so long, and why she took these precautions; but she approached him again before going to summon her mistress.

"Señor Atherton," she said, "my young lady is about to see you alone, although I begged her to let me be present at such a distance that you might say what you liked to each other without my overhearing it. Now it is very plain to me, of course, what this means, as well as her solicitude about your breakfast, and the pretty message conveyed in those flowers, which I understand as well as she, (and I hope you will take care my master does not see that bouquet.) She loves you, señor, as you doubtless know well enough; and it can't turn to good, for although she says that you believe our holy law, and worship only the God of Abraham, it makes no difference, since you are not of her race, and she is betrothed since she was twelve years old to her cousin Joséf. Ah, señor, my mistress is not yet eighteen: she is as simple-hearted as a child, with all her lofty manners, and though she is loyalty itself, and chaste as the daughter of Jephtha, the blood which flows in her veins is not like that of your northern damsels; you must not treat her as you would one of them. You have one of those calm glances, Señor Atherton, which show self-command; think, then, for her as well as yourself, and do not by words, still less by caresses, to which, however innocent you may think them, she is wholly unaccustomed, awaken the sensibility of my mistress, which the more it has hitherto lain dormant, the more violent and uncontrollable will it be when it is roused."

The manner of the young Jewess was animated in the extreme, and her language tinged with a Southern poetry from the earnestness of her feelings. Alban was naturally much embarrassed for a reply, and before he had time to frame one, the quick ear of the maiden caught the step of her mistress on the stair, and she darted away with an appealing look. Miriam's voice was heard without in a tone of impatient reproof, and the maid submissively answering. The young lady rejoined more softly, and immediately entered. Rebecca closed the door, but before doing so, looked in again and made Atherton a quick gesture of warning.

The first address of Miriam was always characterized by a lowly bending modesty. On this occasion she approached with a look of peculiar submission almost amounting to fear, and curtseyed to him without raising her eyes from the ground. The usual richness of her habits was wanting also, her attire being a fine white wrapper, such as Rebecca had described, to which she had only added a Spanish veil or mantilla of black lace, placed with care over her head, and which she gathered around her as if to hide the light robe beneath. Her black hair, which never was glossier, took a gleam from the fire, and her eyes, when she raised them for a moment, darted a strange soft light which might be partly from the same source. Alban had never felt her presence so softening, and this manner, united to what Rebecca had said, disconcerted the apology he had intended to make, and left

him in a perfect perplexity how to address her. He thought of
the bouquet which he held in his hand. The flowers, doubtless,
did speak a language.

"I wished to thank you for this," said he, somewhat coldly,
perhaps. "It is a kind answer to my last night's presumption."

"I thought not of seeing you when I sent it, Señor Alban."

She slightly turned from him, and bending her head, seemed
to struggle with a feeling which he could in no wise interpret;
then she advanced with a quick movement to the table, and
opened the ebon casket with a key which she held concealed in
her hand. It was filled with cases of red silk, containing a most
surprising quantity of jewels. She drew out the glittering contents, and spread them on the table before Alban's wondering
eyes. They were apparently the ornaments of an Eastern lady,
and of enormous value,—bracelets and necklaces of emerald and
turquoise; great strings of pearls; a girdle composed entirely of
brilliants; a Turkish dagger hilted with rubies; ear-rings, ank-
lets, slippers, and velvet caps for the head that were alike absolutely one mass of diamonds.

"Take these," said Miriam, extending her hand to him with
an inexpressible air of sweetness and humility, "and go raise the
standard of Israel on the land of our inheritance, if perhaps God
will deliver us by the hand of a believing Gentile, in whom must
flow, I cannot but think, unknown to himself, the blood of our
sacred tribe. I have loved thee unawares. *That* I can no
longer help," she continued, laying her hand on her heart, "but
my faith, thou knowest, is plighted to another, and I must keep
it. A holy enterprise cannot begin with an act of treason. Take
these, then, and go; it is all Miriam can give thee, though she
would willingly have given all."

He was thunderstruck.

"Except thou fly with me, Miriam," he exclaimed, adopting
her own tone, while he involuntarily drew near to take her hand,
"this is impossible."

She drew back a step or two, with haste, and made a repellant gesture, as if to warn him not to touch her.

"It is all mine," she said ;—" the portion of my Smyrniote mother. 'Tis a poor restitution for the heart which I owe thee and the person which is not mine to bestow. I shall be deeply grieved—inconsolably—if thou refuse it at my hands. What if thou fail in thy daring enterprise ! Have I not thought of that ? It will still be a thing to remember for ever, that, after ages of contempt, the sword was drawn again for Judah."

The more enthusiasm the young Jewess displayed, the more Alban's embarrassment increased. To her the whole was real ; to him it had been but a dream—a wild revery of imaginative ambition. He was not, and never could be, a Jew. Why, in his moments of greatest estrangement from Christianity ill-understood, the cold reasonings by which Seixas had concluded against even the possibility of a *Divine* Messiah, had deeply offended him. Alban's heart was never really divorced from Christ, and he felt that truth, now when a Jewess of whom he was deeply enamored, whose benevolence he had witnessed, and whose present generosity, as well as the sincerity of her virtue, excited his admiration, offered him an immense treasure to take arms against nothing else in reality but that name of sweetness and benediction. Never !

It was a delicate ground to break, to let Miriam know that she was deceived in regarding him as a young proselyte of the gate. She faltered and changed color at the most cautious statement he could frame to insinuate the error into which she had been led in this particular.

"I am not ashamed of my faith in Moses and the Prophets," said he. "I still believe a perfect unity in God, and freedom in man, in spite of his weakness, Miriam. I believe that our justice must be in truly fulfilling the Divine Law. But I believe also that grace has descended from the Most High to implant this justice in our souls. I believe that a Jewess like thee, a virgin like thee, and bearing thy very name, blossoming like Aaron's rod, conceived and bore the Hope of Jew and Gentile alike—the JEHOVAH whom thou adorest."

Alban pronounced the sacred name in a manner known only to the Jews, and in which it is uttered by them only on certain rare occasions of awful solemnity, and Miriam who had been listening in a startled attitude, threw herself hastily upon her knees and bowed her head to the carpet at his feet.

" Yes, worship Him, Miriam," continued Alban, with emotion, " the Notzry whom thy fathers in their ignorance slew, but thy God and theirs."

" It was not that I intended, thou knowest," replied Miriam, rising with agitation. " But be brief, Mr. Atherton. I comprehend now that you are still a Christian, but of which of the numberless sects of Christianity ? or will you found a new one ?" she demanded sarcastically, and haughtily averting her face. Alban's reply was probably not unexpected, for her expression in listening to it altered only by being rapidly heightened into violence.

" The God of Israel has never wanted a people, Miriam. Yes, beautiful but unbelieving one, thy race is not more widely diffused by its exile, than the Catholic Church by its conquests."

" It is then a woman whom you will adore ! I thought so," cried Miriam, in a bitterly scornful tone. " Is it not in the dark eyes of one that you have read the proofs of your new faith ! How easily I discern your falsehood !" She drew herself up to her full height. " Gracious Heaven," she exclaimed, " why do I not repay this man's treachery as in my country the females of his own religion would !"

In her sudden jealousy and sense of slighted love, Miriam forgot every thing else. Her forehead grew purple with the dark blue veins that started up upon it. It seemed that her passion would stifle her. She caught up the Turkish dagger from the table, and raised it with a motion quicker than thought. The armed hand descended with such celerity and force, that, though Alban caught her wrist, he could not so far divert the blow but that the edge of the weapon divided her fine robe, and the point grazed her breast. He wrested the dagger from her relaxing fingers and held her in his arms. She looked at him wildly.

"Tell me," she said, hardly able to speak from panting, "why did you make me think you loved a Jewess, and extort from my bosom a secret of which else I had myself been unconscious? And now I stand before you a woman—a maiden—whom you love not, but who has humbled herself to say that she lov.. you!"

"I *do* love you!" said Alban, with fondness, though shocked. "Be a Christian, Miriam, not adoring, but venerating the blessed Mary, your namesake, and worshipping her Son, the King of Israel, as you did just now in outward act, and I will joyfully take you away, with the treasures you would so generously have bestowed upon me. But overcome this wild emotion, proper to guilt and shame, not to virtue and honor like yours."

"Ah, thou mockest me, Alban. Yet thanks for holding back my wicked hand. God of my fathers, what would I have done! But release me;"—with a peculiar expression, struggling with that of pride and anguish—"see, I bleed; release me."

The dagger had barely grazed the skin, but the blood trickled fast from the scratch, and Miriam stanched it with her handkerchief, heedless of Alban's eyes. Her look was of complete abandonment and desolation. Like most women of her half Oriental education, although sumptuous in the adornment of her person, she owed nothing of its shape to art. Miriam wore the black silk petticoat and chemise of Spanish Central America, the latter surrounded in the neck with rich yellow lace, within which swelled the untortured bust "like two young roes that are twins, which feed among the lilies," to use the comparison of Holy Writ. What lover could behold, unmoved, his mistress thus despairing, with her own hand unveil her chaste bosom? Pity, delicacy, gratitude, a generous desire to heal the wounds of her pride, (the same feelings which had carried on our hero further with Mary De Groot in five minutes, than in months of an intimacy full of interest,) blended now with a kind of sentiment which Mary had never inspired ; and, truth to say, the wisest and strongest have seldom come off conquerors in this strife.

" Hearken to me, Miriam," he said, in tones very different from those which he had lately employed, and the young daughter of the South instantly felt the change—" that which has touched thee so nearly, in my recovered faith, bears another aspect, which thou hast not considered. Had I, in spite of the reluctance of thy people to receive proselytes, become a Jew, thy betrothal to thy cousin, scarce just as it seems to me, would separate us more than ever, as thyself didst but now admit. But if *thou* becomest a Christian, thy conversion necessarily dissolves thy contract. To wear a mixed garment of linen and wool is forbidden by the Law of Moses ; so, for the baptized and unbaptized to be joined in wedlock is contrary to the Law of Christ. You will be free to bestow your hand upon me, Miriam, from the moment that the waters of baptism shall have separated you from your nation, as the Red Sea divided your fathers from the Egyptians. I would not seduce thee, Miriam, even from thy unbelief, as I must term it, by the power I may possess over thy earthly affections ; but thy human love may be His instrument, Who made and controls the heart, to open thine eyes, hitherto blinded by prejudice, to the light of heavenly truth. Think of that ungovernable violence of passion which has so long been hidden under thy virgin serenity of mien. Thy law condemns, but can it impart the inward strength thou needest to restrain it ? Has it power to banish the keen remorse thou feelest, by the sense of innocence restored ? Christ can do this for thee, Miriam. He can remove, in a moment, the shame that bows thy head, and calm the tempest which agitates thy bosom."

Even during this address, Miriam had gently concealed her bosom, and a further attempt to hide the spots of blood upon her wrapper, by drawing the veil over it, showed that hope was reviving in her humiliation, and the faith that she was beloved. Alban, perhaps, ascribed those symptoms to a conviction produced by his arguments, which were really due to a sense of her sex's power reviving in the woman. Miriam, on the other hand, was not sufficiently reassured on that point, to dare resist the caresses with which her lover, giving way to his passion, now seconded his eloquence. He recurred to the picture which, in his delirium of the night before, he had drawn of their mutual existence in a remote land. The young Jewess, who passed from one extreme of feeling to another with Southern facility, murmuring a condemnation of her own weakness, tacitly consented to all that he proposed, when the door flew open, and Rebecca burst in, announcing that her master was approaching the house, and that madam, also, was just risen. The position of the young people gave a different turn to her exclamations.

"Oh fie, Señor Atherton! is this your fine self-command? your arm round my mistress! Oh, sir, pray begone!"

"You don't understand it, Rebecca."

"Oh, yes, indeed, too well! Will you go, señor? What's to be done with these trinkets?"

Miriam, regardless of her maid's presence, leaned her head and clasped hands on Atherton's shoulder.

"This is base, Señor Atherton. You will ruin my young lady without benefiting yourself. There's my master's knock. Now, if you wish my assistance in future, señor, run yourself and open the door for him, while we escape with these things!"

At this suggestion, Alban extricated himself from Miriam, and darted off; yet hardly had he taken a step, ere he felt tempted to return, for Miss Seixas stood rooted, as if despairing, to the spot where he had left her. Rebecca, seeing his irresolution, when every moment was precious, and observing, for the first time, the tell-tale spots of blood on her lady's dress, became frantic, forced him out of the room with a violence approaching to fury, and locked the door. Even while he threw on his cloak, however, in the hall, the white raiment of the Hebrew maiden appeared above, at the top of the stairs, and Miriam's hand, mournfully waving, bade him farewell.

CHAPTER XIV.

IT will be seen that our hero is gradually emerging into light,
amid all the confusion which his passions and the world have
raised.   It is in the hour of temptation that the battle of life is
lost or gained.   Many are they who fall ; few the victors.   But
to be wounded, however severely, is not to lose the battle ; to be
covered and defiled with blood and dust is nothing.   The point is
to see who, after the *mêlée* is over, stands with his sword drawn
in his hand, and his enemy gasping at his feet.

Alban has made some points and certainly lost others.   This
entanglement with Miriam Seixas is very much in his way, and
is likely to injure the simplicity of his course.   He will be afraid
to submit himself immediately to the Church, which is the true
and generous course for him to take, lest he should be required to
abandon his Jewish mistress.   Any way, dispensations would be
required, a formal marriage in the face of the Church must be
resorted to, whereas Alban thinks of nothing but a civil contract
and instant flight to a foreign land.   As for poor Mary De Groot,
her image recedes away into the distance again.   In fact, her im-
maturity has been too much against her with a youth of Alban's
age—which is the period of impatience, and will not wait for the
slow ripening of the fruit it covets.   If we represent love as so
powerfully influencing our hero, and show his heart so inconstant
and open to so many impressions, it is because the heart of youth
is so in fact.   Alban is far from being a perfect character.   His
intellect is first-rate, and his will has hitherto, upon the whole,
acted virtuously, so that it seems congruous that light should be
afforded him, but not too much.   A man like him ought to act
on less evidence than would be required to satisfy inferior persons,
and if his passions do not prevent, he probably will readily corre-
spond to whatever measure of grace may be vouchsafed him.

Alban has arrived at a sufficient truth, viz., that Christianity is one organized body. This truth, which pervades the New Testament, he has seized upon, and we may see how, if we attend for a few moments to his meditations on the day of his interview with Miriam Seixas, after his return home. Let it not excite surprise in any one, that Alban reverts to these topics after such a scene ; for the soul which is tossed on the sea of passion and circumstance, like a landsman on shipboard, naturally endeavors to fix its gaze upon the permanent object of revelation, as on steady stars.

His parents did not question him closely in regard to his staying at the Seixases' the night before. His father asked about the house ; his mother inquired in what room he slept, and whether it seemed familiar to him. She hoped that he had remembered to ask for the ladies in the morning before coming away, and then she recurred to the party at Mrs. Clinton's. As Alban knew that Miss De Groot was not in his mother's good graces any longer, he was particular to mention her refusal to waltz, and going away so early when every body begged her to stay. As Mrs. Atherton could not find fault with either of these things, the conversation languished, and when dinner was over, both his parents disposed themselves for a siesta. His father took the settee, his mother dozed in her rocking-chair, and Alban, after a short revery—much shorter than usual—took down the Episcopal prayer-book. Action indisposes us to dreams. He took the common-sense view of every thing now, and nothing disgusted him so much as unreality.

When our hero first went over the Episcopal order of Baptism with Mr. Soapstone, he thought it beautiful. Now, with the solemn baptism of Mary De Groot fresh in his memory, it naturally seems nude as well as unpractical, and he is struck with the sign of the cross being left optional with the candidate. This Church in the very rite of initiation, allowed the catechumen his private judgment in opposition to her own. The postulant for faith was permitted to dispute and make terms at the font itself,

with those who pretended a commission to teach and baptize all
nations.   Nay, he rejects the sign of Christianity!   " You are not
to make a cross on my brow," he says, " I object to that old superstition."   And the Church lets him have his own conceited,
unhumbled way about it.   Where is the firm, unhesitating, au-
thcritative tone of God's conscious Prophet and Priest ?   Where
is the conviction that truth and power are hers ?

    " No wonder the other old ceremonies of Christian baptism
are omitted altogether.   Of course it is foreign to the notions such
a Church entertains of her own powers, to suppose that insufflations, or touching the ear with spittle, or the tongue with salt, or
the body with holy oils, can have any spiritual efficacy by virtue
of the name of Jesus, or that devils can be cast out now-a-days by
invoking it ; but still, where was her *sense* when she failed to see
that these rites associated Christ's sacrament of spiritual healing
with its designed types, His miracles of bodily cure, in a way far
more instructive and more productive of faith than her cold textual
deductions !   And when the regeneration is at length complete,
and the new-born Christian stands before her, with the dew of
the new birth upon him, what inexplicable want of tact leads her
to substitute an exhortation of her own for those touching allu-
sions to the Lord's parables, which the ancient Church employs,
when she gives her neophyte the lamp of the virgins, and bids
her wear and keep undefiled the white garment of innocence and
sanctity, that she may have eternal life !"

    Alban laid down the book and thought of that character of
objectivity, and almost of personality, assumed in this great action
by the Catholic Church.   She appeared on the threshold of her
temple as a regal and sacerdotal society, dispensing truth and
grace.   Her every step, as she preceded her postulant to the font,
was the step of a queen.   Yet how tenderly she reiterated the
name of the ignorant, defiled, and demon-bound, whom she was
about to enlighten, cleanse, and loose !   What is like this majestic
mother !   You know her by her accents of blended authority and
love.   No false step-dame can imitate the sweetness that tempers

the dignity of the true Spouse of Christ. How coldly on the ear
fell the " Dearly Beloved," with which the English State-church
begins, and the abstract tone in which it calls upon the congregation to pray for " this person," compared with the individualizing
address of *sancta mater ecclesia :* " What is thy name ?"—
"*Mary*, what seekest thou of the Church of God ?" The mother
knoweth her own though future, and calleth it already by name,
but the hireling nurse is not so. In the Episcopal order of Bap-
tizing, Alban noticed, neither previous to, nor after the act, is the
name of the baptized mentioned, but only in the act of baptism
itself, where, indeed, it is the Catholic Church who suddenly
speaks, *and by the womb of her handmaid, brings forth children
to God*. And not otherwise was the difference at the close.
When the exhortation which this State-functionary, or this fashionable, secular, money-holding Corporation, addresses to the new-
baptized is concluded, it has, of course, no parting salutation to
intimate the existence of a new bond between itself—soulless
thing—and the neophyte's spirit : but the Church Catholic, true
to Her maternal instinct, turns not her back thus coldly upon her
offspring : " *Mary*," she says, as if it were a mother's kiss upon
her infant ere she lays it down—" Go in peace, and the Lord be
with thee."

All this was but physiognomy, although as truly indicative
of character to those who have the gift of reading it, as the lineaments of a human face. A deeper and more essential mark
of difference between the true, living Church and the Shadow
which mimics her functions, arrests Alban's intelligent and scru-
tinizing gaze. The Church takes original sin for granted, or
that mankind are naturally lost, and regards herself as the incor-
porate Society of the saved ; consequently she knows no other
way of salvation but by being incorporated into her, which in the
case of infants, who have not the use of reason, and cannot join
her by will and choice, can only be by baptism. Hence she
declares, without hesitation, that infants dying unbaptized cannot
enter heaven or see God—that supreme happiness which God

owes no man and grants to no mortal out of Christ. The Church
of England follows this view of the state of infants dying unbaptized, and consequently refuses them the rites of Christian burial,
for the just reason that she cannot speak of them as " resting in
the Lord," (since they do not,) or imply in any way that they are
among the " *blessed*" dead.

Imagine this vast multitude of souls lost out of the innumerable redeemed, wandering like pale stars in the illimitable outer
night; neither offenders nor yet just; untormented, yet not at
rest; the undeveloped germs of spirits which might have shone
brighter than angels in the blissful Presence, or groaned, haply,
with demons in the lowest caverns of penal fire; the unlighted
lamps of Heaven; the unkindled brands of Hell; the failures of
the Eternal Designer; the mysterious abortions of the Universal
Parent! Flowers of Adam's race coldly budding forth into the
unhallowed light and air of this world, and swept down by the
destroying scythe to which their lives were forfeit ere they began,
before the hand of pity could transplant them into the garden of
the Lord! we weep over them hopelessly as they lie, without honor
or beauty, on the cold, dead earth. Alas! Rachel mourneth for
her children, and will not be comforted because they are not!

But the American Episcopal Church gives unbaptized infants
Christian burial, as our hero observed, singing over them, " Blessed are the dead who die in the Lord!" And she omits the significant declaration of the Church of England, that " children
which are baptized, dying before they commit actual sin, are undoubtedly saved." The meaning of which is, that the American
Episcopal Church cannot believe that the Church is the elect
people of God, or that all who are not of the Church are lost.
" The consequence is," thought Alban, " that she cannot be any
part of the true Church, which of course knows its own relation
to God and to the rest of mankind. Any doubt or wavering
about the terms of salvation is impossible in the Society of the
saved," said he. " This is trifling with us. I had rather be a
Jew, than a Christian on such a plan."

The inquirer meditates and concludes, but at the end comes some regular duty of his existing position. Mrs. Atherton sighed with pleasure when her son at length laid aside the prayer-book, and took occasion to remind him of the Friday evening prayer-meeting. Alban recollected that he was a member of the Presbyterian Church, in good standing. Whether getting tipsy at a dancing party, toying with a wanton girl, (though he repented,) and proposing in the morning to run away with a Jewess, particularly fitted him to "take a part" in an evening prayer-meeting, he doubted. These little circumstances, if known, would scarcely edify, if they did not subject him—which was more than probable—to the somewhat inquisitorial discipline of the brethren. On the other hand, such was the nature of these societies, that a failure to comply with this duty would excite suspicion, either of some secret guilt or some heterodox bias. Alban went to the prayer-meeting, and Dr. —— did not fail to call upon him to pray. A young man from college is always a relief to the tedium of these occasions. When the brethren and sisters spoke afterwards of the exercises, young Atherton's prayer was singled out for warm approval. There was a freshness in his performances which agreeably roused the mind, and an unction that gratified the sensibility. Certainly, his prayer, that night, was unhackneyed. The rich quality of his voice, and its perpetual variety of modulation, contributed not slightly to the charm, and some of the females declared that, on this occasion, it affected them even to tears.

CHAPTER XV.

AFTER meeting, Alban walked down to the Battery, and watched the house in State-street for more than an hour, in the hope of seeing Miriam at her window. It was with difficulty, when he saw a light in her room, that he refrained from scaling the balcony—a feat he had a thousand times performed when a boy—and endeavoring to obtain a fresh interview, in which something definite might be agreed upon. His father and mother, who kept early hours, had retired when he reached home, and in his own room he found three notes, and a neat little parcel lying on the table. All were directed to himself, in female hands ; and after some hesitation which to open first, and trying to guess the writers, all being alike unknown to him, he opened that of which the handwriting looked simplest, and read as follows :—

"FIFTH AVENUE, *Friday.*

" DEAR ALBAN,—I gather from your note of this morning, (it startled me very much at first reading,) that you have done something which you feel to be wicked and silly, under the influence of wine. I am very, very sorry, of course, for you are a dear friend. There is no presumption, I assure you, in your taking that for granted. I wish you had a confessor, with whom you *could* be explicit, and who, besides advising you, could relieve your conscience from its burden. Sometimes we are left to sin, to humble our pride and teach us our frailty. You may live (I am sure you will) to thank God for letting you fall. Whatever you have done, I beg you won't speak of yourself any more in that unnatural strain, as unworthy of my friendship. We are all weak, and if God left me to myself, I might become the most degraded creature that breathes. Assuredly, I shall never cease to pray for you. I send this by Margaret, whom papa kindly lets me keep as a maid. She knows little of her duties yet, but is willing to learn, and I take a great deal of pleasure in teaching her. I thought it best to ask papa's permission to answer your note, of course without saying any thing to him about the matter of it.

"Your affectionate friend.

"M. DE G."

" She is an angel !" cried Alban. It was like a ray of purest heavenly light shining in upon a gloomy scene, illumined only by red and smoking torches. He kissed the note devoutly, read it over twice or thrice, and placed it in his bosom. The next was in the third person.

" MISS CLINTON sends her compliments to Mr. Alban Atherton, and acknowledges the receipt of his note. Her delicacy was deeply wounded, she need scarcely say, by what escaped him last evening, under a temporary excitement, for which she readily believes he was not to blame. She would be glad of an opportunity to explain more fully than she can trust to paper, an occurrence which appears to have come to his knowledge, in which her conduct and *motives* were misunderstood. At present she would only observe that even last night she felt grief rather than resentment, in regard to what happened, and that she accepts Mr. A.'s frank and gentlemanlike apology as a full atonement.

" Miss C. has observed the strictest secrecy in regard to *all* that has occurred, and trusts to Mr. Atherton's honor to do the same. Will he have the goodness to burn this when he has perused it.

" *Friday Evening.*"

Alban read this note also twice, and then, agreeably to the request of the writer, committed it to the flames. He opened the third epistle, trembling, yet eager, and read :—

" My brother found the poniard on the sofa, where you flung it when you had wrested it from my guilty hand, in that moment

of passion. Other circumstances had already awakened his suspicions. He questioned Rebecca, and she betrayed all she knew.
Manuel is not angry with us, Alban. I think he is flattered that
thou lovest me. He forgives me for loving thee, whom he also
loves. But he has convinced me—indeed, I knew it as well as
thou—that unless I become a Christian I cannot be thine. Alban,
I would abandon all else for thee but the religion of my fathers.
I must see thee, therefore, no more. I have promised Manuel to
accompany him, forthwith, to the city where Joseph Seixas
resides, and there, if he will overlook what I shall confess, fulfil
my early contract. How my hand can trace such words I know
not. You are young. One lovelier, worthier, perhaps even now
better loved, will console you for the loss of Miriam. 'Twere
base and wicked, indeed—so Manuel has truly said—to take
advantage of your inexperience, and inflict upon you a Jewish
wife. You must not seek then—it would be vain—to bend my
purpose. To-morrow is the Sabbath, and on the day after, we
shall be gone. I send you a remembrance of Miriam and her
weak love. Keep it for her sake. May the God of Abraham
watch over you. Farewell!"

It was all distinctly written. The parcel was a jewel-case,
and contained the Turkish dagger. Alban could see Manuel
Seixas taking it up deliberately, and fastening his keen Eastern
eye on its ruby hilt, and crooked inlaid blade.

CHAPTER XVI.

ALBAN slept soundly for six hours. Now-a-days, when you want a light all night you turn down the gas to a blue, imperceptible flame, but in '35, our hero's lamp was burning on the hearth. He took his watch from the pocket purchased of Mary at the New Haven fair. It was half-past five, and he sprang out of bed. There was no flowing Croton then, and in our turn we have almost forgotten the mahogany lavatory with its service of blue porcelain. It was a cold morning, and the ewer became full of ice the instant Atherton moved it. Hot water-pipes have put an end also to that : still, there was a generous hardihood in it which we half regret.

Alban dressed and sallied forth, bending his course to the cathedral—somewhat distant. It had snowed again in the night, and a gusty wind had whirled the sleet into drifts. Over head it was clear and starry, and the morning star glittered in the south-east with a brilliancy which must be seen to be appreciated. On account of the weather, mass was said in the chapel, more easily warmed than the church. The congregation, although it was not any particular day, (as the phrase is,) quite filled it. When Alban arrived the vestry door was open, and the confessional was visible, with a priest hearing the confession of a woman. After hearing three or four, he took off his stole and left the box ; the rest were obliged to wait, and he soon came out vested for mass. A considerable number of persons received communion. It was over in half an hour ; the congregation partly dispersed ; but a second had come in, and the same process was repeated ; and now the confessions were going on without intermission. Alban waited. He did not perceive Mary, and began to think that the snow had prevented her coming. He was surprised, at the communion in the second mass, to observe her among the females returning from the altar.

She resumed her place in a remote corner, and he perceived that she had been there when he arrived. She staid through the third mass, and directly it was over, went out, accompanied by Margaret Dolman, evidently not aware of Alban's presence. He joined them in the street. The two girls made their way with difficulty through the drifts and against the gusty wind.

Atherton took Miss De Groot's arm familiarly and helped her along : " Really, Miss Mary, you ought not to walk on such a morning as this."

" Mr. Alban !" with a pleased surprise, and she went on, struggling with the snow and wind.

A covered sleigh stood ready harnessed before the livery stable in Houston-street ; Alban ran forward and engaged it to take them home. In a minute it had dashed through the drift, and drew up jingling at the young lady's side.

" How very kind you are, Mr. Alban !"

He handed them in and paid the driver in advance, as if Miss De Groot had been a little girl. She thanked him in a simple, cordial manner, and asked him to ride.

" My way lies in another direction, you know. Yet I wish to see you to-day, Miss Mary. At what hour shall I find you disengaged ?"

" At any hour which is convenient for you," with great sweetness. " I shall stay at home all day to finish some work. Come when you like."

" It will be in the afternoon, then ; as early as I can make it."

The young heiress began to expect her friend at twelve. At half-past four she was still expecting him. The southwest drawing-room began to grow dusk, for the day had continued overcast with spells of snowing. Since Mary's return home this apartment had acquired an aspect of feminine inhabitation which it did not possess previously. There were flowers on the stands ; the piano was open ; a cozy group of seats had got formed in the corner where the young lady worked, between the fire, glowing in its mantel of statuary, and the richly-curtained south window, with its balcony of stone overlooking the street, hereafter to become so beautiful. At this time Mary could see all the way down the Avenue. She was at work on some strange little garments of muslin. Not to affect mystery where there is none, we may say that they were baby's chemises, which Miss De Groot was making for a poor woman who lived in a shanty on one of the Avenues. Through Margaret she was rich in cases of real want of the most touching kind. She had finished a certain number of the little things, which were neatly folded and laid in a pile on a dark rosewood workstand. Close by stood an embroidery frame, with an incipient chalice-veil stretched upon it, and the bright silks for working it lay ready sorted on a tabouret. It was clearly the young lady's intent to change her other work for this and hide the former, as soon as her friend should come in sight.

At last, when it was so dark that she had already put away the baby garments, a cab came up the Avenue. There was a ring—a gentle ring which she knew—and presently Atherton came into the room. She did not rise to greet him, and he came to her cozy corner. They shook hands in friendly fashion, and Alban dropped familiarly into a chair.

Had Miss De Groot been at work he would probably have begun by some commonplace observation, but it was not light enough even for embroidery, and she sat playing with the pencil that hung at her waist. He alluded at once to her kind reply to his letter of confession.

" I feared that you would feel so disappointed in me," he said.

Mary waited some time before answering. " You Puritans are so self-righteous. You can't bear to be thought weak like others."

" That's the way you view it ?"

" Certainly. It has given me great hopes of you, to learn that your self-complacency had received a wound," with a smile. " I was quite discouraged about you, Alban."

" I believe I showed my irritated pride, rather than virtue,

30

in that part of my conduct which at the time I thought most commendable."

"I dare say," said Mary hastily. She played with her pencil. "Let us not speak of it any more, I pray you, Mr. Alban. I am sorry you thought it necessary to accuse yourself to me at all. I knew you were human without your telling me." And the smile became arch.

"I am going to consult you now in regard to an affair that will be a new proof of my humanity."

"I dare say," replied the young lady, her dark eyes gleaming with witchery in that blended fire and twilight.

"I must premise," said Alban, with some confusion, "that I have got over my Jewish notions."

"I am glad to hear it."

"I believe you would say that pride and earthliness were behind the fact of so strange an aberration."

"I don't know. Father Smith says that sincere and humble persons who have never known the truth, may wander very strangely in seeking it."

"I had sincerity enough, but precious little humility, I am afraid. And how worldly—really how sensual—shocks me to think. The hope of another life—the trampling upon this—offended me. I desired my Paradise here.

"God has been teaching you, Alban," said Miss De Groot, with awakened interest.

"Indeed, I think so. I am sure there was never any one more unworthy of the gift of faith."

"Do you mean," said Mary, dropping her pencil and leaning forward,—"do you mean that you will be a Catholic?"

There was something in his face which answered her before he said with his lips—"By God's grace."

She uttered a faint cry of joy, sprang up hastily, and throwing her arms round his neck, kissed him on both cheeks. She sank back immediately upon her low seat, and buried her face in her lap. Alban turned paler than when he read Miriam's letter.

He could not say a word, while she sobbed in her apron like a child. She lifted her face at last, glowing red, and dried her eyes, without loooking at him.

"The Blessed Virgin has heard my prayers I knew she would, but I did not expect so soon. Tell me how it happened. How did God give you faith?"

"It was this morning at the mass in which you received communion, that I was first able to say with all my heart—*I believe*."

"I offered my communion for your conversion," said Mary, in a quiet, natural tone.

"Did you?" replied he, quite in the same, as if not at all surprised. "I went to a Presbyterian prayer-meeting last night and took part in the exercises," laughing. "But as soon as I got into the chapel this morning, (I came there full of any thing else,) and knelt down, pretty much, I think, with the intention of acting like others, but feeling tolerably sure, too, that there was at least nothing wrong in it, an indescribable certainty stole over me that this was the true, divine religion. I envied the poor people going to confession; the Presence in the Tabernacle penetrated me with awe, and the image of our Lady with the Child, above it, carried me back to Bethlehem. I saw as clearly as could be that let the world think as it might, He was here the same as there, in a form of weakness, but still the Almighty Saviour of Israel. I had concluded thus before from mere reasoning, you understand, nay, I had *said* it, but now I saw it. I heard the first mass in that state of mind. And yet—do you know, all the while I was uncertain what I should do in consequence, or how long I should retain this clear conviction. I felt as if I just saw into the other world, but what would happen when the vision vanished was beyond me. There was an obstacle—something to be given up—a great deal to be given up; more particularly the power of deciding upon my own conduct in a certain case where my feelings, my interests, my honor as a gentleman, and every thing I held dear in this world, were concentred. I felt as powerless, Mary, to surrender my own settled plan on this point, as to lift the cathedral from its base. I *knew* that I should go on with it as I had determined and as I wished, even if Hell-fire were before me as the inevitable end of the path I had chosen. Even now my feelings are as strong as ever, but my resolve is changed. And this happened in the second mass. The priest read so distinctly that I could follow a great deal of it, and the gospel, rapidly as he articulated, sank like molten lead into my heart—' If any man will come after me, let him take up his cross and follow me. For he who will save his life shall lose it, but he who shall lose his life for my sake shall save it. For what doth it profit a man, if he shall gain the whole world, but suffer the loss of his own soul? or what shall a man give in exchange for his soul? For the Son of Man shall come in the glory of his Father, with his angels, and then will he render to every man according to his works.' "

" I remember thinking of you as I followed it in my missal,' said Mary, with evident awe.

" The rest of that mass passed in a struggle with myself. I knelt down again after the gospel with the rest, I joined in the worship of the people as far as I understood it, I adored at the elevation, but with the dreadful feeling that when I looked at last without a veil upon His face who was then lifted up, it might be a face of wrath for me. After the elevation, I began to pray earnestly, until the perspiration, notwithstanding the coldness of the chapel. ran down my body in streams. I appealed to Mary, the Gate of Heaven and Refuge of sinners, as she is called in that beautiful litany you showed me the other day. Then you all went up to communion, (although I had no idea of your being there,) and the thing flashed upon me again. For the love of a woman—a mere creature and of a fallen race, a fair corruption, whose body would soon be dust, and her soul, without faith, go down to eternal night—would I forego the sweetness of the Creator !"—Mary clasped her hands.—" For one draught from the filthy puddle of sensual pleasure—for it was that after all which attracted me —would I lose the beatific vision, and never know what it was to possess and enjoy God ! ' O my Author and my End,' I exclaimed, 'take from me every thing which thou hast made, but give me Thyself.'"

Mary had listened with mixed feelings to this burst. After some little delay, several things being said which were of little importance, she inquired what it was that brought him to mass.

" This very affair in regard to which I still wish to ask your sisterly advice."

He drew from his pocket a letter which the reader will not be slow to identify, observing that it would put her in possession of the facts. He thought that under the circumstances, he was justified in showing it to *her*.

Mary received Miriam's letter with a grave, curious face, glancing first at the feminine superscription of the envelope. She turned towards the fire to read it, spreading it open in her lap. Before she began, however, covering it with both her hands, she looked up to Alban and said—" Is it from Miss Clinton ?—Oh, it is not !"—with a relieved air—" I asked because if it had been, I should have been unwilling—but no matter."

Thus saying, she began to read. Blank astonishment was first depicted on her countenance. As she went on, leaning on the elbow, she shaded her face with one hand, and the other stole softly to her heart. She perused the letter evidently more than once, seeming, by the motion of the eye, to dwell on particular expressions. She remained a good while after as in thought, with her eyes closed ; but when she addressed Alban, it was with a countenance quite free from emotion. She laid her finger on a passage of the letter.

" I understand from this that you have proposed to Miss Seixas ?"

" Precisely," said Alban.

" She is contracted to another person—is she ?"

" A cousin—a Jew," replied Alban, dropping on one knee by Miss De Groot's side, and looking over the letter still spread in her lap.

"There is another ottoman, Alban."

He drew it near her and sat down.

"I don't see what you can do in such a case," said Mary. "She is going somewhere with her brother, to be married to this cousin of her own faith—isn't she? And that will be the end of it."

"Unless I can contrive to see her before she goes, and induce her to change her mind again."

"Is that what you propose?" asked Miss De Groot, with some quickness, and giving him back the letter.

"I will presently tell you. You must know that I have ascertained that Miss Seixas is going to Smyrna. They sail in a Spanish bark, the *Manuel*, with as ugly a looking crew and desperado-looking captain as you would wish to see. Now it is easy to foresee that when they reach Smyrna, which is a voyage of not less than seven or eight weeks, and may be longer, and Miriam finds herself among her own people, she will marry Joseph Seixas. I cannot abandon her thus without a struggle," said Alban, with a resolute air. "If I cannot obtain an interview with her before her departure, in which I may fairly try the experiment of combating a resolution, which, you must have observed by her letter, springs in part from womanly pride and a sense of justice to me— I say, unless I can obtain such an interview—I am resolved to make this voyage with them. To let a woman from whom I have obtained a confession of love go away to misery here and hereafter, without an effort—a strenuous effort—to save her, comports neither with my principles nor with my feelings. What think you?"

Mary kept her eyes on the carpet, except when she gave Alban now and then a glance of surprise.

"How old are you, Alban?"

"Just twenty," replied the youth.

"You have tried to see Miss Seixas to-day?"

"I went to the house and was refused admittance. Miriam sent down word by her maid that she was particularly engaged and could not see me. After that I found Seixas at the synagogue. He was mild as possible, but inexorable. He said that Miriam was free, and had a right to refuse me an interview. On his part he considered it her duty, and therefore he could not be expected to interfere, even for my sake. He was deaf, in short, to my entreaties, and only smiled at my threats; for I got very angry at his immovable obstinacy in sacrificing his sister's soul and happiness."

"Why don't you go to a priest," said Mary, "and impart every thing to him under the seal of confession? He will tell you exactly what to do."

Alban shook his head. She gently took the letter from him again.

"I should be sorry to seem unwilling to act the part of a sister and friend, when you appeal to me in that character. But how can I advise, not knowing all the circumstances? In your note to me you accused yourself of some mysterious sin. It had nothing to do with Miss Seixas?"—"No, no; she is innocent as nature can be."—"I thought so. Well, I will tell you what I think: that Mr. Seixas, considering he is a Jew, is very kind and wise—more so than most Christians would be in like circumstances, Alban; and that Miss Seixas's conduct is noble and dignified—like a true-hearted woman,"—with gentle warmth. "But her passions must be naturally violent. True, she is not to blame for that. Still, dear Alban, the less any of us have to do with poniards, the better. She has permitted herself to love you, although she was already betrothed. That is what I least like. It must have been voluntary in part; all love is. I must say that my notions of fidelity between plighted, or conscious, lovers, do not allow *any* deliberate thought of that kind about another person."

She spoke in a rapid, unpremeditated, earnest sort of way, as a girl naturally talks. Alban shaded his eyes and seemed lost in thought.

"I need not a priest's counsel in this matter," he said at length. "No priest can tell me what I want to know."

Mary bent over the letter as if it could tell her what Mr. Alban wanted to know. She murmured rather shyly, that it was strange he should want to know any thing but what he must know better than any one—the state of his own affections. It seemed to her a very wild idea though—that of his going with the Seixases to the East against their will—leaving his college—he such a youth. Where would he get the funds for such a voyage?

He explained to her that he had some money left him by an aunt, and that even as a minor he could easily obtain an advance on it from the Jews. An old Israelite had promised him a sum which he deemed sufficient.

" You will be betrayed by these people, Alban. It makes me shudder to think of that dreadful Spanish captain and his crew. How do you know that they are not pirates? or slavers, which is just as bad?" She began to cry.

Alban was provided with an answer also to this. It was true that piracy was then not unknown in the American seas, and he conjectured that this Spanish shipmaster had been at least in the African trade ; but he was a devout Catholic. In his cabin hung a picture of the Holy Virgin, with a lamp perpetually burning. In short, it was by appealing to his religious feelings that Alban had obtained from him the information in regard to the movements of the Seixases. The skipper and he had made a conditional bargain.

" If I can obtain her previous consent, I am to be on board when they come to the vessel in the morning. The skipper will then haul up the ladies first—that is, Miriam and her maid. As soon as they are on deck, instead of lowering the ladder down the side for Manuel Seixas, the boat in which they come is to be dropped loose, and we shall make our way out to sea with what promises to be a most favorable wind. Now the question is, shall I, in the interview which I have the means of securing, simply ask her consent to this plan of a mutual flight, saying nothing of a change of faith, or shall I make the latter a prerequisite? Without vanity, I think that could I see Miriam, I should infallibly succeed on the former plan, and should almost certainly fail by taking the latter alternative."

"I dare say," said Mary, changing from pale to red by turns.

"When Miriam is under my protection—after having broken thus irrevocably with her own people and family—she will be readily won, I doubt not, by my arguments and entreaties, to embrace the Christian faith."

"Alban," interrupted Miss De Groot, "say no more on that point. I am sure, that not even to save Miss Seixas's soul, ought you to persuade her to elope with you as a Jewess. It would be a sin on your part, and shame to her. You cannot go to her except to persuade her to be a Christian."

"So I think," said Alban, "but shall I use the means which I possess of obtaining an interview for that purpose before to-morrow's light? For it must be by night—nor sooner than mid-night—and by means of a step which, for any other end, would be unjustifiable. Still, that is not the point. Would you have me make the attempt under the properest circumstances?"

The dinner-bell rang. A glance at the mantel-clock showed the hour of six.

"You must stay and dine with us, it will give me time to think."

With the natural manners of American life, the young lady herself conducted Alban to an apartment where he could freshen his morning toilet, as well as circumstances allowed. A servant came in to help him, and preceded him down stairs; and just as he arrived at the door of the dining-room, a step, like a bird on the wing, came down the last flight. She was in her wonted evening array, without a trace of haste or negligence. Mr. De Groot was ever enlivened by Alban's presence. He ordered a bottle of champagne to be put in the cooler. Our young hero, who begins to be more heroic than heretofore, was not sorry, like his predecessors since Homer, to renovate his energies by a stimulating repast, after a day of labor and excitement.

CHAPTER XVII.

DINNER lasted about an hour, Mr. De Groot indulging in an extra glass of wine, and displaying a cheerful courtesy. Mrs. De Groot inquires respecting "the state of feeling" in Dr. M.'s congregation, having understood that the last night's prayer-meeting was one of "special interest." Alban is self-possessed, occasionally gives in to a concealed humor in answering the questions of Madame. Mademoiselle regards him with wonder, sometimes smiles in spite of herself, and sends away her plate almost untouched.

The half-hour after the ladies have withdrawn (Mr. De Groot adheres to that old custom) passes slowly, although the host wakes into animation, and wondering at Alban's apparent disgust for champagne, regrets again and again that the vacation is so nearly at an end. Then comes tea in the drawing-room, and the card-table set with candles and counters, and two fresh packs. The patroon claims his rubber on account of Alban's being there.

"After which, Mary (I see her impatience) may take you into any snug corner she likes. I declare, Atherton, I believe I shall miss you as much as she will."

Miss De Groot, having employed the interval between dinner and tea to visit her own room, had regained her serenity: still she revoked in the first hand and thereby lost the game ; whereat her father, being her partner, was irritated, and talked of people being so much in love that they could not mind their cards. Mademoiselle blushed a little, and became more attentive ; they won the rubber, which restored the patroon's good humor.

"Now take Mr. Alban where you please, child. The library has a fire, and is a famous place for *tête-à-têtes*. Please to consider, Atherton, that I give in to this New England custom. on the ground of your being too thorough-bred a Knickerbocker to abuse the concession."

The young lady flitted before him. The library was darkish
and light by fits, as the flickering fire of Liverpool coal allowed,
and Mary, after a glance at the sentimental locale, passed on to
the lobby, which she had once pointed out to Alban as fit for the
interviews of lovers. It was worse than the library, but she
stopped there, going to the oriel as the lightest spot; for the only
illumination came from a street lamp, through the stained glass,
shedding a mystic, patchwork beam upon the dark wainscoting.
It sufficed to render visible on the young lady's face the reserved
expression natural to one of her sex who remembered that her
companion had so recently enjoyed similar interviews with others;
and presently she put her handkerchief to her eyes and wept—a
still, silent shower of tears that soon wet through the cambric.

"How can I give my sisterly advice," she suddenly exclaimed,
with a sort of gentle passion, "when I am a party interested.
Really, Alban, your coming to me about this, is the most indelicate thing I ever heard of."

"Mary!"

"If you run away with Miss Seixas, every body will say that
you have jilted *me*. Papa will be very angry. Now let me
finish; don't speak, Alban, till I have said all I have got to say.
I have never formed any false notions myself in regard to your
friendship. I knew all along that you considered me as a little
girl. Because you are such a scholar, and take the lead, in college, of men grown, you seem to yourself very mature : whereas,
in society, you are only a youth, a boy under age, a college student, which is nothing at all;—a girl like Henrietta Clinton
thinks she can twist you round her little finger; and nobody
else would have taken any notice of you, unless they had supposed, from your appearing with us, that I had been so silly as to
engage myself, before I am seventeen, to an under-graduate.
Now *I* am a young lady in society—girl as I am—and if I were to
be married in six months, people might say it was a pity, but no
one would think it strange. 'Twas but yesterday that the *Count*
called on papa, with Mr. Seixas to back his representations of his

family and fortune, and made proposals for me in the foreign way ; and papa told him he did not wish me to marry out of my own country, and besides, that my affections, he believed, were already engaged. You see, Mr. Alban, how the case stands. Papa took a fancy to you from the first. I saw by the way he acted and talked, that Sunday evening at Mr. Everett's, and by his choosing to go down with you to New York, instead of staying a few days, and then turning me over to you on the steamboat, that his mind was made up to have you for a son. I am sure you have every reason to be flattered by his partiality. I observe, indeed, that other people who have experience, like you ; and, for myself, it seems to me quite natural they should ; but I never dreamed of your doing such a thing as to fall seriously in love with a Jewess, who is espoused to another person, and audaciously winning her affection, (she must be very susceptible,) and proposing to elope with her, and that at the moment when you profess to have been converted to the Catholic faith. Least of all would I dream that you would come to ask my advice on the subject. All this is strange to me, Alban, and places you in a perfectly new light. It makes me almost wish I had never known you, and quite that I had never given you so many marks of an affection, which, I take Heaven to witness, a sister, so far as I know, might have felt without blame."

" It appears," said Alban, when she had finished, " that what I thought is true. You have a claim upon my delicacy, which I should disregard by pursuing this affair. I might have seen it without trying your feelings thus, if I had not been blinded by the remains of passion and the obstinacy of my will. To recede, after taking a step, is so painful to me. Yes, I might have saved this if I had gone to a priest at once."

She spoke of his parents. Any clergyman would tell him that it was sinful, in such matters, to act without their advice and consent. Then the rashness ! It made her wonder to hear him speak of a voyage in the company of that beautiful Jewess—so ardent and impulsive.

" Yet see her, Alban, if you can obtain an interview without violating decorum, and try to persuade her to become a Christian. If she consents, bring her here. I will receive her as a sister, and I answer for my father's not objecting. She can stay with me until you have graduated and are of age, and then you can be honorably married. I would be bridesmaid and all that"—speaking quick—" and happy as Miss Seixas herself."

" But if I cannot see her without violating decorum—without scaling her window at night, for instance," said Alban, blushing in the dark. " As a young inexperienced brother, I ask the question of a sister the instincts of whose sex are wisdom."

" Don't dream of such a thing," said Mary, with a candid glance and an extremely gentle accent. " Dear Alban, we have no means of securing our virtue except by never putting it voluntarily in peril. When you have been a Catholic a very little while, you will not ask such questions."

" And what return shall I make for your kindness ?" said Alban. The whole scene inspired him with a sudden impulse. Something he felt was due to this blameless friend, whose pride, if not her affection, he had wounded, yet who showed no resentment. He sank on one knee and took her hand. She tried to withdraw it, but did not till he had kissed it. " I have been far from a true knight, Mary, but you are the truest of ladies ever heard of—the tenderest and most forgiving mistress that ever was. The only return I *can* make is to ask you to love and pray for me as heretofore, and one of these days, perhaps, I may be more worthy of you."

She bade him good night in a less composed voice, and moved shyly towards the door of the private stair. She paused with her hand on the lock.

" Be faithful to your religion, Mr. Alban. No human respects will now be mixed with it. Do not defer seeing a priest, and pray for me when you have been received into the Church."

She opened the door quietly and stole up the stair. He listened till the sound of her steps was lost in the corridor of the story above

BOOK V.

Alban Confronts the Powers of Darkness.

———•———

CHAPTER I.

WE must take the reader once more to New Haven, and introduce him or her to the interior of a room in North College, fire-glowing, red-curtained, book-shelved, study-tabled. The student sat in a rocking-chair by the fire, with his feet on the Franklin, his trowsers strapless, his waistcoat unbuttoned, neckcloth laid aside, his dilapidated frock-coat showing the shirt-sleeves at the elbows and at wide gaps beneath the arms, the buttons off, and the button-holes torn through, and the silk lining completely in tatters. But for two or three other points, the young man would have seemed as great a sloven as could be found in an American college. His morocco slippers were whole and not turned down at the heel ; the white cotton stockings protruding from the strapless trowsers were spotless as a young lady's, and the linen so liberally displayed by his open waistcoat and gaping elbows would have dressed an Englishman for a dinner party. But the careless brown locks clustering and curling over the ears would not have satisfied English precision, notwithstanding the clearness of the brow and cheek they shaded, and of the hand half-buried in them, as the student leaned on his elbow. Being the study-hour, he had in hand a volume of Plato's Republic, while a great folio lexicon lay open on the floor by his side, so that he could reach it by stooping a little, as he half sat, half lounged, in the low chintz-cushioned rocking-chair, which no American collegian is willingly without.

There was a short authoritative rap at the study door, and a gentleman entered, without waiting for an answer to the warning. The intruder was a man of about thirty, pale but in good flesh, scrupulously attired in black, with a neat white neckcloth. The student sprang up and remained standing. The tutor's duty is to make such calls, and generally it is absolved by opening the door, exchanging a bow with the occupants of the room, and retiring. But this gentleman came decidedly in, and the young man offered him a chair.

" Where is your cousin ?"

" Henry is out somewhere, sir. I have not seen him since breakfast."

" I am glad to find you alone. I want to have some conversation with you, Atherton."

Alban had already laid his Plato carelessly on its face upon the lexicon. The Professor took it up.

" You have made beautiful recitations in the Republic I hear, Atherton. It is agreed, I understand, that you are to have the last ' oration.' It is really a higher honor than the valedictory, and all the initiated people present at commencement understand it so. I expect to enjoy your oration, as I enjoy every thing you write."

" You have always been too partial to me, sir."

" You told me last term that you had some difficulties about the evidences of religion. I suppose you have settled that point with yourself, eh ?"

" I think so, sir."

" And you are convinced of the truth of revelation, I hope ?"

" Quite convinced, sir. I am sorry and ashamed to have ever doubted."

" I am rejoiced to hear you say so," said Professor B——, with emphasis. " In fact, from some things you have let fall in your answers, or some questions you have asked, at the Natural Theology Lecture, Dr. —— got the impression that you were—as he expressed it—a concealed infidel. I told him you were the last man in the world to be a 'concealed' any thing. I have always found you frank to a fault. But you did not partake of the sacrament last Sunday, they say, although you were present. Some of our quidnuncs, in fact, are a little excited about you, Atherton. Just give me a word to quiet them. I suppose you are fancying that you are not worthy, or something of that sort."

"I went to chapel with the intention of receiving," said Alban, "but—I did not dare."

"I thought so. Oh, well, you must get over that. It is discreditable to your clear judgment. We are all unworthy, in one sense."

"It was not my own unworthiness—great as it is—which deterred me," said Alban, uneasily.

"What then?"

"Really, sir, I would rather be excused from answering. It is a matter which I have confined strictly to my own breast."

"That is not wise, my dear Atherton. Really, I did not suppose that there was this weak spot in your manly organization. I never should have suspected *you* of brooding over these morbid scruples."

"I feel no such scruples as you suppose, sir," said Alban. "I doubt whether the Lord's Supper, as administered among us, is the sacrament at all."

"Oh!" said the Professor, "you have been too much with that weak fellow, Soapstone. You are going to turn Episcopalian, eh, Atherton?"

This was said in a tone of undisguised contempt.

"I am not going to turn Episcopalian, I assure you, sir," said Alban, much annoyed.

"Oh, yes, you are. If you have got doubts into your head about ordination, and apostolic succession, and all that sort of thing, you will become an Episcopalian sooner or later. I never knew a case that turned out otherwise. It indicates a weak spot, as I told you ; and weak spots always betray themselves."

"Harry is going to join the Episcopalian Church," said Alban, "and yet I have done every thing in my power to dissuade him from it. But Miss Ellsworth's bright eyes, and the charm of the beautiful Liturgy, are more than a match for my arguments. I have actually lost all my influence over Henry by the ground I have taken in reference to the subject."

"You hope to introduce Episcopacy and Liturgies among ourselves ? I have heard of such an idea. It is the first thought of a youth who begins to see, as he says, 'the importance of these things.' Well, try it, Alban. But take my word for it, you will only do yourself harm. You will pass for a silly visionary. Every body will laugh at you. Our own people, of course, will ; for they don't want to be turned into Episcopalians ; if they did, they would take the shorter way of joining the Episcopal Church. And Episcopalians will only say that you are grossly inconsistent, and that you ought to come into 'the Church' at once."

"They would be quite right," said Alban. "It would be the height of absurdity to go about to reconstruct the Church on a supposed divine model, when, if the Church be a divine thing at all, it must exist in the world ready made to our hands. If I were satisfied with the Episcopal Church, I would join it ; but I am not. The Church, it seems to me, is, at least, the faith that believes Christ and the love which embraces Him, made visible. The Episcopal Church neither believes nor loves as I do. Its articles outrage my faith, and its Liturgy disappoints my heart."

"Well, and heartily said ! I declare, Atherton, you have no idea how you relieve my mind. To see your fine understanding beclouded by this fog of Episcopacy,—a mere unmeaning, superstitious formalism—would have been too pitiable. But what do you mean then about the Sacrament ? I hope you are not getting into the mystical line, and renouncing outward forms altogether. This has ensnared some choice intellects, refining too much for humanity. We need memorials. It is not philosophical, Atherton, to overlook the immense influence that the Lord's Supper has exercised over the feelings of Christians in all ages. It has revivified their love for the Redeemer almost morè than every thing else. Don't you feel, now, that this is true?"

"Certainly."

The Professor was nonplussed. He thought he had explored the whole ground. What point was left? He began to feel provoked with Atherton.

"Pray, let me know what *is* your difficulty," he said with irritation. "My whole wish is to serve you, and it is hardly treating me well to let me go on beating about the bush in the dark."

"I have been in some confusion as to my duties, sir, from my being actually a member of the College Church. Obedience to my father, and love for my mother keep me from openly avowing a change which has taken place in my faith. I had persuaded myself that I might innocently join a company of Christians with whom I was providentially associated, in partaking of bread and wine in memory of Christ's death. But when it came to the point, I shrank from doing it, for whatever it is to them, to me it could be nothing but a sacrilegious substitution for the adorable sacrament of love in which I believe."

The Professor stared as if he thought him deranged.

"At one time, not long ago," continued Alban, with some excitement of manner, "I was forced by the manifest contradiction between our New England religion and the Bible to retreat upon the Hebrew position. I found there an ancient revelation and a living witness in perfect harmony."

The Professor gave him a look of piercing scrutiny, but was silent.

"It was deeply painful to me to have these ideas. Christ was dear to me:—yes, He was dear to me through it all. I could never bear to hear Him spoken of with irreverence. Somehow, I had an idea that He was the real Messiah, but that neither His own nation, nor His actual followers had understood him. I grew more and more bewildered. I began to look for Him to reappear. I was desirous of going to Palestine, in the hope, mixed with many a carnal aspiration, of seeing Him. My heart cried out for Christ."

Alban shed some quiet tears. The Professor now regarded him with a mixture of fear and pity.

" We will talk over these things another time, my dear Atherton. You are excited at present."

" No, no," exclaimed Alban. " Now I have begun, let me finish. I can do it in a word. I have found Christ where alone He really is on this earth. I have not as yet found Him, indeed, as I hope to find Him, but I know where to seek Him ; and he who knows where to seek has already found. It is not in Syria, sir, but it is in Jerusalem, in a city set on a hill, of which all men know at least so much as this, that He is said to be there. In faith, sir," continued Alban, recovering his usual quiet manner of a sudden,—" in faith, I am now, what you, perhaps, will consider worse and more foolish than an Episcopalian :—namely, a Roman Catholic."

" Poor Atherton ! I do believe his head is turned," thought the Professor. " Next he will say that he is a Mahometan. Or if not crazy, he is dangerous. His influence is unbounded over certain minds. There are a dozen fellows in the senior class alone, who would follow him anywhere he chose to lead. This must be looked to in time. A Roman Catholic ! oh, he is clearly not sane. I must talk this over with you another day, Atherton," he added aloud. " At present, I see, you are busy with Plato. Good morning. And Atherton,—I hope you will keep this matter to yourself. That's right. Hem !" concluded the Professor, as the door closed upon him. " I must communicate this forthwith to the President."

CHAPTER II.

ACCORDING to the interpretation of many Catholic expositors of
the mystical Book of Revelations, it is a little more than three
hundred years ago since the star fell from heaven upon the earth,
to whom was given the key of the bottomless pit.   This is agreeable to the rules of symbolic interpretation recently laid down by
Mr. Lord, and now, we believe, generally received by his Protestant brethren, viz., that a star signifies a Christian teacher, and a
star falling from heaven the apostasy of such a teacher.   That
the star fell upon the earth intimates (agreeably to the same system) that this teacher fell from the divine to the human sphere
in his doctrine ; and the key of the bottomless pit being given him,
that he opened an abyss to which there is really no bottom, by
appealing to human reason as the interpreter of the divine word ;
from which arose a smoke which darkened the sun and the air,
(the infinite heresies, and gross, light-obscuring prejudices of Protestantism,) and from the smoke came out locusts upon the earth,
or the military and civil powers by which Protestantism was prop-
agated, the Church plundered, and the people persecuted to
make them fall from the faith.   These hateful and violent powers,
however, could not hurt the truly faithful, but only those whom
mortal sin, whether sensual vice or intellectual pride, or covetous-
ness, rendered deserving of it, that is, the men who had not the
sign of God in their foreheads, who readily fell away and perished.
They were as horses prepared to battle, to show the rapidity of
their conquests ; they had crowns of gold, to show that the movement against the Church was conducted by princes, like the sovereigns of Saxony, Brandenburgh, and England ; their " faces were
as men," to indicate their pretensions to human learning and better
reason, criticism, philosophy, and so on, (Humanitarianism ;) and
" hair as the hair of women," to indicate the effeminacy of their

doctrine, in rejecting celibacy, authorizing polygamy, dissolving the bonds of sacred marriage, rejecting the ascetic principle in Christianity, and denying the merit as well as the possibility of heroic virtue, (the αρετη of the N. T.) Their teeth were as lions, to show their destructiveness, evinced in the ruin of those splendid institutions and monuments wherewith centuries of piety had enriched Europe. They had "breastplates as breastplates of iron," to indicate that they would be insensible to reason or pity, as in the cruel proscription of the Catholic religion and the bloody persecution of its professors and ministers; and "the noise of their wings was as the noise of chariots and many horses running to battle," to show their great conspicuity and importance and apparent triumph, their skill in filling literature with their doings, and their semblance of being the great movement of the age and of time. The double period of five months during which they were to torment and hurt, is supposed to intimate a duration of three hundred years, which now happily is come to an end; the Church is already, we may say, emancipated everywhere from their power; they may threaten, but can no longer injure; their "scorpion sting" is lost. However all this may be, and we don't undertake, like Aunt Fanny, to determine positively the sense of so mysterious a prophecy, the application is extremely pat in every particular, even to the succession of sovereigns, (doubtless of various countries,) by whom these symbolic locusts were to be led. "They had a king over them," that is, says Mr. Lord, "many kings reigning successively," the angel or representative of their principles; if, indeed, this does not rather refer to the sect-leaders, to whom they always appeal, and whose destroying names flourish in regal pomp at the head of their armies. But we leave so subtle a point to those who can understand a proverb, and the interpretation thereof.

We suppose that even at the date of our story the scorpion sting in the tail of Protestantism could no longer hurt. It was true the "teeth as lions" were shown about that time by the burning down of a convent in Massachusetts, and of a church or two in Philadelphia, by an anti-popish mob, but as neither of these proceedings made any converts to Protestantism, but rather the reverse, the sharpness of the bite was wanting.   And our Alban, in a Puritan college, although there is an immense dust kicked up and an unearthly clamor made, is in no danger of life or limb.   He will neither be hung nor burned, nor even set in pillory, nor whipped at the cart-tail, of all which he might once have stood in danger, even in New England ; still less will he be embowelled, as priests used to be in Old England for saying mass, or pressed to death, as women used to be in the same country for hearing it.   Still he is a culprit, and must " suffer some."

The thing was whispered.   It got about in the town before it did in the college, which shows that some who were in the secret had female friends.   Then the case was mentioned in a social prayer-meeting in college, that the unfortunate young man in question might be unitedly prayed for !   A hundred young men, by the way, in a college lecture-room at five in the morning, some on their legs, some kneeling on the floor, some resting their heads on the back of the bench before them, so as to conceal their faces entirely, while one of their number, standing with closed eyes and extended arms, or clasped hands, is pouring forth an extempore prayer,—measured, deliberate, long, rather in the manner of reasoning than supplication—is an impressive scene.   There was a faint stirring of the waters for a revival in college at that time, as there generally is in the spring term, and prayer-meetings were held every morning before chapel in the Rhetorical Chamber. Alban was prayed for without mentioning his name, but the absence of a " professor" hitherto so shining, and always conspicuous from his talents, could not escape notice.   It was easy to put this and that together ; the secret was soon nominal ; and one morning, not long after prayers had been mysteriously requested in his behalf, a coarse but fervent youth—a Western man—ripped out the name in full in a long supplication, in which the speaker took occasion to enter into all the circumstances, for the benefit of such as might yet be ignorant.

Alban's friends fell off at once. Even Henry Atherton, as we have intimated, had grown cold. His class no longer cheered him ; the Brothers' Society listened to him in unsympathizing silence. The new President was applauded in turning his palmary argument in a debate, into ridicule, and the Society decided for the first time against the side he had supported. Society, in any of its spheres, is never so unjust as when it turns against a former idol. He is still great by the memory of her favor, and therefore she feels no pity. O'Connor, who was a plucky fellow, and would have stood by Alban, had left Yale and gone to St. Joseph's Seminary. The gentlemanly Charles Carroll was cold to the supposed convert.

It was felt by Alban's religious friends that it would not do to trust wholly to prayer. Charitable charity students, whom Alban had befriended or loved in the days of his fervent experimental religion, called to pay the debt by earnest warnings. Hardly a day passed without one such visit. Some came repeatedly. Old ladies in the town sent for him to touch his feelings by reminding him of his grandfather and mother, of his departed aunts and living uncles, and missionary cousins, and a host of good people of his all but sacred name and blood, who dead, would be ready to start up in their graves, or living, would almost break their hearts, to hear that he was fallen into such fearful errors.

Our young friend answered the old ladies that his *living* friends might err, and that the present opinions of such as were dead might be very different from what they supposed.

His pious classmates, his friends in the Theological Seminary, and the Divinity Professors, opened upon him a terrible battery of arguments. Alban smiled when they told him that Popery was pointed out in the New Testament as the Man of Sin, by the clear marks of forbidding to marry and commanding to abstain from meats. It was as clear a case as Aunt Fanny's notion that the "Church at Philadelphia" meant the Quakers. Did that Church forbid to marry, he smilingly demanded, which declared matrimony to be a Sacrament ? which interrupted its august sacrifice for one purpose alone—to bless the new-married pair, and invoke for them fruitfulness in the bed and peace at the board, chaste constancy in love and length of mutual days ? It was not forbidding or dishonoring marriage, he argued, to say that celibacy was more excellent ; for St. Paul himself expressly said it, affirming that it was " *beautiful to remain a virgin.*" These were Christian ideas, he assured them, not Popish.

" But the Papal Church forbids *priests* to marry—a clear proof that matrimony is considered impure," said one obstinate reasoner. It was a theological student who was engaged to be married to a daughter of one of the Divinity Professors. He was ever harping on this string. He came every day to see Alban about it, and Alban at first declined to meet the objection. At length our hero's patience and modesty were alike exhausted.

" Do you pretend to talk to me in this way," he cried, with a deep flush on his own virginal cheek, " when I have the Bible in my hands ! Do I not know that God Himself enjoined a sacred abstinence, not on a few priests only, but on the whole nation of the Jews, for three days before he descended on Sinai ? Do I not know that God laid a perpetual obligation of this sort upon all priests during the time of their service ? Did God *Himself* in this signify that union to be impure which He had hallowed in Paradise ? Yes, or no ?"

" No."

" Then neither does the Church insinuate that marriage is other than a holy estate, although she requires a better choice of those who are to serve continually at her altars, daily handling mysteries of which those of the Old Law were but the shadows. It is painful to me to talk of these things," added Alban, " I am shocked at your notions of Christian sanctity, and of the power of grace."

It was pretty much in this style that the aggressive Protestantism of the College was met by him. One candid classmate said that Atherton had a " fatal familiarity with the Bible," and that Scripture, as he handled it, was a two-edged sword.

Mr. Soapstone, too, who did not confide so much in the Bible, interpreted, as he said, by private judgment, but who was strong in Patristics, could not suffer his interesting young friend to fall a prey to Romanism without stretching out an arm to save him. When Alban however heard that the Church of Rome had committed schism in separating from the Church of England, he laughed outright.

"As if the button should say to the coat—'Why did *you* fall off!'"

In reply to this irreverent squib, Mr. Soapstone developed his great idea of local Catholicity.

"Our Catholic and Apostolic bishops," said he, "having received consecration in Scotland and England, came to the United States and set up their jurisdiction here, several years before the See of Baltimore was created by the Pope, and the Romish Bishop Carroll consecrated for it. Consequently the erection of that see, and the exercise of Episcopal authority by the said Carroll and his successors, were acts of intrusion into our jurisdiction, and schismatical. The Romish communion in the United States is therefore in a state of schism, consequently it is no part of the Church of Christ; and the encouragement of this schismatical communion by the Church in France and Italy, is culpable in the extreme."

"Your Catholic and Apostolic bishops, as you term them," replied Alban, rather tartly, "were themselves heretics and schismatics when they came here, like the Church of England from which they derived both their doctrine and their orders."

"Prove it," retorted Mr. Soapstone, triumphantly. "Prove that the Church of England was guilty of heresy or schism at the Reformation, or since. For if you cannot *prove* this, then she must be allowed to be a branch of the Catholic and Apostolic Church, and the consequence as to the exclusive jurisdiction of the daughter Church established in these United States follows of course."

"I see the point you make," said Alban, thoughtfully.

"I never knew it fairly met by a Romanist," cried Mr. Soapstone.

"One does not like to enter into single combat with a woman," replied Alban. "If you, whom I personally respect, had not urged this argument, I could scarcely regard it as meriting a serious refutation."

"Where is the fallacy?" asked the young clergyman, a little trembling before the logical reputation of the quondam President of the Brothers.

"Grant you valid orders and an orthodox faith," said Alban.; "then you say you came to these countries *first* with your bishops. You claim on the score of priority. But what you claim is territorial jurisdiction."

"Certainly, exclusive territorial jurisdiction."

"Good. Now jurisdiction is a thing that cannot exist where it is not claimed publicly, and in such a manner that all whom it may concern are bound to take notice of it. It must be claimed in the mode which custom authorizes. My neighbor has no right to complain of my trespassing upon his field if he neglects to inclose it, or to mark his right by some other customary sign of property. There is a regular way, as I understand it, of claiming the Episcopal jurisdiction of a territory, and that is by taking a territorial title. When a man calls himself 'Archbishop of Canterbury and Primate of all England,' we know what he means to claim for himself—a territorial spiritual jurisdiction over Canterbury and all England, for such is the customary style of bishops with such jurisdiction. Pray, what was the style taken by *your* bishops when they established themselves here?"

"Bishops of the Protestant Episcopal Church in the States of New York, Pennsylvania, &c.," returned Mr. Soapstone, reluctantly.

"That is not a claim of territorial jurisdiction," said Alban, "but distinctly the reverse. The adoption of a new mode of designating themselves, and taking a sectarian appellation, was a tacit repudiation of territorial claims, and, unless I am mistaken, was so intended by your first bishops. But whether intended or not, the fact remains. In abandoning the system of local sees, you abandoned what was signified by it. What does your Church call itself?—'The Protestant Episcopal Church in the United States.' Such a title claims nothing. Can you lay your finger on any other thing—any act, any document, any notification, of what nature soever, emanating from your Church, in which she claims exclusive territorial jurisdiction? If not, how can a Catholic bishop be guilty of schism, by coming into a country where such a Church exists, and establishing a new see? What has the erection of the See of Baltimore, by the Pope, to do with the existence of the 'Protestant Episcopal Church in Maryland?' The Pope could not dream that he was invading jurisdiction where none was asserted, and must be pardoned for overlooking what you yourselves ignore."

"I have always regretted the sectarian title assumed by our Church," said Mr. Soapstone, rather pale and worried, "as well as our not establishing sees like other churches, but I never thought of its vitiating our jurisdiction."

"It does more than that, on your principles," replied Alban, following up his advantage. "For, observe, while you have neglected to occupy, the Roman Catholic Church (I take your own point of view) has extended its jurisdiction, in form, over the whole of the United States. It has established its sees, in the old recognized manner, so as to cover every square mile of the territory of the Republic. Consequently, by your own doctrine, she is in possession, and unless you can *prove* that she requires sinful terms of communion, you are in schism, cut off from the true Church, and from eternal salvation. You can't mistake *her* claim—it is patent to all the world. Her style is unequivocal, royal, and supreme. Those who reject *her* jurisdiction, do so, therefore, at their own peril."

Mr. Soapstone sighed.

"If I may be candid," concluded Alban, "I will tell you what I think of these High Church claims, unsupported as they are by facts, repudiated by the majority of your own members, and ridiculed by all the rest of the world. Without having the antiquity or the immense numbers, or any thing to be likened to the curious civilization of the Chinese, you remind me of their pig-tail arrogance, when they talk about the ' Celestial Empire,' and term all other nations, though far more civilized than themselves, ' outside barbarians.' You High Church Episcopalians, prating about ' *The* Church,' and ridiculing ' Dissenters,' are the Chinamen of the West."

CHAPTER III.

At the first blush every body had deserted our young friend. But by degrees his old admirers gathered round him, heard his reasons, and at least in part, espoused his cause. The standard of religious liberty was raised. Two parties were formed in college ;—the Protestants, and "Atherton's friends." The dispute ran so high that one-half the senior class would not speak to the other. Every man felt bound to take a side. Atherton—the quiet, philosophical, regular Atherton, the favorite of the tutors—was become a disturber of the peace of the University.

Alban's enemies—for the rancor of religious prejudice made them such—were not content to assail his principles and decry his talents ; they attacked his private character. They had, indeed, no handle for this except some incautious admissions of his own, dropped in pure frankness and humility, when defending the doctrine of penitence. 'Twas said that Atherton had been guilty of card-playing, drinking to intoxication, and other immoralities, in New York ; that, in consequence, he had "lost his religion," and was given up to this delusion—"to believe a lie." Others said that he did not really believe in Popery any more than they did. But what excited a greater, because vague horror, was that, a Catholic priest coming into town for a few days, Atherton was seen in his company, and (it was even rumored) received a visit from him at his rooms. The popular idea of a Catholic priest, at that time, was of a fiend in human shape, who knew too much of his religion to believe it, but exercised a fearful tyranny over the minds of some poor ignorant people for the sake of gain ; who abused the confidence of the confessional to corrupt innocent women, and committed the greatest crimes every day without compunction. Regarding young Atherton as the voluntary associate of such a monster, even grave elderly folks turned away their heads, or stared in wonder, as they passed him in the streets, and shy maidens hurried by him with downcast eyes and pale cheeks, instinctively gathering their garments closer to their shrinking forms.

Alban would not have minded these things if he had not feared a more tangible infliction in the shape of a college censure. Perhaps it might be suspension, or the loss of his oration, or even of his degree. He heard that there was talk of sending him away, or making him lose a year, and the privilege of graduating with his class. Besides the mortification, this would have been a serious injury to him at the outset of life. Indeed, any academical censure at that period of his course must be a wound to the pride and feelings of his friends and family, and consequently a misfortune to him. Still he trusted that by circumspection in his conduct he should avoid it. He was more regular at chapel than almost any Senior, nor was there any change in that calm attention which he had always given to the chapter at prayers. During the long extempore prayer, he stood, as had always been his custom, with folded arms and eyes downcast. Some asserted that his lips were always moving, as if he were praying by himself, and that he carried for this purpose a string of beads under his cloak, but this was a mere calumny. Alban had adopted few of the devotional practices so much esteemed by Catholics, inasmuch as he knew not of them. His prayers were mostly mental. In chapel he used to meditate on the acts, and if his lips ever moved, it was unconsciously. This purely spiritual worship grew upon him the more because he was entirely cut off from the service of the Church. Father Smith's place had not yet been supplied, and the priest who had left his own district to visit the flock at New Haven, only said mass on a few week-days, at an hour when Atherton could not attend without being absent from chapel.

Matters were in this state when a grave complication occurred. One day the post brought him a note, in a feminine hand, without a signature, requesting him, in somewhat mysterious terms, to meet the writer on the road to East Rock, during the afternoon study hours. It concluded with the expression, that if Mr. Atherton was a sincere Catholic, he would not fail to come, as, according to his doctrine, the salvation of a soul was at stake. Alban was extremely perplexed. He did not like to take no notice of the communication, and it might be only a hoax, or any way, might get him into a scrape. However, on the very afternoon appointed, a visit from the Divinity Professor saved him from the necessity of deciding.

He was thinking over this interview in the evening, and wondering how so mild and genial a man as the Professor could be so bitter against a religion of whose doctrines he was entirely ignorant, when a tap at his door aroused him. It was a little black girl with another note from his unknown correspondent. She reproached him for not meeting her at the time appointed.

" I must, if possible, see you this evening," pursued the note, "and shall wait on the Green for that purpose till my messenger returns. If you fail to come, (but surely you will not,) I shall lose that good opinion of you which I have hitherto preserved, in spite of all the nonsense that people talk,"

Henry Atherton had gone to a Wednesday evening lecture with Mary Ellsworth, (for it was Lent,) and Alban, after a single question to the sooty little messenger, threw on his cloak, put out the study lamp, and followed her. The paschal moon (then a few days old) shed a pale illumination over the white Doric pile of the State House, and it was thither that the black girl directed her way. When Atherton arrived at the foot of the lofty steps, he perceived a dark female figure between the columns. She drew behind a column as he ascended towards her, but when he stood by her in the portico, addressed him in a firm, pleasant voice, quite free from nervous trepidation.

" Mr. Atherton, I am Miss Hartshorn," said the lady.

" I remember you, Miss Hartshorn."

" Mr. Atherton," said Miss Hartshorn," I won't detain you by apologies for the step I have taken, since I owe none to you.

There is a theological student boarding at our house whom you know."

"Walker. He is licensed and gone somewhere to preach as a candidate,—is he not ?"

"He went away, and came back sick with inflammation of the lungs. He has been lying at our house a fortnight. Pa thinks he will not live through it, and Mr. Walker himself expects to die. He wants to see you, Mr. Atherton, but they won't let him. Mr. Walker has prevailed on me to tell you about it. I suppose it is wrong, but I am not a Christian, and I mean to take my chance of getting him a little peace of mind while he lives, at any rate. He has been out of his head, and they have allowed no one to see him but Professor ———, and one or two of Mr. Walker's most particular friends."

"Is he out of his head still ?"

"Pa says not."

"Dr. Hartshorn has been his physician, I suppose."

"Pa and Dr. Reynolds both. Dr. Reynolds was for letting Mr. Walker see you, but pa and the ministers would not consent to it. Mr. Walker says he must die a Catholic, and wants you to get a priest for him, and all sorts of things. I think he is more distracted by what he has on his mind, than delirious from the fever ; and always has been."

"Walker used to call on me frequently to dispute. I thought him very far from such a change."

"He was always talking against you, Mr. Atherton—for ever ! You see it was because he was disturbed by what you said. They say that his mind is weakened by disease, (for he was a man of strong mind, Mr. Atherton,) and perhaps it is, but the horror he has of dying is awful. I promised him that I would see you myself, and I did not know any better way than this. He gritted his teeth like a madman when I told him to-night that I had not succeeded in obtaining an interview with you. 'In twenty-four hours,' said he, 'I shall be one of the damned. Have you no pity on me, Miss Hartshorn ?'—You see that I could not refuse him, but how you will manage to see him, Mr. Atherton, I cannot tell."

Walker was the same theological student whose mind had been so exercised in regard to the celibacy of priests. Alban was surprised that he had not even heard of his illness. Miss Hartshorn observed that " they had kept very still about it." She did not believe that Mr. Atherton would be suffered to have an interview with the dying man, and as for a priest, her father, who was a deacon in the Congregational Church, and the two ministers who daily attended at Mr. Walker's bedside, would as soon think of admitting " the old gentleman himself;" by which Miss Hartshorn meant to signify a personage whom many people dislike to name.

" Shall you see Mr. Walker to-night so as to give him a message ?" asked Alban, after a little thought.

" Oh, yes ; I see him every night. His room is next to mine. I used to have to keep it locked pretty strictly when Mr. Walker was well, poor fellow ! But I don't mind now, except on account of his watchers. They are theologues too. Very well-behaved young men. I have nothing to say against them. But I can go in when I like, to speak to Mr. Walker, and offer him his drink."

" Well, tell him that you have seen me, and that I am going to send for a priest. I shall send an express this very night. Can you let me know, Miss Hartshorn, if any change occurs ?"

" Hetty here," pointing to the little black girl, " shall bring you word. I will run that risk. She is safe, but if any body should see her going to your room—why she lives with us, you understand."

" Exactly. Let her come in the evening, if possible. I shall go openly to your father's and ask to see Mr. Walker. Good-night, Miss Hartshorn. May God reward you for this."

" I might have been afraid if it had been any one else," said Miss Hartshorn, descending the white steps with him, " but Mr. Walker told me that I might rely on Mr. Atherton's treating me with as much respect alone as before a hundred witnesses. I hope that I am not a bad girl, and that you won't think me one, Mr. Atherton, although I don't pretend to be a Christian."

Miss Hartshorn meant that she had never experienced a change of heart, not that she was either a Mahometan or an infidel.

"I would trust you further, Miss Hartshorn," said Alban, "than some bright professors I know."

CHAPTER IV.

If the affair at which our story is arrived concerned such a thing as that Mr. De Groot's tenants were going to ruin him by refusing his rents ; if the hero's life were in danger from an African despot or Spanish brigand ; if the matter were the abduction of a lovely heiress, or the fall of a princely house, we might hope to interest our readers. Yet a greater thing was at stake than the perpetuation of the Howards, or the rights of the Bourbons, or the liberty of the French, or the credit of the Rothschilds, or the nationality of Poland. The burning of the Industrial Exhibition, or the destruction of the Vatican Gallery with all its masterpieces—the Apollo, the Laocoon, the Stanze of Raphael, the ceiling of the Sistine ; or the oblivion of a science—say chemistry or astronomy ; or any other like or worse misfortune that the civilized world would feel as a universal calamity, or all together, could not make an unit wherefrom, by infinite multiples, one could express that catastrophe which now hung in the delicate balance of Providence, and depended, under the Supreme, upon the clearness of our hero's judgment, and on the energy of his will.

A week had passed, and the paschal moon was past the full. The white State House on the green—modelled from the Temple of Theseus—shone like an earthly Luna, reflecting the beams of the just risen satellite. A youth, involved in a cloak, paced to and fro under the portico. By and by a little girl appeared at the foot of the vast white steps, and began to ascend them. When she got to the top she gave a billet to the young man in the cloak. While he read it she turned her face to the moon, and the face was black almost as the hood that surrounded it. When the young man had read the billet, he also looked up to the sky.

" Tell your mistress," he said at last—

" Miss 'Liza ?" demanded the little negress.

"Miss Eliza—that I will come at eleven to-night."

The child of Afric sped her way home.   Dr. Hartshorn's
house stood in a garden ; it was an old double house, with mighty
elms before it, for Dr. Hartshorn was an old and respected inhabit-
ant, an established physician, although as his family consisted of
Mrs. Hartshorn and their daughter Eliza, he was willing to take
a theological student as a boarder : for Dr. Hartshorn had been a
deacon of the Congregationalist Church for thirty years, and was
a very shining Christian, which your deacon sometimes is not.
Little Hetty, (Dr. Hartshorn kept one female "help," a stout lad
to do the chores, and Hetty,)—little Hetty went round to the
kitchen door and admitted herself silently into the house.   Ike—
the lad that did the chores—was carrying in an armful of hickory
from the well-piled wood-house to replenish the "sittin'-room" fire,
for "them ministers" were there, as he gruffly informed the little
negress.   Hannah—the female help—was ironing, and made
Hetty shut the outside door after Ike.

The house was planned in this wise.   In front, on one side of
the hall was the best, or drawing-room, and on the other, the common sitting-room, where the family took their meals.   Back of
the sitting-room was "the bedroom ;" back of the best parlor was
the kitchen, which extended across the hall, so that the only way
out on that side of the house was through it.   The doctor's office
was a sort of offset or wing, opening into the bedroom internally
and having a direct exterior door, as well as separate front gate,
so that professional calls needed not to disturb the house.

Above stairs there were the usual five bedrooms, to wit : two
over the kitchen—one of which was small, corresponding to the
width of the hall—and one over each of the other rooms.   Thus,
over the drawing-room, was the best or spare chamber.   Back of
it was the chamber of the female servants, Hannah and Hetty ;
for although Hannah was white, she condescended to share her
sleeping apartment with such a "little nigger" as Hetty.   But
Hetty, of course, had a separate cot.   Hannah would as soon have
shared her bed with Ike, and Hannah was a girl of the starchest

virtue. Opposite the best chamber was the door of the sick-room ; and Miss Hartshorn's apartment, as she has already told us, was the one back of that ; while the little room at the end of the chamber-entry—situate, of course, between Miss Hartshorn's and Hannah's—was occupied alternately during the night by the sick man's watchers, who thus were enabled to relieve one another—a matter of some moment, as it was considered desirable not to summon a greater number of persons to Walker's bedside than absolute necessity required. A sort of low piazza (painted red) ran along the back of the house ; and at the corner, where the office wing projected from the main building, it was easy for an active man to climb, by the aid of a window-shutter and the lightning-rod, which there descended, and so to get upon the "shed," or roof of the piazza ; whence again, it was easy, by the windows, (at least if one had a friend within,) to enter either Hannah's room or the little chamber which the watchers occupied ; or, finally, Miss Hartshorn's apartment.

The ministers were assembled in Dr. Hartshorn's sitting-room, and conversed on the perplexing affair of their sick brother. There was a difference of opinion between them, in regard to the course proper to be pursued.

" For my part," said a dark, diffident-looking, but meditative man, who spoke in a rich voice, and very quietly, " I am disposed to concede to Brother Walker in the matter of his wish to see young Atherton. I do not see that principle is involved in denying such a request, nor do I apprehend the evil consequences from granting it, which the rest of the brethren seem to forebode."

" I think on the contrary," said a massive, practical-looking man, somewhat advanced in life, " that there is jealousy enough, and bitter theological hatred enough, entertained in reference to the New Haven Seminary, without letting it go abroad that one of our licentiates has died a Papist, and that we have made ourselves, at least, accessories after the fact. It will be laid to the door of the New Haven divinity, depend upon it, Brother F."

" I think the admission of Atherton is inconsistent with our position and his," said a very calm, still-voiced personage, who seemed to be a dignitary of no slight mark, as both the others directed their observations rather to him.. " The only middle course that occurs to me, is what I have already suggested—for I only suggest—namely, that we request one of the Episcopal clergymen in New Haven to visit Mr. Walker. Their Church uses a form of absolution, and it is possible that they may thereby quiet the conscience of this unhappy young man."

" I would prefer to call in a Roman Catholic priest at once," said a young clergyman who had not spoken before. " If there is any thing in a human absolution that can benefit the soul in the presence of God"—he spoke in a hoarse and hollow voice—" let us have it from an authentic source. None of this double-shuffle in religion—this miserable trumpery of the form, without even the profession of the power, which real Popery claims. Away with it, I say !"

This speaker was thin, narrow-shouldered, long-necked, (which his white neckcloth exaggerated) and sallow in complexion. His forehead was high and broad, and his dark, saturnine eye was piercing. Near him sat, in the corner of the sofa, a minister (evidently such) of about the same apparent age, (say thirty-one or two,) but a strong contrast in other respects—light-haired, blue-eyed, softly florid, and graceful in figure. He was now appealed to by the mild dignitary, and spoke with great gentleness—almost too great for a man, and in a voice almost femininely sweet.

" As a stranger I feel diffident in expressing, and indeed in forming an opinion. Are the brethren satisfied, may I ask, that this dying brother is now in the possession of his faculties ?"

" Perfectly," said his dark-eyed neighbor, in his hollowest tone.

" It is, therefore, a case of wilful departure from God, and turning to a refuge of lies—at least so far as poor human eyes can judge ; for it may be—we should trust so—but a permitted temp-tation of Satan, meant to cloud, for a time, our brother's evidence, but from which he may yet emerge triumphant. In either point of view ought we not to wait on the Lord for him in prayer, and leave the rest to God ?''

This advice was like oil on the waters. The colloquy was turned into a prayer-meeting. One after another, (all kneeling,) at the request of the most forward, poured out a long and earnest supplication in behalf of the dying Walker. The deep monotone of their voices, changing in pitch from time to time, rolled on for nearly an hour. Eliza Hartshorn. who was working in the parlor opposite and keeping her mother company, thought they would never get through. In fact, the perplexity of the ministers was great and real. Humanity pled strongly with some of them in the dying man's behalf, but theological prejudice, the fear of stultifying themselves, and awe of the opinion of their world restrained the impulse.

At ten o'clock Mrs. Hartshorn laid aside her knitting, read her chapter, and prepared to retire. She recommended to her daughter to follow her example, but Miss Hartshorn said that she should certainly sit up till the ministers were gone. Finally Dr. Hartshorn and Dr. Reynolds came in together from the office of the former, visited the patient, and, after a short consultation on the stairs. joined the clerical conclave.

" Well, doctor ?"

" Mr. Walker, gentlemen, draws near his end."

" Will he last out the night, doctor ?"

" He *may* do so."

" But you do not expect it."

" It is our *opinion* that Mr. Walker will not live two hours."

" Is he aware of the close proximity of death ?"

" We have thought it best that one of you gentlemen should communicate it to him. It is the duty of the priest rather than of the physician," said Dr. Reynolds.

After some consultation the dark-eyed, hollow-voiced ——, and the mild Professor F——, who had been Walker's immediate pastor before the latter became a licentiate, were deputed to this office. The —— took leave, pleading the hour and his age. Dr.

Reynolds also went off with the air of a man who felt himself no longer needed.

Walker was not greatly changed, except in color and expression. A sort of green pallor overspread his features as he sat, supported by numerous pillows, in a position almost erect, on account of his impeded respiration. Only one of his watchers was in the room ; the other had already retired, and was asleep in the little bedroom at the back end of the chamber entry. A study-lamp with a shade, stood on Walker's table, and the watcher sat by it in a rocking-chair. On the table were books and vials, glasses for medicine, and a decanter of wine. It had been necessary for some time to support the patient's strength by stimulants.

"How do you do, Mr. Wiley?" said the Professor, addressing the watcher in his softest voice.

"How do you do, brother Wiley?" said the other minister in a deep tone.

Mr. Wiley placed chairs for them by the bedside. Professor F——, took Walker's hand kindly and felt his pulse. It was imperceptible, as the Professor gently intimated.

"What does that imply?" said Walker. "Death?"

"We cannot hope that you will continue long with us, Walker, unless God should choose to make a change."

"What do the doctors say? How long have I to live? Tell me the truth," said the dying man, "as you hope for God's mercy."

"We have no desire to conceal the truth from you, brother Walker," said the other minister, more gently than he was wont. "The doctors say that you are sinking. They fear that you will not live many hours."

"How many?" asked Walker, gasping slightly.

"Perhaps not two hours more," said the minister firmly. "You are quite pulseless, and there is effusion in the chest, which increases. These are fatal symptoms, brother Walker. We tell you in kindness, that you may use the time you have left to make your peace with God, if so be that you have not made it already."

"For the love of God," said Walker, beginning to breathe hard and quick, "send for Alban Atherton. I must see a priest before I die. For God's sake, Professor F., send for a priest to absolve me before I die. I shall go to hell. Oh, my God! I would go to purgatory willingly for a million of years—but everlasting perdition! These men have no mercy. God forgive you."

He seemed strangling; but Mr. Wiley calmly brought a draught from the table; the patient coughed and raised a quantity of frothy and sanguineous mucus; then drank, and became quiet, though his eyes glared wildly from one to the other of his persecutors.

"There is no priest to be had, brother Walker," continued the same minister; for Professor F., pushing back his chair, seemed to abandon the case as beyond human reach: "and besides, the hope you place in that source is but a refuge of lies—a reliance on which is the true cause that threatens your perdition. Who can forgive sins but God only? Go directly to him. Not that it would be improper to unburden your mind to one of us, if you have any load of special guilt upon it. 'Confess your sins one to another, and pray one for another, that ye may be healed.' Not a word there about a priest."

"We have been over this ground so often with brother Walker, that I think it is useless to recur to it now," interposed Professor F.

"I wished once more to direct brother Walker's mind away from priests and human absolutions, to the Lamb of God who taketh away the sins of the world," said the hollow-voiced minister solemnly.

"How am I to apply His blood to my soul?" asked Walker.

"By faith," responded the minister, "appropriating him as your Saviour, and renouncing all dependence on your own righteousness."

"Will you pray?" said Walker, addressing the Professor, "and then leave me? I wish to be alone."

The ministers and Mr. Wiley knelt, and Professor F. began to pray.   He was not very fluent, but commenced, apparently from habit, by addressing Almighty God "who by thy apostle hast said, ' If any be sick among you, let him call for the elders of the Church, and let them pray over him'—"

" ' Anointing him with oil in the name of the Lord,'—why don't you go on with the text ?" interrupted Walker.

This disconcerted Professor F., who soon brought the prayer to a conclusion, and his hollow-voiced ministerial brother sighed deeply as they rose from their knees.

People moved through the passages, and on the stairs.   Some were females, from their lighter tread and rustling garments.   By and by the house became quiet.   Mr. Wiley was to call the family if any change occurred, and Hannah, before going to bed, stopped at the door to let him know that there was hot water in case it were needed.   Dr. Hartshorn came in again before retiring. As he quitted the sick-room he tried the door communicating with his daughter's to ascertain if it was locked on the other side, which it was.   But Miss Hartshorn was still in the parlor, and her father looked in upon her.

" Come, Eliza, it is time you were in bed.   It is already considerably past eleven."

" I cannot bear to go to bed, pa, when any person is dying in the house."

" Nonsense, child.   I desire that you will go up stairs, at all events, immediately.   I shall not retire as long as any one is stirring below.   Come."

So Miss Hartshorn took her candle and slowly went up the stairs.   Her father tried the outer doors, and withdrew the key from the lock.   He did not go into his chamber till his daughter's figure was no longer visible from below, and even then he left the door ajar, so that no one could descend the stairs without his knowing it.

Miss Hartshorn did not repair directly to her room ; she went to the sick-room and tapped.   Mr. Wiley came to the door.   She asked a question, and Mr. Wiley came out—nay, he gently closed the door all but a crevice—while he answered her. They whispered awhile, Miss Hartshorn, who was an engaging girl of five-and-twenty, looking very modest, but much interested.

"Don't stand there in the entry with your candle, Eliza," said her father's voice from below.

"No, sir," cried Miss Hartshorn, and with a saucy air, by signs, invited Mr. Wiley into the opposite or spare chamber, to finish what he had to say. Without much hesitation the young man complied, and the candle no longer shining in the entry, her father returned to his room.

Meanwhile Alban was kneeling by Walker's bedside.

"I am dying, Atherton. I want a priest. Confession—absolution! I am a great sinner."

"I expected a priest to-night, but he has not arrived. To-morrow he will certainly be here."

"To-morrow! I have not two hours to live," said Walker feebly, and struggling for breath. Weak as he was, he suppressed the inclination to cough, but the blood flowed from his lips. "No hope for me!"

"Say not so, my dear Walker; God does not require impossibil-ities. An act of perfect contrition, with the desire of the sacrament which you have, is sufficient to blot out your sins in a moment. I have never confessed. I am preparing to do so when Father O'Ryan comes. But if I were to die to-night, I trust I should be saved. The doctrine of the Church is, that perfect contrition—which is genuine sorrow for sin from the love of God, whom sin offends—suffices without the sacrament, if we desire the sacrament and purpose to receive it when we have opportunity, as you and I both do."

"But who can give me perfect contrition! Alas, my sorrow for sin proceeds almost wholly from fear of hell. I think of naught else, day and night, but those eternal flames. I have sinned so grievously. Let me whisper in your ear."

Alban turned pale as he listened to Walker's whispers."

"There is no hope for me! you feel it?"

"You have sinned grievously—"

"Oh, that is only one—the greatest—"

"But the blood of Christ cleanseth from all sin. It matters not how guilty we are ; one drop of that precious blood is sufficient to make us whiter than snow."

"But how is it to be applied to my soul?" It was the same question which he had put to the ministers.

"The sacraments apply the blood of Christ to the soul, if they are received with suitable dispositions," replied Alban ; "but there is no minister of the sacraments here, unless of baptism. Are you sure that you have been baptized?"

Walker had been baptized in infancy by his father, who was a Congregationalist minister of the old school, and was accustomed to use trine affusion with great particularity. Walker had seen his father baptize often.

"There cannot be a doubt that you have been baptized," said Alban. "Perhaps I must teach you a little. Life is the direct gift of God, Walker, yet it comes to us by the ministry of our parents, by the sacrament, if one may say so, of natural genera- tion. It is God who sustains us, who heals us ; but it is by the natural sacraments of food and medicine. Nor can it be other- wise in the spiritual world. There is a ministry and a sacrament of spiritual birth, healing, sustenance. God seems to do nothing without a form, which united to a certain appointed matter, con- veys to us his manifold benefits. You have not feared, my dear Walker, to profane the innocence and the life of grace which God gave you in baptism, and now you need another sacrament of Divine institution to heal your wounded soul, to renew within you the justice which you have lost. Christ's blood has purchased for you the right to such a renewal—to such a medicine. Christ's word has provided it for you in the sacrament of penance ; but a minister to whom He has said 'Whose sins you shall forgive they are forgiven,' is wanting to apply it."

"Ah, you plunge me in despair," said Walker, whose eyes were fixed on Alban's lips.

"*Man doth not live by bread alone, but by every word that proceedeth out of the mouth of God,*" answered Alban, solemnly and tenderly. "The compassion of our Creator and Redeemer is infinite. You must have perfect contrition, certainly, and perfect contrition is *very difficult* to elicit ; it is impossible without special grace, as the Church teaches. I know of but one certain way to obtain it—to interest the Saints in our behalf. God will grant to their prayers what He justly withholds from ours. St. James assures us of it. The sacred heart of Jesus, and that of His blessed Mother, are the refuge of sinners. Fly to them, dear Walker, in these straits. No one, however stained with sin, was ever lost who had recourse, with perfect confidence, to Jesus and Mary. All the Saints say that. For in every exigency God devises means to bring His banished back. Weak, alone, cut off from the ministrations of the visible Church, your faith, Walker, places you in the fellowship of the invisible and triumphant Church. From their bright thrones they watch you, expecting that cry which claims their aid. It is not in vain for us that they *reign* with Christ—believe it firmly."

Walker's eyes filled with tears. He was prepared to believe all. A great scene opened upon him with the clearness of death-bed vision—a great and holy society, partly visible, partly unseen, but travailing in charity for him ; the Lamb of God, the Fount of all that love, its bond the Divine Humanity. If he had been left without the ordinary means which God, as Alban cited from Holy Writ, "devises to bring His banished back," it was only that that charity might reveal itself by overflowing its appointed channels, which is nothing but charity when it restrains itself within them.

Mr. Wiley, having whispered as long as he thought decency permitted with Miss Hartshorn, in the spare chamber, returned into the passage ; but behold the sick-room door was shut. Mr. Wiley tried the handle in silence, but the key had been turned on the inside.

"Good gracious, Miss Hartshorn !"

"Really ! what can have happened ?"

"May I pass through your room, Miss Hartshorn ?"

"Oh, sir, through my room, indeed !"

"Your door is locked, too, Miss Hartshorn"—after trying it, in spite of her reclamations.—"What is to be done, indeed !" The cold sweat stood on Mr. Wiley's forehead. "Can he have got up ?"—listening at the door. "Some one is talking to him," he said, with great agitation.

Miss Hartshorn's quick ear caught her father stirring. She blew out the light with great presence of mind, and whispered her companion to be still. In fine, the doctor came groping up stairs. Miss Hartshorn drew Mr. Wiley, confounded at the dilemma, into the spare room again. The bright moon shone in at the window of the entry, but the closed shutters excluded it from the spare room. The doctor came to the door of the sick chamber and listened ; he heard a low voice as in prayer. The rigid countenance of the Congregational deacon, supposing that he heard Mr. Wiley himself, smoothed in the moonlight into an expression of contented piety. With noiseless steps he returned to his own sanctum below.

It must not be supposed that Mr. Wiley abused the opportunity of the situation by any reckless act of gallantry towards Miss Hartshorn. It is true that she kept herself as far as possible from him ; but he was also too conscience-stricken, and too full of apprehension in regard to the fault which he had already committed in deserting his charge. With slow, agonizingly-muffled steps he again approached the fatal door.

They could both faintly hear the Litany of the departing.

"Lord have mercy ; Christ have mercy ; Lord have mercy.

"Holy Mary, pray for him.

"All you holy Angels and Archangels, pray for him.

"Holy Abel, pray for him.

"Whole Choir of the Just, pray for him.

"Holy Abraham, pray for him.

"Holy John Baptist, pray for him.

"Holy Joseph, pray for him.
"All ye holy Patriarchs and Prophets, pray for him."

Soon the strain altered.

"Be merciful, Spare him, O Lord.
"Be merciful, Deliver him, O Lord.
"Be merciful, Receive him, O Lord.
"From thy anger,
"From the perils of death,
"From an evil death,
"From the pains of hell,
"From every evil,
"From the power of the devil,
                            Deliver him, O Lord.
"By thy nativity,
"By thy cross and passion,
"By thy death and burial,
"By thy glorious resurrection,
"By thy wonderful ascension,
"By the grace of the Holy Ghost,
"In the day of judgment,
                            Deliver him, O Lord.
"Sinners, we beseech Thee hear us.
"That Thou mayest spare him, we beseech Thee hear us.
"Lord have mercy; Christ have mercy; Lord have mercy."

"Is it a Catholic priest who is with him?" whispered Mr. Wiley, in a tone of awe.

"I don't know. Listen."

But all was a low confused murmur of question and faint reply, till the same clear, soft voice was heard reciting, deliberately, the Acts of Faith and Hope, and of Divine Love, and the Act of Contrition; and something that might be supposed to be an *Amen* followed each. Miss Hartshorn knelt all the while at the door, and was weeping. Twice again the low accents repeated the Act of Contrition, which, if indeed it be assented to with all the heart, this sinner's salvation is secure.

"O holy and compassionate Virgin, Mother of Mercy and

Refuge of sinners, suffer not this soul to perish for lack of thy all-powerful intercession, which in its last hour turns to thee the eye of hope.   By the sword of suffering that pierced thy heart beneath the cross, be his advocate with thy Almighty Son, his Redeemer.

" O Jesus, who hast shed every drop of thy blood for him, melt his heart by one glance of thine infinite charity ; remember him, Lord, in thy kingdom ; say to him as Thou didst to the thief who confessed to thee on the cross, ' This day thou shalt be with me in Paradise.'   From all eternity Thou hast foreseen this hour.   Behold he is the child of time, and he has abused thy gifts, but his sole hope, O Saviour of men, is in thy mercy.   Shed abroad in his heart a ray of that perfect charity which effaces in a moment the multitude of sins, for this gift also is thine ; or else, O Lord, all-powerful, preserve him yet a little while for the sacrament of thy reconciliation, which he so fervently desires."

These prayers were interrupted by Walker's coughing.   The fit was severe, and was succeeded by panting moans as of one struggling for breath.   Wiley could not refrain any longer from tapping on the door, and Alban came presently and opened it. Wiley went in with a cowed and guilty look.   Walker was now suffering fearfully,

" Air ! Air ! Air !" he articulated ; his countenance was of a darker lividity, and his lips bubbled with bloody foam, which Wiley wiped away with a handkerchief.   A draught which the latter offered he put away with his hand.   His strength was so great that he raised himself entirely from the pillows and sat unsupported save by Wiley's arm.

" Give me—Air !"

Wiley motioned to Miss Hartshorn who stood within the threshold.   She understood him and ran down for her father.   In a moment Dr. Hartshorn came up, with his dressing-robe thrown round him.   After a glance at the bed, not even noticing Alban, he took a vial from the table and administered to the sick man a spoonful of liquid.   A smell of ether was diffused through the apartment. Walker ceased to cry for air and fell back slightly panting on the pillow. His eyes sought Atherton, who had knelt again by the bedside. Having never seen death, Alban was not alarmed.

" Do you believe in God," he said in a low voice, " and in all that He has revealed to His Church ; the Trinity of Persons in the Unity of the Godhead, the Incarnation of His Son Jesus Christ of the Ever-virgin, His death for our sins, His resurrection for our justification, the perpetuation of His sacrifice and the presence of His Body and Blood, Soul and Divinity in the adorable Sacrament of the Altar, the Remission of Sins by the power of the Keys which He has left to His Church, and in general all that is believed and taught as of faith by the Holy, Catholic, Apostolic, and Roman Church, out of which there is no possibility of salvation ?"

" I believe all," said Walker, with a faint eagerness.

" You hope in the infinite goodness of God, and in His gracious promises to you, though a sinner, for salvation through the blood of Christ, that is, the infinite merits of his sacred passion ?"

" It is all my hope."

" It grieves you to the heart to have ever offended by thought, word, or deed, this God and Saviour ?"

" To the heart."

" You desire to be reconciled to the Church by penance and absolution, were it possible ?" continued Alban, in a trembling voice.

" God knows that I desire it—I ask not to live one moment longer than may suffice for that."

" Yet once more," pursued Alban, hurriedly ; " you are willing, however, to die whenever it pleases God, and you accept your death in the spirit of penance, humbly offering it to God in union with the death of His beloved Son ?"

Walker raised his eyes to heaven, but answered not with his lips. He seemed so collected and so calm, that no one but the physician could believe that the end was so near. Dr. Hartshorn had stared at Alban wildly at first, and then fixed his gaze upon the sick. Mrs. Hartshorn had come up from the room in the garb of haste, and stood with her daughter at the bed's foot. Little Hetty had also somehow glided in, and stood with her black arms crossed on her breast, in her coarse chemise and petticoat.

Alban began to murmur prayers, to invoke the sweet names of Jesus and Mary. He took a crucifix from his bosom and offered it to Walker's lips.

"Behold with faith Him whom your sins have pierced, but who has washed them out in His heart's blood."

The dying man looked at the image of Him who was "lifted up like the serpent in the wilderness," with an expression of unutterable tenderness and compunction. His eyes wandered round as if he saw something in the room. He made an attempt to speak, but could only articulate faintly the words "Jesus! Mary!"

There was a slam of the outer gate, followed quickly by a firm, loud knock at the street door. Little Hetty disappeared at a sign from her mistress, for Dr. Hartshorn was wholly absorbed The eyes of Walker were glazed; his jaw had fallen; he lay motionless. Mrs. Hartshorn was about to draw away the pillows from under the corpse, but her husband prevented her. Little Hetty came running in again, and whispered to Miss Eliza, who in turn whispered Atherton. The latter started up and went out. He returned in a minute, bringing in a gray-haired man in a long overcoat, and wrapped up as from night travel. The stranger approached the bedside, (even Dr. Hartshorn giving way before his air of quiet authority,) and uttered without delay some words in a voice almost inaudible, making a rapid sign in the air with one hand. The dying drew one soft breath, that just raised the linen over the breast. All waited in silence for another, but it came not, and at length it became manifest that all was over.

CHAPTER V.

WALKER's funeral, agreeably to the custom of the country, took place on the second day after his decease. His father and only sister had arrived but the day before ; they had been sent for at an early period of his danger, but their journey was from far and by winter roads. They were plunged in the deepest grief, for he was their hope and stay, and the trying circumstances of his last illness, considered in a religious point of view, could not be kept from their knowledge. The father, a respectable Congregationalist minister in Western New York, was profoundly humiliated by his son's death-bed apostasy : the daughter (now a sole surviving child) seemed stunned. A grave and stern sympathy pervaded New Haven ; Alban Atherton's name was hardly mentioned without some indignant sentence which on other lips would have been an execration ; the Episcopalians alone secretly exulted in the blow inflicted on the pride and bigotry of the "standing order."

Early in the morning (it was Good Friday, but the college routine was not interrupted for that) a young student visited the house where the dead lay. He was shown by little Hetty into the best parlor, where a white-haired but hale-looking man, clerically attired, and a pale girl in black, already were. Mr. Walker, senior, was placid in mien, but his mouth had that stern compression of the thin lips over the jaw, which is so common in New England. He spoke not, but his look said to the student, "What do you want with me ?"

"My errand," said the young man, after a brief but earnest expression of sympathy with the affliction of those whom he addressed, "regards the performance of the last rites of religion at our friend's burial."

"The Reverend Doctor ——, is to conduct them," said the senior Walker quickly.

" At the house, pa," said Miss Walker.   " The Reverend Mr. —— is to officiate at the grave."

" I have no wish," said the young man, " to propose any thing that can conflict with these arrangements, which have been adopted in accordance with the feelings of survivors.   The sole request which I would prefer in the name of the Catholic priest now here, is that on the way from the house to the grave the remains of your son, sir, may be taken to the Catholic chapel.   The object, I need scarcely say, is to pay them those rites of respect which are due to one who died in our holy faith."

Mr. Walker started as if stung.   Miss Walker stared at the speaker, as if she for the first time understood who he was, and was petrified at the presumption of his request—indeed, at the audacity of his coming.   The father only answered quietly,

" My son, I hope, died a Christian.   I want no mummeries over his body."

There was something so definitive, so absolute in the tone in which this was uttered, that the youth felt it would be vain to urge any thing further.   Yet he turned to the daughter.   Women are more accessible, more open to conviction than men.

" Let me claim your intercession, Miss Walker," said Alban.

" You cannot have it, sir," answered Miss Walker.   " Why do you come here to add to our affliction by such proposals ?"   Her frame, which was slight, trembled with passion.

Alban rose.

" I have a message to deliver to you, Miss Walker, which your brother, a little before he died, requested me to impart to you alone."

Miss Walker's pale face changed to crimson.   Her father, gazing sternly out of the window, evidently listened not.   In a minute the daughter rose, pale again, paler than before, and beckoned Alban to follow her.   She preceded him up stairs to the room which had been her brother's.   The door was locked, but the key was outside, and she turned it.   The room was cold, but cheerful with the sun.   The bedstead had been stripped of its furniture; the books, toilet, and table were arranged with the formal precision of a vacant chamber; but supported on three chairs was the open coffin with its stiff and white tenant. There were no flowers, as in the half-heathen Germany; no candles burning, as in Catholic lands; the dead lay coldly, but not unimpressively, alone.

"Here," said Miss Walker, seeming to lean on her brother's coffin for support, "we shall not be interrupted, and this cold presence is propriety."

Miss Walker's features were not beautiful; she was too dark and pale; but she had a fine brow and large, dark, piercing eyes, full of melancholy. Her figure, in deep mourning, was remarkable only for its extreme fragility. Her attitudes and movements were somewhat rigid and ungraceful. She bent on Alban those mournful eyes with an expression of fear, expectation, and distressful curiosity, mingled with something of womanly embarrassment, perhaps of maiden shame.

"Your brother fell into a grievous sin, not unknown to you," said Alban, "and he crowned the sin, as you also know, by a great injustice, and added a falsehood, which came little short of perjury, to shield himself from the consequences; finally, when driven to desperation, procured the commission of what even human laws punish as a crime, and which certainly is a great one in the sight of God. A great part of this is irreparable; but the person whom he has injured is known to you; it may be in your power to save her from further degradation and eternal ruin. He implores you to do it, even if his reputation should be thereby endangered. Do not be so overwhelmed—Miss Walker. God has pardoned your brother, we trust, and that is the important thing. Perhaps but for this fall he had not been saved. It is only a divine restraint upon us that prevents any of us from rushing into wickedness."

"I never knew his sin till it was too late to do more than conceal it as best I could."

"If concealment had not been unjust to another," said Alban.

"She deserved her fate," said the sister of Walker, looking

34*

up. "Not that I excuse my brother; but he was a man. A woman who forgets what is due to her sex, Mr. Atherton, must and ought to bear the penalty."

"Would *he* say so now, who has met, face to face, the justice of God?" said Alban, glancing down at those features locked in the tranquillity which knows no earthly comparison.

Miss Walker bowed herself over the calm, white face, from which Alban had lifted the light fall of muslin that covered it, and burst into sobs. Their violence racked her delicate frame. Some low words escaped her in which nothing but "Brother," was distinguishable.

"And now I may say," continued Alban, "that we are not anxious to claim your brother as a convert for the sake of any credit that would hence redound to our religion. He fled to the Church as an ark of safety from the wrath of God. The Divine mercy inspired him with such dispositions, so far as we can judge, that the priest, whose word and sign in the last unconscious moment of existence swept away the airy barrier which yet separated him from the visible communion of God's Elect, entertains no doubt of his salvation, and is ready to attest the fact of his reception into the Church by granting his mortal remains the last honors of the flesh which is to rise in Christ's image. For the repose of his soul, masses shall be offered. Whatever measure of just retribution his spirit suffers, the merits of the Divine sacrifice are applicable to expiate and relieve. Body and soul he belongs to Christ—not to Satan. That is what we wish to say, Miss Walker,—what we *dare* to say—let the cruel, harsh-judging, unforgiving·world talk of him as it will."

Now the sister's tears fell fast, but in silence. Although the quick transitions and delicate links of reasoning, than which adamant were more easily shivered, baffled a female attention in most that Alban would say on such subjects, the main drift was intelligible to a woman through her heart. A certain apprehension of punishment is inseparable from the knowledge of guilt in ourselves or those near to us. Hence Alban had touched the right string when he pointed out to Miss Walker that the Church extended over her brother in death, the arm of courageous love and the ægis of the name of Christ. She was softened enough to.reason with the young student whom at first she had regarded but with indignation and horror,

" I cannot imagine," said she, gently replacing the muslin over the face of the dead, " how an absolution which seems to have been pronounced when my brother was unconscious, and actually breathing his last, should affect his state. You attach a value to forms, Mr. Atherton, which appears very strange."

" Because behind the veil of the form we see something that you do not—Jesus Christ gliding into the chamber and saying to the departing, ' Thy sins be forgiven thee.' But I must not tarry longer." The young man bowed for a moment over the dead, and turned away. " It is not good for you to remain here long," he said, allowing her to pass out before him. When they reached the bottom of the stairs, he extended his hand without alluding to the business which had occasioned his visit.

" I will get pa to consent to your proposal about—" said she, avoiding the conclusion of the sentence. " And in regard to the other matter—it rests between us, I hope, Mr. Atherton ? We may never meet again, sir, but you may be assured that my brother's dying request is something that I shall consider sacred."

The funeral was in the afternoon. A crowd of students and citizens of New Haven, with many ladies, filled every room within the house. Without were collected a great number of Irish servants and laborers, mingled with the more ordinary class of town-people. At one time, from the excited feeling between the Catholic and Protestant portions of the crowd outside, an excitement fanned by various reports, there were symptoms of a battle, but the arrival of the ministers produced a calm by diverting the attention of the multitude.

The exercises consisted of an address to those assembled, and a prayer. Both were made in the hall at the foot of the stairs, and were listened to, in breathless silence, by the men who filled the lower portion of the house ; with tears and some audible sobbing by the females in the chambers. The address of Professor —— was cautious and painful. He spoke of the lessons to be drawn from the death of one so young—"in the opening bud of manhood and usefulness, and so recently full of health and strength." He applied to the surviving friends the ordinary topics of instruction and consolation ; but he said very little of the departed, which, considering that it was almost a clerical brother, seemed a significant omission, and struck a chill into the breasts of his auditors. The Rev. Mr. ——'s prayer was more fluent, and his hollow tones reverberated with an awe-impressing effect ; but he, also, much more slightly and vaguely alluded to the deceased than was his wont. He made amends by praying fervently that all present might be preserved from false dependences, from every refuge of lies, from all the cunning devices of Satan, even when he disguised himself as an angel of light, (here every eye was directed, or at least, every thought, to the form of Atherton, who stood in the doorway among the bearers,) and that every stronghold of his, whether pagan or papistic, might speedily be overturned by the power of the Word of God, and so on, which was listened to eagerly, and found in every listener a ready interpreter.

The procession was formed. The pall-bearers took their places. There was only one carriage, occupied by the mourners ; the citizens followed on foot ; the students walked on before the hearse. It proceeded by an unusual road, which many, indeed, did not understand, until a pause occurred before the low building with a cross on the gable. Those whose duty it was to bear the coffin, when taken from the hearse, here refused to act ; but six Irish laborers, decently clad in black, came forward and supplied their places. However, curiosity carried most of those present into the chapel, and it became filled. Unfamiliar, and some of them apprehensive, the crowd gazed upon the black hangings, which had not been removed since the morning service, (it was Good Friday,) and the candles burning by day.

The body of Walker passed a threshold, which living it had never crossed ; and psalms were recited in the ear of the dead, which living it had never heard ; holy water was sprinkled on the inanimate flesh, which living had never used that salutary aspersion ; lights burned and incense waved around that body, which living had never rendered like honors to the glorious Body of the Lord. Such was the Church's acknowledgment of penitence and faith, though testified at the final hour. Nor did she avoid his name, which once before she had uttered, when she bore him in baptism. She breathed it now in prayer, commending his spirit to the mercy of Him Who created it.

> " Requiem eternam dona ei, Domine.
> " Et lux perpetua luceat ei.
> " Requiescat in pace.
> " Amen."

CHAPTER VI.

" A BOY like this cannot be permitted to triumph over us all."
—" The spirit of insubordination appears already. Nothing else
was talked of in commons to-night, and those who were opposed to
Atherton's views sympathized with his victory over the faculty."—
" The weakest thing was brother ———'s speech at the grave—
why should he speak at all ?"—" The students dispersed smiling
and laughing. But I wonder that more decided measures were
not taken to prevent that significant demonstration at the Catholic chapel."—" It was a mistake all round. Atherton, who
(between us) is the very deuce among the women, persuaded
Walker's sister, and she made the old man consent. But Master
Alban has laid himself open to discipline in that visit to Walker. I
suppose you know that he entered Dr. Hartshorn's house near upon
midnight, by Miss Hartshorn's chamber window."—" Shocking !
scandalous ! and he a professor ! Isn't it a misdemeanor, a trespass, or something of that sort ? Dr. Hartshorn should bring
him before a justice of the peace."—" His daughter's share in it
prevents his doing that. But there is nothing to prevent an investigation before the faculty."—" That 'll be rich. Atherton
will be expelled—don't you think ?"—" I am sorry for him,"
with a look of mysterious knowledge, " but he has brought this
thing upon himself."

Thus a pair of tutors gossiped as they returned from their
evening walk.

These subordinates but echoed a determination of the superior
members of the college government. The proceedings of the faculty of Yale College are always marked by promptitude. The
morning of the day following Walker's funeral, Alban was summoned before them ; few witnesses were required, for the culprit
admitted most of the facts alleged against him.

A majority of the younger members of the faculty, and one or two of the older professors whose natures were more despotic and their religious antipathies more violent, were in favor of expulsion, or at least dismission. But the venerable President, the amiable and gifted Professor F., and others, opposed so extreme a measure. This body is one of a remarkable sagacity, which has ever tempered its instinctive jealousy as a government. There was danger, as the acute and practical S. pointed out, in carrying Atherton's punishment beyond what was necessary to save themselves from contempt ; it was wiser to fall short of the severity desired by the public feeling than to awaken sympathy for the sufferer by the semblance of vindictiveness. These temperate counsels prevailed, and Alban Atherton, more humiliated by his trial than aggrieved by a sentence which virtually acquitted him of every thing not openly acknowledged by himself, was *rusticated* for three months—being the entire remainder of his college course.

The President's room was directly under Atherton's—" Awful handy for you !" said St. Clair, who tried to keep up his cousin's courage under these painful circumstances by a fire of constrained jests. All Saturday afternoon he heard the voices of those who were sitting there and deciding upon his fate ; at six o'clock he went in to hear his sentence from the lips of the President, as well as to receive the " admonition" which was a formal part of the punishment.

The day which he had thus spent had been fixed for his first confession, and as soon as he could get away, he hurried to the Catholic chapel. He found it full of servant-girls and laborers waiting their turn, and crowding, not to say pushing, each other round the door of the sacristy in order to secure it. It might be nearly half-past seven when Atherton came in, and he remained more than three hours kneeling at one of the back benches, trying to recall the matter he had previously prepared, and to excite himself to contrition. In spite of his efforts at recollection, his mind wandered —now to the sentence which, in all its mild wording and severe sense, rung in his ears, now to the mortifying details of his trial, in which he might have said so much that he did not say, (in reply to attacks,) and omitted so much (that was indiscreet) which he had said ; then to Walker's death and funeral, his interview with the father and sister, and the probable effect of all upon his own parents, the De Groots, and all his near or distant friends.

At about eleven o'clock the chapel was at last cleared, and he entered the sacristy with a beating heart. The old priest rose from the confessional and met him.

"My dear sir, you must not think of coming to confession to-night. If I had had a suspicion of your being here I would have come out of the sacristy to tell you so. It is impossible, my dear young friend, that after what you have passed through to-day you can be sufficiently recollected to make a first confession. God will take the will for the deed. Return to your room and sleep upon it. To-morrow you will hear mass quietly, and in the afternoon, or Monday morning, whichever you prefer, I will see you here, and we can take it leisurely."

"On Monday morning, Father O'Ryan, I must quit New Haven. I am rusticated."

"Have they gone so far?—Well," giving Atherton's hand a warm pressure—"thank God ! thank God ! you begin to suffer a little for the faith. What a favor to *you*, my dear friend ! Now *don't* trouble yourself about this confession. Let me see. You go on Monday morning. Perhaps you will like to make a beginning to-night, and I dare say you can finish to-morrow."

"I think I will not attempt to do any thing to-night, if I can have an hour to-morrow all in a lump," said Atherton.

"Then I will hurry to my hotel and take a bite before twelve o'clock," said the priest, "for I have two masses to-morrow, and to-day, of course, I have had but one meal. As that was ten hours ago, and I have been in this dreadful confessional ever since, I feel rather used up."

"My dear Father O'Ryan ! and you talked of hearing my confession !"

"Why, to tell the truth," said the missionary with a gruff

cheerfulness, " I hardly knew how I should stand it if I didn't get something to eat before midnight. Not but that I've done it in my day, but this has been a hard week. *In vigiliis, in jejuniis* often comes to my mind, Mr. Atherton. We stagger under a trifle of fasting for twenty-four hours—what would we think of the watchings and fastings of St. Paul ?"

So on Sunday Alban came in the afternoon to the chapel, but found it closed. Not a soul knew why. He went round to the hotel. The missionary was gone, having been called away to a place thirty miles off to visit a person at the point of death. He had left a pencilled note for Atherton, which thus concluded.

" Thank God, my dear friend, for this fresh disappointment, it being His will to try you a little longer. To be perfectly resigned to the will of the Almighty is better than to receive absolution with ordinary good dispositions. Be humble enough to say from the heart *fiat voluntas tua*, and grace itself can do no more for you."

With faint steps the young convert approached his boarding-house at the hour of the evening meal. He was fasting, although it was the Queen of Festivals—the first Easter he had ever observed.

Looking forward to confession, and feeling pretty sure that under the circumstances Father O'Ryan would give him absolution at once, he had entertained the innocent desire of making his first communion on that sacred day. The disappointment of both these expectations coming upon his academical disgrace,—conspired, with the exhaustion of his bodily powers and the moral reaction after the somewhat exalted state through which he had passed, to produce an extreme depression. His very faith appeared to have left him. The sublime Hope on which his soul had fed, identified itself with the illusions of the imagination. Could his eyes have been opened he would have perceived a dark and formless Being walking by his side, triumphing that his power was not yet at an end, and that one more temptation was permitted him to which those of the world and the flesh were weak.

Mrs. Hart met him in the hall with some letters which had
arrived on Saturday, for Alban had lately taken a fancy to have
his letters left at his boarding-house. By such a batch coming to
hand at once, he divined a crisis, such as indeed he had reason
to expect. As in duty bound he opened one from his father
first.

"NEW YORK, April 17, 1835.

"DEAR SON,—Your mother and myself have been astonished
at the communication just received from you. What you propose
is an act of perfect lunacy. I can with difficulty realize that
you are serious in it. I omit all reply to your long argument. I
am astonished that the college faculty should not have informed
me, when they knew that you were diverting your mind from your
studies to these frivolous questions, which the whole world settled
hundreds of years before you were born. You mentioned to me,
before leaving home last vacation, that your mind was occupied
in this manner, and I thought I then signified my wish with sufficient clearness, to the effect that you would postpone such matters
until you have completed your college course. Indeed, it would
be far better never to take into consideration any subject which
has no practical bearings.

"The recent rise in ——— (which has very much surprised the
rich 'bears') has realized the expectations which I had confidently
formed, and I anticipate a still further improvement. Thinking
you may be short, I inclose you a check for fifty dollars, which
please acknowledge.

"The proposed change of religion would be decidedly injurious
to you in a quarter to which I need only allude. I speak from personal knowledge when I say that the opinion entertained of your
sound judgment and liberal views, is the ground of the approbation which has been given by her parents to the preferences of a
certain young lady.

"Yr. aff. father,

"SL. ATHERTON."

The next letter was from his mother.

"GREY STREET, *April* 16, *Thursday.*

"MY DEAR ALBAN,—Your letter has plunged me into the deepest grief. Words, my beloved son, cannot express the feelings with which I have again and again perused it. Surely it is a transient bewilderment. You confess that you were for a time skeptical, then (singular and incomprehensible) almost a Jew! These notions will also pass off if you give them time.

"What you say in condemnation of the religion of your sainted grandfather, your aunt Elizabeth, your cousin Rachel, (who is going on a mission,)—not to say of your own mother—is dreadful! But you have not looked upon it in that light. When you do, you will repent, I am sure, of such thoughts as you seem to have had. It would break my heart, Alban, if I thought that you could really be given up to this awful delusion.

"Your father (although he has promised me to write you temperately) is very angry about your letter. He says that if you turn Papist or Jew (for he cannot make out which it is you mean) he will never see you again.

"Before you were born it was my prayer, day and night, that (whatever else you were) you might be one of God's true children; and indeed I had hoped that my prayer was answered. Oh, Alban, I would rather have followed you to your grave than see you forsake the truth, and lose your soul!

"Put away the books which have perverted your mind, my dearest son; give up your proud reliance on your own talents, (ah, that is the great point,) and study your Bible with prayer to God for guidance—He will not fail to direct you.

"I have no heart to add more at present. If you will not take the counsels of those who are older and wiser than you, I foresee your ruin for this world and the next, and for your parents nothing but shame and grief, where they have hitherto felt so proud and happy.

    "Your affectionate mother,

        "GRACE ATHERTON.

"P. S. I have just heard, from a reliable source, that Miss De G., who has no doubt influenced *you* more than you are aware, is herself not too well satisfied with the step so hastily taken in opposition to the known wishes of her parents. Oh, Alban, will you not be warned?"

These letters touched our hero deeply. Could any thing be so certain as the evil of outraging these kind affections—the prime religion of nature and basis of piety?—*A man's foes shall be they of his own household. He that loveth father or mother more than me is not worthy of me.*—"How true the prophecy! How precise the warning!" thought Alban, as he broke the rich seal of a third letter.

"FIFTH AVENUE, *Fer.* 6 *in Parasceve.*

"DEAR ATHERTON: Addressing a new-blown votary of the Christianity of the Middle Ages, I can do no less than adopt an ecclesiastical date. Your father tells me you are going to make a fool of yourself as Mary has done, but with infinitely less excuse.

"Speculate as you will, Atherton. Protestantism is a shallow thing, no doubt, but do not think that because there are truths which it cannot measure or fathom, its opposite must necessarily be truth without alloy. It is but a few months since you hesitated between Judaism and Episcopacy, and but a few more since you were a fervent Puritan. Now you regard these past states as blindness. Wait a few more months and you will deem the same of your present stage of development. I do not mean (as some vulgar people would) that you have gained nothing, but that you have something yet to gain. You are young, and although you have a wonderful head for your years, no genius can compensate altogether for the want of that grandest and most fruitful experience whose domain is the inner world of reflection,—which time and self-study alone can give.

"I do not wish to appeal to any feeling or interest which you would regard as beneath the dignity of such a question. At the same time I think it right to tell you that since she has looked upon you as a convert, Mary's interest in you has sensibly diminished. Her imagination is no longer excited about you, and that is a fatal incident to the love of a devotee. Mary thinks more of the cloister than of wedlock already, and if you were actually to join the Roman Church at this premature stage of your friendship, I greatly fear that she might never arrive at that passion-point where maiden resolutions melt like snow before the fire.

"Win and wed my daughter *first*—then profess her faith. The world will then appreciate your change, which now will be assigned to an interested motive.

"Let me hear that you have chosen the wise course of postponing an irrevocable step, at least until you can take it with dignity.

"Truly yours,

"E. De Groot.

"Alban Atherton, Esquire."

"How sage and how confident he seems!" thought Alban. "And Mary! It would be strange if she ceased to love me, because I had become actually a Catholic. And yet it would not be strange, for it is not like the ways of the Highest to bestow a rich earthly reward on those who leave all for His sake. I see how it will be. Flower of chastity! My bosom is not pure enough on which thou shouldest repose! He whose 'name is as oil poured forth,' has attracted thy virgin steps."

A sudden faintness overcame Atherton; the room swam around him; he looked about for help, but Mrs. Hart was gone; he rose and staggered to the sofa, on which he had just time to throw himself ere a darkness swept the room from his sight.

He lay motionless, but not unconscious, till on that black depth, as in a mirror, a bright scene became gradually distinct.

It was the interior of a beautiful chapel, the morning sun shining in at the high east window. A pure yet brilliant altar of white marble was crowned with a constellation of starry lights.

A meek prelate in a rich robe stood before it; the sides of the chapel were lined with black-robed nuns, each in her oaken stall, the snowy wimple covering her breast, the snowy *band* across her temples. At the rail knelt two young females in pure white, one of whom was habited as a bride.

Alban could hear no words; but the brief and beautiful cere-mony·of taking the white veil took place in dumb show in the small, brilliant chapel. He knew what it was, although he had never seen it. When the novice turned from the altar with the plain veil of religion upon her head, in place of the rich bridal lace which had previously shrouded her, Atherton saw her features of incomparable loveliness :—they were those of Mary De Groot, and the bright vision gradually dissolved again till only her youthful form, still advancing towards him, remained visible. It approached till it seemed that he could have touched her, and then vanished.

CHAPTER VII.

The place to which Alban was rusticated, was a retired country village in the interior of Connecticut. Early on Monday morning he took stage for Hartford, the semi-capital of the little State, not content with one metropolis. From New Haven to Hartford was a day's journey in those times, and in the early spring, a tedious one. The heavy and well-balanced vehicle went swinging and swaying through the mud, crawling up the hills, tearing down the declivities with a rocking and sweeping whirl that for the moment stirred the blood and half took away the breath, then crept on as before.

Atherton was too busy with his own brooding thoughts to heed much his fellow-travellers, or their conversation, which was slight and desultory. At noon they stopped for dinner, after which several new passengers were taken in ; the stage received its compliment of nine inside, and two with the driver. The new company were more talkative. The recent events at New Haven were discussed, and Alban heard his own name freely mentioned.

" This young gentleman is a Yale student, I believe," said one of the old passengers.

" Are you acquainted with the young man Atherton ?" asked a new passenger.

" I have some acquaintance with him," said Alban, in the dry New England manner.

" Is he so talented as they say he is ?" inquired the new passenger. " I heard that it puzzled the Doctors of Divinity to answer his objections."

" There is generally exaggeration in these reports," replied Atherton.

" Is it true that he let himself down the chimney into a young lady's chamber and hid himself under the bed till she had retired ?"

" No, not under the bed, but in the closet," said a morning passenger, with an air of information.

" What a bad, impudent fellow he must be !" said a lady on the back seat.

" I never heard those circumstances mentioned," said Alban.

" Oh, I assure you they are quite true," said the morning passenger. " I was told by a friend of Miss —— Hornheart herself— was not that the name ? Miss Hornheart was dreadfully shocked, as you may suppose, ladies," (turning to the fair occupants of the back seat.)

" How old is Atherton ?" inquired one of the ladies, addressing Alban.

" I should say he was something past twenty, ma'am."

" Young scapegrace !" ejaculated the afternoon passenger.

" He has been dreadfully dissipated without any one's ever suspecting it," said the morning passenger.

" Sly boots," interposed the afternoon passenger, with a wink at the eldest of the ladies.

" And worse than dissipated—a very *dangerous* young man in a family."

" Oh, really !" exclaimed the two elder ladies.

" Dear me !" softly breathed the youngest, with a blush.

" I think you rather calumniate Atherton, sir," said Alban, coloring. " I belong to the same class in college, and I certainly never heard any thing insinuated against his moral character."

" Oh !" cried the morning passenger, contemptuously, " I dare say you never *heard* any thing against him, young gentleman. Nobody had heard, till this came out. Sly boots ! as you were saying, sir," (to the afternoon passenger.)

The afternoon passenger was a tall, large-framed, and well-fleshed man, in a suit of rusty black, with a narrow white cravat; quite evidently the minister of some Episcopal congregation in a rural district. He sat on the middle seat with his great, heavy arm over the strap, and exchanged many little courtesies with the ladies behind him.

"I should like to have a talk with this Popish classmate of yours," said he, addressing Alban. "He and I would agree on many points. For instance, the Roman Catholic Church has always set its face against modern science. I like that," turning to the rest of the company; "modern science is little better than dealing with the devil, after all. These great discoveries! gifts of Satan all. Steam, Chemistry, Galvanism, and last but not least, Animal Magnetism!"

"Do you rank Animal Magnetism with acknowledged scientific facts?" asked Alban.

"There is a girl here in Hartford at the present time," replied the clergyman, with a keen look at the young student, "a girl in the clairvoyant state, who can see through blankets, and tell you what is passing hundreds of miles off."

"'Tis true as the Gospel," said a gentleman in the corner of the front seat, who had not before spoken. "She sees all the interior organs in any one's body, (that wishes it, of course,) and describes all their conditions, so that a physician by her aid can prescribe as exactly for any disease as if he could take you to pieces like a watch. I have witnessed this myself."

"For my part I should object to being seen through in that fashion," exclaimed one of the ladies.

"And I too," said the second lady, who had a slight cough, "though I should like to know if I have tubercles."

The young lady only blushed.

"The first time that the Mesmerist made this clairvoyant girl see the inside of a human body—with the heart beating, the blood rushing through the great arteries, the lymph circulating, and so on—she was terribly frightened," said the stranger who had last spoken. "Now she is used to it, and thinks nothing of examining any body that the operator requires."

"But where is the evidence that her seeing these things is not all pretence?" asked Alban, skeptically.

"Of course you must take her testimony as part proof," said the stranger, "but if you have sufficient evidence of her preternatural sight in many incontestable instances, you cannot refuse to believe."

"I will tell you what happened to myself," said the Episcopal clergyman.

All expressed a desire to hear the clergyman's story.

"I visited this clairvoyante with a determination to test the genuineness of her pretensions. She was not in the mesmeric state when I arrived at the house, but the operator, a medical man, called her in, and she consented, not without some difficulty, to be mesmerized in my presence. It seemed that she had been under this physician's care for a nervous disease, for which he had been induced to try mesmerism as a remedy. I dare say you are all familiar, gentlemen, with the process of mesmerizing—the thumbing, the passes, the flourishes, and all that. In about fifteen minutes the effect was produced. In the earlier period of the experiments on this girl it had taken sometimes two or three hours to accomplish a like result. She seemed to be in a natural sleep, paying no attention to any thing I said, although she readily answered the questions of the mesmerizer. Well, not to be tedious, after showing some of the common tricks of mesmerism, he placed the girl, at my request, in *rapport* with myself." Here the narrator pulled out his watch. "You observe, ladies and gentlemen, that mine is what is called a hunter's watch, with the outside case entirely closed, so that it is necessary to touch a spring (thus) and make the face-side fly open in order to tell the hour. I had taken the precaution before entering the house to set the hands about six hours and a half in advance. The girl's eyes were at this time closely bandaged, with a strong silk handkerchief over some six or seven thicknesses of common linen roller. I stood behind her and asked, 'What is this I have in my hand, Eliza?' 'It is a watch,' she replied. 'And what time is it by my watch?' She hesitated before answering, somewhat impatiently, I thought, 'How can I tell?'—'Nay,' said I, 'if you can see through a blanket, and all those bandages, and the back of your head, you can surely see through a plain silver case. Is it harder to see the inside of a watch than the inside of a body?' 'The case dazzles my eyes,' she answered, putting her hand before them. All this while I held the watch directly at the back of her head, and in such a position that the doctor—the Mesmerizer—could not see it. I touched the spring. 'Can you tell me now what time it is.'— 'Yes,' she answered, removing her hand from her bandaged eyes, 'it wants a—quarter to ten.' I glanced at the doctor, whose face wore an expression of slight disappointment, for the real time was about a quarter past three, P.M. ; but I relieved him by showing the hands of my watch, which indicated just sixteen minutes to ten. The minute hand was a mere line past the sixteen. 'Does it want just a quarter?' I asked. 'Well,' she replied, pettishly, 'it *will*, in less than a minute.' For my part, ladies and gentlemen," concluded the clergyman, "I was thunderstruck."

"And was that all?" inquired Alban.

"Oh, by no means. I tried her with a short sentence, which I had previously written on a slip of paper and inclosed in a brown paper envelope. She read it with facility, altering only a word." The clergyman paused. "I tried her with some other experiments in which she failed partially or entirely, and the Mesmerizer remarked that all the circumstances on which the perfection of the clairvoyant state depended were not known, and it was probable that these mistakes, which perpetually occurred amid things alike wonderful and inexplicable, were due to some violated condition, or decline, or oscillation of the mesmeric extasy, as he termed it. In conclusion, however, after, at my request, he had renewed the passes, and placed me once more in the most intimate *rapport* with the girl that he was able, I asked her some questions relative to a room which I had privately prepared in my own house, before setting out for Hartford. The distance is about fifty miles, and no one, I am certain, was in the secret of these arrangements but myself. Her answers I cannot divulge," said the clergyman, with a dark shade passing suddenly over his countenance, " but they satisfied me of the existence of a power beyond my comprehension, and previously, beyond my belief. Suffice it, that she not only described the most secret arrangements which I alone had made in my own parsonage, but revealed to me also circumstances which were occurring in my absence, of which otherwise 1 should have had no knowledge whatever."

"In time we shall arrive at more wonderful things," observed the stranger in the corner seat. " Or rather, all miracles will be explained by some very simple principle. A few passes, you observe, sir, effected that extraordinary phenomenon which you witnessed in the mesmerized girl. By and by we shall learn to cure diseases with a touch. In fact, it is not more wonderful than that they should now be cured by some simple herbs."

" And what do *you* think of it, young gentleman ?" said the clergyman, addressing Atherton.

" Why, sir, it appears on your own showing, that you have had dealings with Satan," replied Alban, gravely.

" Pshaw !" said the stranger in the corner seat, " there is no such person as Satan."

The evening lights already sparkled in the windows when the stage rattled into Hartford. At the tea-table of the hotel the conversation was renewed upon Mesmerism, demoniacal possessions, and the forbidden arts. The stranger believed in magic, which he maintained was only the consummation of science. Matter, in itself nothing, was meant to be subject to the human will as a slave to a master. He thought that the world was on the eve of great discoveries, before which the barriers which separated us from the unseen would fall. His conversation breathed an intense desire to penetrate the profoundest secrets of nature and of time, and Alban, as he listened, could with difficulty withstand the contagious influence of these daring aspirations.

CHAPTER VIII.

In the northeast part of Connecticut, among the hills where the Yantic takes its rise, extends a bleak, almost woodless table-land, of some miles in length by about one and a half in breadth. It is not destitute of farm-houses, and a great road passes through the middle of it, which, for one reach of about a mile, expands into a wide common, where the housen (this old Saxon plural is still used in New England) are more frequent, and form the straggling village of Carmel.

At either extremity of this common rises a steepled meeting-house; for the old Congregationalists have split in Carmel, and the new school have raised a rival house of worship, at the distance of a mile from their neighbors. On the road-side, nearly equidistant from the two meeting-houses, stands an old, white, pillared mansion, with fine old button-balls planted in a long line before it, and a garden in the rear; meadows and orchards on either side. The house formerly belonged to a great family in the State, and one to which our hero was nearly allied; but it had passed out of the name, and at this time was the parsonage, or rather the residence of the old school minister. This gentleman eked out his pastoral income by pupils, and was willing to receive, now and then, a rusticated student from his *alma mater*.

The stage-coach drew up, by a gray sunset, before the Rev. Dr. Cone's. The driver took off Alban's trunk, and set it down for him in the long piazza. The Rev. Dr. Cone himself came out to greet the new-comer. He was a man past the middle age, of a grave and dignified aspect.

"President ——," said Alban, offering a letter, "assured me that this would procure me the pleasure of pursuing my studies for a few months, under your roof, Dr. Cone."

"I understand," said Dr. Cone, balancing the letter vacantly

36

in one hand. "Walk in, Mr. Atherton"—glancing at the name
written in the corner. "You have come to a queer place, but
you are welcome, sir."

A hall of small dimensions, with a square balustraded staircase, opened on one side into a spacious parlor, sparely but handsomely furnished. The chairs were high-backed, solid, and heavy;
a large wood-fire burned on the ample hearth. The room contained a piano, at which a little girl was sitting. She turned her
head as the door opened, and Alban saw a sparkling brunette,
with the wildest black eyes, and a shower of jetty ringlets falling
on bare, slight shoulders.

"Ah!" said Alban's future host, and withdrew from the room
which he had half entered. "Perhaps you had better walk into
my study," said he, addressing Alban, and with the word went to
an opposite door.

The study was lined with rude book-shelves, but well laden.
Here, too, was a wood-fire, but burning in an old Franklin. A
school-desk ran along the front windows, with a bench. But
there was no one in the study, and the doctor, pointing Atherton
to a seat by the Franklin, assumed what was evidently his own
study chair.

"With your permission, doctor, I will lay aside my cloak,"
said Atherton, for the room was very warm.

"Certainly, certainly, sir," said the doctor, abstractedly.

Atherton threw off both his cloak and overcoat, and Dr. Cone
regarded him curiously, glancing from him to the letter of introduction, which was still unopened.

"Perhaps I have mistaken—the nature of the affair," said the
doctor, slowly breaking the seal of the letter, and looking at the
young man with surprise. "I was under the impression—"

Here Alban was startled by his host's apparently chucking the
open, but unread letter of the President into the fire. It was in
flames in an instant. The doctor made a sort of effort to recover
it, but it was consumed before he could seize it. He drew from the
Franklin only a bit of blackened cinder, that quickly fell into ashes.

"Hem! disagreeable these things are," said Dr. Cone, in a low voice.

"Surely, then," thought Alban, "you might have been more careful."

The doctor looked so embarrassed at the destruction of the letter that our hero felt the position of culprit, in which he had entered the house, entirely reversed. While he was reflecting how far he was bound, or even authorized, to supply the information which the burned epistle had doubtless contained, the door of an inner apartment opened, and a plump, well-looking dame of forty entered the study. She stared slightly at Alban, and looked at the doctor.

"This is Mr. Atherton, my dear, (Mrs. Cone, Mr. Atherton,) from Yale College, who has come to pursue his studies, (did you not say so, sir?) for a few months, at Carmel."

"Mr. Atherton?" said Mrs. Cone, courteously. "It is not the son of Mr. Samuel Atherton, of New York, surely! Indeed! What, Alban Atherton! I am very glad to see you, sir. Why I have known your mother ever since I can remember. Mr. Atherton is a grandson of General Atherton of Yanmouth, my dear. *Little* Alban! Why I have had you in my arms a thousand times!"

Mrs. Cone poured out a flood of questions relative to his parents. She had heard of his being at college, and distinguishing himself greatly. A mother could hardly have greeted him with more warmth.

"And what is it brings you to Carmel, Alban? You have not been rusticated, I take for granted," said Mrs. Cone, laughing.

"Unfortunately, I have," replied Alban, with a slight blush.

"Why, what have you been doing to merit such a sentence?" demanded Mrs. Cone, with some surprise.

"The President wrote a letter to Dr. Cone, informing him of my offence," answered Atherton, with embarrassment.

"Where is it, husband?" said Mrs. Cone, imperiously.

"It is burned," replied her husband, meekly.

"Burned !" exclaimed the lady.

Her husband glanced significantly at the young man.

"How provoking," she added in a low tone, and with a sudden change of countenance. "I am really wearied at these annoying occurrences. I shall quit this house soon, that is certain !"

In uttering these ejaculatory sentences, which considerably mystified Alban, the lady seemed to have forgotten her curiosity in regard to the cause of his rustication. She abruptly asked how long he would stay with them, and where his trunk was; then saying that she must give directions to get a room ready for him, quitted the study, with a disturbed air.

In a few minutes she called to him from the hall. He found a couple of healthy-looking Irish lasses carrying his trunk up stairs, at her bidding.

"I fear it is too heavy for them to carry," said Alban, observing that the girls panted under the weight.

"Oh, never fear," said one, "this"—pointing significantly at the other—"is a strong girl."

"There's them in the house 'od take it up a dale asier," replied her companion, as they rested on the landing, "if they could but turn a hand to any thing useful."

"Hold your tongue, Bridget," said Mrs. Cone.

They got the trunk at last into a comfortable chamber, and Mrs. Cone dismissed her handmaidens. When they were gone she turned to Alban with an air of authority.

"Now, Alban—I must call you Alban, for you seem quite like my own child—I knew your aunt Betsey so well, and your mother, too, at Yarmouth, when I was a girl—and a wild thing as ever breathed—and you a delicate little boy—how you have grown ! I am very proud of your college distinctions, your prizes, and being President of the Brothers' Society—they say that you are the best writer of your class—but what is the cause of your having been rusticated ?"

"According to the best of my knowledge and belief, Mrs.

Cone, the real cause why I have been sent here is that I have become a Roman Catholic."

" A what ?"

" A Roman Catholic," said Alban, smiling at Mrs. Cone's blank consternation.

" I have a great mind to box your ears," said Mrs. Cone. " Why what do you mean ? Your grandfather's grandson a Roman Catholic ! Don't talk such nonsense to me, Alban ! What have you been doing at New Haven that they sent you here ? Come, I love you for your aunt Betsey's sake, and your mother's, too. Tell me the truth."

It was with difficulty that Alban could make Mrs. Cone comprehend the truth, no part of which he concealed from her. In the course of his narration, the conviction, however, gradually dawned upon her mind that the young man was, at least, not sporting with her credulity. She was ready to overwhelm him with arguments, but luckily the bell rang for tea.

" Hurry down to tea," said Mrs. Cone, leaving him, " and let me charge you not to breathe a syllable of this to my husband, nor to any one else in the house. I have my reasons, which perhaps will appear in due season."

36*

CHAPTER IX.

THE tea-table was set (it is the New England fashion in country districts) in an ample and well-kept kitchen. On the side of the table opposite Alban sat three hearty boys, from twelve to fifteen years of age, Dr. Cone's private pupils; next to himself was a lady to whom he was introduced by Mrs. Cone as her sister. Her name was Fay, and the party was completed by the black-eyed little girl of whom Alban had caught a glimpse at the piano, and whom Mrs Cone named, " my niece, Miss Rosamond Fay." Mrs. Fay was pale, and of an extremely delicate appearance ; she coughed frequently and with singular violence ; but when Alban turned to offer her some civility, he perceived that her features were eminently beautiful. Her eyes were the brightest and most finely set he had almost ever seen. Her voice, too, was soft and plaintive as a dove's.

The two Irish lasses, one of them blooming and luxuriantly made, the other darker, plainer, and a trifle stouter, remained in the background during the meal. It passed nearly in silence. Dr. Cone indeed attempted to put a courteous question or two to his new-arrived guest, when one of the boys opposite, as Alban thought, commenced kicking violently under the solid mahogany table. To his great surprise, neither Dr. Cone nor his wife took any notice of this indecorum, although the latter frequently reproved one or other of the lads for some trivial impropriety.

" Sit up, William ! Charles !" in a tone of grave remonstrance, " is that the way in which a young gentleman should help himself ? Certainly, use a spoon for your honey."—Here there was another kick under the table, so violent that Alban wondered the tea-things did not rattle, and Mrs. Cone became silent, while the boys grinned, and little Rosamond Fay but half suppressed a laugh.

Immediately after tea, family prayers were attended in the same apartment. Dr. Cone read a chapter from the Epistle to the Romans, accompanying it with a short exposition. Then Rosamond Fay, at a sign from her mother, went into the next room, where, on the doctor's giving out the evening hymn, she played a well-known tune on the piano, and the whole family joined in singing it with a very sweet effect. Alban took notice that the prettier of the two Irish girls, whom Mrs. Cone called Harriet, sung with a clear voice, but her less attractive companion, whose name was Bridget, did not sing, and sat with folded arms and downcast eyes. Harriet had rich, pouting lips, ripe and inviting as cherries; Bridget's mouth was of a different character quite; it possessed a chaste sweetness not unfamiliar to Alban, and which diffused a charm over her plain physiognomy. As soon as the hymn was finished, the family threw themselves on their knees, and the young Rosamond gliding in from the parlor, knelt by her mother's side. Alban, on the contrary, unwilling any longer to join, even in appearance, in Protestant worship, took the opportunity of the noise this general change of position occasioned, to escape into the room which the young girl had quitted. Seating himself by the parlor fire, he could listen to Dr. Cone's prayer.

Suddenly, in the midst of it, while the good minister was praying, as our hero thought, with unusual earnestness for protection during the night, particularly from the malice of demons and the assaults of evil spirits, there was a scream in the kitchen, followed by a crash of porcelain and a heavy fall. Alban sprang to the open door; the tea-things were half off the table; some broken cups and plates strewed the floor, and Mrs. Cone was endeavoring to save others which were just on the point of falling. Dr. Cone concluded his prayer rather abruptly, and the family sprang to their feet with a variety of exclamations.

"I told you that you had come to a strange house, Mr. Atherton," said Dr. Cone, passing his hand over his forehead, and drawing a deep sigh.

"Oh, look what they have done in the parlor!" cried little

Rosamond Fay, and Alban, turning, beheld, to his astonishment, all the heavy chairs in the room behind him piled one on another, nearly to the ceiling, the stool of the piano being perched on top of all.

" Who are *they* ?" Alban innocently demanded of the child.

" The Spirits !"

" My daughter !" said Mrs. Fay, reprovingly.

For the little witch clapped her hands with glee.

It seemed, indeed, that the devil was really in the house. The tea-table was again lifted up at one end, sending some half-dozen more cups and plates upon the floor with a crash ; the pretty Harriet, while picking them up, screamed, and cried out that some one pinched her ; Bridget fell on her knees and began to call upon the Virgin and Saints for help, and in the midst of all, a noise like some heavy body rolling down stairs was heard in the front entry or hall, the door leading from which into the parlor was suddenly burst open with violence, and Alban's trunk hurled into the room as if from a battering-ram. The hasp of the lock snapped with the violence of the concussion, the lid flew open, and with another turn the entire contents of the trunk, consisting of books and clothes, were scattered over the carpet.

Alban flew out of the room, and up the stairs, but in a few minutes returned with an aspect of blank astonishment. He had found the outer door of the hall bolted on the inside, and every thing in the story above quiet and orderly as a sepulchre.

The loud and deafening raps now recommenced below, and from several quarters at once, on the table, on the floor, the walls, the doors. Some were feebler than others, and they were repeated at longer or shorter intervals, and the family listened in silence ; Dr. Cone and the females were pale, and even the children began to look frightened. The youngest boy sobbed, and having seized Alban's hand, held it with a convulsive force. Little Rosamond alone, although excited to the last degree, and clinging to her mother for protection, showed more curiosity than fear. And all at once she approached Alban and the little boy who still grasped his hand, and whom our hero had taken upon his knee.

"What is the matter with your clothes, Eddy?" she said. She touched the little fellow, but instantly drew back screaming, and ran away, covering her eyes with both hands.

The boy's garments were cut in strips from head to foot.

CHAPTER X.

It was midnight.   Alban and Dr. Cone kept a sort of vigil over the kitchen fire.

"It is a month since we began to be persecuted in this way," said the Doctor.   "At first I fancied that the boys were at the bottom of it.   Then I suspected the servants of complicity, and that men were concealed in the house.   Very soon, however, things came to such a pass as to preclude every hypothesis of natural, human agency.   You have seen nothing yet !   My books have been flung into the fire before my eyes by invisible hands, and with difficulty saved.   A good deal of property has been destroyed, particularly clóthing, as you saw that little boy's jacket and trowsers to-night cut into ribbons.   Mrs. Fay and Mrs. Cone have had their bonnets secreted, (usually it was discovered, just as they were going to meeting,) and when found, it was behind some heavy furniture, crushed, and completely ruined."

"Human agency might have done this," observed Alban.

"True, and the suspicions of the ladies fell upon Bridget, our Catholic girl.   They thought she might have done it to prevent their going to church."

"Why not as well suspect Harriet—or is she a Protestant ?" asked Alban.

"She is, and has been one of the greatest sufferers all along. Her clothes are spirited away, and found, half-destroyed, in some out-of-the-way place.   And the girl has been pinched (the ladies say) black and blue."

"Pinching the maids !   It is the old trick attributed to the fairies," observed Alban.   "What is Harriet's character !"

"She is such as you see her : a pretty girl !" said the Doctor grimly.   "She would have left us if I had not promised to make good her losses,   Of course it would be very disagreeable to engage new servants under these circumstances, and difficult too. Bridget was frantic for going, at first, but her priest, whom, at my instance, she went some thirty miles to consult, advised her to stay. She was the first to say they were spirits, and *then* we all laughed at her superstition."

"And suspicion fell upon *her*," said Alban, with a grave smile. "It is the only thing like a *motive*, that I have discovered yet, sir, in the acts of petty mischief which you relate, or which I have witnessed."

"At times," observed the doctor, looking round apprehensively, and lowering his voice, "I doubt there may be a motive, even for what looks like mere wantonness."

"And that is, sir?"

"The desire to communicate with the living," whispered the doctor.

Rap, rap, rap; rap, rap; rap, rap:—the whole kitchen resounded! Even Alban turned pale. The cold sweat stood on Dr. Cone's forehead.

"The petty, but irritating injuries inflicted seem to proceed, if I may venture to say it," proceeded the doctor, still lowering his voice, "from impatience that we cannot or will not understand them."

Rap, rap; rap, rap.

"Do you hear? It is an answer."

"Have you ever communicated with them in this way before?" asked Alban, rather solemnly, and giving the minister a piercing glance.

"Occasionally at night, after the family have retired," replied his host trembling. "I sometimes fear that I have done wrong."

There was a crash, simultaneous with the last word. Both looked round startled. A pane of glass had been broken. Yet the outside shutters were all fast closed.

"It is written," said Alban in a firm tone—"'tis but last night that a peculiar conversation led me to examine the passage

—'Neither let there be found among you any one that consulteth soothsayers, or observeth dreams and omens, neither let there be any wizard, nor charmer, or that consulteth pythonic spirits, *or that seeketh the truth from the dead.*' "

There was a faint scream—faint and peculiar : Alban had never heard aught like it.

"Had you never a dream to which you could not refuse credence ?" asked his companion, unheedful of this strange sound. "Knew you never a dream exactly fulfilled ?"

"I must answer both questions in the affirmative," replied Alban with emotion, "but one of those dreams, I had reason to suppose, came from above, and the other I yet doubt."

Both were now extremely startled to observe all at once, that chairs had been placed on either side of them, so as to form with those which themselves occupied, a complete semicircle around the ample fireplace. Alban's blood froze in his veins at the sight (if one could say so) of this awful session of viewless beings, prepared to participate in their midnight colloquy.

"They wish to converse with us," said the minister, with a sudden energy, and pressing Alban's arm. "Let us gratify them. I have thought of a way, if you have no objection. It is by calling out the letters of the alphabet. When they rap at a letter, you shall write it down, and so we can spell out word by word into a regular sentence."

An intense curiosity, despite his fears and scruples, overcame Atherton. The host, with wild eyes, extended to him some tablets and a pencil, which he hesitatingly received.

"I have no doubt but they can inform us respecting the future world and its employments"—(rap, rap, rap, on the floor at their feet)—"the state of the soul after death—(rap, rap.)—"Do you hear."

A heavy step was heard on the kitchen stairs, some one slowly descending. After a minute of expectation they were interrupted by the entrance of the girl Bridget, with a shawl thrown over her half-bare shoulders, and a large ruffled cap, as if she had hastily risen from bed. She looked frightened, and her great, black beads were clasped in her hands.

"What do you want?" asked her master, roughly. "Have you no more sense of decency than to come down in that garb at this hour of the night, while there are young gentlemen in the house?"

"Och, indeed, sir, and I big a thousand pardons for comin' down, but surely I dramed them spirits was a murthering this young gentleman, and it was on my mind, sir, to ask you to step to his room (bein' I couldn't) and see if all was right."

A sharp reproof evidently hovered on her master's lips, but Atherton interposed.

"Thank you, Bridget. You see I am safe. The Blessed Virgin will protect me, you know."

"Indeed, sir, and that's true, if you have light and grace to ask her. But maybe you'd condescend to put these beads round your neck for to-night. They are the beads of St. Bridget that I brought from ould Ireland, and there's a hundred days' indulgence for every one that slips through your fingers. No harm 'd come near you, sir, with it round your neck, and I am safe with the scapular, sir, let alone that I said the third part of the rosary before I laid me down."

"Thank you, Bridget—thank you kindly. Keep your rosary, and pray for me."—He kissed the small metal crucifix attached to the bead-string, and returned it to her, with a smile peculiar to Atherton.

The girl retired, not without offering the beads once more.

"You are a humorist, I perceive, Mr. Atherton," observed Dr. Cone, when the girl had disappeared. "I question, however," he added, somewhat gravely, "whether it is right to countenance such superstitions, even in jest."

"You had better put that question to the spirits, doctor," replied Alban, rising. "And, by the by, if you will excuse me, sir, I will retire."

The kitchen was now quiet. Quiet was the hall and his

own chamber. But as he was entering the last, the door of Mrs. Fay's room, which was just opposite, opened with some fracas, and Mrs. Fay appeared with a candle in her hand. She attempted to shut the door instantly that she saw Atherton, but some obstacle prevented its closing, and while she quickly stooped down to remove it, he caught almost involuntarily a glimpse of the interior of the chamber.

The fair occupant had been writing ; for a table, with an additional candle, some writing implements, and an unfinished letter upon it, was drawn close to the fire. The bed was directly over against the door, and little Rosamond, who had apparently just started up, was hiding herself again under the bed-clothes. The object which had prevented the door from closing was an inkstand, and Alban perceived large and numerous stains of ink on the tasteful white wrapper of the beautiful Mrs. Fay.

CHAPTER XI.

THE season advanced, and even the dreary table-land of Carmel assumed somewhat of the smiling aspect of early summer. The great button-balls, lining the road before Dr. Cone's house, were covered with delicate green leaves, and spread a checkered shade on the old front piazza. The orchards were white and pink with apple blossoms; the garden was gay with those of the cherry trees and hardy plums. The cool air that blew from the hills over the plain, carried their fragrance on its wings. Still the indoor fires glowed night and morning, and only slumbered in white embers during the warmer hours of mid-day.

The singular visitation by which the old mansion-house was haunted had not ceased. Sometimes, indeed, perfect quiet would reign for a week, so far as any supernatural disturbance was concerned; then the mysterious agency would break forth in manifestations of greater violence than ever. As time went on the character of these singular phenomena changed. A great deal of petty mischief continued to be done, nearly exhausting the patience of every one except quiet Dr. Cone, and the ever elastic Rosamond Fay. It was wonderful how patient Dr. Cone was, although he suffered considerably in his property, and something more in the reputation of his family. They kept it secret as much as they could, but events so marvellous could not be prevented from transpiring. Hundreds of persons came to see the operation of the "spirits," and although the family resisted such applications wherever they could, and both Dr. and Mrs. Cone assured their visitors that the stories which they had heard were exaggerated, and that some natural method would probably yet be discovered to account for what at present seemed inexplicable, the idea gained ground that it was the work of the devil.

But within the family itself a system of communication with

these unseen agents of mischief, was now quite established.   It
was ascertained, for example, that a request to them, couched in
civil terms, would procure at least the temporary cessation of any
peculiarly vexatious demonstration.   The method of interpreting
the rappings, suggested by Dr. Cone to Alban, the former did not
venture publicly to adopt, for nearly all the adult members of the
family were of the opinion that it would be criminal to hold such
an intercourse with beings who could only belong to the infernal
hosts.

"They can only be 'spirits in prison,'" observed Alban ; "for
angels and good spirits, if permitted at all to hold communication
with the living, would not be restricted to such imperfect methods.
These attempts to hold parley by inarticulate noises and acts of
mischief, prove restraint.   These beings might and would do
more if they were permitted, or if they dared."

"Good beings would not do mischief at all," said Mrs. Cone.

The justice of our hero's reasoning was soon made apparent
by a freer communication suddenly taking place.   Books were
found lying open with paper marks adhering to significant passages.   The Bible was much used in this manner.   A large family
copy which lay on a reading stand, would fly open spontaneously
in the midst of a conversation, and at some wonderfully apt text
would be found a narrow slip of paper, sticking as fast as if it had
been glued, yet apparently by mere atmospheric pressure.   Sometimes the texts selected were expressive of pious and appropriate
sentiments, such as the hope of the resurrection, the reality of a
future state of rewards and punishments, and so on ; at others
the passages marked were among those which, particularly as
found in the common Protestant translation, are by no means suitable for indiscriminate perusal, and which caused the females to
retire from the book with a blush.

The communion season of Dr. Cone's Church was now approaching.   They had it once in two months, and some of the
family remembered that the last occasion had been marked by
peculiar outrages, bearing more the impress of malignity than any

which had occurred before or since. In all instances of this kind it was remarked that one or two individuals were the special objects of attack. The pretty Harriet, and Eddy, the youngest of Dr. Cone's pupils, have been already mentioned; but there was a boy employed by the minister about his stable, the son of one of his poorer neighbors, who could not enter the house without some strange missile being hurled at him, and *he* averred (but Mrs. Cone declared it was only his imagination) that he felt himself dragged towards the well, whenever he accidentally approached it, as if some one were endeavoring to throw him in. He was certain that when sent to fetch wood he was frequently hurt by the fall of large fagots; and once a tall wood-pile suddenly precipitated itself upon him as he was filling a basket for the Franklin. It was a miracle that he was not killed, and the lad made it an excuse for fetching no more. It was a half-simple lad, was Jake, and some of the stories which he told of his persecutions were too marvellous for belief. Harriet said that Jake pulled down the woodpile upon himself, and that for her part she was more afraid of him than of the spirits. Like many beings of that unhappy class, Jake's animal propensities were more fully developed than his mental powers, and if ugliness could provoke the malice of demons, his ungainly slimness and satyr-like countenance would account for their hostility.

The sacrament Sunday at Carmel happened to synchronize with a festival of the Church, on which Episcopalians also usually celebrate the rite of communion, and Mrs. Fay being a pious member of that denomination, proposed to go down to Yantic Falls to receive on this occasion, because there was an Episcopal church there. The distance was not more than ten miles; Dr. Cone lent his gig, and Alban had offered to drive. All that week the disturbance in the house was nearly unremitting. The knockings were incessant, day and night; the furniture was thrown about remorselessly, panes of glass were broken daily, clothes and books were burned; a bed was found in a blaze at noonday, and the flames with difficulty were extinguished; Harriet was wounded in the cheek by a pitcher, and a new dress which she had purchased at Yantic was missing from her chest, and not to be found on the strictest search. But what was more alarming, Eddy was taken with fits of screaming every evening. Dr. Cone punished him in vain. Mrs. Fay's delicate health suffered from the incessant nervous agitation which all this produced, besides that she had her private troubles which she concealed as much as she could. Little Rosamond told Alban that her mother was visited by the spirits every night. It was singular that the most earnest and polite requests for a cessation of the infliction, had no longer any effect. Mrs. Cone would sometimes fly into a passion and abuse the unseen mischief-workers, but that only procured an increase of annoyance.

"I would leave the house, Mr. Atherton, were it in my power," said Mrs. Fay, on Saturday afternoon.

They were walking in the piazza, arm in arm, for Alban had become a favorite with the invalid. As they passed the parlor window there was a crash; a dark object shot swiftly by, and fell upon the grass of the court-yard. The window pane showed only a round hole as large as a grape-shot; the dark object was a common poker. The force necessary to effect a passage through the glass without producing a larger fracture, was at least equal to that of a well-charged rifle. There was no one in the parlor.

"If I could only get a peaceful night before going to communion to-morrow," said Mrs. Fay, in a sweet, but despairing tone.

"You have never tried the experiment of asking them to desist," observed Alban.

"Never yet, but I really think I must try it. Lately it has not succeeded so well."

"I object to it on principle," responded Alban. "The favors of the devil, or of spirits malicious and lost to goodness, are more to be dreaded than their hostility, which after all is controlled by a higher power. They can do nothing but what is permitted them, as they have repeatedly confessed."

"Yet if I could gain a tranquil evening and an undisturbed night before communion," urged Mrs. Fay. "Really I feel that I must. If that boy's screams should be renewed to-night, I think I shall go distracted. Besides, Mr. Atherton, they knock upon my head-board at night."

"Do they really?"

"I have fancied it was Rosamond, you know, and then, as if they read my thoughts, it would occur when her little arms and limbs were fast imprisoned in mine—oh! it is beyond endurance. And such temptations as are suggested to my mind in order to escape. *You* are never troubled in your own room, Mr. Atherton?"

"Never."

"Is it because you are so good, or because you are so bad? I have thought at times that if I would do some wicked thing they would let me alone."

"If you will be patient under it till to-morrow," said Alban, "as we ride down to Yantic, I will explain to you a way by which I think you may be exempt from future annoyance."

"You have several times spoken to me in that mysterious manner, Mr. Atherton. You talk as if you had a charm, such as that poor, superstitious Bridget believes in."

"Yet Bridget is never assailed as the others have been. Neither her person or property have been injured."

"Well, do you suppose that it is because she crosses herself and mutters her prayers, whenever any strange thing happens? For my part," said the beautiful Mrs. Fay, "I believe the secret is that she is not so pretty as Harriet. You laugh, but these beings certainly have the strangest caprices. Now, there is my Rosamond. Why should they not cut her clothes into ribbons as well as Eddy's? To be sure it would be shocking to treat a little girl so."

"You think that Rosa is spared for the same reason that Harriet is persecuted? I believe, my dear Mrs. Fay, that we shall be entirely foiled in endeavoring to penetrate the motives of beings who are in a state so different from ours—beings devoid of hope, freed from concupiscence and passion, yet possessed of power, will, and understanding. I have perplexed myself much to arrive by analysis at what must be their condition, but humanity winds itself too closely round me. How know you that the spirit within you—the familiar tenant of your own clay—is not endued with a latent malice exceeding that of any of these disembodied ones whose presence we have been made so strangely to feel? They were our companions but a few days since, if we may believe them. The sweet chains of flesh and blood bind us still, and if they enslave, restrain us. A moment—I think of it often with a shudder—may convert a polished youth or a modest-seeming woman into a malicious and obscene demon."

Mrs. Fay coughed—her violent cough. She applied her handkerchief to her mouth, and took it away again dabbled with blood.

"Do not be alarmed," said she, sweetly smiling on him. "This is a common occurrence. But I must go in. I fear that your conversation has induced me to remain out longer than was prudent."

It was evident, however, to Alban, that she was considerably agitated. He supported her into the parlor, and persuaded her to recline on the old-fashioned chintz sofa.

"Don't call any one," said Mrs. Fay. I shall be better directly."

A very singular rap commenced, apparently over the invalid's head. None of the sounds which Alban had heard in the house were any thing like it. At the same instant the great Family Bible on the stand slowly opened. Mrs. Fay in a low voice implored him to ascertain for her the passage marked. Atherton had always refrained from gratifying his curiosity in this way.

"Of what use is it?" said he, earnestly.

She sprang up and went to the book. He was extremely surprised to see her tear away the mark with violence. She closed the Bible, and returning to the sofa with an air of desolation, clasped her hands. The rapping continued. Suddenly the door of a closet flew open, and a large blue junk bottle danced out, and went dancing and tumbling round the room. It was fearfully ludicrous. Presently out flew another.

"Oh, heavens!" exclaimed the unhappy invalid in a tone of misery, "I can bear it no longer. I ask a truce till to-morrow night. Let me pass this night in quiet. Whoever you are, I beg it as a favor."

The bottles rolled over on the carpet and were quiet; the rapping ceased; and a bit of white paper came floating down as if from the ceiling, falling into Mrs. Fay's lap. She took it, glanced at it, and passed it to Atherton. It was inscribed, in a singular but legible hand, with the following words:

*"You shall not be disturbed:"**

---

* This incident was related to the writer by the estimable and intelligent lady to whom it occurred. "I was about to receive the Sacrament on the following day," she observed, "and I was extremely desirous of passing a tranquil night, particularly as not a single night had passed without some disturbance. So I said something to that effect, and feeling warranted by the occasion, although I entertained scruples as to the lawfulness of holding communication with these beings, ventured to request that for this night they would leave us unmolested. The words had hardly escaped my lips before a paper fell at my feet on which was written—*You shall not be disturbed.*"

CHAPTER XII.

THE house was filled with the peculiar bustle, prophetic of a religious quiet, that belongs to a New England Saturday night. Jake brought in armful after armful of wood from the pile, to fill the boxes for Sunday, and flung it in without a word. Biddy strained the contents of her foamy milk-pail into the pans, and ranged the latter on the pantry shelf without one being overset. Hatty finished mopping the painted floors, set the tea-table, and relieved the mighty oven of its hot and fragrant loaves, of the vast pan of baked beans, and the flat cakes of gingerbread, without once complaining of being pinched, or pouting her pretty lips in despite, because her table was lifted some inches from the floor, or a beautiful crusty loaf was sent spinning into a distant corner. The family partook of the evening meal and attended evening prayers with the feelings of ship passengers in a calm after boisterous weather, or just arrived in port, and who can scarce believe the absence of that restless and dizzy motion to which they have become accustomed.

The boy whose screams had lately alarmed them, as the hour of his seizure approached, became drowsy, and falling asleep at prayers, was carried up to bed. Whether it was the sudden withdrawal of excitement, or some other cause, the whole family seemed to drop off much earlier than usual, nor did they fail to sleep so soundly as to make the next morning's breakfast considerably later than was usual even on Sunday. Jake brought round Dr. Cone's smart-looking chaise, (this was Madam's innocent vanity,) with the shining-coated bay horse and well-appointed harness. Alban was not displeased to drive a lovely and elegant lady into Yantic, on one of the finest Sundays in June, himself attired in his sprucest gear.

Mrs. Fay had a lovely spring bonnet, trimmed with lilac. It

was a New York hat, ordered as a pattern by the most fashionable milliner in Yantic, of whom Mrs. Fay had taken it at no
extravagant price, about a week previous, with fear and trembling in regard to its probable fate. Well might she tremble, for
she had had one bonnet hidden in a drain, and another (but that
was only a straw) ruthlessly crammed behind a sofa. And if the
beautiful invalid—who, to those around her, seemed on the verge
of the grave—had an apparent weakness, it was her love of
elegant costume. But perhaps that was a part of the facile propriety, the fine perception of the becoming in conduct, which
eminently distinguished her. Rosamond was always most suita-
bly dressed. Being only turned of twelve, she wore shortish
frocks and pantalets. This bright Sunday morn the little girl
was arrayed in a cherry-colored silk, neatly made, with a
shadowy Leghorn crowning her jetty ringlets and dark-bright
countenance. Mrs. Fay very properly placed her daughter betwixt herself and Alban, and the trio were a snug fit for the gig.

And now, lest the reader should imagine some romantic
mystery in the domestic relations of Mrs. Fay, inasmuch as we
describe her certainly not as a widow, yet living it would seem
apart from her husband, of whom we have hitherto made no
mention, we will observe that she was the wife of an officer in
the U. S. Navy, and that Lieutenant Fay was absent on a cruise.
There was undoubtedly a reason why his name was so much
avoided in the family of his wife's sister, that Alban, for instance,
during a stay of seven weeks, did not remember to have heard it,
except that once or twice Rosamond had, as if inadvertently,
spoken of "papa." But our hero was aware that Mrs. Fay corresponded regularly with her husband, and the brightest glow he
had seen on her pale cheek was on a day when he brought her
from the Carmel P. O. a thick letter, stamped, in red ink, " U. S.
Ship Pacific."

For one thing, Atherton knew that the pay of a lieutenant
was moderate, and he guessed that Mrs. Fay had very little
money to spare. He had inferred from occasional expressions

which she had let fall in regard to her prolonged stay in a house
where she suffered such terrible agitations, that considerations of
economy made it necessary. But as they were drawn along
swiftly and silently over the smooth turnpike, Mrs. Fay seemed
to him to have shaken off an incubus. She had never conversed with him, or prattled to her daughter, so naturally and
gayly.

"Sister,"—so Mrs. Fay termed Mrs. Cone—"sister would
have been glad to prevent your being my beau this morning, Mr.
Atherton," with a smile.

"I cannot comprehend why," returned Alban, very sincerely.
"Certainly I am a more suitable one than Jake, in every respect,
I flatter myself," and he also smiled.

"Sister talked to me quite seriously about your being a handsome and agreeable young man, and my husband being away,
and so on, till I was half persuaded that I was going to do something very improper ; and then I thought that it was too ridiculous. Why, I remember you when you were a baby, as I told
sister, and am almost old enough to be your mother. And finally,
I could not abide the thought of such a gallant as Jake."

"Oh, mamma, _I_ would never go to Yantic if Jake was to
drive the chaise—would _you_ ?" cried Rosamond.

"I feel quite flattered, Miss Rosa, that you prefer me to Jake,"
said Alban, gravely.

Rosa blushed and was silent.

"You are a great favorite with Rosa," said her mother.

"Oh, mother ! how can you say so—right to Mr. Atherton's
face ! He is not a favorite of mine any more than William Rus-
sel, or Eddy Edwards is. I like Mr. Atherton, mamma, because
he is so polite to you—you know I always told you so."

"And because aunt Cone told you that you must not, on any
account, fall in love with him," said her mother, archly.

"Oh, fie, mamma ! _My_ mother tells tales out of school, Mr.
Atherton, don't she ? But she will never let _me_ do it."

"Aunt Cone seems to think me a dangerous character," said

Alban ; " but really, her precautions do not strike me as the most judicious."

" I asked sister," observed Mrs. Fay, still smiling, " if there was any thing against your moral character, and she was obliged to confess that, so far as she knew, it was unimpeached. She said, indeed, that you had been ' rusticated,' but declined telling me what had been your offence."

" I am capable of committing very bad actions," replied Alban, evasively. " You would be shocked if you knew to what sins I am sometimes tempted—and which perhaps I should commit, if Providence did not mercifully put it out of my power."

" The life of a Christian," piously observed Mrs. Fay, " is a continual conflict with the corruption of his own heart."

" If one could be sure that one was really combating," answered the young man. " Mrs. Cone, now, tells me that she is *sure* she loves Christ—she is sure she has passed from death unto life. Nothing can convince *her* that religion (her own religion, of course) is not a reality. Do you suppose, Mrs. Fay, that she has any conflicts, or is ever worsted in them ? or how is it that she does not feel what a great saint once said, that *no man knows whether he is worthy of love or hatred ?*"

" I do not like the Presbyterians—they are so self-righteous," said Mrs. Fay, " although I believe that there are good Christians in all denominations."

Alban smiled.

" I was brought up in the Episcopal Church," continued Mrs. Fay, " and so was Fanny ; but she married a Presbyterian minister, and of course she joined that Church. Now that is what I would not do, Mr. Atherton—leave my Church ! My husband never interferes with my religion. To be sure he is not a religious man."

It was natural for Alban to inquire under what form of faith Lieutenant Fay was nominally ranked, and he was greatly surprised when Mrs. Fay, after a glance at Rosamond, replied that her husband was a Roman Catholic.

"He fell in love with me at a ball, when I was only seventeen," she said, with a beautiful smile. "My friends opposed it on the ground of his being in the navy and a Catholic. But I was captivated by his careless, manly manner, his ardor, and his handsome uniform, I suppose, and about two years after we were married. Rosamond was born before I was twenty, and her father never saw her till she was three years old. That was the hardest absence I ever had to bear, although our next—our little boy"— Mrs. Fay dashed away a tear—"my husband never saw. Then he was ordered to the West Indies, and I went to Pensacola to be near him, and there my other little girl was born. She was a delicate child from the first, and as her little brother had been carried off in teething, I resolved not to wean her as long as I could help it, and that is the way I lost my own health. And after all, she took the scarlet fever in that fatal year, and died of it. Her father was absent too, but, by that time, I was used to bear such things alone ; nor have I seen him since ; you see I have had my sorrows, Mr. Atherton."

"Dear mamma," exclaimed Rosamond, drying her eyes, "papa will be made a commodore one of these days, and then he will take us to sea in his ship, and we shall have better times."

"Now that I have been so communicative, Mr. Atherton," resumed Mrs. Fay, after they had driven on in silence for some time, "I hope that you will tell me what is that charm you spoke of yesterday by which I can be free from the persecution of these spirits (if such they are) while we stay at my sister's. I assure you that I shall be glad to have recourse to any thing reasonable, for apart from the agitation which I suffer from their attacks, I really cannot afford to lose so many valuable articles from my wardrobe. We are too poor, ain't we, Rosamond ?"

They were now entering the beautiful town of Upper Yantic, and the bells were already tolling for service. Alban did not reply to Mrs. Fay's question, while they were driving past some of the old Atherton homesteads, which he had visited thirteen years before, with his aunt Elizabeth and cousin Rachel. But when they emerged into the open road again, and saw the white spires of the Falls gleaming in the leafy distance, he said,

"Did it never strike you, Mrs. Fay, what a curious religion is depicted in the New Testament ? I mean about demoniacal possessions, and the power given by Christ to His ministers to cast out devils. He seems to give it as a perpetual sign : '*In my name shall they cast out devils*,'—'*they shall lay hands on the sick, and they shall recover*.' This power certainly must exist still in those to whom it was given, if our religion be divine."

"But miracles have ceased," said Mrs. Fay.

"Is that in the Bible ?"

"No, I believe not."

"Since the devils are come back," said Alban, "it is time to have recourse to the power which formerly expelled them. I am not at all surprised, myself, that the Kingdom of Darkness should be making a bold push in New England, to regain a portion of its old dominion over the bodies of men. Unless it be driven back by the old spiritual arms of the Apostles, we must look to see demoniacal possession soon re-established. These Presbyterians, certainly, can do nothing in this line ; but the ministers of your Church pretend to derive their orders from the Apostles. Why don't you get your pastor here in Yantic to visit Carmel, Mrs. Fay, and compel the man-hating demons to return to their abyss ?"

Shortly after, the easy-going gig glided into the rural street of Yantic—a sunlit road, an umbrageous common, a wild hill-side, villa-like mansions. The organ was playing when they reached the church door. It ceases even while Alban is carefully handing out Mrs. Fay and half lifting down the dark-eyed Rosa ; and as they enter, they see the congregation already standing, and the white-robed minister is saying the *Dearly beloved brethren*. There were two ministers in the desk, in one of whom Alban was surprised to recognize his friend, Mr. Soapstone, and in the other, his mesmeric acquaintance of the stage-coach.

CHAPTER XIII.

As soon as the service was over, Alban went up the chancel to speak to Mr. Soapstone. A careless group of the male communicants, standing at the rail, were eating the remainder of the consecrated bread, and draining the huge chalice, passing the latter from hand to hand. The whole floor along the rail was white with crumbs, and Alban blessed God that he could be morally certain it was nothing but bread and wine. Poor Mr. Soapstone, who thought differently, looked daggers at his irreverent communicants, or glanced down in despair at the Body of the Lord, as he considered it, trampled under foot, and left to communicate mice upon the chancel carpet. In that glance of mingled wrath and horror the future convert to Rome might already be discerned in the zealous Anglican minister. Mr. Soapstone gave our hero a cordial shake of the hand, and introduced him to "the rector of the parish," the Rev. Dr. Patristic.

" Mr. Atherton and I have met before," said the latter, with a jovial glance; "and I can't say that even his name is a surprise. By the by, Mr. Atherton, you came in, I noticed, with an old friend of mine, Mrs. Fay, (lovely woman.) I knew, of course, that you were staying at Dr. Cone's. Well, you must both come and take pot-luck with us. I will speak to Mrs. Fay as soon as I have changed my cassock for a coat."

So saying, the rector hastily withdrew into a sort of dark closet or passage under the pulpit, whither Mr. Soapstone had already retired, and whence both speedily emerged in their ordinary garb. Alban waited at the rail to say, in reply to Dr. Patristic's invitation, that he meant to take Mrs. Fay to his uncle's.

" What, old Deacon Atherton's on the plain ! Is the boy mad ! You'll get a fine dressing if you show yourself there. And with Mrs. Fay of all persons ! Why, your uncle is the bluest and bitterest Puritan in all Yantic. And besides, you will get nothing to eat but cold dough-nuts and gingerbread, for they never cook any thing on Sunday. No, no ; come to the rectory. We have got a prime quarter of lamb and mint sauce, and I rather think Mrs. Patristic has a batter pudding in preparation, which you will find vastly more agreeable than the rod which is in pickle for you at your uncle's."

The rectory truly seemed the abode of creature-comfort. Mrs. Patristic, a fresh-colored and plump dame, preluded the dinner by an egg beaten up with wine for her husband and Mr. Soapstone, the latter of whom really required something, having made a step in advance since the preceding Christmas by receiving the communion fasting. Alban, too, played a very good knife and fork, for although so dreamy and so gentle in manner, the boy was no milksop, and here the host encouraged him both by precept and example. The ample frame of the rector of Yantic required a large pasture. The sociability of the party was aided by some choice wine, (which your sound churchman never finds amiss,) and it was soon very difficult for Mrs. Fay and our hero to realize the scenes they had lately witnessed otherwise than as an ugly dream. Certainly there was nothing ghostly about Dr. Patristic. His commanding, yet seductive eye spoke of the world of sense, and his rich masculine voice had nothing in it of the hollowness of the tomb. A goodly number of "olive plants" surrounded his table, from a fine girl of eighteen, his eldest, to a rosy-cheeked boy of five, his youngest born. Of course the doctor made himself agreeable to Mrs. Fay, and Alban divided his attention pretty equally between the fresh-looking Mrs. Patristic and her no less blooming daughter. The latter had a cheek soft and rich as a peach, and while Atherton chatted with her, Mrs. Fay's beautiful gray eye often roved to them from her imposing and fluent host.

Alban had promised Mrs. Fay to bring forward the subject of the spirits, but for some time he found no opportunity. At length the conversation turned on Mr. Soapstone's asceticism. Dr. and

Mrs. Patristic both considered that the young clergyman carried the mortification of the flesh to a frightful extent.

"What think you of tasting no food till sunset, Mrs. Fay? Nothing else deserves the name of fasting, according to Mr. Soapstone. He says it was the mode of the Jews and primitive Christians."

"He is more strict than the Roman Catholics," replied the lady. "Lieutenant Fay once kept Lent when we were at Pensacola, but we always dined at noon."

"No Romanist ever fasts," observed Mr. Soapstone, austerely. "As you say, even in Lent they are allowed a full meal at twelve o'clock. Then there is the collation in the evening, and 'custom has introduced,' a cup of tea or coffee in the morning, with a bit of bread. This is not fasting, unless it be fasting to take three meals a day."

"If it be true that 'this kind can come forth by nothing but by prayer and fasting,' Mrs. Fay," said Alban, "Mr. Soapstone is just the person to rid us of our persecutions at Carmel."

"What persecutions?" demanded the rector.

Dr. Patristic's countenance sobered into an expression of profound interest, as he listened to the account which Mrs. Fay and Alban now proceeded to give of the disturbances in Dr. Cone's house.

"We have talked over similar matters before," said he, with a significant glance at Atherton. "Dr. Cone has always been a believer in Mesmerism. I remember that several years ago he was full of certain revelations delivered by a clairvoyant boy."

"It is not the first time, then, that the doctor has meddled with forbidden knowledge," observed Alban.

"I have heard strange reports about noises being heard at Carmel," said the rector, "but I took for granted that it was the silly exaggeration of some old women. Mrs. Fay and you have astonished me. How very strange is that incident of the billet being thrown down! And that horrible junk bottle dancing out of the closet!"

A thrill of horror ran round the table, but Rosamond Fay laughed.

"It is the greatest amusement of this child," said Atherton, "to run and pick up the things that are thrown about the house."

"I must pay you a visit at Carmel," said the rector, "and see for myself. No human hand could do what you describe as being done."

The rector's curiosity was excited to such a degree that he resolved to visit Carmel that very evening after the second service. To the scandal of the Puritans at Yantic, and even of his own flock, who marvelled at such style in a minister, Dr. Patristic kept a pair of fine bays and a sort of curricle which he was accustomed to drive on Sunday evenings, really to exercise the horses, but ostensibly to hold service in a neighboring village. Mrs. Fay and Atherton readily agreed to stay for an early tea, and start at the same time with their host. Mr. Soapstone was to accompany his ecclesiastical superior, to try the effect of an exorcism. Alban never ceased to impress upon Mrs. Fay that if any minister of her Church could lay the evil spirits at Carmel, Mr. Soapstone, being full of faith, an ascetic, and a sort of confessor, would certainly be able. For we must not omit to mention that Mr. Soapstone had been finally driven from New Haven in consequence of the unpopularity of his views, the strong anti-popery feeling excited in the community by the death of Walker having required a victim more important than our Alban. The whole thing, indeed, was now traced up to his Christmas-eve sermon, the evergreen cross, and candles on the communion table.

Dr. Patristic, not being an ascetic, but a husband and father, insisted on Mrs. Fay taking a seat in the curricle, an arrangement which Atherton was at first minded to resist as an impudent invasion of his rights, but a gentle whisper from the lady herself procured his acquiescence. The gig received the two young men and Rosamond. A red, red sunset soon faded over the hills, and the nearly perfect orb of the already risen moon brightened the stern-featured landscape. Over the moon-lit road, now rising to surmount a hill, now sinking into a valley, the chaise chased the curricle, the single horse the pair, and the former lost no ground, though flecked with foam from the ardent rivalry.

" And what news from New Haven ?"

" Not much. Your cousin Henry is engaged, they say, to Miss Ellsworth."

" Is that all ?"

" Miss De Groot passed through on her way to enter a convent."

" Ah !"

" You knew of it, I suppose ?"

" I am not surprised."

" An immense grief to her family, it was understood. Some said that she had quitted them clandestinely, but the Everetts told me that was entirely false."

" Of course—it is too absurd."

" She was travelling with a couple of nuns, and the mob of New Haven with a lot of students came near attacking the hotel."

" Miscreants !"

" The notion was that these terrible nuns were carrying off this young girl, and that once they got her into a convent, she would never be allowed to come out."

" And so they wanted to rescue her, even against her will ? It was rather a generous idea, after all."

" The New England people, Atherton, hate Popery in every shape. The more amiable in appearance, the more they suspect it."

" It is a spiritual system, and they are carnal."

" The common impression is exactly the reverse."

" Yes, because by spirituality is understood vagueness. A positive spiritual power is offensive to those who judge after the flesh. It is not simply incredible to the Protestant mind, it is hateful, that the Church should cast out devils, work miracles, forgive sins, impart the Holy Ghost, and possess the gift of truth. Yet all these are what Christ does. Protestantism knows Christ only as a lovely abstraction, and shrinks like a scared fiend from his bodily presence."

"And yet," said Mr. Soapstone, "they are never tired of telling you that it is the indisposition of the carnal heart to the truths of the gospel, which makes you turn from pure evangelical Christianity and justification by faith alone, to a system of forms and works."

"'Every spirit that confesseth not that Jesus Christ is *come in the flesh* is not of God, and this is antichrist.' This is the Protestant translation ; the Vulgate says, ' that dissolveth Jesus,' which means nearly the same. To separate the human and divine in our Lord, either in His person or His religion, is antichristian. But how very strange, Soapstone, that people should fancy it to be a mortification of the carnal heart to pick out a religion for one's self from the Bible instead of receiving it from the Church. Why, the Protestant principle, in this respect, is the most flattering to spiritual pride that it is possible to conceive."

Mr. Soapstone gravely assented to all these propositions, for fancying himself quite pure from all stain of Protestantism, no one more ready than he to send Protestantism to Coventry. Alban was irritated by this conceit, which indeed renders your high Anglican the most impracticable animal in existence. As our hero became silent, the Anglican minister began to talk about his present superior.

"I came to Yantic," said he, "supposing that Dr. Patristic was a true Catholic-minded man. But he has only a smattering of the Fathers, and no idea at all of the Church. Yet he thinks he knows every thing. In regard to the sacrament, he adopts the Non-juring hypothesis of an Eucharistic body distinct from the natural, and that the consecrated bread itself is the only Body of Christ we ever receive."

"And what do *you* think of it ?" inquired Alban.

"I believe with the Greek Church and the whole body of the Fathers, that after consecration what was bread before is the real Body of Christ, and the cup His real Blood. From Justin Martyr and Ignatius down, there is but one voice on this subject in all Christian antiquity, although the word Transubstantiation did not come into use till a comparatively modern period."

"I suppose then," said Alban, "that when Dr. Patristic to-day after service gave you a double handful of the communion-bread to consume, this was the reason you knelt down in the chancel to eat it, instead of standing as he and the rest did. It looked rather funny, but you believed it was the real body of Christ?"

"Assuredly."

"And the contents of that huge chalice which one or two nervous girls, I noticed, came near spilling when they took it into their hands for communion, you believed to be the real Blood of Christ?"

"Certainly, Atherton."

"To-day being a great feast, nearly all the devout members of your Church must have received communion—say half a million of persons in all, (a large estimate perhaps,)—how many of these, do you suppose, believe as you do about it?"

"Perhaps two or three individuals—perhaps not one," replied Mr. Soapstone, heroically.

"And the rest had as little idea what they were receiving as the mice who took what was left on the floor this morning. If the Ark of God smote the Philistines with plagues, and slew the men of Bethshemesh for prying into it, I wonder greatly at the impunity of your people in eating without discerning the Body of the Lord. Does God, year after year, permit the commission of such horrible wholesale sacrilege?"

"True," groaned Mr. Soapstone. "It is very distressing, especially when we remember what the Fathers say even in the second century, of the care used by the primitive Christians to prevent a particle of the sacred Body falling to the earth, or a drop of the precious Blood being spilt. I am quite with you there."

"But how can you remain in your present communion with such feelings?"

"With a view of calling it back from its errors," replied Mr.

Soapstone. "Our Church does not claim infallibility. If fallible, she may be in error. If in error, she ought to be set right. Before Henry the Eighth's time, the Church of England held Transubstantiation. I believe as she believed then."

"What nonsense!" exclaimed Alban. "The essence of a Church is in the profession and inculcation of truth. Where there is not identity of doctrine, the identity of a Church vanishes. You are no more the same Church which existed in England before Henry the Eighth, *than a changeling is the same child with that whose cradle, name, and inheritance it usurps.*"

After some desultory conversation on this point, which the Anglican minister would by no means concede, to Alban's surprise, his companion fell back upon some of the popular objections to Transubstantiation itself, urging them not against the tenet indeed, but against the practice of communion in one kind.

"To reason in this way," said Alban, "is to fall below the region of pure, unclouded ideas into the mist of the senses, and to betray as gross an ignorance of spiritual laws as the clown does of natural, who, because his ponds are not emptied by night, refuses to believe the revolution of the globe on its axis. Come now, with this pretended philosophy, and analyze for me the *germ*. Explain how it is, that in a speck of albumen, so minute that it needs a microscope to discover it, are contained all the manifold characteristics of the class, the order, the genus, the species, and the variety, to which the future individual belongs—all the transmissible peculiarities of both his parents, bodily and mental—the red hair of one, the club-foot of another, the insanity or genius of a grandparent. And how does that same speck of albumen (the flesh of the first Adam) communicate the spiritual effects of the fall, and cause the new being to be infected with concupiscence, devoid of justice and sanctity, and an alien from God? These questions solved, I will explain the rationale of *concomitance*, and the life-giving virtue of communion."

The young Rosamond, nestling in her corner of the gig, with her slender limbs crossed, to take up as little room as possible, listened with an attention which verified the proverb about the ears possessed by " little pitchers." But ten miles of good road are soon got over by willing steeds. At a trifle past nine the curricle and gig stopped almost at the same moment at Dr. Cone's gate. Mrs. Cone came out into the piazza to reprove her sister for choosing to return by moonlight with her young beau, but her thoughts were driven into another channel when she saw Dr. Patristic, with a half fatherly, half courtierly air, conducting Mrs. Fay up the gravelled walk to the house.

CHAPTER XIV.

THE first sounds which saluted the ears of the visitors on entering, and indeed before entering, were the shrieks of the child Eddy, who had been going on terribly, said Mrs. Cone, ever since sundown. The quiet of the Sabbath had not been disturbed till that hour, when just as the sun dropped below the rim of hills, stifled cries were heard proceeding from the chambers. After a brief search, following the sounds, Eddy had been found in the closet of Mrs. Fay's room, perched (goodness knows how he ever got there !) on a shelf so high that a grown woman could barely reach it by the aid of a chair. The lower part of the closet was a press, with hooks for ladies' dresses. It was with difficulty that Dr. Cone and the eldest pupil had succeeded in dislodging the poor little fellow from his dangerous position, for he resisted with screams every attempt, until it was discovered at last that a cord was noosed round his neck, and attached to one of the hooks before mentioned, as if with the design of hanging him. This was the most horridly malicious purpose yet betrayed by the invisible persecutors of the family. Ever since, or for more than an hour, the boy had lain on the floor of the room into which he had been conveyed, uttering incessant screams, but apparently unconscious of what was going on, The village doctor had been sent for, and had administered a powerful medicine, which hitherto had produced no effect, Such was the account given by Mrs. Cone to her visitors, and confirmed by their own observation, as they stood by the child himself in his dim chamber. The two elder pupils and the two Irish girls were watching by him.

" It's a divil he has," observed Bridget, pausing in her beads. " If yer riverince could but spake a word to cast him out."

" Nay, it's but fits, the doctor says," returned Harriet, " and what could his reverence do for fits ?"

"This is demoniacal possession," said Dr. Patristic, preparing to retreat from the room.

Some low raps on the dusky walls quickened considerably the rector's flight. In the cheerfully lighted parlor, the nature of the visitation was further discussed. Dr. Patristic betrayed a good deal of timidity, particularly when Rosamond Fay, who was visibly delighted at the rector's fears, finding that the spirits were slower than usual in their demonstrations, slyly pushed over one of the heavy chairs when no one was looking.

"Rosamond," said her mother, after reproving the child for this feat, and checking the untimely mirth which followed its success, "Rosamond is the only person in the house who has never shown fear on these occasions. The only instance, I remember, which at first looked like it, was when Eddy's clothes were cut to pieces on the night that you arrived, Mr. Atherton. She screamed *then*, but I afterwards found it was from another cause. Rosa is sensitively modest."

The young girl grew red, and at the final word hid her face in her mother's lap. Mrs. Fay merely stroked the black-ringleted head with a quiet motion of the hand which could scarcely be called a caress.

"I wish Mr. Soapstone would begin his exorcism," said Alban. "I have great faith in that."

"If Dr. Cone has no objections, I think we might do something in this case," said the young clergyman, modestly.

Dr. Cone observed with patient courtesy that several of the neighboring brethren had given him the benefit of their prayers. If these gentlemen thought that those of a minister of their Church would prove more efficacious, they were welcome to try. The truth was that the good doctor, as well as the family in general, would have been glad of relief from any source. He had felt compelled to write to the friends of the afflicted boy to take him home, and justly apprehended, with the continuance of the infliction, the loss of all his pupils, not to speak of the injuries he received in his property, reputation, and comfort. In former times the whole world believed in demoniac agency, but now-a-days few people would be found to credit any thing of the sort, so that the least imputation to which he was liable was that of being easily imposed upon.

There then arose a brief contest of professional courtesy between the rector and his assistant, which should officiate on this trying occasion. But Dr. Patristic was resolved not to meddle more than he could help with spirits of darkness, and the younger clergyman, not without some appearance of uneasiness, yet overcoming natural fears by an undaunted spirit and a faith in his own vocation, left the room to assume his cassock and bands, surplice and stole, from a bundle which he had brought in the curricle box. He reappeared a figure calculated to awe even spirits. In one hand he bore his prayer-book, and in the other a large vial, from which he presently poured a colorless liquid into a bowl placed by Mrs. Cone, at his request, on the table.

"What is that?" demanded Dr. Patristic, aghast.

"Some water from the font, which I saved after the baptism this evening," returned the assistant. "It has been solemnly blessed in the administration of the sacrament, and I deemed it could not but possess some power to quell the evil spirits whom baptism has ever been held to dispossess."

"It is Protestant holy-water," said Alban.

"Really, brother S.," returned the rector," I doubt if our Church ever contemplated, much more authorized, such an application of the water of the font."

"She authorizes us to bless it, and does not prescribe what shall be done with it afterwards," replied the young clergyman. "And in the reign of Charles I. I find that holy, or blessed water was used in the Church of England by Laud, Andrews, and some others. So I am not without precedent."

Mr. Soapstone, therefore, proceeded. First, he opened the great Bible and read with much solemnity a chapter from the gospel containing the promise of our Saviour that his disciples should cast out devils in his name. The scene was deeply impressive, and even awe-inspiring, but less so, perhaps, when the young minister, closing the book, invited those present to join him in the Litany. When, however, those petitions were recited which pray that " Satan may be finally beaten down under our feet," and " that those evils which the craft or subtlety of the devil or man worketh against us, may be brought to naught," the voice of the reader became earnest, and most present were sensible of an emotion of awe. All were kneeling except Alban and Rosamond Fay. The latter had begun to laugh when Harriet, who was sent for on the score of her being an Episcopalian, responded somewhat louder than her wont ; and in order to conceal her merriment, the little girl was forced to retreat behind the sofa, where she remained curled up on the floor till the prayers were concluded.

It was a favorable sign that the knocking, which was usually troublesome at prayer-time, ceased entirely during the litany. As the prayer-book did not contain any collect expressing the precise intention of the present devotions, the young clergyman offered one of his own composition, brief and pointed, appealing to the promise made to the ministers of Christ, and imploring its fulfilment in the deliverance of this family, and particularly of the most suffering member thereof, from the malicious persecutions of Satan. Mr. Soapstone used not many vain repetitions. Rising from his knees, he sprinkled the font-water round the room, and upon the persons present, except Alban, who, with a grave gesture, declined any share in the aspersion, and the youthful Rosamond, who, apprehensive perhaps for her cherry-silk frock, when she saw her turn coming, sprang to her feet and took refuge behind our hero.

" It is quiet now," said Mrs. Fay to the latter, in a half-whisper, when Mr. Soapstone had left the room to say a prayer and sprinkle some of the consecrated element over the little sufferer up stairs.

" Perhaps it is going to succeed," replied Alban, in the same tone of voice. " We shall see presently."

The minister returned, and all being indeed hushed, even to Eddy's shrieks, concluded with an appropriate collect and the benediction. Scarcely was the latter uttered, when the great Bible from which he had read the lesson, flew open. The passage marked was in the Acts, the xixth chapter and 15th verse. All crowded to read it, but ere it could be finished by Dr. Patristic, whether it was that he leaned too heavily on the stand, or from a supernatural cause, one end flew up; the Bible, the candles, the holy-water, bowl and all, went rolling off in all directions. One of the candles blazing up on the carpet, caught Mr. Soapstone's long surplice, and in a trice the minister was enveloped in flames. Every body fled from him, the women loudly screaming, and but for Atherton's presence of mind in throwing him rather irreverently down and rolling him in the rug, Mr. Soapstone might have paid for his temerity with his life. A scene of confusion and clamor followed such as had never occurred before. The raps were deafening, several windows were broken, various objects were thrown with violence. As one of the candles had been extinguished in falling and the other had been intentionally put out by Mrs. Cone, when the conflagration of the surplice was arrested, the room remained in darkness except for the moonlight shining in at a side window. There was much wild running hither and thither from purposeless alarm, so that the scene was like an incantation of witches. The pretty Harriet, uttering loud exclamations, did not perceive that her gown was becoming slowly inflated, till it suddenly flew over her head. Shrieking, she attempted to fly from the room, but unable to see where she was going, ran against Dr. Patristic, who lost his balance and tumbled over a chair, dragging the girl with him in his fall. All the Episcopalians, in fact, were ridiculously prostrate; Mrs. Fay lying on the sofa terrified rather than hurt. Rosamond sat on the edge of it, bending almost double with suppressed laughter, and over all rose Eddy's piercing screams.

A loud knock was heard at the front door, and all other sounds suddenly ceased.

All listened. The knocking was repeated. It was in vain that Mrs. Cone, coming in with a light, commanded now the boys, now Harriet, to go to the door and see who was there. Such terror had been struck into every heart that no one dared stir, till, on the knock being heard a third time, very quick and impatient, Alban, who with Rosamond, had been inquiring into her mother's situation, seeing that no one else would, himself went to the door.

"Sir," said the stranger, "your horses have run away with your carriage."

"My horses!" exclaimed Dr. Patristic. "Give me my hat! Soapstone, the horses have run away—let's after them at once!"

And the rector of Yantic, forgetting his fears and recent discomfiture, rushed from the house, followed, with an inferior degree of impetuosity, by his less interested assistant.

"Won't you walk in, sir," said Dr. Cone, now advancing and courteously addressing the stranger, who still remained on the threshold.

"Nay, my good sir," replied he, "I have myself met with a misfortune. The runaway equipage came violently in contact with the light wagon in which I was just passing your house, and we find that a bolt has been broken, which must be repaired before we can proceed. The young man who is with me has gone on to your neighbor, the blacksmith's; but I do not like, at this hour, to trespass so long as I may be obliged to wait."

A renewal of the invitation, and cordial assurances that it would be no intrusion, overcame the stranger's scruples.

He entered with a frank air, and took a seat near the stand which had been overset, but which was now on its legs again, and the candles replaced on it. His appearance was rather prepossessing. He wore a black frock-coat and black neckcloth, notwithstanding the warmth of the weather, and had a red ribbon round the neck, probably serving to suspend a locket, or other memorial, in the pocket of his waistcoat. His thick black hair was closely cut, and the razor had not spared a single vestige of whisker or beard, to break the outline of a dark but regular physiognomy. A piercing eye and a calm gravity about the mouth gave him a commanding aspect, although the facial muscles were quite free from the wooden sternness of New England, and it seemed as if it would take little to relax his features into a smile.

This further appeared when he entered into the usual topics of conversation, courteously started by his hosts, such as the weather and the roads, and met their characteristic inquiries as to his destination and motive for travelling so late on Sunday evening. The stranger evaded this inquisition with good humor.

" You are bound to Yantic, I suppose, sir ?" said Dr. Cone.

" They say it is a wise man who knows whither he is bound till he arrives at the journey's end," replied the traveller, laughing. " Pray, sir, to return your question, what place is this ?"

" It is called Carmel," said Dr. Cone.

" Carmel !" said the traveller, thoughtfully." "A name of many associations. Was it not at Carmel that the prophet Elias defied the worshippers of Baal to a trial ?"

" The prophet Elijah," observed Dr. Cone.

" Ah, yes, Elijah or Elias, I believe it is the same," said the stranger, with simplicity.

It might be that twenty minutes thus elapsed ere the two Episcopal clergymen returned, having abandoned the pursuit of the fugitive horses in person ; but the rector had engaged a countryman to follow and bring them back. And while Dr. and Mrs. Cone were yet offering a hospitality for the night—which their guests perforce accepted—the young man of whom the belated traveller had spoken, returned with the blacksmith himself, to say that it would be impossible to repair the accident of the wagon before morning.

" I must have daylight to do it, sir," said the son of Vulcan. " And, any way, I could not get you started before midnight. It's well on towards eleven, and my fire is out."

" Good reasons, my friend," interrupted the stranger. " But is there a public house in this Carmel ?"

Dr. and Mrs. Cone consulted each other apart, and then cordially offered the stranger a bed. In retired places in America, a passing traveller is always welcome, particularly if he be intelligent and gentlemanlike ; and in this instance, the hosts might be conscious that they were partly responsible for the stranger's mishap ; while the fact that his arrival had been marked by a complete cessation of the frightful disturbance in their house, coupled perhaps with a fear that it might recommence at his departure, animated their hospitality still further, and made them press the offer with a warmth to which the traveller, not without surprise, at length yielded. The broken wagon was drawn to the smithy, the stranger's horse received into the doctor's stable, his valise brought into the house, his travelling companion was accommodated by the smith himself, and Mrs. Cone, bustling and cheerful, got out fresh bed-linen, and caused supper to be prepared for her unexpected guests.

"Alban," she whispered to our hero, "you must put up with the sofa for to-night, and resign your room to Dr. Patristic and Mr. Soapstone, (I wish they were both in Guinea !) for the strange gentleman must have the little room, (the prophet's chamber.) I suppose he will be contented, as he doesn't seem difficult."

The traveller had resumed his seat and was fallen into a profound revery, from which he at length emerged only to take a book from his pocket and settle himself quietly to read, saying, " May I ask the favor, madam, to be shown to the apartment you intend for me, a few minutes before supper ;"—and forthwith he became completely absorbed in his book. Supper in due time was ready, the stranger was shown to his room, and Rosamond Fay, whose bright eyes had scarcely been taken off from him since he entered, immediately whispered, turning to her mother and Alban, " I wonder why he wears that red ribbon round his neck."

When the stranger returned the red ribbon had disappeared ; whether he had taken it off or merely concealed it, could only be matter of speculation. The first thing on his re-entrance, the great Bible, now replaced on the stand, flew open, and he started. Rosamond ran to read the passage aloud.

" Oh, mamma! it is marked with a red cross.—*Be not forget-ful to entertain strangers, for thereby some have entertained angels unawares.*"

" What is the meaning of that?" asked the traveller, ap-proaching the book with a frown.

Rap, rap, rap! Rap, rap.

" What is that?"—And he started again. " Is the house haunted?"

" By demons," said Alban.

" Come in to supper, sir," said Dr. Cone, " and we will tell you all about it."

And the stranger slowly made the sign of the cross from the forehead to the breast.

CHAPTER XV.

NOTHING had been said but a brief grace by Dr. Patristic, when a light-colored, glittering object fell heavily upon the table before Mrs. Fay. It was a portrait-cameo, which she had worn that morning to Yantic, but had taken off with the hat and shawl on her return. The fact was that it was a portrait of Lieutenant Fay, and she never wore it at Carmel from a feeling of delicacy towards her sister and brother-in-law, to whom her husband was odious, in the same way as she avoided mentioning his name before them. Faintly blushing, Mrs. Fay took the ornament from the table, and attached it in the usual manner of a brooch to the neck-ribbon of her dress.

"Whence came it?" demanded the stranger, casting his eyes up to the ceiling.

"Twenty minutes or half an hour ago, sir, I locked it up in my trunk, in my own room," replied Mrs. Fay, quietly. "These things are of hourly occurrence in this house, sir."

The stranger, who left his plate untouched, again demanded an explanation, which could only be afforded by narrating more instances of the same kind. Piece by piece—some of the family rather exaggerating, others perhaps falling short of the truth—the whole history of the visitation came out. When Alban described (for the rest shunned that point) Mr. Soapstone's attempted exorcism, the stranger smiled.

"Still," observed he, "the principal object seems to have been gained, or why do I not hear the cries of the lad you speak of?"

A shriek, up stairs, from Eddy, causing a general start and shudder, answered the question almost ere it had escaped the lips of the questioner.

"Have you or any of your family," demanded the traveller, addressing Dr. Cone, "ever sought intercourse with spirits, by consulting fortune-tellers, or pythonists, (that is, persons having familiar spirits,) or pretenders to the second sight, or clairvoyants, or by using any charms or divinations yourselves ?''

Dr. Patristic and Dr. Cone both looked guilty, and the latter confessed to having had to do with clairvoyants, but maintained, with some warmth, that theirs was but a natural state in which the latent faculties of the soul were extraordinarily developed. Dr. Patristic shook his head at this, while the stranger replied,

"So the professors of magic have ever reasoned. Every thing real is natural in one sense, but there is a lawful order in the acquisition of knowledge, as well as in other things. Our natural senses, reason, and divine revelation, are the only legitimate sources of knowledge. If, in attempting to pass these limits, you find yourself in the power of demons, you have only yourself to blame.''

Supper done, the ladies retired ; but before the gentlemen could follow their example, first Mrs. Cone and then Atherton were summoned by Rosamond to her mother's room, and presently Alban called the whole family to witness the singular exhibition there presented.

Mrs. Fay's table was covered with a white sheet, arranged in a peculiar style, and upon it were set a pair of lighted candles, an open book, and a bowl of water. A number of figures, in male and female attire, knelt around in various attitudes of devotion— one kneeling at the table itself, being arrayed in the half-burned surplice, bands, and stole of Mr. Soapstone. The effect was startling, and it was difficult to believe they were not real personages till Rosamond, venturing, as usual, to approach, pushed one of them over, with a laugh, and it was seen that they were figures dressed up with the aid of garments belonging to the family.

"Did you ever see any thing so curious in your life?" said Dr. Patristic. taking up a figure dressed in a silk gown of Mrs. Fay's, fitting more perfectly, too, than it ever did on the fragile form of its owner.

But Harriet, in her good-humored Irish way, going to undress this life-size doll before everybody, excited some merriment, mingled with blushing reproofs from the ladies, by showing that it was arrayed as scrupulously in all respects as one of themselves ; and yet the inside of all these figures consisted of a few pieces of household linen, and old carpet, and, wonderful to relate—as showing the inconceivable quickness with which this display had been got up—in the very centre of the carefully dressed one, representing Mrs. Fay, was found a sort of crumb-cloth or drugget, which had been spread under the table during supper. With one rude shake they tumbled to pieces.

The mixed wonder, amusement, and strange surmises occasioned by this singular representation were put to an end by a new and startling incident. Bridget came to the door and said—" Please, ma'am, send some of the gentlemen here, for sure Eddy has stripped himself as naked as the day he was born, and is a-running about the house."

The screams of the demoniac boy, though only occasional, for his strength seemed somewhat exhausted, impeded sleep. Few in the house but listened awe-struck on their beds. Dark and malignant was that spirit from the deep, who, the first perhaps for ages, had burst the restraint imposed upon his accursed race, and dared openly to manifest his ancient lust and power of torment. So at least deemed most of those who heard him.

Alban had volunteered to sit up with Eddy, who could not safely be left alone for an instant, and Mr. Soapstone charitably insisted on sharing his watch. Dr. Patristic was at first considerably nervous about sleeping alone in the adjacent room, until Dr. Cone, after visiting the child for the last time before retiring, went in to confer with the rector of Yantic, and these two worthies were soon in deep conversation on the mysteries of the spiritual world. Atherton and the young Episcopal clergyman insensibly fell to whispering on the same topic.

" My greatest difficulty in ascribing these things to diabolical agency," said Mr. Soapstone, " is the absence of apparent motive.

Satan, why should *he* play such tricks ? They are unworthy the prince of darkness."

" Well, I think there are several clear marks of his presence," returned the clear-headed student :—" a power above human ; malice in its use ; a restraint upon its exercise ; and a general tendency of the whole in the long run to glorify the Eternal Ruler by whom it is permitted."

" Yet seems it not strange even to you, Atherton, that these infernal powers are permitted to defy and insult our religion in any form, to mock it by sacrilegious representations ?"

" Not stranger than that heretics are permitted to travesty the priesthood, the sacrifice, and the Sacrament of the Lord's Body, in their profane and perverted rites. Is it not enough," said Alban, warmly, " that you impose your trumpery notions upon men, but you expect the very devils to revere the cheat ! Earth, no doubt, has some respect for solemn shams : Hell has none !"

Eddy half rose up and grinned horribly. He was but half-clothed, for except by tying him it was found impossible to prevent his stripping off his garments. While the family were at supper he had made one desperate attempt to get into the stranger's apartment, but Bridget had fortunately locked the door. Bridget had shown the stranger to his room, and after he had left it might have been seen to kneel outside the door and pray.

The young men were about to resume their conversation, when the demoniac again showed signs of trouble ; a step was heard in the passage ; Eddy made one bound into the furthest corner of the apartment, and the strange traveller entered.

He was not habited as before. A coarse, dark-brown woollen robe, with a long scapular hanging down before and behind, flowed to his feet, unconfined even about the waist by cord or belt. The red ribbon was again around his neck. Slightly bowing to the young men, he said, with quiet authority, " I want to see this boy," and immediately approached the possessed. To the astonishment of all, Eddy broke forth in a torrent of curses and abuse. It was not loud, rather muttered like the rolling growl of some incensed animal, but such abominable oaths and imprecations, such a filthy stream of obscenity and blasphemy never issued from human lips.

" *Immundissime spiritus, tace!*" said the stranger, laying his hand firmly on the boy's crouching head. " *In nomine Jesu Nazareni adjuro te.*"

The boy spat in his face and was silent. Eddy had naturally a sweet countenance. It was now upturned to the stranger's with an expression of revolting malignity.

" What is thy name ?" demanded the latter sternly.

" Elias Walker," said the boy, between his teeth.

Alban started.

" Speak truth in the name of God."

" Edward Fay—"

" Remember—*in nomine*—"

" *Legio!*" shouted the boy at the very top of his voice.

" Is there a cause wherefore thou art come, and what cause ? *In nomine*—"

" Ask *him*," in the same tone, and pointing to Atherton :— " him and yonder woman."—The boy used the coarsest of appellatives, and pointed with his index finger in the direction of Mrs. Fay's apartment.

" Speak truth," returned the stranger, " as thou fearest Him who is so near us both."

The boy faintly clutched at the red ribbon which was just visible at the stranger's throat, and sank on the floor as if senseless.

The stranger slowly turned to the appalled witnesses of this scene, and fastened upon Alban his dark, penetrating eyes.

" You are a Catholic, young sir ? That good girl Bridget told me you wanted to see a priest. Please step into my room for a few minutes. This gentleman will not fear being left alone with the child."

The " prophet's chamber," in truth, had in it little more than the Sunamitess gave Eliseus :—a " little bed, a table, a stool, and a candlestick." The stranger's large valise, to economize space, had been put beneath the table. On the bed lay a fine Roman surplice and purple stole, which the monk, (as he evidently was,) without asking Alban any further questions, immediately put on. Having thus done, he seated himself in the solitary chair which the little apartment afforded, and laying his hand authoritatively on the table at his side, said, " Kneel there."

For a moment the haughty blood rushed to Alban's face, at being thus ordered, but in a moment the emotion had passed, and the youth humbly knelt, while the monk, having murmured, " The Lord be in thy heart and on thy lips,"—with a rapid motion of benediction, added, in the same tone of abrupt command as before, " Say the *confiteor*."

Alban obeyed in a tremulous voice. The moment he reached the *mea culpa*, the stranger demanded, shortly, " When were you last at confession?"

" Never," replied Atherton.

" Never?" said the priest, slightly turning round, for he was leaning with his elbow on the table, and his hand over his eyes.

" I am only a convert, and have never had an opportunity of being received into the Church."

The Carmelite was silent for a minute, and then said in a kind, softened voice,

" You have been baptized?"

" In infancy, by a Congregationalist minister."

"Accuse yourself, my son, with candor, but without scrupulosity, of those things in your past life by which you are conscious of having offended God."

Alban continued on his knees nearly two hours. Unexpectedly as this confession had come upon him he was abundantly prepared for it. If he faltered, the priest, without appearing anxious that he should proceed, assisted his memory by a quiet, skilful question. His tears wet the little table. At length his voice died away in the conclusion of the *confiteor*, and he covered his face with both hands.

"My dear son," said the monk, "you have made a confession marked, to all appearance, by those qualities which are requisite in a good confession—sincerity and integrity. The humility you have displayed cannot but call down upon you the benediction of the Almighty, who has said in words familiar to your ears, *I dwell with the man that is of a contrite and humble spirit, and to whom shall I have respect but to him that is poor and little and of a contrite spirit, and that trembleth at my words?* You have had your evils—enough to teach you that in yourself you are no better than others, but with the proof they have afforded you of your own frailty, you ought to be thankful that you have been kept, perhaps by Providence as much as by grace, from that 'foul and lavish act of sin' which, as the poet says, inflicts such deep and lasting wounds on the soul. In regard to what is more recent—those violent inward temptations of which you speak—think not too much of *them*. The motions of concupiscence being natural we cannot feel horror at them ; it is sufficient that we refuse to yield, and wish to be freed from them, if it were possible. Despise the movements of your rebellious flesh, which is not and cannot be subject to the law of God, or regard them only to deepen your humility. Neither be over-scrupulous in regard to intercourse with certain persons. You may easily thus ensnare your conscience. Preserve a right intention in all things, and go forward with a sweet and holy courage. Lift the eyes of your heart above this sphere of vile temptations, and fix them on the perfections of your God. Meditate, my son, on the tender love of the Holy Trinity for the race of men : the Father's goodness in creating you, that of the Son in redeeming you, and of the Holy Ghost in effecting your sanctification. Consider Jesus Christ expiring on the Cross for you, or lingering in the Blessed Sacrament to be your food and victim. Remember that this life must be to you as it was to Him, one of unceasing conflict, humiliation, and suffering, in order that the life to come may be one of happiness, triumph, and rest. Avoid, of course, all consent to sin, and especially every outward act, which of itself proves the consent of the will ; but these apart, be courageous, calm, serene, hopeful, manly. Yes; let your piety be manly. You pray a great deal, it seems. It is well; it is necessary. But remember that one act of unfeigned humility is a prayer more efficacious than if you recited the whole Breviary from beginning to end. Use every means of grace, and confide in nothing but God."

Alban felt a deep surprise at the lightness of the penance which his strange confessor imposed for the sins of his whole life, it being only to read the eighth chapter of the Third Book of the Imitation of Christ, and add the *Veni Creator* to his devotions; both every day for a week. It was true that he had accused himself of what were doubtless mortal, though interior transgressions, but the shame and compunction which he evidently suffered in thus laying bare the secrets of his heart, were so great, that what with his innocence in the exterior point of view, it was a case for binding up the wound, and pouring on the oil of consolation. The priest had questioned him in regard to his baptism. Alban had never doubted its validity.

"It may seem strange," observed the monk, " that so great a gift as regeneration, which is the gate to eternal life, should be suspended on the right performance of an external act of this kind. But it is not more strange than that the gift of existence, which in one sense is greater, (for unless we existed, we could not be regenerate,) should be suspended on the coincidence of outward circumstances far less solemn. It is necessary to a valid baptism that the matter and form, that is, the water and the words, be morally united, so that while the baptizer is pronouncing the latter, he may be fairly considered to wash the baptized. The sect-ministers generally have no idea of matter and form in a sacrament, or of the necessity of uniting them, and as they generally *sprinkle*, often while the infant's head is covered with a cap, it may easily happen that only a few drops of water, too minute to *flow* upon the surface, may touch the child. Now that would not be baptism. I have seen even an Episcopal minister first pronounce the child's name, pour his hollow hand full of water

40*

upon its head, and then say, *I baptize thee, &c :* that would not be baptism either. In short, as the slip-shod notions of these sects do not permit them to prescribe, as the Church does, such a manner of administering the sacrament as to preclude the possibility of these defects, we cannot safely assume the validity of their baptisms, and they must be repeated as doubtful, unless we have positive proof to the contrary."

" The two ladies in this house were present at my baptism," said Alban.

" By all means, then, we must question them before proceeding further," said the monk.

As soon as Alban, confessed but not absolved, had risen from his knees, the monk said to him with a smile,

" What meant the evil spirit by referring me to you and the beautiful lady ? You know not ? The enigma may be solved one day. At present we must try the effect of an exorcism, for which I have a competent general authority. We shall need holy water—*real* holy water. Will you get me a little salt and a capacious bowl."

Alban departed on this errand. The back stair descended from a room occupied by the older boys, both of whom were asleep. Breathless quiet reigned throughout the house. Just at the landing of the stair was a low door opening into a garret-room where the servant girls slept. As Alban passed it, he heard the raps, not loud but decided. These raps upon doors had been of frequent occurrence, and were always understood as implying an invitation to enter, or if it was a closet, to open it. He disregarded the hint and went down stairs. Returning in about ten minutes with a salt-cellar and large bowl, he perceived the smell of fire in passing the same door, and the raps were repeated. Having carried in the articles to the priest, he returned hastily and knocked at the girls' room. There was no answer, and the smell of fire being now strong, he opened the door. A dim lamp burning on the floor discovered a slight smokiness in the air, yet the two Irish girls slept profoundly on separate cots. Since Eddy had ceased to scream, slumber had sealed all eyes and steeped all senses but those of the monk and Alban. The latter passed on between the beds of the girls to a door in the side of the apartment. This was the room of Mrs. Fay. A red flame illumined it, proceeding from the bed. Breathless he approached, lifted the muslin valance of the white-curtained bed, and lo, on the carpet a little pile of kindlings all in a light blaze, which already darted its snake-like tongues along the hempen sacking towards the light valance and curtains. Above, two soft faces lay still and close together on the dusky white of the pillows. He touched Rosamond ; she wakened her mother.

" Your bed is in flames—nay, be not alarmed."

Rosamond's limbs gleamed for a moment in the red light, as she sprang out ; her mother glided from the bed like a spirit. Alban threw on water—what the pitchers contained—then flinging the curtains within the bed, out of reach of the flames for the moment, proceeded to uncord the bedstead. Meanwhile—more thoughtful of their modesty than their safety, or that of the house—the mother and daughter robed themselves, with palpitating hearts. It seemed an age that passed ; the valance was in flames before the bed's head was uncorded. Alban stepped boldly on the bed, which sank through upon the soaking carpet, drew the curtains quite out of reach of the flames, which now encircled him, and completed the work of uncording. The fire beneath was smothered, the light valance went out like paper, and darkness descended upon the room.

" Is it Rosamond ? Ah, Mrs. Fay !"—The voice trembled.— " I was trying to find the door and went the wrong way. I will find it now and fetch a light."

He brought the lamp from the girls' room. Mrs. Fay took it to light her candle. Her hand trembled, but her face was calm. She was already dressed. At least a snowy wrapper hid all.

" Rosamond, my love, thank Mr. Atherton,"—half reproachfully, for the little girl was shrinking behind.

Rosa, whose ringlets were in wild disorder, and her frock half hooked, at her mother's word, sprang forward, threw her arms round his neck, and kissed him. Even a little girl's warm, quick kiss seemed to embarrass Atherton. He was retiring, with a downcast glance, when Mrs. Fay detained him.

" Mr. Atherton, one moment pardon me. You were speaking of your baptism the other day. I was then just going to tell you of a dispute, which arose at the time, about its validity, but sister made me a sign to hold my tongue. Your family, you know, was of great importance in Yanmouth ; and as there were several Episcopalians like ourselves present at your christening, we described the way it was done to our clergyman, who said it was no baptism. He was a terribly high churchman, to be sure, and afterwards turned Roman Catholic. After what you have done for Rosa and me, I cannot keep from you a fact which you may regard as important. When it occurred, I was just of Rosa's age."

He passed out between the cots of the sleeping maids, and having deposited their lamp where he found it, without a glance to the right or the left, rejoined the monk in the " prophet's chamber." The Carmelite listened, with his piercing eyes wide open, to Alban's relation.

" What was the maiden name of these ladies ? And yours is Atherton ? Is it so indeed ? Strange are the ways of Providence. *I* was that Episcopal clergyman, Mr. Atherton—now, by the mercy of God, a poor Carmelite. Well, we will examine into the matter more closely in the morning ; but let us now return to this demoniac."

Eddy was still lying in the corner of the chamber where he had fallen. Soapstone had thrown some clothes over him, and had afterwards fallen asleep himself in his chair. He became roused from his doze to behold the grave Carmelite, with book in hand, and holding the end of his stole over the prostrate child, reciting rapidly the prayers prescribed in the ritual for the exorcising of persons possessed by the devil. Alban held a light and a vessel of holy water, from which, at intervals, the exorcist sprinkled.

In the midst of the third exorcism, at the words *et ignis arde-bit ante ipsum*, the boy threw off the clothes and arose. It seemed that he was going to make a dash at the holy water, but he stop-ped short, gazing at Atherton with a horrible look of fear. Thrice the boy shrieked—an unearthly shriek, a cry of anguish unutter-able, sinking into a deep, hollow, vanishing moan—and fell lan-guidly. The priest caught him. They all together raised and laid him on the bed.

CHAPTER XVI.

DAY has dawned. Minute crimson clouds—the *avant gardes* of the sun—floated in a sky clear as a bell. The glittering plume of the morning star trembled, to speak poetically, in the rosy East. Dewy were the plains ; misty and dark blue the hills. The cock, as the old epopee would not fail to notice, crowed in the farm-yard ; the horse already cropped the June meadow with crunching teeth and snuffling nostril; the fresh-breathed maids came forth with their milk-pails from the brown farm-houses.

In Catholic countries the *Angelus* bell would invite to prayer and the tapers kindle on the altar for early mass, whither the laborer would repair to sanctify the day by assisting at the morning oblation. The Church loves early hours. Protestants delight in the sentimental witchery of evening, in the exquisite languor of sunset, the unreal charm of moon and stars throughout the year. They enjoy "night services," with bright gas-light, and crowds like a theatre, and a fervent preacher, soothing and exciting at the same time an exhausted nervous system. The religion which begins and ends in feeling is necessarily so ; but a religion of practice cannot thus arrange itself, because the evening being followed, not by action but repose, whatever impression could be made at this unseasonable hour, would pass away without fruit. *Compline*, which is the last sweet and brief office of the day in the Roman Church, and never varies in more than a few words, a hallelujah in the Paschal time, a doxology on the feasts of the Lord—*Compline* is supposed to conclude ere the last fading of the vesper twilight. In practice it is said much earlier. Catholic priests almost universally rise early, and are engaged in the duties of their calling, personal and public, for hours ere Protestant ministers quit their conjugal beds. The moral influence of this early activity, in the long run, is incalculable. *His* heart is not easily made impure by the foul illusions of a bloated sensuality, who rises before light to meditate and pray. That first victory over sloth fortifies the will ; the cool breath of morn assuages the fever of concupiscence ; and the matin worshipper feels upon his soul a cooler breath, from the Eternal Mount, imparting to it an adamantine temper, against which the edge of temptation is quickly turned.

The wagon-bolt was replaced by sunrise, and the monk's companion waited for him at the gate. In the little chamber a pair of candles stood lighted on the table, whereon a narrow white cloth was spread. The priest took from a sort of wallet of silk, having a red ribbon attached, a square piece of linen, which he spread, and a silver case resembling a locket. He opens the latter ; he adores, kneeling ; he lifts the sacred victim of salvation. Alban and the girl Bridget are kneeling, and he communicates the latter. He adores again ; he closes the pix, replaces it, with the corporal and purificatory, in the bursa, and passes the ribbon round his neck.

It was a question whether Dr. and Mrs. Cone would permit their house to be blessed, and holy-water to be sprinkled through the rooms as a defence against the future incursions and return of the demons ; if, indeed, the quiet which had continued since the exorcism of Eddy, intimated their effectual expulsion. Father Xavier, (such was his name in religion,) refused to do any thing without the express permission of his hosts. The fear of being burned in their beds overcame the repugnance which they naturally felt to avail themselves of his assistance. At their formal request, he passed from room to room, reciting the appointed prayers, and sprinkling the element which the Church blesses with the expressed intention that " *whatever in the houses or abodes of the faithful this wave shall sprinkle, may be free from all impurity, be delivered from harm ; that no pestilent spirit may reside there, nor corrupting air : that all the snares of the latent enemy may depart ; and if there is any thing which is hostile either to the safety or the quiet of the inhabitants, by the asper-*

*sion of this water, it may flee away : that the salubrity which
is sought by the invocation of Thy holy name, may be defended
from all assaults."*

They came upon Dr. Patristic snoring in bed in spite of the
sunlight streaming betwixt the half-open shutters, and hallowed
the room without disturbing his slumbers.

The astonishment and displeasure of Mrs. Cone were great when
her departing guest declined to break his fast. He had not tasted
their salt ; he had not even pressed the couch provided for him.
He assured her that he was accustomed to vigils ; and as for
taking food ere his departure, he regretted to decline the hospitable
offer, but decline it he must, since his first duty at Yantic would
be to say mass for the small colony of Irish laborers and servant
girls, whom the factories had collected around the Falls of the old
Indian river.

Good Mrs. Cone was further astonished and afflicted to find
that Alban was going to accompany the priest. The questions in
regard to his baptism next came up and made her dart a reproving
glance at the blushing Mrs. Fay.

" Nay," said the grave Carmelite, " I myself remember something. Have you quite forgotten an old friend, Mrs. Cone ? Time
has altered us both, but I can retrace the laughing Fanny Cleveland
in my sedate hostess."

" Mr. Hewley !" cried Mrs. Cone, blushing as vividly as her
sister.

" And how about this young man's baptism ?" said the monk.

Mrs. Cone brought out a new feature of the case. Old Mrs.
Atherton, Alban's grandmother, had been annoyed at the talk,
and had got his uncle, the bishop, to make all right, as she
deemed, in private. Mrs. Cone herself, then an Episcopalian, had
been godmother, and her brother, a clergyman and the bishop's
chaplain, had been godfather, when Dr. Grey baptized his great-
nephew in the old Yanmouth church on a week-day Festival, and
in the old marble font taken with the bell from the Spaniards.
This was just after Mr. Hewley resigned the parish, and when

the child was about eighteen months old. Mr. Cleveland read the Church service, and the Bishop baptized the child after the second lesson, although, except old Mrs. Atherton, the two clergymen, and the narrator, not a soul was present. The Rev. Mr. Cleveland was since dead.

"I don't care if they read the whole prayer-book," said the monk, "or if the church was empty or crowded. All I want to know is how the bishop performed the simple act of baptism."

"Oh, sir, he did not use the conditional form, I remember, because the bishop considered all Presbyterian baptism invalid."

"That was a heresy. But did Bishop Grey use much water?"

"The hand brimming full," said Mrs. Cone, affecting to pour from her hollow hand as from a cup. "The quantity of water made Master Alby cry lustily. When I took him back from the bishop, his fine light hair was wet enough to drip, and it ran all into his neck. I shall not soon forget it. For he was a year old at least."

"So far is highly satisfactory," said Father Xavier, glancing at Alban. "One point more remains, and it is one of great delicacy as well as importance. At what moment did the bishop pour all this quantity of water, or did he pour it thrice?"

"Only once, I am sure, or I should have noticed it," responded Mrs. Cone. "He poured it, I presume, while he was pronouncing the words. The child cried so that I thought of nothing else at the time but that flood of water which the bishop scooped out of the old font. No doubt Bishop Grey did every thing as it ought to be done, sir. A bishop, sir! of course!"

"The truth is," said Father Xavier, as Alban and he drove away from Dr. Cone's gate, "evidence is worth little after so much time has lapsed, unless the witness had her attention called particularly to the point."

"And am I still to remain suspended thus between heaven and earth, not knowing whether I am a Christian or not?" asked Alban, with a painful smile.

41

" Through no fault of Holy Church, my son. It would sim-
plify the matter very much if we could say that all baptisms out
of the Church are invalid. But the Church never seeks simplicity at the expense of truth. Sometimes an adherence to truth
may involve her in perplexities which others do not feel ; but she
is patient, and in the end order is developed under her unerring
hand out of the most intricate seeming confusion."

" To be baptized *three times* is very repugnant to my feelings," said Atherton.

Father Xavier would say no more until they should again be
alone. The missionary (for although merely on a visit to his
native country, the monk was discharging the duties of an ordinary priest of the mission) heard a number of confessions at
Yantic, said mass, and baptized some children. At length Alban
was alone with him in the humble room overlooking the Falls,
where the temporary altar had been erected. The young convert
again knelt, and added some brief words to his previous confession.

" Think not of these things," said the priest, who in the confessional seemed another person. " Without grace it is impossible
not to fall. Satan throws these seeming opportunities and suggestions in your way to tempt you partly, and partly to make you
despair of God's goodness. If you had really had the opportunity
of committing the sin which you say was suggested to you, probably
in your present state of mind, you would have repelled it with
horror, or at least with decision. The real impossibility made it
seem to you as if you consented. It was an illusion of the devil,
who is always ready to afflict us in that way if God permits.
You have made a good and sincere confession, I am very sure,
and the Church cannot mean that you should make it fruitlessly.
She cannot withhold from you the grace of which she is the dispenser. I really think it probable that you have been baptized,
and I shall therefore absolve you, on the invariable condition of so
far as you need and I am able. You must write to your right-
reverend uncle, and if his answer be satisfactory, you will need
only to have the ceremonies supplied, and you can go to commu-

nion at once. But whatever his answer may be, you will never be obliged to repeat this confession. Remember that. For if you have been baptized, the absolution you are about to receive will be good, and if you have not been baptized, no absolution whatever will be necessary. Does this meet your wishes, my dear son ? It is just the ordinary case of receiving absolution, but deferring communion. Bow your head, then, and renew your contrition for all the sins of your life."

In a moment it was over, and the sins of Alban's youth had passed away, we may believe, like darkness at the entrance of a bright light, and his star-like soul, formed to know and love its Creator, shone once more in the sight of the angels, brighter than Hesperus, or Lucifer, with the glorious beams of sanctifying grace. Hell had failed with all its arts.

CHAPTER XVII.

In July Alban visited New Haven by special permission, to attend the final examinations of his class. He was almost forgotten. The class feeling was already dissolving. College had sunk into its true place, and men had their eye on the world. There was talk of keeping up old friendships, but it was mere talk. The Popery excitement had died a natural death. The President received Atherton kindly, and informed him that he would be allowed to deliver his oration. This great honor, so long anticipated and the cause of so many heart-burnings, seemed now a very small affair. Alban loved his *alma mater*, and that iron New England of which it was the intellectual representative, but he had taken the dimensions of them both. In all this ancestral land of his, and in its university, not one thinker was to be found who dared maintain that the human will was truly self-determinant, or who deemed that grace had any other office than to compel the affections.

"Oh glorious liberty of the sons of God !" he exclaimed, as he walked under the endless arbors of the grove-like Academe, " you are here unknown !"

The rustication was now at an end, and Alban might have gone where he pleased ; but he returned to Carmel to write his oration. His mother, whose health was delicate, was spending the summer with their relatives at Yantic, and he wished to be at least in her vicinity ; for it was not pleasant either for Alban or the Athertons, to associate much, his apostasy from the New England, or rather from the family faith, rendered him so odious. He frequently drove down to the Falls with Mrs. Cone or Rosamond Fay, and once they penetrated as far as Yanmouth, where Alban paid a visit to the " castle," which had been sold, modernized, and new furnished. But the stone-bound, iron-gray hills, and broad, breeze-ruffled waters were unchanged, and the white, massive

brick pillars, black, many-sloped roof, and shrubberied terraces
of the old Atherton house, still commanded the town and bay and
fort-crowned heights.

At length the seniors' six weeks were over, and from the open
window of his chamber Alban watched for the last time the sun
set upon the table-land of Carmel. The fiery orb sank behind the
low blue ridge-line of the remote hills as beneath the rim of ocean.

It grew dark : the sounds of evening began to be heard ; the
katydid and the cricket made a concert ; the fire-flies sparkled on
the dusky green ; a bat flew back and forth under the leafy button-balls.

The student's revery was broken by the entrance of a maid
to perform certain neat duties about his room. It was the pretty
Harriet. Alban spoke to her in a kind tone, slightly tinctured
with gayety. She laughed, and busied herself with filling his
pitcher, and setting in order his wash-stand. He turned again
to the embrowned landscape and faded sky. Presently the girl
sobbed. The young man took no notice till just as she was about
to leave the room, when he called her to him.

" Harriet," said he, " of all the people in this house who have
seen the wonderful works of God in it, you are the only one who
has been led to faith. They laugh at you and call you a fool ;
they say other things harder yet for a young woman to bear. I
have never spoken to you much. Now I am going away. What
will you do when *you* leave this house ? Will you go straight
forward and do your duty ? It will be a hard struggle for your
pride—to ' turn,' as they say."

" I will never die what I am," said Harriet, weeping.

" Ah, Hatty ! if you *live* what you are, it may not be in your
choice what you will die."

" I know it, sir."

" Is it so hard to give up *your* little world ? In your rank of
life, Hatty, a pretty face and person expose to great temptations :
how will you resist them when your conscience all the while tells
you that you have turned your back on grace and Heaven ? Are

you not afraid that God will punish you by letting you be drawn
into sin and shame by those very persons whose opinion you fear?"

"Oh, sir," cried the girl, with a toss of the head, "I have no
fear of that. I am above that, I hope."

"None of us is above any kind of wickedness, Hatty—if God
lets us fall."

The girl applied the corner of her apron to her eyes and cried
again. The youth glanced at her as she stood near, but indistinct,
in the dusky chamber, and then he looked away again into the
sparkling summer night, the warm breath whereof came in at the
casement. Hatty was doubtless just as attractive to the senses as
if she had been a lady—perhaps more so. The bat which had
been flitting under the trees flew suddenly in at the open window.

"So flies the evil one into the heart," thought Alban, looking
round again. "Go, Hatty," he added aloud, and in a composed
manner. "You will be as good a girl, I hope, when next we
meet, as I believe you are now. Only remember as my last
words, that it is safer to fear our weakness than to rely upon our
strength."

Hatty departed from him; the youth knelt at his chair, and
the swift-circling bat flew out like a winged shadow.

"How degrading," exclaimed the young man, rising, "to feel
these coarse external temptations! A ruby lip and springing
waist—can they allure him whose cleansed vision beholds the
dread realities of faith? And yet it is well for me to have something positive and tangible to conquer. Haply a victory here,
though inglorious, may arm me for the subtle conflict which is all
fought within. Those infinite suggestions of forbidden pleasure in
the sweetest guise, and seemingly so pure,—shall they never end?
How hopeless, then, to struggle, since I cannot hope always to
stand!"—The winged shadow flew in once more, unseen.—"Yet
let me fall fighting. O Michael, Prince of the heavenly hosts,
come to my assistance."—Again the bat darkened the casement
as it flew out.

There was a light tap at the door; he sung out "Come in,"

and little Rosamond Fay entered. Rosamond was clad in deep
black. Alban sighed, kissed her forehead, and taking her hand,
led her down into the piazza.

Something supernatural lingered to the last about the old house
in Carmel. They say that strange noises are heard in it yet,
particularly at night, and in certain chambers. The night that
Alban slept there last, a certain wild inarticulate cry began soon
after the family had retired, and never ceased till he was gone.

In a few days, our hero arrived with his mother in New
Haven, where his father was already installed at the Tontine.
The beautiful little city was full of strangers. The graduating
class gave a ball. The Phi Beta gave a dinner. Commencement
day came, all music and orations, a church full of black coats
and gay bonnets, degrees tied with blue ribbons, youths wearing
mysterious society badges, and more valedictories said than were
pronounced from the carpeted platform, where sat and listened,
with unwearied gravity, the elders of New England.

It is not often that a commencement oration attracts much
attention, except for the fifteen minutes which it may occupy in
delivery. Atherton's was one of the exceptions which now and
then strike between wind and water, and hold such an audience
as he had, profoundly interested from first to last. The subject—
" The Necessity of Patience"—had already excited curiosity,
augmented by the whispers floating about in relation to the singular opinions of the author. A nearly beardless youth, loosely and
scholastically attired in black summer cloth, with the golden sym-
bols of the Φ. B. K. and X. Δ. Θ. glittering on his watch-guard,
and the badge of the Brothers' on his breast, stood in the circle—
the triple, chaired corona—of gray-beards, bald intellectualities,
and reverend white cravats. Two things struck people in Atherton's oration, its life-like reality and the absence of ornament in
the style. The matter was important and original ; the manner
simplicity itself, showing that he had studied only to make his
meaning perspicuous. And yet the peroration was highly rhetorical. It was almost impassioned, as the words of a human being

speaking from a deep personal experience and sustained by an invincible faith.

The conferring of degrees was an imposing ceremony, particularly when the President put on his hat. Any thing symbolic is so rare in New England that it never fails to impress. The only want which our hero felt at the time arose from the absence of the De Groots. Mary, it was understood, was in a convent—but whether as a boarder or a postulant no one exactly knew, and her parents were at the Virginia Springs.

Henry Atherton was to be married the day after commencement, and Alban was to be one of the grooms-men, but such was the hurry of all parties that he could learn little about the arrangements except the necessary particulars of time and place.

The day before commencement, going from the hotel to the colleges on an errand connected with his graduation, our hero had walked behind a party of some distinction, attended by Professor S——. Alban hated to pass people, and accommodated himself to their leisurely pace. In advance with the Professor walked a large, middle-aged matronly lady, with an imposing gait, and who talked a good deal. Behind them, an officer in the undress uniform of the army, gallanted a young lady of an exquisite figure, in rose-colored muslin and a white bonnet, managing with much grace a rose-and-white parasol. She was like a bouquet in motion under the mighty elms. The bronzed profile of her companion was often turned to her, and she answered the movement by a corresponding one, but that provoking crape bonnet hid her features.

When Alban had finished his business at the colleges, he strayed into the Trumbull Gallery, to take another last look at the pictures which he had once admired, and the same party were there. But Professor S—— had quitted them, and the officer was sitting by the matronly lady, while the graceful wearer of the rose dress sauntered round the room by herself, with a catalogue. Atherton observed her. She stopped longest before the very pictures which interested him ; and at the portrait of Washington, bent down twice to read the names of the donors. Still he could not catch a glimpse of her face, until, upon her friends calling her to come away, she turned back at the door of the inner room, and gave him a perfect view of her features. They were the sweetest mixture of fairness and bloom he had ever beheld—deep violet eyes, golden brown hair, with a fall of ringlets about the white throat; a nose, mouth, and chin indicative of character, vivacity, tenderness, and purity. She caught the student's admiring glance, blushed, and hastily joined her friends.

In leaving the church with his father and mother, after the exercises were over on commencement day, he again saw this party, somewhat in advance. The gentleman and older lady looked back on this occasion—and at him, he thought—as if they meant to stop and speak; but after some hesitation, they proceeded without doing so. Their way was the same, and at last they all entered the Tontine, at the ladies' door. Alban hoped, with reason, to see the beautiful face again at tea.

He was not disappointed, for the ladies and their naval companion came to the tea-table and sat opposite them. The young lady, unbonneted, was lovelier still, for her head was perfectly classic, and the light summer evening toilet showed a neck and shoulders not less finely formed, and of dazzling whiteness. The purity and even bloom of her complexion yielded, as it were, to a visible blush the moment that her eye rested on Alban; nor did she quite recover from the suffusion while the brief sunset repast lasted. After tea, while his father and mother, worn out with the excitement and fatigue of the day, retired to their own room, he went into the general parlor of the Tontine. The same party were there, grouped in a window that looked upon the green. The officer immediately advanced towards him.

"Mr. Atherton, I believe?"—Of course, any body who had been at commencement knew his name.—"There is a young lady here who says she has a right to be acquainted with you, Mr. Atherton."

Alban went forward, wondering and not a little fluttered, notwithstanding his being now so used to ladies. She extended her hand with maidenly frankness and a look of affectionate archness, quite irresistible.

" You have forgotten your cousin Jane, Alban ?"

" Jane ! Is it possible that you are Jane !"

He embraced her, and she drew back confused, whereupon the elder lady, who was her aunt, observed with a smile that Jane and her cousin had been brought up like brother and sister. He found that Jane was to be one of the bridemaids on the morrow.

" We shall stand up together," said Alban. " I owe Hal a turn for not telling me of this, nor even that you were here."

We arrived but yesterday," said Jane, " and it has been such a busy day."

Moreover Jane had promised to accompany Henry and his bride on their wedding-tour, (Niagara, of course,) and the grooms-men were to be of the party. It is a custom yet in the States, and often makes one wedding the fruitful parent of several others.

We intend not to enter into the details of this interesting excursion ; the transitions from the shady steamboat deck, on the noble river, to the flying rail-car that pierces the beautiful valleys ; the walks from lock to lock in the deep cuttings of the great canal, still used for travel ; rocking on the seat of an American stage, hanging over waterfalls, gazing at mountains and lakes by moon-light, drinking Spa waters from bubbling fountains before break-fast, rolling nine-pins, satisfying keen young appetites at plentiful tables, dancing in the evening saloons at the Springs. We may suppose that Jane had heard, from time to time, of Alban's college distinctions, and that she was not insensible to the romance of their meeting. She had listened to his beautiful oration with pride ; she was making her first summer journey as a young lady in his company, and although young, " Alban was a graduate, and a graduate was a Man."

But at an early period of the tour, Jane became aware that a great change had taken place in her cousin. The day on which they were steaming up the Highlands was the first of the discovery. The immense boat—not three hundred feet long indeed, like those which now ply on the same river, but able to accommodate some eight hundred passengers—was moving with scarcely a perceptible jar in its huge frame at a speed of nearly eighteen miles an hour, against the broad stream, shut in like a lake by green hills, under a sky of motionless *cumuli* and deep blue. They sat on the promenade deck, with perhaps a hundred others, all forming little circles apart, keeping carefully beneath the awning, and the ladies protecting their complexions by thick green veils, Some read novels ; some studied the map of the river ; in which the chief thing that seemed interesting, after some historic sites, were the old seats of the Livingstons, Van Rensselaers, Van Brughs, and De Groots. Overlooking a beautiful sweep of the river, from a lawn-like opening in an extensive park or wood which ran for miles along the water's edge, a noble, bluish-gray mansion with a tower and wings, attracted general attention.

"The De Groot Manor !" said Mrs. Henry Atherton.

"What a beautiful situation !" exclaimed Jane. "I like it best of all we have seen."

"Your friend Mary's father, cousin Alban," said Mrs. Atherton.

"Who is your friend Mary ?" asked Jane.

"The daughter of the Mr. De Groot who owns the fine mansion you see, and who, as well as his daughter, is a great friend of mine," said Alban.

"A *young* lady ?" inquired Jane.

"When I saw her last she called herself sixteen."

"Oh ! a little girl !" said Jane.

"Her father is not merely very rich," continued Alban, "but an elegant scholar, a collector of rare books and pictures, and a man of very peculiar and subtle powers of mind."

"What remarkable friends you seem to have," observed Jane. "Mr. Clinton—of whom you were telling me this morning, Mr. Seixas, and this Mr. De Groot. Is he of some strange out-of-the-way religion too ?"

"He is professedly a Unitarian, really, a Pantheist."

"At least you won't apologize for *his* views."

"Yes," returned Alban, smiling. "The Unitarians have their good points. They recognize the importance of careful moral culture, and reap the fruit in great moral excellence. No Protestants are more famous for truth, justice, amiability, and active benevolence. And those whom I have known pushed their ideas of decorum to prudery."

"Was your friend Mary a little prude?" said Jane, smiling. "I think that is so odious in such young girls."

"What do you say, Mrs. Henry?" said Alban, turning to Mary Ellsworth. "Was Miss De Groot a little prude or not?"

"I have seen her box a gentleman's ears for a pretty slight cause," cried St. Clair, shrugging his shoulders.

"Oh! was she that sort!" cried Jane, with some disgust.

"I think," said Alban, "we may say that she had a delicacy of conscience on those points where your sex is supposed to be bound to a greater strictness than ours." And he still appealed to Mrs. Henry Atherton.

"Mary was propriety itself: I never thought her prudish," said Mrs. Atherton, with a slight bride-like blush.

"Well, I understand Unitarians," said Jane, "and Jews: but how an intelligent, shrewd man, as you describe Mr. Clinton, Alban, can be a sincere Roman Catholic, passes my comprehension."

"The only way to account for it is by the power of divine grace," said Alban.

"I hope we shan't get into any religious discussions," interposed Henry Atherton, rather severely.

"Nothing was further from my intention," said Alban. "Only Jane's remark made me feel queer."

Mary Ellsworth, (as for convenience we shall still call her, for there was another Mary Atherton of the party,) leaned over towards Jane and whispered to her audibly to ask Alban what he thought of the Church of Rome's prohibition of the marriage of cousins. Jane blushed.

"Is it prohibited?"

" Don't you know that ? You and Jane are within the prohibited degrees, cousin Alban,—are you not ?"

" Certainly, we are second cousins. We could not marry without a dispensation."

" You see, Jane, you will have to get the Pope's leave."

" Nonsense," said Alban. " Every bishop, and I believe, every parish priest in this country, can dispense in that degree."

" Where do you find in the Bible, Alb, that cousins must not marry ?" asked Henry Atherton. "This appears to me one of those traditions and commandments of men which the Church of Rome is famous for imposing on men's consciences. It was a great instrument of her tyranny in those middle ages that you so much admire, as well as a rich source of emolument through the dispensations you speak of. First she forbade what God's Word permitted, and then she took money to let you do it."

" Yes, Alban, you can explain every thing," cried St. Clair, " pray give us an explanation of this. Jane looks for it anxiously."

" Since you appeal to me, I will answer," said Alban, quietly. " The Primitive Church forbade the marriage of cousins long before you suppose the Papacy to have arisen, and the Greek Church forbids it still, understanding the terms brother and sister in Scripture to include cousins. The example of the Patriarchs, which I know you will quote, proves nothing, for Abraham married his niece—his sister, as she is called in the Bible. The Church is a chaste and tender mother. It is true that she has drawn the bonds of consanguinity closer than under the old carnal dispensation. Her heart is more sensitive to the slightest claim of nature ; she takes a wider circle of kindred into the nearness of blood affection ; she is more jealous of that purity which refuses to mix the two kinds of love. Do you blame her for it ?"

" Very fine, Alb, but it proves too much. If it is a question of Christian delicacy, no dispensation ought ever to be allowed. Why should the Church dispense with the slightest obligation of purity ?" asked Henry, coldly.

" Why, indeed !" exclaimed Jane, in an indignant under tone.

" Still you misunderstand her. I am bound by the law of purity to regard Jane as a sister, notwithstanding my knowledge that the Church may for good reasons remove the barrier between us and permit us to forget our common blood."

" Well, if that is not impertinence, I don't know what is," cried Mrs. Henry. " If I were you, Jane, I would remember it."

" Jane understands me better than you do," replied Alban, " and I am convinced that she is not offended because I say that no sister could be dearer to me than she is."

" I understand perfectly," said Jane.

" You all talk of Jane," exclaimed Mary Atherton, Henry's sister, who was older than her brother. " But no one seems to think that *my* feelings are outraged. Jane is only a second cousin after all, and as Alban says so pointedly (encouraging Jane) ' Any priest may dispense.' But I am a first cousin. No help for me short of the Pope ! As Jane says"—mimicking her—" I understand perfectly."

This sally made every one laugh, and brought the conversation back to safe ground. Alban promised that if Mary Atherton would give him any encouragement he would write to Rome for a dispensation at once.

" No, no !" she replied. " I shall take care how I expose myself to the charge of wanting delicacy towards my near relations. Henceforward, Alban, I regard you simply as a brother."

Henry Atherton told Jane afterwards that Alban was very eccentric. He had been nearly or quite an infidel, then almost a Jew, and now he talked as if he were going to turn Papist. They all hoped he would get over these crotchets as he grew older, and he (Henry) hoped a great deal from his affection for Jane herself.

From that time the subject was avoided, but Jane found it hard that wherever there was a Catholic church, however mean, Alban would go to it when they rested on the Sundays. This happened first at Babylon, and she knew not how to bear it to sit by herself in the square pew in the old meeting-house, where she and Alban in the old times occupied opposite corners, and thought more of each other than of long prayer or pleasant hymn, or even stirring sermon. And to think that he had gone and strayed away to that great brick structure outside the village, where crowds of common Germans in blouses or petticoats of blue, according to their sex, and of the low Irish, filled the whole space and even knelt outside upon the steps of the portico; and she did not care at all that the building realized a wish of Aunt Fanny's, being dedicated D. O. M. under the invocation of the Prince of the Apostles.

Nor must we omit that they had some narrow escapes on this tour—Jane and Alban. One was at Niagara, where they two went under the Fall, and Jane slipped on the stones amid the spray, wind-gusts, and darkness, and the water-snakes that crawled up from the boiling caldron below. The detention caused by this saved their lives, for on coming out again they found that a piece of rock had fallen directly upon their path, strewing it with fragments, any one of which was sufficient to have killed them both. Jane fancied that Alban's "guardian angel" had pushed her down, and Alban wondered, if he had been killed, what would have become of his soul. After that, a boiler burst on the St. Lawrence, a minute after they had passed it, and when Jane had been desirous of staying in its dangerous vicinity to look at the machinery, but Alban, who since the Niagara business was nervous either for himself, or her, or both, would not let her. In that case his guardian angel must have inspired him, they both agreed : for several persons were scalded to death by the accident.

Another incident was their visiting the cathedral in Montreal, and Alban's kneeling before the altar where burned the solitary lamp. His friends thought it "too absurd," "quite a display," and Jane too was ashamed ; but when Alban rejoined her, he looked so strangely calm and sweet, that she loved him with all her heart in spite of his singularities.

And so our party sailed up Lake Champlain, while the flying mists now hid, now revealed, the wild mountains of Essex. They landed at the picturesque and historic Ti. Then their keel, steam impelled, cut swiftly the transparent waters of St. Sacrament, blue as the Rhone at Ferney—a sacred lake.

THE END.

THE AMERICAN CATHOLIC TRADITION

An Arno Press Collection

Callahan, Nelson J., editor. **The Diary of Richard L. Burtsell, Priest of New York.** 1978

Curran, Robert Emmett. **Michael Augustine Corrigan and the Shaping of Conservative Catholicism in America, 1878-1902.** 1978

Ewens, Mary. **The Role of the Nun in Nineteenth-Century America** (Doctoral Thesis, The University of Minnesota, 1971). 1978

McNeal, Patricia F. **The American Catholic Peace Movement 1928-1972** (Doctoral Dissertation, Temple University, 1974). 1978

Meiring, Bernard Julius. **Educational Aspects of the Legislation of the Councils of Baltimore, 1829-1884** (Doctoral Dissertation, University of California, Berkeley, 1963). 1978

Murnion, Philip J., **The Catholic Priest and the Changing Structure of Pastoral Ministry, New York, 1920-1970** (Doctoral Dissertation, Columbia University, 1972). 1978

White, James A., **The Era of Good Intentions: A Survey of American Catholics' Writing Between the Years 1880-1915** (Doctoral Thesis, University of Notre Dame, 1957). 1978

Dyrud, Keith P., Michael Novak and Rudolph J. Vecoli, editors. **The Other Catholics.** 1978

Gleason, Philip, editor. **Documentary Reports on Early American Catholicism.** 1978

Bugg, Lelia Hardin, editor. **The People of Our Parish.** 1900

Cadden, John Paul. **The Historiography of the American Catholic Church: 1785-1943.** 1944

Caruso, Joseph. **The Priest.** 1956

Congress of Colored Catholics of the United States. **Three Catholic Afro-American Congresses.** [1893]

Day, Dorothy. **From Union Square to Rome.** 1940

Deshon, George. **Guide for Catholic Young Women.** 1897

Dorsey, Anna H[anson]. **The Flemmings.** [1869]

Egan, Maurice Francis. **The Disappearance of John Longworthy.** 1890

Ellard, Gerald. **Christian Life and Worship.** 1948

England, John. **The Works of the Right Rev. John England, First Bishop of Charleston.** 1849. 5 vols.

Fichter, Joseph H. **Dynamics of a City Church.** 1951

Furfey, Paul Hanly. **Fire on the Earth.** 1936

Garraghan, Gilbert J. **The Jesuits of the Middle United States.** 1938. 3 vols.

Gibbons, James. **The Faith of Our Fathers.** 1877

Hecker, I[saac] T[homas]. **Questions of the Soul.** 1855

Houtart, François. **Aspects Sociologiques Du Catholicisme Américain.** 1957

[Hughes, William H.] **Souvenir Volume. Three Great Events in the History of the Catholic Church in the United States.** 1889

[Huntington, Jedediah Vincent]. **Alban: A Tale of the New World.** 1851

Kelley, Francis C., editor. **The First American Catholic Missionary Congress.** 1909

Labbé, Dolores Egger. **Jim Crow Comes to Church.** 1971

LaFarge, John. **Interracial Justice.** 1937

Malone, Sylvester L. **Dr. Edward McGlynn.** 1918

The Mission-Book of the Congregation of the Most Holy Redeemer. 1862

O'Hara, Edwin V. **The Church and the Country Community.** 1927

Pise, Charles Constantine. **Father Rowland.** 1829

Ryan, Alvan S., editor. **The Brownson Reader.** 1955

Ryan, John A., **Distributive Justice.** 1916

Sadlier, [Mary Anne]. **Confessions of an Apostate.** 1903

Sermons Preached at the Church of St. Paul the Apostle, New York, During the Year 1863. 1864

Shea, John Gilmary. **A History of the Catholic Church Within the Limits of the United States.** 1886/1888/1890/1892. 4 Vols.

Shuster, George N. **The Catholic Spirit in America.** 1928

Spalding, J[ohn] L[ancaster]. **The Religious Mission of the Irish People and Catholic Colonization.** 1880

Sullivan, Richard. **Summer After Summer.** 1942

[Sullivan, William L.] **The Priest.** 1911

Thorp, Willard. **Catholic Novelists in Defense of Their Faith, 1829-1865.** 1968

Tincker, Mary Agnes. **San Salvador.** 1892

Weninger, Franz Xaver. **Die Heilige Mission** *and* **Praktische Winke Für Missionare.** 1885. 2 Vols. in 1

Wissel, Joseph. **The Redemptorist on the American Missions.** 1920. 3 Vols. in 2

The World's Columbian Catholic Congresses and Educational Exhibit. 1893

Zahm, J[ohn] A[ugustine]. **Evolution and Dogma.** 1896